Commercial Loan Officer's Handbook

From Basic Concepts
to Advanced Techniques

Robert H. Behrens

BANKERS PUBLISHING COMPANY, BOSTON

Library of Congress Cataloging in Publication Data

Behrens, Robert H., 1931–
    Commercial loan officer's handbook.

    Bibliography: p.
    Includes index.
    1. Bank loans—Handbooks, manuals, etc. I. Title.
HG1641.B43 1984   332.1'753'0685   84-14510
ISBN 0-87267-049-X .

Printed in the United States of America

BANKERS PUBLISHING COMPANY
210 South Street
Boston, Massachusetts 02111

Robert M. Roen: Vice President and Executive Editor
Nancy Long Coleman: Managing Editor
Karen Mason: Cover and Jacket Designer

About the Author

Robert H. Behrens is currently vice president and senior loan officer at The Commercial Bank, Champaign, Illinois. During the course of his career, Mr. Behrens has been involved in every aspect of commercial lending as the head of a loan review department and a commercial lending division.

Mr. Behrens has contributed articles to *The Bankers Magazine,* the *Journal of Commercial Lending,* and the *Mid-Continent Banker.* He is also a frequent speaker at state and national banking conferences and meetings. A graduate of both the Stonier Graduate School of Banking and the National Commercial Lending School, Mr. Behrens holds the ABA's professional designation of Certified Commercial Lender.

He is the author of *Commercial Problem Loans* and co-author of *Lending to Agricultural Enterprises,* both published by Bankers Publishing Company.

CONTENTS

Chapter 11   Legal Documentation   142

Chapter 12   The Uniform Commercial Code—Secured Transactions   163

Chapter 13   Credit Files and Monitoring Loan Performance   192

Chapter 14   Dealing With the Problem Loan   199

Chapter 15   Collections and Bankruptcy   217

Preface

Commercial banks are primary providers of credit to the nation's businesses and industry. Although many large corporations now use the commercial paper market to supply a substantial part of their credit requirements, most businesses depend on the commercial banking system as their primary source of credit for both working capital and capital needs. Bank credit may be said to be the lifeblood of business and commerce.

Lending can be considered the heart of the commercial banking business.

In October 1983, domestically chartered U.S. commercial banks had loans and leases totaling $1,060 billion dollars in their portfolios, constituting the largest single asset category of commercial banks. According to the Federal Reserve Statistical Release of November 21, 1983, $367 billion dollars of these loans were classified as commercial and industrial loans. Since the majority of its deposits are invested in loans, and a significant percentage of its loans are commercial and industrial loans, every commercial bank is vitally concerned with the quality of its commercial loan portfolio and the proficiency of its commercial lending operation.

The professional knowledge and technical expertise of the men and women who make, administer, and collect a bank's commercial and industrial loans is therefore vitally important to the performance of a commercial bank. With the exception of top management, a bank's commercial lending staff often makes a more significant contribution to the profits or losses of a bank than any other segment of its staff.

This book is written for the benefit of commercial loan officers. It is comprehensive and covers both basic concepts and sophisticated lending techniques. It covers the complete spectrum of the lending process from formulating loan policy to interviewing applicants; from making the loan decision to collecting the problem loan. This book covers in detail the legal aspects of lending, including a discussion of legal entities, legal documentation, secured transactions under the Uniform Commercial Code, law as it applies to loan collections, and the Bankruptcy Code. It also contains many sample loan forms and a case study covering the financing of a start-up business. Finally, it covers several specialized areas of lending, such as U.S. Small Business Administration loans, commercial letters of credit, aircraft financings, and equipment leasing.

Commercial lending is constantly becoming more challenging. In my contacts with working loan officers at many conferences and seminars, I have observed a sincere desire on the part of these lenders to improve their professional knowledge. Many have expressed a need for practical, pragmatic information concerning the techniques lenders use on a daily basis in dealing with their customers. This book is my endeavor to meet that need, and to make a useful and significant contribution to the honorable and challenging profession of commercial lending.

Unless otherwise noted, all references to the Uniform Commercial Code in this book pertain to the 1972 version of the Uniform Commercial Code as embodied in Chapter 26 of the Illinois Revised Statutes. I know that there are significant variations in the Uniform Commercial Code from state to state, and therefore recommend that the reader consult the applicable sections of the Uniform Commercial Code of their own state. Other statutes also vary considerably from one jurisdiction to another, and in referring to law, I have concentrated on generally accepted principles of common law. Again, the reader should become familiar with the provisions of the specific applicable statutes of his/her own state.

The loan forms and legal documents shown in this text are for the purpose of illustration only. A lending institution should consult its attorney when revising its loan forms and legal documents.

Acknowledgments

A work as comprehensive as this book could not have been completed without the assistance and support of a number of individuals to whom I owe a debt of gratitude.

James W. Evans, co-author of Chapter 12, legal advisor for the book and author of the Addendum, generously made his immense legal knowledge available to me on a continuing basis. His advice and guidance have been invaluable.

J. L. (Jan) Bennion, author of Chapter 19, added an important additional dimension to the book by sharing her comprehensive knowledge of equipment leasing.

Alene Landreth, manuscript typist, proofreader, and problem solver, played a vital role in production of the manuscript.

Delores Behrens, my wife, whose support and encouragement means a great deal to me.

Richard M. Jorgensen, President of The Commercial Bank of Champaign, who generously permitted me to use various bank forms as exhibits, and whose support is greatly appreciated.

David White, James J. Jesso, and Anthony Milano, my fellow bank officers, who advised me on topics within their particular fields of expertise.

Robert M. Roen, Vice President and Executive Editor of Bankers Publishing Company, without whose guidance and encouragement this book would probably never have been completed.

1

The Commercial Loan Officer's Job

The job of commercial loan officer is a key position in any commercial bank. Commercial loan officers have the challenging dual responsibility of making recommendations and decisions concerning the investment of a major portion of the bank's funds, and that of dealing with the needs of the bank's business customers on a day-by-day basis. Since a bank's business customers are often its largest depositors, it is imperative that their needs be met on a prompt and professional basis. In many banks, the commercial loan officers are the bank's principal contact with the business community, and their relationship with the community's business people may be the prime determinant of the community's attitude toward the bank.

The specific function performed by a loan officer will vary greatly depending on the size and staff organization of the bank. In a large bank, the commercial loan officer may be a specialist, dealing with a limited number of large loans concentrated in one specific industry. In a medium-size bank, he or she may deal with a wide variety of businesses, varying from small retail and service businesses to sizeable manufacturing concerns. The commercial loan officer in a small bank may have any number of duties, including installment and personal lending, collections and marketing. Whatever his or her specific duties, every commercial lender must have the twin basic objectives of adequately and equitably serving the needs of the business customer and of profitably investing the bank's funds on a safe, sound basis. In addition, the loan officer has the responsibility of supervising those loans already on the books, of obtaining periodic progress reports from the borrower, and of continually evaluating trends in each of the loans he or she services, in order to identify problems as soon as possible. The success of the bank's commercial lending operation is directly dependent upon the ability, initiative, and dedication of the loan officers who staff that operation.

The following basic functions of a loan officer might be shown in a typical job description for a commercial loan officer in a medium-sized bank:

1. To be charged with the responsibility of originating, servicing, supervising, and collecting loans in compliance with the policies and procedures of the commercial loan department.
2. To ascertain that every loan made meets the bank's standards for safety and soundness.
3. To ascertain that each loan complies with state and federal regulations.
4. To compile a proper, adequate, well-documented file on each loan.
5. To competently and adequately service the day-to-day needs of each loan customer, and to maintain proper working relationships with the customers, advising and counseling them in their financial affairs.
6. To make loan decisions within the limits of their authority granted by the board and the chief executive officer, and as outlined by the loan policy of the bank.
7. To periodically report his or her activities, and especially all loan problems, to the departmental supervisory officer.
8. To actively cooperate with the departmental supervisory officer in all collection cases and legal proceedings.
9. To perform such other duties as may be assigned by the supervisory officer or the chief executive officer, including participation in the bank's business development and customer service programs.

In specific terms, the commercial loan officer's job will ordinarily include interviewing the applicant; obtaining necessary financial information; ascertaining the nature of the loan request; organizing and analyzing the financial information submitted by the borrower; obtaining and compiling background information on the borrower; performing or having performed a search of the public records; preparing a presentation and recommendations for the loan committee; negotiating terms and rate with the borrower; inspecting and appraising collateral; completing or supervising the completion of the necessary loan documents; verifying that all documents are properly executed and filed; disbursing loan proceeds; monitoring borrower performance; identifying potential problems; and instituting collection action if necessary.

In addition, most commercial loan officers have duties related to, but not directly connected with, the lending operation, such as calling on existing or potential customers; cross selling the bank's other services; counseling their customers concerning their financial affairs; and keeping their customers informed concerning the national economy.

Attributes of a Successful Loan Officer

The successful loan officer must have a wide range of technical skills, including a thorough understanding of the principles of lending, law, and commercial practice. He or she must also have a working knowledge of business management, accounting, economics, and finance as well as the technical skills necessary to interpret and analyze statistics, and the ability to organize and compile information in a meaningful manner.

Above all else, a loan officer must have the ability to make sound decisions. As noted above, this requires a wide range of technical knowledge. However, technical knowledge alone is not sufficient for making a sound loan decision. It also requires basic good sense and an ability to judge the character of the borrower and the feasibility of the borrower's request. A professional loan officer must have an almost intuitive sense of the risks involved in a loan. This involves a capacity for gauging the ability, integrity, and motivations of the borrower. Since this involves subjective judgments, it is doubtful that a scientific formula will ever be developed that can be exclusively relied upon for loan decisions.

Making a judgment of the human element involved in every loan is more an art than a science. It requires that the loan officer have a basic understanding of psychology, a sensitivity to the attitude of the borrower, and a keen sense of perception. A highly competent loan officer is almost invariably a meticulous observer of the reactions and attitudes of the borrower. These attributes enable some seasoned loan officers to develop an almost instinctive sense of what is sound and what is unsound, what is true and what is false.

The decision-making process for the loan officer, therefore, involves an analysis of financial information, a weighing of the weak and the strong factors, judgment of the future performance of the borrower based on both past history and projections, and the loan officer's assessment of the human element involved in the loan. Making a proper decision on this basis requires not only technical knowledge, and a perceptive understanding of the human element, but also experience. The job of the loan officer, more so than most, is a continual learning experience. True competence is developed to a great extent through a number of years' experience in a lending operation. It takes time to develop a loan officer's credit judgment. It cannot be done overnight, or in crash courses. An exposure to a tremendous number and variety of lending situations is what is required to develop the necessary skills and depth of perception that are the hallmark of the professional loan officer.

Experience in the business world is extremely helpful. The greater the commercial loan officer's knowledge of business practice, of the manner in which businesses conduct their day-by-day transactions, and of the businessman's perspective, the greater his or her ability will be to communicate with the bank's business customers. These attributes will increase the customer's respect for the loan officer.

Successful commercial loan officers will be empathetic with the borrowing customer, and be genuinely concerned for the customer's success. This means being able to see the businessman's problems from his or her perspective, and to take a constructive approach to those problems.

Finally, the competent commercial loan officer must be an able negotiator. Most loans involve a certain amount of negotiation of terms, and a complex business or industrial loan proposal may involve weeks or months of intricate negotiations regarding rate, security, guarantys, loan agreement convenants, and compensating balances. Negotiations of this kind require flexibility, an ability to identify alternatives, and resourcefulness. The loan officer must be able to structure a deal satisfactory to the customer without violating the bank's policy or making pricing concessions that would render the loan unprofitable to the bank.

Professional Qualifications

As the banking and business environments have become more complex, banks have increasingly demanded that their lending staffs upgrade their professional qualifications. Contrary to past practice in some banks, where employees were often promoted to lending positions based on time of employment and seniority, with little regard for professional competence, most banks now require that candidates for lending positions have academic degrees in finance, accounting, or business administration, or commensurate business experience and training. Many of the larger city banks now require that candidates for lending positions have Master of Business Administration degrees. In view of the fact that many modern business managers have similar academic qualifications, it appears prudent for banks to endeavor to retain lending personnel at least as qualified as the businessmen they serve.

Although adequate academic qualifications provide the potential loan officer with an excellent foundation for becoming a competent commercial lender, considerable further professional education is required. This is ordinarily achieved by on-the-job training, self-study programs, and through educational programs provided by professional organizations like the American Bankers Association and Robert Morris Associates. While many large banks have formal training programs, most banks' training programs consist of on-the-job training in which the trainee works very closely with an experienced loan officer on a one-to-one basis. Knowledge is gained by the trainee through observation, participation, informal discussion, examination of credit files, and reading assignments. The next step is often to allow the trainee to review or analyze loans. Then, as the trainee progresses, he or she is allowed to make loans under the supervision of an experienced officer, and finally, as proficiency is gained, the fledgling lender is allowed to operate more or less independently. One-to-one training is no doubt the best way for a trainee to gain knowledge of the day-by-day operation of a loan department.

Many educational resources are available to both the beginning and the experienced commercial lender in the form of schools, conferences, seminars, self-study programs, and books. A number of these, especially those sponsored by the American Bankers Association and Robert Morris Associates, are described here. Since commercial lending is a complex, constantly changing profession, it is important that every loan officer strive to improve his or her expertise on a continuing basis.

American Bankers Association Educational Programs

The National Commercial Lending School provides a specialized training program in commercial lending for middle management level bankers. Practical aspects of financial analysis and cash flow are stressed. Established in 1969, the two-week school is highly regarded as a basic professional training program for loan officers. Sessions are held two or three times per year at the University of Oklahoma at Norman, Oklahoma. Educational requirements for admission are completion of AIB courses or the equivalent in accounting, credit administration and financial statement analysis. Three years of experience in commercial lending or credit analysis is generally required, although bankers with five years of experience in areas other than lending who are recommended by their superiors will be considered for admission. The curriculum includes lectures and case studies in accounting, agricultural finance, asset based lending, financial forecasting, statement analysis, bankruptcy, leasing, loan documentation, and workouts.

The National Commercial Lending Graduate School provides an advanced training program for experienced commercial loan officers. The curriculum emphasizes the concepts of loan administration and theory involved in policy decisions. All aspects of profitability, risk, and liquidity are considered. The curriculum includes lectures and case studies on asset/liability management, business development, problem loans, loan policy, credit administration, and portfolio management. The school consists of two one-week sessions held at the University of Oklahoma. Applicants must hold a responsible position in formulation and administration of loan policy, and must be a graduate of the National Commercial Lending School, or have completed graduate AIB courses or the equivalent in credit administration, accounting, financial analysis and management. Applicants must also have at least five years commercial lending experience. This is an excellent educational program for the seasoned commercial lender or loan administrator.

The National Advanced Agricultural Banking School, established in 1981, provides officers at middle and upper management levels an opportunity to develop and broaden the skills necessary to manage an agricultural department or bank. Although not exclusively devoted to lending, the school does provide much information that is useful to loan officers involved in agricultural lending. The two-year school is held annually at Iowa State University, Ames, Iowa. It is recommended but not required that applicants be graduates of state level agricultural banking schools. Five years of agricultural banking experience or the equivalent is required, and the applicant must hold or have potential for a management position, and be endorsed by the bank CEO.

The National School of Real Estate Finance was established in 1963 as a specialized training program for bank officers involved in real estate lending, including commercial, residential, and construction lending. The two-year school holds annual sessions at Ohio State University, Columbus, Ohio. The curriculum includes lectures and case studies on income property analysis, construction financing, compliance, legal aspects, servicing, the secondary mortgage market, appraisals, and real estate development. Applicants must be management personnel at junior or intermediate levels with at least part-time assignments in real estate finance.

The American Bankers Association's two-day National Credit Conference is held in a different major city each year. It is a working conference for commercial lenders and presents general sessions featuring nationally known speakers, workshops, and special interest sessions that address topics of interest to commercial lenders. One of the greatest benefits of this conference is the opportunity it gives a working loan officer to exchange ideas and viewpoints with other bankers actively involved in commercial lending.

The National Leadership Conference on Real Estate Finance is also held annually. It's program is specifically structured for commercial bankers who are active in real estate lending, and covers such subjects as the economic forecast for housing, and legislation affecting the real estate industry.

The National Agricultural Bankers Conference is held each year in a major U.S. city and presents a comprehensive program for agricultural bankers. Although not devoted exclusively to agricultural lending, many workshops and special sessions are devoted to lending related subjects, and this conference presents an excellent opportunity for agricultural loan officers to obtain current information and exchange ideas with peers.

American Institute of Banking

The American Institute of Banking is the major educational arm of the American Bankers Association, and offers excellent educational programs for bank personnel at all levels. It has 450 chapters and 150 study groups serving a membership of over 300,000 bank personnel. The programs of AIB are operated primarily by volunteer bankers. AIB chapters are permanent educational institutions, locally organized and administered by bankers. The larger chapters offer a wide range of educational programs in all areas of commercial banking. Many chapters have working arrangements with area colleges under which AIB courses are co-sponsored by the chapter and the college, and which bankers and students may take to earn simultaneous college and AIB credits. Many of these programs lead to two or four year degrees in banking and finance.

Many communities which are too small to support chapters have study groups that are organized from year to year as the need arises. Bankers may also enroll in correspondence study. The correspondence student is provided with a textbook and a set of practical exercises which he or she must complete and return for grading. Qualified experts review the correspondence work. A final examination must be completed satisfactorily for the student to receive credit for the course.

Diplomas are awarded to those students who complete a prescribed series of courses, including an applied diploma in commercial lending. Some courses currently being offered which are of interest to commercial loan officers are analyzing financial statements, introduction to commercial lending, lending to agricultural enterprises, loan documentation, loan and discount, real estate finance, and written lending policy. These courses are an excellent way for personnel in all areas of lending to improve their professional expertise by class attendance or study on a part-time or spare time basis.

Robert Morris Associates

Robert Morris Associates, which was established in 1914, is the national professional association of commercial bank loan and credit officers. One of the principal objectives of RMA is to publish materials for the continuing education of bank loan and credit officers. The *Journal of Commercial Bank Lending* is published monthly, and each issue contains a number of articles covering various aspects of commercial lending. RMA also has books and manuals covering a wide variety of lending topics. Its *Annual Statement Studies* provides composite balance sheet and income data on over 300 different categories of businesses and industries, which is widely used by banks for external analysis purposes. RMA also sponsors conferences and workshops on financial statement analysis, loan review, and commercial loans to businesses.

Other Resources

Many state bankers' associations offer excellent state level schools for the banker, and prior to attending one of the national level schools, it is usually advisable for the loan officer to attend one or more of the schools sponsored by his or her state bankers' association. The American Bankers Association's

Bankers Schools Directory is an excellent source of information on over 100 resident banking schools. Most of the state associations also offer annual conferences and seminars on various aspects of commercial lending.

Many excellent books and manuals are available to the commercial lender, and every bank commercial loan department should have a library of texts on basic lending subjects. The following are suggested basic texts that should be useful to every commercial loan officer.

1. *Commercial Loan Documentation*, William C. Hillman, Practising Law Institute, 810 Seventh Avenue, New York, New York, 10019.
2. *The Law of Secured Transactions Under the Uniform Commercial Code*, Barkley Clark, Warren, Gorham & Lamont, Inc., 210 South Street, Boston, Massachusetts 02111.
3. *Banker's Guide to Financial Statements*, second edition, Thomas J. O'Malia, Bankers Publishing Company, 210 South Street, Boston, Massachusetts 02111.
4. *Bankruptcy Manual: Guide for Bankers to the Bankruptcy Act of 1978*, American Bankers Association, 1120 Connecticut Avenue N.W., Washington, D.C. 20036.
5. *Annual Statement Studies*, Robert Morris Associates, The Philadelphia National Bank Building, Philadelphia, Pennsylvania 19107.
6. *Real Estate Financing*, American Bankers Association.
7. *Commercial Problem Loans*, second edition, Robert H. Behrens, Bankers Publishing Company.
8. *Effective Loan Management*, Robert Morris Associates.

In addition, each commercial loan department should have a current, complete set of the statutes of the state in which it operates.

2

Loan Policy Considerations

Every lending institution has a loan policy of one kind or another. This policy may consist of a very formalized written statement or a series of informal memoranda. In some instances, it may consist only of verbal guidelines voiced by management. In others, it may be a set of attitudes, precedents, and traditions which are hardly recognized as constituting a "policy" at all. No matter how nebulous they may be, every lender has a set of constraints and guidelines that forms the parameters for the lending operation. This chapter examines the function and importance of a clear, comprehensive loan policy, and includes guidelines for the formulation of a written policy. A sample commercial loan policy is included as Exhibit A.

An institution's loan policy may be defined as a statement of its basic philosophy and concept of lending. This includes standards, guidelines and limitations to guide the decision-making process. The distinction between loan policy and loan operating procedures should be recognized. Loan policy should be a broad statement, while loan operating procedures may be quite specific, and may include step-by-step instructions for handling various situations. The importance of a written loan policy cannot be overemphasized. Written procedures (usually in manual form) are also recommended, especially if the lending institution's staff is large, and includes relatively inexperienced personnel.

Most lending operations of any size have found it necessary to formulate a written loan policy to achieve consistency, coordination, and control. Also, the various bank supervisory agencies strongly recommend that banks prepare a written loan policy. A well-conceived loan policy should be stated in concise and positive terms and should be specific enough to provide guidelines for handling various categories of credit. It should give the loan officer a sense of direction and a definite frame of reference in which to consider a given loan application. However, a loan policy should never be so restrictive that it stifles the loan officer's initiative or prevents exceptions in those cases where a sound, safe loan can be made, even though the specific situation is somewhat outside the limits of lending policy.

A written loan policy is one of bank management's most effective yard-sticks for measuring the performance of the bank's loan officers. While loss experience over an extended period of time may be the most crucial measure of performance, certainly the next best measure of performance is the extent to which the loan officer adheres to the bank's written policies. A well written loan policy can also be a major tool for communication within an organization, and an educational tool for inexperienced loan officers.

Criteria for a Loan Policy

Establish Objectives

Most lending institutions have established or should establish objectives in these areas:

1. Growth—in assets, loan volume, capital.
2. Profitability—in dollars, as a percentage return on equity or on assets.
3. Portfolio quality—holding delinquency and losses to a stated ratio; limiting loan concentration.
4. Customer service—guidelines for properly serving the customer.
5. Community service—guidelines for the institution's involvement in the community; social responsibility.
6. Compliance with regulations—regulatory and supervisory authorities are now requiring lending institutions to include a compliance policy in their general policy statement.

Establish Lines of Authority

1. Recognize the responsibility of the board of directors.
2. Outline the authority and function of the loan or discount committee.
3. Outline the duties and responsibilities of the chief executive officer and the loan supervisory officer.
4. Establish the duties and responsibilities of the loan officers.
5. Establish the lending authority of each loan officer, taking into consideration the title, lending experience, past performance, and duty assignment of each officer.

Establish Credit Criteria

1. Establish which types of loans are acceptable and which are not. Unacceptable loans might include illegal loans, those that are

purely speculative, loans made on a subordinated basis or secured by a subordinate security interest, or made against a restricted stock, or loans linked to brokered deposits.

2. Outline the credit factors to be considered in making loan decisions.
3. Establish criteria for unsecured loans.
4. List the types of collateral that are acceptable and what percentage of value may be loaned against each type.
5. Outline what deposit relationship will be required on the part of the borrower.
6. Establish guidelines for acceptable maturities, based on loan type and purpose.
7. Outline the extent to which a credit investigation will be conducted on each type of loan application.
8. Establish criteria under which loans may be renewed or extended.
9. Define the bank's attitude toward loans to borrowers outside the bank's normal trade area.

Establish Procedures and Controls

1. Describe what information and documentation will be maintained in credit files, and at what intervals information is to be updated.
2. Set standards for loan supervision—including frequency of visits to business premises, frequency with which the file is to be reviewed, and monitoring of compliance with the repayment plan loans.
3. Establish a procedure for reporting possible problems to management.

Establish Policy for Loans to Directors, Officers, Employees, and Other Insiders

1. Prohibit favorable treatment for insiders.
2. Procedure for approving these loans.
3. Limitations of amounts and other terms.

Establish Criteria for Handling Problem Loans

1. Determine who is to be responsible for handling problem loans.
2. Establish guidelines for instituting legal action.
3. Establish procedure for periodically reporting status to management.

Establish Criteria for Charge-Offs

1. Identify those conditions that will require the charge-off of a loan.
2. Establish accounting procedure for handling the charge-off.
3. Establish guidelines and procedure for the follow up and collection of charged-off loans.

Establish Procedures for Compliance with Regulations
1.   Statement of intent to comply with all statutes and regulations.
2.   Guidelines for training of lending personnel.

Establish Procedure for Periodic Review of the Credit Policy
Annual review probably sufficient.

Summary

The importance of a written loan policy cannot be stressed enough. The general loan policy statement should be the institution's major statement of its philosophy toward risk, profitability, and growth. It should be approved by the Board of Directors and periodically reviewed by them. Management should see to it that all lending personnel are thoroughly familiar with the loan policy, and it should be used both as a measure of loan officer performance and a communicative and educational tool.

EXHIBIT   A   Commercial Loan Policy Crossroads National Bank

I.   *Objectives*
    1.   The bank shall have the following objectives in its lending operations:
        a.   To invest a prudent proportion of the bank's total deposits in loans, but loan deposit ratio shall not exceed 70%, without permission of the Board of Directors.
        b.   To provide for the reasonable, constructive credit needs of the responsible businesses and individuals in the community, in accordance with the bank's CRA policy, and to counsel those borrowers regarding their finanacial needs.
        c.   To invest the bank's funds at a rate of return adequate to meet the bank's budgeted profit objectives.
        d.   To consider all risks involved in a loan to protect the stockholders' equity, and to continue to analyze the risk factor during the entire term of the loan.
        e.   To collect any loan made with the least possible delay, problem or controversy, and to limit loan losses to no more than .40% of average loans outstanding.
        f.   To maintain a moderately aggressive lending posture to achieve reasonable growth.

II.   *Responsibility and Authority*
    1.   The Board of Directors has the ultimate responsibility and authority for the general supervision of the affairs of the bank, including the loan portfolio. The Board shall review and approve all loan objectives and policies, and changes thereto.
    2.   The Loan Committee shall consist of the chief executive officer and four other members elected annually by the Board at its annual organization meeting.
    3.   The Loan Committee shall have regular meetings twice monthly, and at such additional times as deemed necessary by the chief executive officer.
    4.   The specific functions and duties of the Loan Committee shall include:
        a.   Approval of loan requests, or at their discretion, or if required by regulations, referral of loan requests to the Board for approval.
        b.   Review and approve monthly all loans in the amount of $10,000.00 or more.
        c.   Monitor compliance with loan policy and procedures.
        d.   Give counsel and direction to management in the administration of the loan portfolio.
        e.   Review on a monthly basis the bank's Watch List and all delinquent and problem loans, and make recommendations for the handling of those loans.
    5.   The chief executive officer shall be responsible for the general administration and supervision of the loan portfolio, shall monitor compliance with loan policy, and shall see that proper reports of loans made and other lending activities are made to the Loan Committee and the Board.

6.   The Senior Loan Officer shall be responsible for the day by day supervision of the Lending Departments, shall see that loan forms and procedures are updated from time to time, that all lending personnel are properly trained, that the Lending Departments develop annual budgets, and strive to meet their budgetary goals. The Senior Loan Officer shall also actively work to develop new business.

7.   The Commercial Loan Department Head shall be responsible for the day by day operation of the Commercial Loan Department and shall see that all lending operations are carried out in a prudent and proper manner. He or she shall be responsible for personnel organization and work assignments within the department. It will be his or her duty to develop an annual budget and operating plan for the department, and he or she shall strive to meet budgetary goals set by management. The department head shall also prepare monthly a Watch List of all weak and problem loans in the department's portfolio.

8.   The Loan Officers shall have the primary responsibility for making, approving, monitoring, and reporting loans. It shall be their responsibility to obtain all required loan documentation, perfect a security interest in collateral and establish and update the credit file for each loan.

9.   Lending Authority for each officer shall be established by the Loan Committee and approved by the Board of Directors. In establishing lending limits for each individual officer, the Loan Committee shall take into consideration the individual's title, experience, and capability. The lending authority for all officers shall be reviewed annually by the Loan Committee.

III.   *Commercial Loan Department Functions*

1.   The primary function of the Commercial Loan Department shall be to make, supervise and collect the following categories of loans:
   a.   short term working capital loans to businesses
   b.   capital term loans to businesses
   c.   agricultural loans
   d.   construction loans
   e.   commercial mortgage loans
   f.   in exceptional instances, loans to individuals for consumer purposes, principally in the form of single-payment notes.

2.   In addition to these primary duties, other duties may be assigned to the department by the chief executive officer.

IV.   *Prohibited and Undesirable loans*

1.   Prohibited Loans
   a.   Loans that are illegal, or which will finance illegal enterprises.
   b.   Loans that violate state or federal banking regulations.
   c.   Loans secured by the bank's own stock, U.S. savings bonds, IRA or Keogh accounts, profit sharing or pension plans.
   d.   Loans to individuals or businesses on which the bank has previously had a charge-off, or on which the bank has had to initi..e legal action to force collection.

2.   Undesirable Loans
   a.   Loans for speculative purposes.

    b.   Loans secured by restricted or closely held stock for which an established market does not exist.

    c.   Loans for which the sole security is a second mortgage on real estate, unless the total of the first and second mortgages fall within the bank's parameters for first mortgage loans.

    d.   Interim construction loans which are not supported by a permanent loan (take-out) commitment.

    e.   Loans secured by household goods, jewelry, antiques, art works, etc.

    f.   Loans to an unprofitable business, or one in which management is weak.

    g.   Loans for a term longer than the economic or depreciable life of the assets used as security.

    h.   Loans to a business for the purchase of sizeable non-productive assets which are not required for the operation of the business.

    i.   Consolidation loans to an over-extended borrower.

    j.   Subordinated loans, or loans secured by a subordinated security interest.

    k.   Loans linked to brokered deposits.

    l.   Loans to a borrower whose integrity is questionable, or against whom there is a substantial judgment or tax lien outstanding.

V.   *Credit Standards*

    1.   Credit shall be extended only to honest, capable, responsible individuals and well managed business firms having adequate capability to repay the loan from normal sources of income.

    2.   A specific, workable repayment plan for each loan shall be agreed to by the bank and the borrower and recorded in the credit file. The borrower shall be required to adhere to this plan, but it may be modified from time to time by mutual agreement if a valid reason exists for doing so. The only loans for which a specific repayment plan is not required are those secured by hard collateral such as assignment of savings accounts, cash value of life insurance, listed securities, government bonds, certificates of deposit, etc.

    3.   The purpose of every loan shall be ascertained by the loan officer, and in the case of a loan for $2500 or more, recorded in the credit file.

    4.   Every borrower should have financial strength adequate to support the loan. To substantiate this, a complete financial statement, including income statement, shall be obtained at least annually from each borrower, with the exception of those who borrow less than $2500, and those whose loans are secured by hard collateral in the bank's possession.

    5.   All business borrowers shall be encouraged to provide CPA audited financial statements, and in the case of a loan of $250,000 or more, a CPA audited statement shall generally be required. All unaudited statements shall be closely examined and a reasonable effort made to verify information contained therein to determine each statement's accuracy and the soundness of asset valuations.

    6.   When a borrower has substantial assets held in joint tenancy, the bank generally shall require that the joint tenant(s) execute any security

documents required to perfect the bank's security interest in the borrower's assets.

7. Any loan made to a closely held corporation shall be guaranteed by the principal owners. Exceptions to this will be made only in rare instances, and where there is a significant reason for doing so.

8. Unsecured credit shall be granted only to those individuals and businesses with above average integrity, adequate financial management ability, very strong financial position and repayment capacity, and a history of satisfactory past performance. The strength of these factors shall be the prime criteria in judging the acceptability of a loan on an unsecured basis.

VI.   *Credit Files*

1. A credit file shall be maintained on all loans in excess of $2500, with the exception of those fully secured by hard collateral in possession of the bank. The credit file shall include a complete annual financial statement of the borrower, as well as specific information regarding loan purpose, the repayment agreement, and supporting documentation, so that the status of the loan can be determined at all times.

2. A historical record of each continuing line of credit shall be maintained in the form of a comparative summary of all financial information, which shall be a part of the basic documentation in the credit file.

3. A record of all rejected loan applications shall be maintained containing pertinent information and showing the reasons for rejection.

VII.   *Credit Investigations*

1. A current credit report or a search of the public records shall be obtained for each new loan applicant and for any applicant whose character or financial position is questionable. A complete search of the public records shall also be performed for any borrower upon whom the bank receives derogatory information or in whose loan there is a noticeable deterioration in quality.

VIII. *Loan Supervision*

1. It will be the duty of each loan officer to periodically review the repayment plan and general status of each loan he or she services, and if substantial deviations or problems are detected, to actively follow-up to determine the cause, and to develop a plan for correction with the borrower.

2. It shall also be the duty of the loan officer to visit the premises of each substantial business borrower at least annually, not only for public relations purposes, but with the express intent of observing the premises, facilities, and personnel of the business. Observations made on such visits shall be recorded in the credit file by the loan officer.

IX.   *Compliance with Regulations*

1. It shall be the policy of this bank that all loans shall be in full compliance with the applicable state and federal regulations.

2. All loan forms and procedures shall conform to state and federal regulations, and shall be reviewed periodically and revised to reflect changes in the statutes, or to conform to the requirements of the supervisory authorities.

3. Meetings and seminars shall be held periodically at the discretion of

the department head, to insure that all lending personnel are fully informed of the requirements of the various state and federal regulations.

X.   *Loan Pricing*

1. The bank's base loan rate shall be defined as the rate available to the most qualified applicants who demonstrate financial strength, a history of acceptable performance, and the capacity to repay in a timely manner. The base rate reflects the bank's present cost of funds, and current money market conditions.

2. The bank's base rate shall be determined monthly by the Asset and Liability Management Committee.

3. All commercial borrowers who, in the bank's judgment, do not qualify for base rate, shall be charged a rate higher than base rate, to be determined after consideration of the level of risk involved and the customer's overall relationship with the bank.

4. Commercial loan rates fixed for an extended period of time shall generally be avoided, unless deemed appropriate for the bank's portfolio by the Asset and Liability Management Committee.

XI.   *Participations*

1. Participations in loans may be sold to other institutions from time to time. Participations shall be sold only in loans that are of acceptable quality and on the basis of full disclosure of all facts to the purchaser.

2. Participations purchased from other institutions shall meet all criteria and quality standards for direct loans, and the decision to purchase a participation shall be made in the same manner as the loan decision on a direct application. Documentation requirements shall also be the same as for a direct loan.

XII.   *Problem Loans*

1. A problem loan is defined as one in which there is a major breakdown in the repayment agreement resulting in an undue delay in collection, or in which there appears to be a potential loss.

2. It shall be the bank's objective to identify all problem loans at the earliest possible date, to identify the cause of the problem, and take corrective action as soon as possible. Protection of the bank's interests and the avoidance of a loan loss shall be the first consideration in any corrective action taken. However, the borrower's rights shall be recognized and preserved at all times.

3. All problem loans shall be promptly reported to the chief executive officer and Loan Committee.

XIII.   *Charge-offs and Collections*

1. All loans charged off will be charged against the valuation portion of the Reserve for Loan Losses.

2. Accounts will be charged off as soon as probability of loss or undue delay in collection is established, taking into consideration such factors as the customer's financial condition, value of collateral, and guarantors.

3. All loans are subject to periodic examination by the comptroller of Currency who may require the charge-off of loans of unacceptable quality.

4. All charge-offs of loans shall be approved by the Loan Committee and entered into the minutes thereof.

XIV.   *Loans to Officers and Directors*
1.   All loans to officers or directors of this bank, or to a business entity in which an officer or director has a material ownership interest, shall comply with the provisions of all pertinent federal and state regulations.
2.   A loan to an officer or director of this bank, or to a business entity in which an officer or director has a material ownership interest, shall comply with all credit standards, and shall be made at a rate of interest in line with normal prevailing rates, and on terms not more favorable than those afforded other equally eligible borrowers.

XV.   *Trade and Loan Areas*
1.   The bank's primary trade area shall be that area roughly within a 50 mile radius of the bank's main office as designated by the bank's Community Reinvestment Act (CRA) statement, and shall generally conform to the Adams-Hancock retail trade area as identifed by the local Chamber of Commerce.
2.   The bank's secondary trade area shall be that area comprising the trade areas of its principal affiliate and correspondent banks. It is not contemplated that direct business will be done in the secondary trade area, but that the bank will engage in some business on an indirect basis in cooperation with, and as an accomodation to, its affiliates and correspondents in its secondary area.
3.   The bank's primary loan area shall basically consist of Adams and Hancock Counties with geographic priorities as follows:
    a.   The Crossroads City metropolitan area.
    b.   The agricultural area within the above counties.
    c.   The outlying villages within the above counties.
    Commercial or agricultural loans to unusually strong customers may occasionally be made outside the primary loan area. Real estate mortgage loans will not be made outside the bank's primary loan area except in rare and unusual circumstances.
4.   The bank's secondary loan area shall consist of the normal loan areas of its principal affiliate and correspondent banks. It is not contemplated that the bank will normally make direct loans in its secondary area, but that it will, from time to time, purchase participations in loans made within its secondary area by its affiliates and correspondents.

XVI.   *Policy Review*
The credit policy of this bank shall be reviewed by the senior loan officer and the chief executive officer annually, for the purpose of recommending those changes necessary to update this policy. Changes recommended by the senior loan officer and chief executive officer shall be approved by the Loan Committee and the Board of Directors.

3

Basic Principles of Lending

Lenders have long recognized that to make a proper loan decision, certain basic principles and concepts must be considered. Lenders have devoted much research and contemplation to the identification and articulation of those critical elements which significantly affect the safety, soundness, and workability of a loan. As a result, the banking industry has its "C's" of credit, and other lenders have various "credit factors" or "key factors" which constitute their basic rules of lending. Whatever the terms in which these principles are stated, it is absolutely necessary that commercial loan officers understand the concepts involved, if they are to make good loan decisions. These principles are in effect the ten commandments of the lending business. In this chapter I will discuss the basic principles of lending in some detail. These will be divided into five basic categories—human/management factors, financial position, repayment capacity, collateral, and loan purpose. In addition, concepts pertaining to structuring the loan and determining proper maturity will be discussed.

Human/Management Factors

Every lender realizes that the pay-off of a loan on a satisfactory basis depends largely upon the borrower—on his or her willingness and ability to perform in accordance with the terms of the loan. What specific factors affect the borrower's performance? These factors can be identified and divided into two categories, namely "human" or character factors, and management capability factors.

Human Factors

The human factors encompass such basic issues as the borrower's honesty, moral character, goals, objectives, motivations, determination to meet obligations, and willingness to cooperate with the lender. It is of prime importance that the borrower make complete and truthful disclosure of his or her financial affairs to the lender, and discuss the status of his or her business in an honest and open manner. Otherwise, it is impossible for the lender to make a good loan decision and to develop a satisfactory working relationship with the borrower, and this will lead to trouble for both lender and borrower. Willful misrepresentation is a sure danger signal which may be indicative of fraud, and which cannot be ignored by the lender.

An applicant's general moral character may be extremely difficult to judge, and the lender must exercise considerable caution in making necessarily subjective judgments in this area. The borrower's motivations may be complex, and therefore very difficult for the lender to analyze. A borrower who is lax in honoring marital obligations, or who drinks too much, or who from time to time appears to engage in questionable business dealings, may nevertheless fulfill his or her obligations to a lender in a very satisfactory manner. Conversely, the individual who appears to be a pillar in the community may prove to be a poor credit risk. Probably the most prudent approach for the lender is to judge the borrower primarily by his or her attitude and performance record. At the same time, the lender must remain aware that the borrower's reputation and moral attitudes may provide significant clues to his or her future attitude toward the debt obligation. It should also be recognized that integrity may be relative, and that a borrower who is completely honest when prosperous, may become less honest when faced with financial problems.

The borrower's determination to meet obligations is another important factor. Certainly a borrower with a "will to win" attitude who has the ability to perform well under adverse conditions, and who is willing to curtail his or her personal living standard during lean times is more likely to pay off the loan in a timely manner than a borrower who does not possess these attributes. Another significant factor is the borrower's attitude toward his or her relationship with the lender. If the borrower has a willingness to cooperate and accept the counsel of the lender, a basis then exists for building mutual respect and confidence that will benefit both parties.

To understand the borrower, the lender must strive to understand the borrower's goals, objectives, and motivations since these will significantly affect the manner in which the borrower sets priorities and makes management decisions. Several distinct types of borrowers may be identified, based on their basic motivations.

The empire builder—this is the aggressive, growth minded business manager. This type of manager is dedicated to the business, always searching for new horizons, willing to assume additional risk to facilitate expansion. He or she is not hesitant to borrow to fund expansion and often wants to leverage to a greater degree than the lender is comfortable with. This kind of manager often believes that growth will solve all the business' problems.

The innovator—a major goal of this kind of manager is to be ahead of the competition. He or she is always anxious to introduce new products and services, and new marketing programs, often without adequate consideration of financial consequences and to the detriment of company profits. The lender's major concern often is to "hold him down."

The image builder—this kind of manager is more interested in the appearance of success, rather than in success itself. He or she has a tendency to overspend on facilities, equipment, and incidental amenities, and is very concerned about moving in the right business and social circles. He or she may be a big contributor to community causes, both in time and money, when the business can ill afford it. Debt repayment generally does not have a high priority, and insufficient profits may make repayment performance unsatisfactory.

The stagnant manager—this manager is content to maintain the status quo. As long as the business generates sufficient profits to satisfy the stockholders, or to maintain the sole proprietor's standard of living, any change will be avoided. This kind of manager is slow to react to economic or competitive change, unwilling to adopt new technology, and definitely not growth minded. The business' future is probably uncertain, and it and the lender may have problems when economic or competitive conditions change.

The high liver—this manager has only one objective, that of maximizing withdrawals from the business for personal use. No matter how profitable, the business always has a low equity, and lenders are expected to fund 100% of growth. The lender is probably concerned about debt/worth ratio and repayment performance, since personal withdrawals take priority over debt reduction.

The well rounded manager—this is the ideal business manager who is profit oriented, recognizing that profits are the lifeblood of any business. He or she is also a good planner who anticipates problems, and who is constantly looking for more efficient ways to do things. This kind of manager is not only technically competent in production, marketing, and personnel management, but also recognizes the key importance of good financial management.

Importance of Management Ability

Adequate financial and technical management ability is almost as important as acceptable moral characteristics, and this key factor must be critically analyzed by the lender when making a loan decision. Today's business operation requires a high degree of technical skill in planning, personnel management, production techniques, marketing and accounting, as well as a sophisticated level of financial management. Even small business operations have annual cash flow in the hundreds of thousands or millions of dollars, and the management of dollars has become even more important than the management of labor, production, and marketing programs.

Good business management is to a great extent good cash management, and the capable manager must have sufficient knowledge to prepare a complete cash flow projection, control expenses, recognize profit opportunities, and make wise capital investment decisions. This entails not only knowledge, but also good judgment and a certain amount of experience. Adequacy of management ability is often relative to the economic conditions under which the borrower operates. A poor manager may do relatively well while market conditions are favorable, but be unable to cope with adverse conditions. Flexibility and the ability to adjust to changing conditions are usually a sure sign of a good manager.

How does the lender judge a borrower's management ability? He or she does so primarily by observing the performance of the borrower over a period of time. The decisions the borrower makes and his or her ability to solve problems are indicators of management ability. The nature of the borrower's loan request is also significant. Ultimately, the business' profit performance and financial progress (or lack thereof) are the true indicators of management ability.

Financial Position

Every borrower should have sufficient equity to enable the creditors to recover their funds through the sale of assets, if all else fails. If repayment materialized as contemplated on every loan, the borrower's financial position would likely be of little interest to the lender. However, since problems do arise in loan repayment, lenders want assurance of adequate equity in the borrower's assets to rely on in case repayment fails to materialize.

A lender basically analyzes a business' financial position by examining its balance sheet. However, examination of the balance sheet does not always tell the full story, and often raises almost as many questions as it answers.

What is the quality of the balance sheet information? Is it the result of a fully audited report prepared by an independent CPA firm, or a review compilation of information prepared by management? Is it information prepared internally by the business firm itself? Is the statement a cash basis or accrual basis statement? The quality of the information submitted must always be considered by the lender.

Does the balance sheet represent the right entity? If Joe Smith is applying for a loan as an individual, then submission of a balance sheet on Smith Trucking, Inc., or Smith Trucking, a partnership, raises questions.

Is the balance sheet current? Material changes in financial position may have taken place recently.

Since valuations of assets are estimates, are the quantities and dollar amounts realistic?

What is the condition of such assets as inventory, fixtures, and equipment?

What is the ratio of productive assets to non-productive assets? A proportionately large investment in such assets as recreational facilities or other amenities (or a sizeable investment in an unrelated or speculative business venture), may be indicative of poor financial management.

If there is real estate, it may be shown either at cost or at or near current market value. If listed at market value, there may be substantial potential capital gains tax liability which should be recognized as a contingent liability.

What is the aging of receivables? Has a reserve been established for uncollectible accounts?

Are all liabilities accurately listed? Such accrued liabilities as real estate taxes, income tax and interest are sometimes overlooked.

How does total debt relate to total assets and net worth?

To whom are debts owed and what assets are pledged? Which are short, intermediate, or long term?

How solid is the net worth figure? Is a portion of it "water" due to overstatement of assets or understatement of debt? Where do the equities lie—in land, equipment, inventory on hand, or elsewhere?

What are balance sheet trends? Is debt increasing?

To what extent does the business have "off balance sheet" obligations?

These and other questions will be considered by a loan officer when the borrower's financial position is being analyzed. Also, contingent liabilities, adequacy of insurance coverage, and adequacy of working capital should be considered.

The potential lender should also attempt to ascertain whether the borrower has contingent liabilities, (indirect or potential liabilities), which may become actual liabilities under certain circumstances. Contingent liabilities are discussed in detail in chapter 6.

Adequate casualty and liability insurance coverage to protect the value of the borrower's assets is crucial. No lender wants to be in a position in which his or her "cushion" in the form of the borrower's equity in the assets has disappeared due to fire, windstorm, or theft, and where this equity, or at least a portion of it, cannot be replaced by cash in the form of insurance proceeds.

Importance of Equity

The business' equity or net worth is the difference between its total assets and total liabilities. It represents risk funds that are invested by the owners and are available to creditors as a cushion against loss. Increasing net worth is a principal indicator of financial progress. An increase in a sole proprietor's equity can be achieved only by three basic means—the generation of profits that are retained, the appreciation of assets, or by gift or inheritance. In the case of a corporation, equity can also be increased through the sale of capital stock; in a partnership, equity may be increased by capital contributions from the individual partners.

Many lenders seem to underestimate the importance of equity, which is the best single indicator of the strength of a business and the commitment of its owners. A business with insufficient equity, that is, one that is "overextended," has little ability to weather adversity, or to take advantage of growth opportunities. Debt service costs can be a heavy drain on cash flow. The amount of equity a business should have depends to some extent on the nature of the business, but it appears that as a bare minimum, equity should equal at least 20% of total assets in almost any business, with the exception of financial institutions and businesses, which are often more heavily leveraged.

In some instances, the borrower can offer lenders sources of financial strength other than his or her own equity to support the loan. This may be in the form of a cosignature, endorsement, guaranty, hypothecation, or subordination. These are defined and discussed in chapter 11.

Repayment Capacity

The difference between a good loan and a charge-off lies in one word—repayment. If a loan is repaid in full in a timely manner, then, whatever its weaknesses may have been, the lender generally considers it a good loan. Therefore, the lender's accurate assessment of the borrower's capacity to repay is equally as important as the lender's judgment of the borrower's character and management ability.

How does a lender judge capacity to repay? When dealing with an established business operation, he or she does so in two ways— first, by studying records of the business' past performance, basically in the form of annual income statements; and second, by studying projections of future performance in the form of cash flow projections. Information from income statements is valuable because it gives the lender a picture of the past capability of the business to generate repayment, and thereby provides a relatively sound basis for projecting future income, expenses, and repayment. However, it should be remembered that it is not past performance but future performance that will determine the amount of repayment available for the loan the lender is about to make. Hence, cash flow projections that intelligently estimate the future availability of repayment may be more important to the lender than historical performance data.

In the case of a new business, or one in which significant expansion or other change has taken place, historical income and expense data may be of little relevance, even if available. Since the lender cannot readily use historical data to test projections of future performance, assessing repayment capacity becomes much more difficult. For this reason, lenders generally are less inclined to lend to a new business or one that has significantly changed or expanded its operations, often demanding additional collateral or other changes in loan terms to compensate for the lack of proven repayment performance.

What constitutes sufficient repayment capacity? Every business must generate sufficient cash income to pay all normal operating expenses and income taxes. It must produce enough additional revenue to provide an adequate return to its owners and to repay capital debt in an orderly manner. The amount of capital debt repayment required will depend on the type of debt owed, its terms, and the demands of the holders of that debt. Interest accrued on capital debt is an operating expense. Ideally, a business operation should also produce sufficient cash flow to enable it to establish cash reserves to protect against future adversity and to fund future growth.

In analyzing repayment capacity, lenders must always remember that only cash repays loans! Unsold inventory, uncollected accounts receivable, and work in process are only potential repayment, and do not become actual repayment until converted to cash. Therefore, the lender must project available cash income and its adequacy to meet obligations. This is the basis of all cash flow projections.

There is a significant difference between profits and cash flow. A failing business may have substantial cash flow if it is liquidating its inventory, receivables, and equipment. A profitable but rapidly growing business may be very "hard up" for cash. Profits are essential for the long term survival and growth of a business, but in the short term, a debtor's ability to repay is determined by cash flow rather than profits.

Profits (Net Income) may be defined as the excess of revenue over all expenses during a given period. If a business is to survive and grow, it must produce profits, which are the lifeblood of all business and commerce. Profits are important for a number of reasons, including:

1. Profits provide a return to the investor, who otherwise would have no incentive to risk his or her funds in a business venture.
2. Profits enable a business to increase its working capital.
3. Profits provide funds for repaying capital debt and for new capital investment in equipment and facilities.
4. Profits provide funds for establishing reserves to protect the business against future adversity.

Importance of a Repayment Agreement

If a loan is to be repaid as agreed, two things must happen—first, the anticipated repayment must materialize in the form of cash, and second, the debtor must pay the cash to the lender. For this process to work well, there must be a definite agreement between the lender and borrower, the terms of which are mutually agreed to and well understood by both parties. In the past, lenders have often relied on informal verbal agreements regarding the repayment of loans. In many cases, this agreement has been so vague as to hardly merit the term "agreement." The lender has assumed that the debtor would repay when he or she was able, and the debtor, although fully intending to repay the loan, has had no specific plan for doing so. At best, this has often resulted in confusion on the part of both the lender and the debtor, and at worst, in a serious repayment problem.

As lenders have become more sophisticated, they have come to realize the importance of a specific, firm repayment agreement, which is clearly understood by both lender and borrower. This may be in the form of a verbal agreement with the debtor, but preferably it will be in writing, either in the form of a memorandum in the credit file, as a part of the loan application, or as a separate written agreement. Whatever its form, the repayment agreement should contain the following basic information:

1. The specific source or sources from which repayment is pledged.
2. The approximate amount anticipated from each source. The agreement should state whether *all* repayment generated by a specific source is to be applied, or only a stated maximum, or a certain proportionate part.
3. The approximate date each item of repayment is expected to materialize.

"Split" repayment, i.e., repayment from one source to be divided between several creditors, is always a potential source of misunderstanding and conflict, and should be avoided. Although the repayment agreement should be as specific as possible, it must also be flexible enough to allow modification if changing conditions warrant. A change in marketing strategy or unforeseen adversity often constitutes valid reason for revising the repayment agreement.

Once the loan is disbursed, the lender then must periodically monitor repayment performance. Repayment that has not materialized 30 days after the date it was anticipated in the repayment agreement calls for prompt follow-up by the lender. If contact with the borrower reveals that merely a routine delay has occurred, the lender will probably just make a notation in the credit file, and then continue to monitor the loan until payment materializes. However, if the lender learns that repayment has been diverted, an immediate conference with the debtor is essential. If diversion has occurred due to a misunderstanding, it may not prove a serious problem, provided it does not occur again. If diversion has occurred through the borrower's lack of desire to cooperate or honor his or her obligation, then the lender may well have a severe problem, which may require aggressive corrective action.

In summary, it may be said that the lender who negotiates a firm, specific, workable repayment program with the borrower at the time the loan is made, and who then follows up on the borrower's repayment performance, has taken a major step toward the successful collection of the loan.

Collateral

An institutional lender normally does not lend its own money. It lends funds from depositors or investors and has a prime responsibility to protect their interests. Although most lenders anticipate some losses, those losses must be stringently controlled to safeguard the funds with which they are entrusted, if they are to operate on a profitable basis. Safety is therefore a prime consideration in the extension of all credit. For this reason, a lender will often make a loan on a secured basis in order to make the risk more acceptable.

"Collateral" may be defined as property pledged as security for a loan or other obligation. In modern usage, the terms "collateral" and "security" have become synonymous, each meaning property pledged as security for a loan. The concept of a "pledge" is thousands of years old, and was conceived by money lenders of the ancient world, who took possession of some valuable item of a borrower's property to insure the repayment of a loan. Such transactions are little different from the modern day banking practice of holding stock certificates, bonds, or certificates of deposit as collateral for a loan.

The pledge of collateral normally adds safety to the loan, since the lender can sell the security to obtain repayment if the debtor fails to pay. Therefore, unless the lender has considerable confidence in the quality of the loan being made, he or she will require that it be secured. If a loan is to be acceptable to a lender on an unsecured basis it must generally meet the following requirements:

1. The lender must have strong confidence in the borrower's character and ability.
2. The borrower must have a balance sheet showing substantial financial strength and a strong worth/debt ratio.
3. Repayment capacity must be more than adequate: it must be sufficient to repay the loan in full even under adverse circumstances.
4. The borrower must have a satisfactory record of past performance. A lender is usually hesitant to lend on an unsecured basis to a borrower with whom he or she has little or no experience.

5. The borrower generally must be obtaining all credit of one type from a single source. Few lenders like a split-financing arrangement.

If the borrower meets these requirements, he or she may well be eligible for unsecured credit. In such case, only the borrower's signature on a promissory note (backed by his or her "full faith and credit") is required, but not the conveyance of a security interest in some of the borrower's property. In case of default, the creditor may still attach the debtor's property through court action, but the claim will be subordinate to all prior security interests, judgments, and other liens. If the debtor is in trouble, these prior security interests and liens may be numerous.

For a particular item of collateral to be acceptable to a lender, it must generally meet the following requirements:

1. It must be identifiable.
2. It must be relatively nonperishable.
3. The lender must be able to establish a reasonable estimate of its value.
4. It must be in saleable condition.
5. There must be an established market for it.

A commercial lender normally looks to equipment, inventory, receivables, and other chattel assets for security. It is especially desirable for the lender to perfect a security interest in those assets that are to provide loan repayment, since this provides substantial control of the source of repayment, and precludes another creditor from perfecting an interest in that security.

If a creditor is to realize the value of the collateral, he or she must be able to (1) locate it, (2) identify it, (3) take possession, (4) prevent its deterioration, (5) establish its value, and (6) find a market for it. Therefore, a lender should make every effort to inspect the items being offered as collateral and to obtain complete descriptions, including serial numbers of equipment. Inspecting the collateral will also assist the lender in estimating values and aid in determining its marketability through normal market channels.

Split collateral, i.e., collateral of the same type in which two or more creditors each have partial security interests, should be avoided. For example, if lender A has a security interest in 50 parts bins owned by XYZ Company, and lender B has a security interest in 30 parts bins of the same type, there may be a significant problem of identification, control, and division of sales proceeds, even if XYZ Company does in fact own 80 parts bins. If 20 bins are sold, how are the proceeds to be divided between creditors A and B? If some bins are damaged, which creditor stands the loss or is entitled to the insurance proceeds? Such is the stuff of which court cases are made.

Another area of potential conflict exists where one creditor has a security interest in inventory, and another a security interest in accounts receivable. Since inventory is converted into receivables, it is apparent that both creditors may have conflicting claims against the receivables. UCC9-312 addresses the issue of conflicting security interests in the same collateral. However, when a conflict exists, litigation is often necessary to resolve the problem.

How much collateral is required to secure a loan adequately? Theoretically, collateral is adequate, if, under the worst conditions, enough of it can be located and repossessed and can be sold for sufficient cash to repay the loan in full. From a practical standpoint, the lender must first consider what is available, and then decide how much will be requested for security. If inventory, receivables, and equipment do not provide adequate collateral, the lender may be able to solve the problem by requiring a real estate mortgage, vehicle titles, assignments of cash value of life insurance, or other additional collateral. If collateral is still insufficient, the lender may have to reject the request.

Loan Purpose

Purpose has a significant effect on the quality of a loan. Almost any lender would prefer to make a loan that is sound, i.e., one that enhances the welfare of the borrower rather than one that is detrimental. For example, a lender usually prefers to finance needed equipment for a struggling young business, rather than an expensive new automobile for its chief executive.

Some lenders evaluate loan purpose by classifying loan requests as necessities, needs, and wants. Necessities are those things that are essentials, such as operating expenses, inventory, raw materials, repairs, and taxes. Needs are those items which under some circumstances could be postponed. Replacement of a piece of equipment might be an example of a need. Wants are those items which add to the comfort, convenience, and prestige of the businessman, but without which the operation can continue to function in a normal and efficient manner.

First priority must be given to financing the borrower's necessities and needs if the business is to function properly. In many cases, this means limiting or deferring the financing of wants. Often the lender must help the borrower establish priorities, and it may require considerable counseling to prevent the borrower from over-borrowing for nonessentials.

Loan purpose must also be analyzed in terms of the effect of the loan on the profitability of the business. Does the loan finance sound expansion or more efficient operations that will increase profits, or will it merely place an additional debt burden on the business without any offsetting benefit? Ideally, a sound loan will enable the borrower to increase income by an amount significantly greater than the carrying costs of the loan.

The purpose of a loan will not only affect profits, but also the borrower's overall financial position. For example, a loan for non-productive purposes may increase debt without significantly increasing tangible assets or income. If it is for a capital purchase, it will increase both assets and liabilities, as well as providing additional collateral for the loan. All the potential effects on the borrower's financial position should be carefully analyzed by a lender. This usually requires the preparation of both a pro forma balance sheet and pro forma income statement.

Loan purpose should also be a significant factor in determining loan maturity. Ideally, a working capital loan (except for a revolving loan) should mature when the pledged repayment is expected to become available. The sales proceeds of each production cycle should repay its production costs. Loans for capital purchases can reasonably be expected to be repaid over a longer term from net income. Depending on the size and type of capital expenditure, a proper term may well range from two to ten years, or up to 30 years in the case of real estate.

Types of Loans

Various types of loans are generally extended by commercial lenders to meet the needs of businesses, and these may be broadly categorized as follows:

Short term working capital loan. This kind of loan is usually extended on a 30 to 180 day basis to fund a seasonal growth in inventory and receivables, or to cover a short term need for cash for operating expenses, tax payments, etc. This kind of loan normally will be repaid from liquidation of inventory and collection of receivables.

Capital term loan. This is a loan for acquisition of capital assets such as equipment, furnishings, fixtures, vehicles, and in some cases, buildings or other improvements to real estate. A term loan may be written for a term of from one to ten years, depending on the depreciable life of the assets purchased, and is usually secured by a security interest in those assets.

Revolving loan against receivables and/or inventory. This type of loan differs from other loans in that there is no regular repayment schedule. Reductions come from the application of receivable collections to the loan, and new advances are made against sales and/or inventory acquisitions. The maximum amount loaned is usually determined by a formula based on the amount of inventory and/or receivables shown on the borrower's books as of a given date. As long as the amount of the loan conforms to the formula, which is re-computed periodically (usually monthly) the lender may be willing to carry the loan indefinitely.

Interim loan. A loan made in anticipation of a sale of an asset or the closing of a refinancing. This kind of loan is usually for a short term, although on occasion, the term may be as long as several years, and there is a specifically identified source of repayment—the proceeds of the asset sale or of the refinancing. A construction loan, which funds periodic payments to contractors during a construction project, and which is repaid by proceeds of the permanent mortgage financing upon completion of the project, is one kind of interim loan.

Long term working capital loan. This is a type of loan that most commercial lenders make from time to time, although it often is not perceived to be what it actually is. A loan of this kind becomes very much like capital in the business, and generally must be repaid from profits over a period of time. Risk may be relatively high, since repayment may depend on earnings generated over a period of several years. Generally, a request for a loan of this type signifies that the business' equity position is relatively weak, or that the business is growing rapidly.

Summary

In summary, sound lending decisions are based on well identified concepts and principles. The most important of these pertain to the moral characteristics and management ability of the borrower. Almost equally important is the borrower's capacity to repay, as established by analysis of past performance and projections of future performance. Also of major significance is the borrower's financial position and adequate equity to protect the creditor's position. In addition, the availability and quality of collateral, and the purpose and proper term of the loan must be considered. Lastly, both the lender and the borrower must recognize the importance of a clear, concise, workable repayment agreement.

4

Business Entities

A business entity may be defined as a legal being which is recognized by law as having the capacity to conduct business transactions. It is imperative that the loan officer be familiar with the various kinds of legal entities since the kind of legal entity that the commercial loan officer is dealing with has considerable effect on financial structure and management organization, as well as the kind of documentation required to secure the lender's position properly. The borrower sitting across the desk from the loan officer may be acting in his or her individual capacity, as the sole proprietor of a business, as a partner in a general or limited partnership, as a corporate officer, in a fiduciary capacity as agent or trustee, as conservator, as the executor or administrator of an estate, or in one of several other capacities. It behooves the loan officer to discover early in the initial interview what entity or entities he or she is dealing with, and in what capacity the applicant is acting. Attorneys who deal with commercial collection cases agree that a high percentage of loan documentation problems arise from the lender's failure to ascertain what entity he or she is or should have been dealing with. If multiple entities are involved, the loan officer must then determine the relationship of those entities, including their ownership and the nature of their affiliation. In this chapter we will examine the various legal entities, their financial and legal characteristics, advantages and disadvantages, income tax implications, and the loan documentation requirements for each.

Sole Proprietorships

A sole proprietorship is the simplest and most common form of business entity. It consists of one individual in business for himself or herself, contributing all the equity capital, taking all the risk, making all the decisions, and taking all the profits, or absorbing all the loss. There is little or no organization cost, and minimal legal organization is required. Legally, the sole proprietor and his or her business enterprise are one business entity. There is no legal distinction between personal debt and business debt. However, from an accounting standpoint, it is perfectly acceptable to compile a separate financial statement on each "business enterprise," and therefore a lender may receive a statement, even one produced by a CPA, which shows only assets and liabilities of the business enterprise, with personal assets and liabilities of the proprietor omitted. Therefore, when accepting a financial statement from a sole proprietor, the lender should immediately ascertain that the statement shows all of the assets and all the liabilities, both personal and business, of the proprietor. While a business enterprise statement may be valuable for analyzing the status and performance of the borrower's business, it may fall considerably short of being a complete and accurate representation of the borrower's overall position. Therefore, the lender should always require a complete statement that includes both personal and business assets and liabilities.

The biggest advantage of a sole proprietorship is its simplicity. A charter or other legal agreement forming the entity is not required. The only records required are those necessary to keep management informed, to enable the business to file the necessary tax returns and comply with various government regulations. There is no formal requirement for meetings or minutes, and there are no stockholders or other participants to satisfy. The proprietor-manager has complete discretion and freedom to act. However, there are disadvantages to this form of organization. Backup management may be lacking. Death terminates a proprietorship. There is no ready means for transferring a partial interest to another party. Available capital is limited to the amount the proprietor can raise through his or her own resources. The proprietor has unlimited liabilities for contracts, injuries, etc. In addition, profits may be subject to an income tax rate that is higher than the corporate tax rate.

A sole proprietor often owns assets, especially real estate, in joint tenancy with a spouse. Since in most states joint tenancy property passes to the surviving joint tenant clear of the debts of the decedent (unless the surviving joint tenant is obligated as co-maker, endorser, or guarantor), this may present special problems for the lender. In the past, most lenders prudently made it their policy to request that a joint tenant become an obligor on the loan. With the passage of the Equal Credit Opportunity Act (Regulation B), many lenders have become hesitant to require the co-obligation of a spouse, which ultimately may cause a higher ratio of loan losses for some lenders.

No special documentation is required when lending to a proprietorship. The proprietor's signature obligates him or her and all his or her assets, both personal and business. No documentation regarding authority to act is required.

Partnerships

A partnership may be defined as an association of two or more persons to carry on as co-owners of a business for profit. A partnership may exist under either a written or oral agreement, or through an implied agreement. In other words, even though persons associated together in a business venture may have taken no express action to form a partnership, and do not perceive themselves to be a partnership, if they act as though they were partners, the law may construe that a partnership exists. In the absence of a specific agreement, each partner has an equal voice in management, and a right to an equal share of the profits, regardless of the amount of capital he or she has contributed.

Most states have adopted the Uniform Partnership Act, which governs the formation, operation, and dissolution of partnerships. The following are some of the basic sections of the Uniform Partnership Act, as found in the statutes of most states:

1. Joint tenancy, tenancy in common, joint or common property, or part ownership does not of itself establish a partnership, nor does the sharing of gross returns.

2. The receipt of *a share of the profits* of a business is prima facie evidence that the recipient is a partner, unless such share is received in payment of wages, or of a debt, or as interest.

3. Generally, property acquired with partnership funds is partnership property.

4. Real estate may be acquired in the partnership name, and the title thus acquired can be conveyed only in the partnership name. (Some states may prohibit this.)

5. Every partner is an agent of the partnership for the purpose of conducting its business. The act of every partner, including the execution of any instrument for carrying on in the usual way the business of the partnership, binds the partnership.

6. Generally, the partnership is liable for the wrongful act, omission, or loss or injury to a third party, caused by a partner acting in the ordinary course of business of the partnership.

7. All partners are jointly and severally liable for the debts and obligations of the partnership. A new partner admitted to a partnership becomes liable for the preexisting obligations of the partnership.

8. Unless otherwise agreed by the partners, no partner is entitled to remuneration for acting in the partnership business.

9. A set of partnership books shall be kept, and every partner at all times shall have access to and may inspect and copy any of them.

10. Generally, a partnership is dissolved upon the death or bank-ruptcy of a partner, the withdrawal or expulsion of a partner, or by mutual consent of the partners. Dissolution of the partnership does not discharge the existing liability of the partners.

Therefore, a partnership is a more formal type of business organization than the sole proprietorship, requiring an agreement, either expressed or implied, among the partners. It also requires a capital contribution by each partner, which may be in the form of cash or other property, or services such as labor and management. The partnership must keep a record of each partner's capital account, and each partner's capital account is generally shown in the partnership financial statement, along with an explanation of any changes in the form of additional capital contributions or withdrawals.

It is advantageous for a partnership to have a comprehensive written partnership agreement. Although such an agreement may be as simple or as complex as the partners wish, every agreement should contain certain basic and vital provisions. These include:

1. The date, and names of the parties entering into the agreement;
2. The name of the partnership, address of its principal place of business, and its purpose;
3. A listing of capital contributions by the various partners, and a statement of the proportionate ownership in the partnership by each partner;
4. The amount of time each partner will devote to the business of the partnership, and the amount of salary, if any, to be paid;
5. Provisions for borrowing funds;
6. The manner in which profits and losses will be shared among the partners;
7. Provisions for terminating or dissolving the partnership.

Exhibit B is an example of a simple general partnership agreement.

A partnership pays no federal income tax, although it must file an information return (IRS Form 1065) annually. All tax liability (or tax shelter) is passed through to the individual partners on a basis proportionate to their ownership of the partnership. The partnership annually must furnish each partner a statement of such tax liability (IRS Form 1065, Schedule K-1), and the information from this form must be transferred to each partner's individ-ual tax return.

There are a number of advantages to the partnership form of legal organization. It may make additional management time and expertise avail-able, as well as a greater amount of capital. It may create a more efficient operation. It facilitates the participation of several individuals in one business enterprise, without requiring that the participants form a corporation, thereby avoiding the more complex requirements involved in a corporation. There are also disadvantages. Each partner is fully liable for all debts and obligations of the partnership, and further, may be liable for the wrongful acts of the other partners. Transfer of partial interests is difficult, and there are generally no significant tax advantages in forming a partnership. From a lender's viewpoint, there are a number of special considerations when dealing with a partnership. It is absolutely *necessary* for the lender to have all information pertinent to the partnership when considering a partnership loan request. The best way to accomplish this is to obtain a signed copy of the partnership agreement, which should be made a permanent part of the credit file. Since the statutes generally provide that one partner may obligate the partnership, should a lender be content to get only one signature on the note and other loan documents? A lender may well have the partnership obligated if he or she has the signature of one partner. However, the rules of prudence dictate that the lender examine the provisions of the partnership agreement to ascertain which partners are authorized to borrow on behalf of the partnership, and how many partners' signatures are required. Ignoring the provisions of the partnership agreement can only lead to disputes and litigation.

If there is no written partnership agreement, or if it does not have a provision as to borrowings, the lender should obtain a written borrowing authorization signed by all of the partners. This authorization should show the name of the partnership, names of the partners, those authorized to borrow and transact business on the partnership account, and the number of signatures required. A sample partnership authorization is shown in Exhibit C.

A cautious creditor may request that individual partners sign a personal guaranty covering the borrowings of the partnership. Why would a lender want a personal guaranty when each partner is jointly and severally obligated anyway? The reason is that there is a general rule of law that personal assets of a partner are first subject to the claims of his or her personal creditors, and thereafter subject to the claims of partnership creditors. If a partner becomes a guarantor of the partnership obligation, it then becomes a personal obligation having equal status with other personal obligations, thereby improving the lender's priority position as to the personal assets.

A joint venture may be described as a partnership formed for the completion of a specific project. The participants in a joint venture may be corporations, partnerships, or individuals. The joint venture type of legal organization is often used in the construction industry.

Limited Partnerships
A limited partnership is a special kind of partnership, similar to a general partnership, with some exceptions. A limited partnership has two kinds of

partners. It must have at least one general partner who provides management, and who is fully liable for all partnership obligations, just as in an ordinary partnership. It must also have at least one limited partner who is prohibited from participating in management, or providing services, and who is liable only to the extent of his or her investment. The limited partner in the strictest sense of the word, is simply an outside investor of capital. Generally, a limited partnership is a "marriage" of one or more individuals who want to engage in a business venture which they intend to control and manage, who become the general partners, and one or more individuals who wish to make a capital investment in a business venture, but who do not want the liability of a general partner and who have no wish to participate in management. Many limited partnerships are formed to provide a tax shelter for the limited partners. A limited partnership which invests heavily in depreciable assets, such as buildings and equipment, may generate sizeable tax losses, while at the same time generating a significant positive cash flow. In this kind of limited partnership, the general partners often receive substantial fees for organizing and managing the venture.

The Uniform Limited Parnership Act, which has been adopted by most states, requires that persons wishing to form a limited partnership sign and swear to a certificate in a form prescribed in the Act, and this certificate must then be filed in a designated county office. The name of a limited partner cannot be used in the partnership name. A limited partner may contribute cash or other property to the partnership, but not services. He or she has a right to inspect the books and receive full information regarding the affairs of the partnership, and to receive a share of the profits.

The limited partnership form of business organization has several advantages. It often enables a venture to attract a significant amount of investor capital which it might have been unable to attract otherwise. The limited partners are able to limit their liability, as they would in a corporation, without the cost and effort of forming a corporation. It enables the general partner to retain control of the business venture even though a majority of the capital being invested may come from outside investors. The biggest disadvantages in this form of business entity are that it does not limit the liability of the general partners, nor does this entity have the favorable tax treatment of a corporation.

When lending to a limited partnership, the lender should remember that ordinarily only the general partners become obligated on the loan. A lender can obligate a limited partner only by obtaining a separate personal guaranty. This is usually very difficult to obtain, since it would negate one of the principal reasons for which most individuals become limited partners— that of limiting their liability. It is not unusual for an unsophisticated lender to make a loan decision based on the financial strength of limited partners, as evidenced by their financial statements, failing to recognize that the "full faith and credit" of the limited partners is not committed to the lender in any way.

Corporations

A corporation is a legal entity entirely separate from its stockholders or officers. It is, in fact, an artificial legal being created by statute. Every state has statutes governing the formation and operation of corporations. A corporation is formed by obtaining a charter, usually from the state, but in some cases, such as that of a national bank, a charter must be obtained from the federal government. By law, the corporation's name generally must contain the words corporation, company, incorporated, limited, professional association, or professional corporation, or an abbreviation of one of these words. Also, a corporation may not have a name deceptively similar to any other corporation existing under the laws of the same state.

A corporation's charter authorizes it to issue certain classes and amounts of stock. Capital is raised through the sale and issue of this stock. Additional capital may be contributed by the stockholders in the form of paid-in surplus. A board of directors elected by the stockholders determines the general policies and management philosophy of the corporation, and corporate officers selected by the board manage the affairs of the corporation on a day-by-day basis. The board usually meets periodically, and a stockholders' meeting generally must be held annually. Corporate records must be maintained as prescribed by law. Common shareholders have a right to share in the profits of a corporation proportionate to their stock ownership. Profits may be paid to the stockholders in the form of dividends, or at the discretion of the board may be retained within the corporation as additional capital in the form of retained earnings.

There are a number of advantages to the corporate form of business organization. Liability of the shareholders is limited, since they are not liable for corporate obligations. A corporation does not terminate upon the death of one of its owners, but continues indefinitely. Transfer of a partial interest is easy, since this can be accomplished by the transfer of shares of stock. Incorporation may result in federal income tax savings. As a result of the passage of the Economic Recovery Tax Act of 1981, federal income tax rates for corporations have been reduced over a two-year period. For tax years beginning in 1982, the rates were as follows: 16% on the first $25,000 of taxable income, 19% on taxable income from $25,000 to $50,000, 30% on taxable income from $50,000 to $75,000, 40% on taxable income from $75,000 to $100,000 and 46% on taxable income over $100,000. For tax years beginning in 1983 and later, the rates are as follows: 15% on the first $25,000 of taxable income, 18% on taxable income from $25,000 to $50,000, 30% on taxable income from $50,000 to $75,000, 40% on taxable income from $75,000 to

$100,000 and 46% on taxable income over $100,000. Since personal income tax rates may be as high as 50%, it is obvious that corporate tax rates may be preferable if taxable income is substantial.

There are also disadvantages to incorporating. A corporation is a complex form of business organization. The formal requirements for meetings, minutes, officers, etc., may be disconcerting to a relatively unsophisticated businessman. Day-by-day financial operations become more complicated. The initial cost of incorporation in the form of fees, taxes, and attorney fees may amount to $1,000 or more. Corporations usually are subject to annual state franchise and capital stock taxes. In some cases, earnings may be subject to double taxation, since the corporation pays taxes upon its earnings, and earnings paid to stockholders in the form of dividends are taxable income to the stockholder (except for a $100 dividend exclusion). However, the use of proper financial management techniques can minimize this double tax exposure.

A lender dealing with a corporation must observe two rules. First, the corporate board must authorize all loan transactions and designate the officers authorized to execute documents. Second, documents executed by the corporate officers in their capacity as officers obligate only the corporation, not the officers or stockholders individually, even in a case where the officer executing documents is the sole owner of the corporation. Prior to making a loan, the lender should obtain a certified copy of the resolution adopted by the corporate board authorizing the borrowing of funds and the pledging of corporate assets. This certified copy should show the date the resolution was adopted, the amount of borrowings authorized (this may be a "no limit" amount), and which officers, and how many of them, are to sign the note and other loan documents. The resolution may authorize a specific borrowing, or it may be a broad resolution, authorizing borowings on a continuing or periodic basis over an extended period of time. The certified copy of the resolution should show the names (and preferably the genuine signatures) of the corporate officers, should be attested to by the corporate secretary, and should bear the corporate seal. A sample of a form for a certified copy of a resolution to borrow is shown in Exhibit D.

Even though the lender holds a broad borrowing resolution, it should be reviewed periodically, and replaced by a new resolution if: (1) aggregate corporate borrowings will exceed the dollar limit established in the resolution; (2) a change in corporate officers has occurred; (3) the terms of the loan have changed significantly; or (4) the resolution is several years old. A resolution may remain valid even though it is several years old, but many prudent lenders prefer to update their corporate resolutions about every four to five years even though none of the above listed changes have taken place.

The policy of most lenders requires that the principal stockholders (who are usually also the managing officers) of a closely held corporation personally guarantee corporate borrowings. This accomplishes several things. First,it provides additional financial strength to support the loan, since the personal assets of the guarantors become subject to the claims of the lender. Second, it results in a stronger personal commitment on the part of the guarantor-managers to work toward the success of the business, since they cannot simply walk away from the lender if the business fails. Third, it minimizes the possibility that corporate assets or income will be fraudulently transferred to the individual owners to avoid payment of the corporate debt.

On occasion, a lender may be offered the stock certificates of a closely held or family corporation as security for a loan. Stock certificates represent only the shareholder's proportionate share of the net worth (equity) of the corporation. The pledge of a stock certificate is therefore only a pledge of a proportionate share of the equity, and in no way represents a pledge of the assets of the corporation. Obviously, a creditor who has a security interest in the corporate assets has a prior claim against the assets of the corporation. The creditor who holds a stock certificate as security has a claim against the corporate assets that is subordinate to all creditor claims against the corporation, including those of the unsecured creditors. A corporation cannot pledge its own stock as security for its borrowings, but one of its stockholders may pledge his or her stock to secure personal borrowings or to secure a guaranty of the corporate borrowings. Also, when accepting the stock of a closely held corporation as security, the lender should ascertain that its marketability is not restricted by the terms of a buy-sell agreement. The law generally requires that such a restriction be shown on the certificate.

In recent years, many small businesses have begun to consider the corporate form of business organization. This is usually due to the perceived tax advantages, or with the objective of limiting the liability of owners, or may be done to facilitate bringing another party, such as a manager or a relative, into the ownership of the business. Anyone considering such a move should consult an attorney who is knowledgeable in the area of corporate law. Such a move is not easily undone, and many businesspeople have learned that coping with the legal and financial complexities of a corporation can be a frustrating experience, at least initially. It may become necessary to ask if you are acting as an individual or as a corporate officer prior to engaging in the most routine transaction. I have dealt with businesspeople who have found it difficult to realize that their corporation is a *separate entity*, and that corporate property is distinct from personal property, and corporate income from personal income. Therefore, the lender needs separate personal and corporate statements. In a few cases, individuals even have attempted to prepare a sort of consolidated financial statement, combining individual and corporate assets and liabilities, an approach that is entirely unacceptable.

Because of the advantages of the corporate form of business organization, lenders undoubtedly will continue to deal with a significant number of businesspeople who are considering the corporate form of business, and it behooves the lender to be well enough informed to be able to advise his or her customer of the advantages and disadvantages of this type of business organization.

S Corporations

The net profits of a corporation are generally taxed at a lower rate than those of a business that is operated as a sole proprietorship or partnership. However, the distribution by a corporation of its after-tax income to the shareholders is subject to a second tax— regular income tax on a dividend payment, or capital gains tax on a distribution of capital. The S corporation (until 1983 called a Subchapter S corporation) provides a means for avoiding this problem of double taxation.

A 1958 change in federal income tax laws allowed the formation of a closely held corporation, which could elect to treat its federal income tax liability as though it were a partnership, and pass through any tax liability or tax shelter to the stockholders. This type of corporation was known as a Subchapter S corporation. The Subchapter S Revision Act of 1982 was passed by Congress in October, 1982. Most of its provisions became effective for taxable years beginning after December 31, 1982. This legislation represents a major effort to simplify the Subchapter S method of corporate income taxation, and also changed the designation of this kind of corporation from "Subchapter S" to "S".

Originally a Subchapter S corporation could have only ten shareholders, with a husband and wife treated as one shareholder. That number was increased to 15 in 1978 and to 25 in 1981. The Subchapter S Revision Act of 1982 increased the maximum number of shareholders to 35, and a husband and wife continue to be treated as one shareholder. Subchapter S corporations were originally permitted to have only a single class of stock. The 1982 Act provides that differences in voting rights in common stock are permissible and do not violate the requirements of a single class of stock. Preferred stock is still prohibited. Since 1958, Subchapter S corporations have operated under a rule that no more than 20% of corporate gross income could come from passive investment income such as rents, royalties, dividends, or interest. The 1982 Act eliminates the limit on passive investment income for corporations that do not have accumulated earnings and profits from years the corporation was regularly taxed.

The election to be taxed as an S corporation can be made either by a newly formed corporation, or by one that previously operated as a "regular" corporation and which may have accumulated substantial earnings. Formerly, a corporation that wanted to become an S corporation had the first 75 days of the taxable year to make that election, and all shareholders on the day of the election had to consent. This has been changed so that the election must be made on or before the 15th day of the third month, instead of 75 days. The election must be consented to by all shareholders on the day that the election is made, and on all days in the taxable year before the day that the election is made the corporation must have been eligible to make the election. All persons who were shareholders during the taxable year before the election is made must also consent. The 1982 Act retains the rule that a member of an affiliated group of corporations cannot be an S corporation. Therefore, an S corporation cannot own 80% or more of the stock in another corporation.

Several events can cause the termination of an S election. These include exceeding the allowed maximum number of shareholders, transferring stock to an ineligible shareholder, creating an ineligible class of stock such as preferred stock, or acquiring a subsidiary.

The S corporation is an ideal type of legal organization for the business-person who wants the advantages of a corporation and the tax flexibility of a partnership. However, the S corporation may have all the disadvantages of a regular corporation, plus some additional potential problems. Income distributed to the individual stockholders is unearned income, which may create a tax disadvantage for the individual. Financial growth may be difficult for an S corporation, since all earnings must be distributed to the stockholders to achieve the greatest tax advantage. Therefore, there is little incentive to accumulate retained earnings in an S corporation. However, the stockholders may reinvest the earnings in the corporation in the form of stockholder loans or subordinated notes. Unless this is done, a potential lender may have a problem, since even a profitable S corporation may have little equity. In such case, the lender is required to look to the individual stockholders for the financial strength necessary to support a loan to the corporation.

From the lender's standpoint, the legal documentation required for a loan to an S corporation is no different from the documentation required for a regular corporation.

Cooperatives

A cooperative is an association of two or more persons established to accomplish a common function or purpose. The majority of business cooperatives exist in the agricultural sector of our economy. Federal legislation has encouraged the formation of agricultural cooperatives, and almost every rural community has a farmers' cooperative grain elevator or livestock shipping association. Huge agricultural cooperatives include major manufacturers and suppliers of fuel, fertilizer, and feeds, as well as operators of major marketing systems for commodities and livestock. The Farm Credit System, a cooperative system, is the largest single supplier of agricultural credit. Most states have statutes regulating cooperatives, and most provide for the incorporation of cooperatives by a special form of charter. Legislation in many states provides for the formation of cooperative corporations which are to be non-profit in the sense that they are not organized to make profits for themselves, but only for their members. Theoretically, at least, all earnings not required as capital and reserves for the business are returned to the members in the form of patronage refunds or dividends. In the past decade we have also seen the formation of a number of relatively small consumers' cooperatives, formed mainly for the purpose of buying consumer goods on a volume basis for the members of the cooperative. Most of these cooperatives have been only marginally successful and have not become a significant factor in the economy of most business communities.

Lending to a cooperative is basically the same as lending to a corporation in that the board of the cooperative must authorize the borrowings by resolution, and designated officers must execute the loan documents. There are however, a number of factors that a lender should consider when dealing with a cooperative. A cooperative may not have as strong a profit motive as a privately owned business, and this may adversely affect earnings performance in some cases. In some small cooperatives, hired management may be inadequate and board supervision may not be as strong as it should be. The majority of cooperatives, especially those in the agribusiness sector, are aggressive organizations with highly competent management. Probably the greatest disadvantage the lender has in dealing with a cooperative is that he or she cannot get the personal guarantys of the principal owners as when dealing with a closely held and privately owned corporation. The average cooperative's ownership is scattered among too many members, and the average member would not benefit from signing such a guaranty. Even cooperative board members usually serve more from a sense of public service and for prestige than from monetary interest. This lack of significant monetary interest on the part of directors and members may be a real problem to a lender if the cooperative gets into financial trouble. Management may quit, board members may resign, and the hapless lender is left to liquidate the remaining assets as best as he or she can. It should be recognized however, that some cooperatives, especially the strong agribusiness cooperatives, are valued customers of the banks who serve them.

The legal documentation required by a lender is much the same for a cooperative corporation as for a regular corporation. Because it is difficult to get personal guaranties, and because management may have no personal financial involvement, adequate cash flow, profits, and collateral are generally even more important in a loan to a cooperative than they are in a loan to a regular corporation.

Dealing with Fiduciaries

Occasionally a lender will be called upon to deal with a borrower acting in a fiduciary capacity, such as a trustee, agent, custodian, guardian, executor, or conservator. A fiduciary relationship is a special kind of relationship in which one party is empowered to act on behalf of and in the best interest of another. When dealing with a borrower who is acting in such a capacity, the lender must first ascertain that the fiduciary is authorized to borrow, and second, that he or she is doing so for the benefit of the beneficiary rather than for himself or herself. A fiduciary legally cannot pledge assets held by him or her for personal borrowings, nor can he or she use funds borrowed in a fiduciary capacity for his or her own purposes. If presented with collateral held by a prospective borrower under the title of trustee or custodian, or some similar designation, and if the loan is to be to the applicant personally, the lender should proceed with extreme caution.

Trusts have become widely recognized as versatile means for the transfer, holding, and management of property for the benefit of individuals (beneficiaries) designated by the persons establishing the trust. Trusts are widely used as an estate planning device, even by individuals of modest means. A trust is established by a written agreement which designates a trustee who holds title to, and generally manages, the trust property. The trustee, who may be an individual, an institution, or a combination of the two, has only such powers as are granted by the trust agreement. Therefore, a lender should ascertain that the trustee is empowered to borrow and pledge trust assets under the terms of the trust agreement before proceeding with the loan. A trustee executing a note in that capacity obligates only the trust, and not himself or herself as an individual. The lender should obtain a copy of the executed trust agreement which should be made a part of the credit file.

An agency is a less formal kind of arrangement. An agent is one who is authorized by a person identified as a principal to make contracts with third parties on behalf of the principal. The agency is usually established by written agreement, but may result from a verbal agreement, or in some instances, stem from an implied agreement resulting from the principal's conduct. A written authorization of agency is commonly referred to as a power of attorney. The burden of proving the existence of an agency relationship rests upon the party who would benefit by such proof. Therefore, a lender should deal only with an agent whose authority is based on a written power of attorney containing a specific authorization to borrow. Lacking that, a prudent lender generally will decline to make the loan. An agent with proper authority obligates only the principal, not himself or herself. However, an agent may obligate himself or herself rather than the principal if the agent enters into a transaction without proper authority.

Executors, administrators, conservators, and guardians are appointed by the courts. When dealing with borrowers acting in such a capacity, the lender should require proof of appointment in the form of a certified copy of a court order, letters testamentary, or similar documents. Borrowings by persons acting in such a capacity usually require court approval, and a lender may be well advised to consult legal counsel regarding the legal requirements for such borrowings prior to entering into a loan.

Unincorporated Associations

A lender may occasionally deal with a type of organization that may not fit into any of the previously discussed categories. Social clubs, fraternal societies, churches, and some other religious organizations may fall into this category, which for lack of a better term, we will call an "unincorporated association." Most organizations of this type are simply a group of persons banded together to further a common interest or purpose. The local Lions Club and the Ladies Society of the local church might be examples found in most communitites. They may have little formal organizational structure, and although not illegal in any sense of the word, may have questionable legal status as to the conduct of business transactions. Generally, the members of an unincorporated association are not liable for the obligations of the association, and the officers of such an organization may be acting upon very questionable legal authority. However, since many organizations of this type are well regarded and beneficial to the community, a lender may wish to accomodate their borrowing needs. A lender usually must rely on the integrity and good will of the leaders of such an organization to insure that the loan is repaid, since there is usually little or no property available to serve as security. In some cases, it may be possible and desirable to obtain the personal guaranty of some of the individuals who are in leadership roles in the organization.

Advising a Customer on Business Organization

What advice should a lender give a customer who is contemplating a change in the legal organization of his or her business? Obviously, if a lender is to give beneficial counsel, the lender must have a certain amount of basic knowledge concerning the legal requirements and advantages and disadvantages of the various types of legal organizations. Sole proprietors have a tendency to underestimate the complexities of a partnership or corporation. They are often better informed of the advantages of a change in structure than they are of the disadvantages. A businessperson should be very sure that he or she wants to make a change before doing so, since dissolving a partnership or corporation may be difficult, costly, and time consuming, and may cause significant tax problems. It is imperative that anyone considering a change in legal organization consult competent legal counsel and a good accountant before making a decision. Ideally, the businessperson, his or her attorney, accountant, tax consultant, and lender, working as a team, should participate in making the decision.

Importance of Correct Name

Because names are considered important, each state has statutes regarding their usage. Every business entity has a correct legal name, and use of the correct legal name is very important to the lender if the loan documentation is to be valid. A person may use any name he or she wishes, as long as that name is used without intent to defraud. Business entities may also use assumed names, also referred to as "trade names," and provided that they fulfill certain basic legal requirements, the use of a trade name is entirely legal. The statutes usually require that an assumed business name, whether used by a proprietorship, partnership, or corporation, must be filed in a designated office of the county in which the business is conducted. Disclosure generally must be made of the true name or names, and the post office addresses of the persons conducting the business. Notice of such a filing usually must be published in a newspaper of general circulation within the county in which the certificate is filed. When dealing with a borrower operating under a trade name, the lender should inquire whether proper filing and publication has been made.

Use of the term "doing business as," usually abbreviated "dba," denotes the use of an assumed or trade name. Therefore, the name of a sole proprietor using an assumed name might be shown as "John Jones dba Jones Trucking Company." A partnership or corporation may also use a trade name such as "Western House Inc., dba Western Publishing Company." It is vitally important that the lender determine both the proper legal and assumed names of a business entity when preparing loan documentation. It is absolutely necessary that the legal name be used in all loan documentation, and it is usually desirable to show the trade name also. Failure to use the proper legal name may result in a defective UCC filing and documentation that is unenforceable or invalid. In spite of the importance of using the proper name, many lenders are quite careless about this aspect of completing their loan documentation. Many lenders have learned to their sorrow that the answer to the question "What's in a name?" is a great deal indeed, if they are ever required to enforce their legal documentation.

EXHIBIT B   Partnership Agreement

THIS AGREEMENT, made and entered into this 7th day of November, 19X4, between Alice C. Smith, Jean Donovan, and Martha J. Cross, doing business as Tradewinds Travel Agency, a Partnership.

WHEREAS, the parties hereto agree to form a partnership for the purposes of operating a travel agency:

1. The partnership shall begin on November 7, 19X4, and shall continue until terminated as hereinafter is provided.
2. The initial capital of said partnership shall be a Twenty Thousand ($20,000.00) Dollar contribution by each partner. Thereafter, an individual capital account shall be maintained for each partner to the partnership and no interest shall be paid or shall accrue on the capital account of any party to the partnership. The respective interests of the parties hereto as partners, in and to the partnership, and in and to the net profits and losses of the partnership shall be:

Alice C. Smith 33-1/3%

Jean Donovan 33-1/3%

Martha J. Cross 33-1/3%

3. The respective interest of the partners hereto shall not be transferred or assigned in whole or in part.
4. Each partner shall have equal voice in the management of the partnership. No partner shall, without the consent of the others, borrow or lend money on behalf of the partnership; enter into a contract to sell, assign, or pledge her interest in the partnership.
5. All funds of the partnership shall be deposited in the name of the above described partnership and all the books and accounts shall be maintained at the partnership business office located at 1212 West Lincoln Street, Center City, U.S.A.
6. The partnership bank accounts shall be established at the Commercial Bank of Center City, or such other bank as the partners shall from time to time agree upon, and all withdrawals shall be made upon checks signed by any two partners collectively. The partnership may from time to time borrow funds and obligate itself therefore. Any partnership borrowings shall require the signatures of all three partners.
7. Partnership books shall be maintained in an adequate and accurate manner, and each partner shall at all times have access thereto. The books shall be closed and balanced at the end of each accounting year. A CPA review shall be made as of the closing date.
8. Any partner shall have the right to retire from the partnership at the end of any accounting year. Written notice of intention to retire shall be served upon the other partners at the office of the partnership at least three (3) months before the end of the accounting year. The retirement of any partner shall have no effect upon the continuance of the partnership business. The remaining part-

EXHIBIT   B (*Continued*)

ners shall have the right either to purchase the retiring partner's entire interest in the partnership or to terminate and liquidate the partnership business. If the remaining partners elect to purchase the interest of the retiring partner, they shall serve written notice of such election upon the retiring partner at the office of the partnership within two (2) months after receipt of her notice of intention to retire.

(a) If the remaining partners elect to purchase the interest of the retiring partner in the partnership, the procedure for purchase of the retiring partner's interest, the purchase price, and the method of payment shall be the same as stated in paragraph 9(a) with reference to the purchase of a deceased partner's interest in the partnership.

(b) If the remaining partners do not elect to purchase the interest of the retiring partner in the partnership, the partners shall proceed with reasonable promptness to liquidate the partnership business. The procedure as to liquidation and distribution of the assets of the partnership business shall be the same as stated in paragraph 9(a) with reference to termination in the event of a partner's death.

9.   Upon the death of any partner, the surviving partners shall have the right either to purchase the entire interest of the decedent in the partnership or to terminate and liquidate the partnership business. If the surviving partners elect to purchase the decedent's interest, they shall serve written notice of such election, upon the executor or administrator of the decedent, or, if at the time of such election no legal representative has been appointed, upon any one of the known legal heirs of the decedent at the last known address of such heirs, within three (3) months after the death of the decedent.

(a) If the surviving partners elect to purchase the interest of the decedent in the partnership, the purchase price shall be equal to the decedent's capital account as at the date of her death, plus the decedent's income account as at the end of the prior fiscal year, increased by her share of partnership profits, or decreased by her share of partnership losses, for the period from the beginning of the fiscal year in which her death occurred, and decreased by withdrawals charged to her income account during such period. The purchase price, with interest at nine percent (9%) on each installment from the end of the calendar month in which the decedent's death occurred to the date of payment, shall be paid in six semi-annual installments beginning six (6) months after the end of the calendar month in which the decedent's death occurred.

(b) If the surviving partners do not elect to purchase the interest of the decedent in the partnership, they shall proceed with reasonable promptness to sell the real and personal property owned by the partnership and to liquidate the business of the

EXHIBIT   B *(Continued)*

partnership. Each of the surviving partners and the estate of the deceased partner shall share equally in the profits and losses of the business during the period of liquidation, except that the decedent's estate shall not be liable for losses in excess of the decedent's interest in the partnership at the time of her death. No compensation shall be paid to the surviving partners for their services in liquidation. Except as herein otherwise stated, the procedure as to liquidation and distribution of the assets of the partnership shall be as follows:

    (i)   To pay or provide for the payment of all partnership expenses, debts, and other obligations.

    (ii)   To equalize the income accounts of the partners.

    (iii)   To discharge the balance of the income accounts of the partners.

    (iv)   To equalize the capital accounts of the partners.

    (v)   To discharge the balance of the capital accounts of the partners.

10.   It is mutually acknowledged that each and every partner has her own individual employment and nothing in this agreement shall be construed to limit the right of said partners to continue in said employment.

IN WITNESS WHEREOF, the parties hereto have signed this partnership agreement as of the day and year first above written.

s/ALICE C. SMITH
_____

s/JEAN DONOVAN
_____

s/MARTHA J. CROSS
_____

EXHIBIT   C   Partnership Authorization

PARTNERSHIP AUTHORIZATION

THE COMMERCIAL BANK OF CHAMPAIGN

Gentlemen:

We hereby certify that the undersigned,   John C. Davis, James E. Carter, Frank P. Sullivan,
and George Bernard

are engaged in business as partners, doing business under the name and style of   Davis, Carter and Associates,
A Partnership   at the following address   1663 South Second St., Center City, U.S.A.

                           and that the undersigned represent and constitute all the members of said partnership.

This will further evidence the agreement and authorization of the undersigned that:

1. The Commercial Bank of Champaign be, and it hereby is, designated as one of the depositaries of the funds of said partnership and that any one of the undersigned partners, their agents or employees be, and each of them hereby is authorized to deposit in said depositary funds of said partnership and for that purpose to endorse in the name of said partnership checks, drafts, notes and other like obligations and that such endorsement may be written or stamped without designation of the individual partner, agent or employee making such endorsement.

2. That any _____two_____ of the following named partners, agents or employees of the partnership   John C.
Davis, James E. Carter, Frank P. Sullivan, George Bernard, and Mark Jones, manager,
are hereby specifically authorized for and on behalf of the undersigned partners and in the partnership name to make, execute and deliver checks against said deposited funds, including checks drawn against the partnership account for deposit to the individual accounts of any one or more of the undersigned partners, agents or employees and the said Commercial Bank of Champaign as said depositary, be, and it hereby is authorized to pay out funds on deposit with it from time to time to the credit of the partnership, upon checks, drawn upon said depository and signed in the name of the partnership, in conformity with the foregoing authorization.

3. That any _____three_____ of the following named partners are hereby authorized, in addition to and not in limitation of the rights inherent in a partner, for and in behalf of said partnership and in the partnership name, from time to time to borrow money from said Commercial Bank of Champaign in such amounts, for such lengths of time, and at such rates of interest and upon such terms and conditions as to said partners may seem expedient, and to secure payment of money so borrowed and to evidence indebtedness thereby created, to execute and deliver promissory notes, judgment promissory notes and other like obligations of said partnership, in such form and containing such terms and provisions as may to them seem necessary and advisable, and to pledge or hypothecate as security for the payment of said notes and other obligations any receivables, securities, or property of any character whatsoever now or hereafter belonging to such partnership; to discount with said depositary any receivables now or hereafter owing to said partnership; to withdraw, receipt for, execute and deliver trust receipts for savings accounts, securities, or other property of any kind whatsoever purchased from, left with, or held by said depositary for safekeeping, or other collateral security, or for delivery and/or collection; and said depositary is specifically authorized to deliver to the person so designated any such savings, deposit, securities, or other property of any kind whatsoever, upon receipt of trust receipts executed by such persons in his or their individual name and without requiring the execution of such receipts in the name of the partnership.

4. That said Commercial Bank of Champaign shall not be in any way responsible for or required to see to the application of any of the funds deposited with it or borrowed from it as hereinabove provided.

5. If any other persons became interested in said business as co-partners of the undersigned or our relations as such be altered in any way, or if the business should become incorporated, the undersigned will notify you promptly.

6. That all transactions above authorized shall be conclusive and binding upon the undersigned and each of the undersigned until written notice of the revocation of the authority hereby granted shall have been delivered to said Commercial Bank of Champaign as its office and place of business in Champaign, Illinois.

IN WITNESS WHEREOF, we have hereunto subscribed our respective hands and seals this ____15th____ day
of ____October_____ A.D. 19_____.

John C. Davis	(SEAL)
James E. Carter	(SEAL)
Frank P. Sullivan	(SEAL)
George Bernard	(SEAL)
	(SEAL)

EXHIBIT D   Corporate Resolution to Borrow

RESOLUTIONS OF CORPORATE BOARD
Authority to Procure Loans
(Certified Copy)

I HEREBY CERTIFY, that I am the duly elected and qualified Secretary of __Johnson Truck Lines, Inc.__
_____and the keeper of the records and corporate seal of said Corporation; that the following is a true and correct copy of resolutions duly adopted at a meeting of the Board of Directors thereof held in accordance with its By-Laws at its offices at __Center City, U.S.A.__
_____on the____18th____day of ___October_____, 19 _84_, and that the same are now in full force.

COPY OF RESOLUTIONS

"BE IT RESOLVED, that the (insert titles only) __President, Vice President and Treasurer__
_____ of this Corporation, or their/his successors in office, or any (insert number required to sign)____two____of them be and they/he hereby are/is authorized for, on behalf of, and in the name of this Corporation to:

(a) Negotiate and procure loans from

The Commercial Bank of Champaign	Champaign, Illinois
Name of Firm	Address

up to any amount not exceeding (if there is no limit, so indicate) _____ $ 500,000.00 in the aggregate at any one time outstanding;

(b) Discount with said Firm, commercial or other business paper belonging to this Corporation, made or drawn by or upon third parties, without limit as to amount;

(c) Give security for any liabilities of this Corporation to said Firm by pledge or assignment or lien upon any real or personal property, tangible or intangible, of this Corporation, and

(d) Execute in such form as may be required by the Firm all notes and other evidences of such loans, all instruments of pledge, assignment or lien, and that none of the same shall be valid unless so signed or endorsed provided, however, that the endorsement of promissory notes discounted may be effected by any one of them."

"RESOLVED FURTHER, that said Firm be and it is hereby authorized and directed to pay the proceeds of any such loans or discounts as directed by the persons so authorized to sign, whether so payable to the order of any of said persons in their individual capacities or not, and whether such proceeds are deposited in the individual credit of any said persons or not;"

"RESOLVED FURTHER, that this resolution shall continue in force, and said Firm may consider the holders of said offices and their signatures, respectively, to be and continue as set forth in the certificate of the Secretary of this Corporation accompanying a copy of this resolution when delivered to said Firm or in any similar subsequent certificate, until notice to the contrary in writing is duly served on said Firm."

I HEREBY FURTHER CERTIFY, that the following named persons have been duly elected to the offices set opposite their respective names, that they continue to hold these offices at the present time, and that the signatures appearing hereon are the genuine, original signatures of each respectively:

(PLEASE SUPPLY GENUINE SIGNATURES HEREUNDER)

Ralph Q. Johnson	President	_Samuel S. Smith_	Vice-President
John W. Samuelson	Treasurer	_____	Asst. Treasurer
Glenn M. Brown	Secretary	_____	Asst. Secretary

IN WITNESS WHEREOF, I have hereunto affixed my name as Secretary and have caused the corporate seal of said Corporation to be hereto affixed this____18th____day of____October____, 19 _84_.

Glenn M. Brown
Secretary

**IMPRINT
SEAL HERE**

I hereby certify that I am a Director of said Corporation and that the foregoing is a correct copy of resolutions passed as therein set forth, and that the same are now in full force.
Roger A. Dunston
(To be signed by a Director other than the Secretary)

5

Financial Statements

Financial statements are the most basic and important tools available to a loan officer for analyzing the strengths and weaknesses of a business. Lenders make loan decisions primarily based upon accounting data furnished by borrowers, including historical and projected data. Since this information is of such key importance, its accuracy, completeness, reliability, and proper interpretation are vital.

Accounting is a systematic method for collecting, analyzing, summarizing, and reporting financial information about a particular business entity. It involves listing in a traditional order all resources (assets) of that entity, and all claims against those resources (liabilities). Financial accounting provides information to parties outside the business, such as creditors; management accounting is information compiled primarily to facilitate management decision making. A lender must have an understanding of financial accounting and certain generally accepted principles of accounting to develop an understanding of the content and quality of information submitted by borrowers. The balance sheet, income statement, and statement of changes in financial position are the basic components of historical financial information.

The Balance Sheet

A balance sheet is a listing, in a traditional format, of the assets, liabilities, and equity of the entity or enterprise represented. All assets or categories of assets are listed and valued first on the balance sheet. Then, all liabilities are listed. Finally, equity (net worth) which is the dollar difference between the value of the assets and the amount of all obligations, is shown. The term balance sheet signifies the equality in the fundamental accounting equation: Assets = Liabilities + Owner Equity. The balance sheet represents the position of the entity at one particular point in time, a position that may have been significantly different one day previously, and which may differ greatly one day later.

The balance sheet tells the loan officer about the kind of assets owned by the borrower, and their probable value. It must be recognized that most asset valuations are estimates, and that these valuations, while often arrived at in a systematic manner, may not always reflect the actual marketable value of the assets. Liabilities, unlike assets, usually consist of claims for a specific number of dollars, and it is usually easier to verify the amount of a liability than it is to place an exact dollar value on an asset.

Assets are also categorized in the balance sheet according to their liquidity. Current assets are those that can be most readily liquidated. These generally include cash, marketable securities, accounts receivable, and inventory. Non-current assets are those that can be less readily liquidated, such as equipment, other fixed assets, or real estate. Liabilities are categorized by their maturity: current liabilities are those that mature in a year or less; non-current liabilities have a longer maturity.

By perusing the balance sheet a lender can therefore learn much about the borrower's position. In addition to information about the nature and valuation of the assets, the lender can make observations about the amount and maturity of the borrower's liabilities, and to some extent ascertain their nature. The loan officer can also observe the relationships between various categories of assets and liabilities, such as that of debt to equity, and current assets to current liabilities. Further, by observing the equity section of the balance sheet, the loan officer generally may determine what kind of entity is involved—sole proprietorship, partnership, or corporation.

However, examination of the balance sheet alone leaves many questions unanswered. Unless it is an audited statement, there may be a question concerning the method by which asset valuations were determined. While an audited statement generally will reflect depreciated cost value of assets, many unaudited statements will reflect appraisal or estimated current market value. If asset valuations are to be meaningful to a lender, he or she must determine their valuation basis. With an unaudited statement, the lender also generally cannot determine whether liabilities are past due, or whether assets are pledged as collateral. In addition, the loan officer may not be able to determine at what point in the business' seasonal cycle the balance sheet is drawn, and the balance sheet may differ greatly at the cyclical peak from the seasonal low. Lastly, the lender cannot determine the business' performance from the balance sheet. For this, an examination of the income statement is required.

Income Statement

The income statement is a listing of all revenue and all expenses for a given period of time. Net income (profit) is simply the excess of revenue over expenses. If expenses exceed revenue, the difference is called a loss. Revenue includes cash inflow plus accounts receivable adjustment. Expenses include operating and overhead expenses, interest, depreciation, and an adjustment for gain or loss on the sale of capital assets.

Lenders generally prefer an income statement that covers a fiscal or calendar year. However, lenders often receive interim income statements covering periods less than a year, and therefore it is important that the lender ascertain what period of time is covered by the income statement. It is also important that the income statement is prepared on an accrual rather than cash basis. A cash basis income statement may give a very erroneous impression about the performance of a business, since it is based strictly on cash inflow and outflow, and does not take into consideration changes in inventory and accounts receivable.

Since profitability is such a key factor in the health of a business and its ability to meet its obligations, the accuracy of the income statement is vital. By studying the income statement, the lender can learn a great deal about the business. Its gross profit margin, relationship of operating expenses to sales, and bad debt losses are all indicators of operating efficiency. The ratio of the amount of interest paid to sales is indicative of how heavily the business is leveraged. The amount of withdrawals by owners in the form of officers' salaries, bonuses, cash draws, etc., tells much about the business philosophy and personal motivation of the owners. The relationship of the amount of depreciation to sales may be an indicator of the efficiency with which fixed assets are utilized. High legal fees may indicate legal problems or litigation.

The lender should also be aware whether profits are before or after tax profits. In a corporate income statement a deduction for income tax liability is generally made from the net profit figure to arrive at a profits after tax figure. This is not true for a partnership income statement, since tax liability is not incurred by a partnership, but rather is passed to the individual partners. In a corporation profits are either added to retained earnings or paid out to stockholders as dividends. In a partnership, each partner's proportionate share of net profits is added to his or her capital account, which may be reduced by withdrawals. In the case of a sole proprietorship, the bottom line represents the owner's compensation for his or her labor and management, and return on equity.

Although the income statement tells the lender a great deal about the performance of the business during a specific time period, it does not tell the user whether performance is static, improving, or deteriorating. Since an accurate assessment of future performance depends on understanding current performance trends, the lender obviously needs income statements covering a number of time periods, usually at least two or three years, to make a sound loan decision.

Statement of Changes in Financial Position

Many lenders are relatively unfamiliar with the statement of changes in financial position. It has been a requirement since 1971 for business' preparing annual reports in accordance with generally accepted accounting principles. Like the income statement, it is a flow statement that summarizes the changes that have occurred in the various balance sheet accounts during a certain period of time. The analysis of these changes revolves around the sources and applications of funds, which are shown in a standardized format. The statement of changes in financial position can be quite useful in helping the lender understand the flow of funds and further analyze the financial performance of the business. It is an excellent indicator of how well the business' resources are used, and tells the analyst a great deal about how the business really functions. Exhibit E contains a sample of a typical statement of changes in financial position.

Types of Financial Statements

Financial statements vary considerably from the standpoint of quality, completeness, and accuracy. When the lender receives a financial statement from a borrower, an effort should be made to ascertain the quality of the statement information. The appearance and format of a statement are not necessarily indicators of its quality. As stated by an experienced loan officer, "The cost of the cover has no relationship to the quality of the statement." In order of their desirability, statements may be broadly classified as CPA audited statements with an unqualified opinion; CPA audited statements with a qualified opinion; CPA review statements; CPA compilation statements; statements produced by third parties who may be neither fully qualified nor impartial; and statements produced internally by the borrower.

The title "certified public accountant" indicates that the accountant has successfully completed a three-day examination administered by the American Institute of Certified Public Accountants. Generally, a college degree in accounting plus one-to-five years of experience is required to qualify for a license to practice as a CPA. The CPA designation also indicates that the accountant observes a strict code of professional ethics administered by the AICPA. When completing an audit report, the CPA issues a professional opinion on the fairness with which the financial statement presents the business' financial position and operating results. Although the auditor attests to the truthfulness of the information in a fully audited statement, this is not necessarily a guaranty to the user that fraud does not exist. Generally, however, the lender may rely on the information found in a fully audited statement. The key to judging the quality of the information found in a CPA audited statement is the auditor's opinion in letter form which is included with the statements.

Audited Statement—Unqualified Opinion

This is the most desirable form of CPA audited statement and is often referred to as a clean opinion. A clean opinion indicates that the examination has been made in compliance with generally accepted auditing standards and included all procedures the CPA felt were necessary to provide sufficient information to enable him or her to form an opinion. The CPA's written opinion will consist of two sections, a scope paragraph and an opinion paragraph, usually worded in a manner similar to the following:

> We have examined the balance sheet of XYZ Company as of December 31, 19___, and the related statements of income, retained earnings, and changes in financial position for the year then ended. Our examination was made in accordance with generally accepted auditing standards, and accordingly included such tests of the accounting records and such other auditing procedures as we considered necessary in the circumstances.
>
> In our opinion, the statements mentioned above present fairly the financial position of XYZ Company at December 31, 19___, and the results of its operations and changes in its financial position for the year then ended, in conformity with generally accepted accounting principles applied on a basis consistent with that of the preceding year.

The first or scope paragraph describes the financial statements examined and further indicates that the examination was made in accordance with generally accepted auditing standards. The second paragraph recites the opinion of the accountant that the statements are presented fairly in all material respects in conformity with accounting principles.

Ideally, lenders should request clean opinion statements from almost all borrowers, but in practice this is not feasible. However, in the case of a large or complex loan, or one in which risk may be greater than normal, lenders should be more demanding for clean opinion statements than they have been in the past.

Audited Statement—Qualified Opinion

A qualified opinion states that "except for" or "subject to," the effects of the matter to which the qualification or exception relates, the financial statements present the financial data of the business fairly. The exception may result from a departure from generally accepted accounting principles, or limitations in the scope of the audit itself. In many instances the qualification may be minor and of little concern to the lender, but any qualification in the auditor's opinion should be carefully examined by the lender. When such a qualification exists, the auditor adds an additional paragraph to the opinion explaining the circumstances. The following is an example of a qualified opinion:

> We have examined the balance sheet of ABC Company as of December 31, 19___, and the related statements of income, retained earnings, and changes in financial position for the year then ended. Our examination was made in accordance with generally accepted auditing standards, and accordingly included such tests of the accounting records and such other auditing procedures as we considered necessary in the circumstances.
>
> Although the proceeds of sales are collectible on the installment basis over a five-year period, revenue from such sales is recorded in full by the company at time of sale. However, for income tax purposes, income is reported only as collections are received and no provision has been made in the financial statements for income taxes on installments to be collected in the future, as required by generally accepted accounting principles. If such provisions had been made, net income for 19___ and retained earnings as of December 31, 19___, would have been reduced by approximately $_____ and $_____, respectively. For the effect on other account balances, see Note ___ to financial statements.
>
> In our opinion, except that provision has not been made for additional income taxes as described in the preceding paragraph, the statements mentioned above present fairly the financial position of ABC Company at December 31, 19___, and the results of its operations and changes in its financial position for the year then ended, in conformity with generally accepted accounting principles applied on a basis consistent with that of the preceding year.

Audited Statement—Disclaimer of Opinion

A disclaimer of opinion is used in a situation where the auditor feels he or she cannot express an opinion. This may result from the auditor being unable to perform all auditing procedures considered necessary, or from the auditor being unable to satisfy himself or herself that significant financial data could be relied upon. It is important that the lender understand the reason for the disclaimer, and the auditor's opinion should be read very carefully. Again, the reason for the disclaimer may be relatively routine, as in the following example, or it may present serious problems for the lender.

> We have examined the balance sheet of GHK Company as of December 31, 19___, and the related statements of income, retained earnings, and changes in financial position for the year then ended. Our examination was made in accordance with generally accepted auditing standards, and accordingly included such tests of the accounting records and such other auditing procedures as we considered necessary in the circumstances, except as noted in the following paragraph.
>
> Because we were not engaged as auditors until after December 31, 19___, we were not present to observe the physical inventory taken at that date and we were unable to satisfy ourselves by means of other procedures concerning such inventory quantities.

> Because the inventory at December 31, 19__, enters materially into the determination of financial position, results of operations, and changes in financial position, we do not express an opinion on the statements mentioned above.

Audited Statement—Adverse Opinion

Adverse opinions are rare. An adverse opinion indicates that the auditor feels that the statements are misleading as to fairness of presentation, or that they fail to conform to generally accepted accounting principles. Rather than issue an adverse opinion, the auditor may refuse to allow his or her name to be used in connection with the statements. An adverse opinion should be a red flag for the lender and requires further investigation into the financial position of the borrower. The following is an example of an adverse opinion:

> We have examined the balance sheet of DEF Company as of December 31, 19__, and the related statements of income, retained earnings, and changes in financial position for the year then ended. Our examination was made in accordance with generally accepted auditing standards, and accordingly included such tests of the accounting records and such other auditing procedures as we considered necessary in the circumstances.
>
> As explained in Note__, property, plant, and equipment are carried in the balance sheet at appraised values as of January 1, 19__. As a result, fixed assets net of accumulated depreciation at December 31, 19__, are carried at $____ in excess of cost to the Company and same amount is included in stockholders' equity as appraisal surplus. Net income for the year ended December 31, 19__, has been reduced $____ by amortization in excess of depreciation based on cost. The recording of appraisals in excess of depreciated cost is not in conformity with generally accepted accounting principles.
>
> Because of the material effect of the matter described in the preceding paragraph, we are of the opinion that the statements mentioned above do not present fairly the financial position of DEF Company at December 31, 19__, the results of its operations or the changes in its financial position for the year then ended in conformity with generally accepted accounting principles.

Unauditied Statements

A certified public accountant will produce two types of unaudited statements—a review or compilation. As part of a review the CPA makes a limited effort to verify information, primarily through inquiries of company personnel and through certain analytical procedures. This allows the CPA to express *limited* assurance that no material modifications need to be made for the financial statement to conform to generally accepted accounting principles. The following is an example of a CPA's opinion letter in a case where a review has been performed:

> We have reviewed the accompanying unaudited financial statements of ABC Company, Inc. as of December 31, 19__ and for the year then ended. Our review was made in accordance with standards established by the American Institute of Certified Public Accountants.

All information included in these financial statements is the representation of management. A review consists principally of inquiries of company personnel and analytical procedures applied to the financial data. It is substantially less in scope than an examination made in accordance with generally accepted auditing standards, the objective of which is the expression of an opinion regarding the financial statements taken as a whole.

Accordingly, we express no such opinion with respect to these statements.

Based on our review, we are not aware of any material modifications required to put the accompanying financial statements in conformity with generally accepted accounting principles.

A compilation is simply information that has been furnished by the client which the CPA has assembled in standard financial statement format. Generally, no effort has been made to verify this information through any inquiry or analytical procedures. *No* assurance is given by the CPA regarding the reliability or accuracy of the statement information. The following is a sample CPA's opinion in a case where a compilation has been performed:

We have compiled the accompanying unaudited financial statements of ABC Company as of November 30, 19__ and for the eleven months then ended.

A compilation is limited to presenting in the form of financial statements information that is the representation of management (owners).

We did not audit or review the accompanying financial statements and, accordingly, we express no opinion or any other form of assurance with respect to these statements.

Management has elected to omit substantially all of the disclosures and the statement of changes in financial position required by generally accepted accounting principles. If the omitted disclosures were included in the financial statements, they might influence the user's conclusions about the company's financial position, results of operations, and changes in financial position. Accordingly, these financial statements are not designed for those who are not informed about such matters.

Many small businesses do not use the services of a certified public accountant, relying instead on the services of a bookkeeping firm, an internal accountant, or on financial information prepared by company management. Statements from these sources may be acceptable to a lender but should always be viewed with a critical eye. Information is often incomplete, or it may not be stated consistently from year to year. Asset valuations may be estimates at best, and liabilities may be understated or omitted. Such statements may contain considerable "window dressing," since the opinions of owners and management as to the worth of the business are hardly unbiased. A prudent lender will attempt to verify information in this type of statement from other sources, if possible. In spite of the problems, a lender who works with very small or unsophisticated business enterprises often must content himself or herself with relatively poor quality financial information.

Statement For the Proper Entity

As the first step in examining statements a lender should ascertain that the statements presented are for the proper entity, that is, the legal entity that is the proposed borrower. If Suburban Printing Company, Inc. is to be the primary borrower, then the statements presented should be for that legal entity. A statement on Suburban Printers, a Partnership, or on John Davis dba Suburban Graphics will not suffice. In addition to statements on the primary borrower, the lender should also request complete statements on any proposed guarantor. If a corporate borrower has a substantial investment in a subsidiary, statements on that entity should generally also be requested.

At times corporate borrowers will present consolidated statements covering the proposed corporate borrower and its subsidiaries. Consolidated statements contain financial information that is valuable to a lender, but the lender should recognize that a consolidated statement is, in a sense of the word, a fiction. No single legal entity exists that has the financial position or operating results shown in the consolidated statement. It is a statement that should supplement rather than replace the financial statement of the individual corporation which is to be the primary borrower. In some cases, the parent corporation is nothing but a non-operating holding company, with all operations and business transactions carried on by its separately incorporated subsidiaries. In this case, it is necessary to examine the financial statements of the corporate subsidiaries to gain a true understanding of the business, and to learn which entity owns which assets and owes which liabilities. Occasionally, a lender will receive a "consolidated" statement purportedly consolidating the assets and liabilities of an individual and his or her wholly owned corporation. This is an unacceptable approach which should not be tolerated by the lender.

In traditional accounting, a financial statement may present the position of a given economic entity as distinct and separate from its owners. In accordance with generally accepted accounting principles, a statement may represent a "business entity" even though that enterprise is not a "legal entity." Therefore, a sole proprietorship may be treated as an entity separate from its owner, even though legally that distinction may not exist. Such a statement on a business enterprise would show only the assets and liabilities of the business enterprise, and should not be mistaken by the lender for a complete financial statement of its proprietor. Exhibit F is an example of a business enterprise balance sheet. To understand fully the borrower's position, a complete financial statement showing all business and personal assets of the proprietor is required.

Statements Projecting Future Performance

Historical financial information as represented by balance sheets, income statements and, statements of change in financial position, shows how a business has performed in the past and what its position is today. This, however, does not answer all the lender's questions. It is future performance, not past performance, that determined a business' ability to meet its obligations. Therefore, the lender must make an assessment of the business' probable future position and performance. This is accomplished primarily by examining financial projections, including a cash flow statement, pro forma income statement, and pro forma balance sheet.

The projected cash flow statement is an estimate of future cash outlays and receipts. It shows anticipated cash inflows from all sources for a given period, usually a year, as well as all anticipated outflows, including operating expenses, inventory purchases, capital outlays, and debt repayment. Inflows and outflows are usually listed on a monthly basis and then totalled for the year. It should be stressed that *only anticipated cash transactions* are reflected in the cash flow projection. By studying the cash flow projection it can be determined when surplus cash will be available for debt reduction, and when cash deficits will have to be funded by additional borrowings. A sample cash flow projection is included as Exhibit G.

Simply defined, a pro forma income statement is a projected income statement. It is usually prepared in the same format as a historical income statement, but reflects projections of future revenue and expenses rather than actual operating results. Contrary to the cash flow statement, which projects cash flow, the pro forma income statement projects profitability. The pro forma income statement takes into consideration several factors that are not considered in projecting cash flow. These include depreciation charges, other non-cash expenses, and inventory changes. A sample pro forma income statement is shown as Exhibit H.

A pro forma balance sheet is a projected balance sheet for the end of a future period, showing the borrower's anticipated financial position at that future date. It enables both the borrower and the lender to estimate what the borrower's future leverage, working capital position, and debt structure will be. It also enables the lender to project what affect the requested loan will have on the borrower's overall financial position.

To be credible, any projection must be realistic and achievable. A cash flow projection based on overly optimistic estimates of future performance will only lead to trouble for both the borrower and the lender. Since meaningful projections of future performance are so vital to the lender's decision on the loan request, it behooves every commercial lender to obtain projections from the borrower, and then to analyze those projections in the light of past performance to ensure that they are realistic. The borrower should be required to justify any projection that indicates that future performance will be significantly superior to past performance.

Other Lender Concerns

A lender should always be concerned about poorly prepared statements. A statement of poor quality may reflect carelessness or lack of sophistication on the part of the borrower, or it may camouflage the borrower's deteriorating financial position. The loan officer should also beware of the borrower who proffers only a balance sheet but no income statement or cash flow projection. Failure to produce an income statement may be an oversight on the part of the borrower, or it may indicate the borrower's reluctance to disclose unsatisfactory operating results. Troubled management, unable to face the true magnitude of its problems, sometimes prepares misleading financial information as much to deceive itself as to deceive a lender.

The borrower who changes accountants should also concern the lender, and a loan officer should always question why a borrower has taken this action. In some instances, the change is made because the accountant refuses to consent to a change in the basis on which information is presented in the financial statement, or to delete information disclosed in a footnote. A change from an audited to unaudited statement may also be a red flag. Lack of consistency in the presentation of financial information from one accounting period to the next can cause problems for a lender attempting to analyze loan trends. When this problem is detected, an explanation should be requested from the borrower and/or the accountant who prepared the statements to ensure that the changes do not obscure adverse trends. An example of this would be writing up real estate to current market value from cost basis to hide a significant decrease in equity due to a substantial operating loss.

In summary, since financial statements are the loan officer's most valuable tool, concern about statement quality, completeness, and consistency is required.

EXHIBIT   E   **Statement of Changes in Financial Position**

ABC MANUFACTURING COMPANY

STATEMENT OF CHANGES IN FINANCIAL POSITION

Years Ended July 31, 19X4 and 19X3

	19X4	19X3
FINANCIAL RESOURCES PROVIDED BY		
Operations:		
Net income (loss)	$ (70,381)	$ 80,236
Items which did not require outlay of working capital:		
Depreciation	71,236	53,249
Amortization	92,484	91,086
Deferred income taxes	696	-
Total working capital provided by operations	$ 94,035	$ 224,571
Other sources:		
Proceeds from sale of equipment	4,010	14,096
Long-term receivables transferred to current assets	-	30,000
Proceeds from long-term loan	775,000	262,500
	$ 873,045	$ 531,167
FINANCIAL RESOURCES APPLIED TO		
Addition to cash surrender value of life insurance	$ 6,004	$ 10,163
Purchase of equipment and leasehold improvements	389,131	177,378
Incorporation expenses	-	12,346
Agreement not to compete	-	270,000
Long-term debt transferred to current liabilities	245,586	92,138
Purchase of common stock for the treasury 1984 none; 1983 150 shares	-	75,000
Cash dividends declared	-	1,000
	$ 640,721	$ 638,025
Increase (decrease) in working capital, as below	$ 232,324	$(106,858)
SUMMARY OF CHANGES IN WORKING CAPITAL COMPONENTS		
Increase (decrease) in:		
Cash	$ (27,305)	$ 30,218
Receivables	(31,073)	86,775
Inventories	178,932	483,245
Other	(36,512)	29,016
Decrease (increase) in:		
Notes payable and current maturities of long-term debt	261,077	(604,919)
Accounts payable and accrued expenses	(112,795)	(131,193)
Increase (decrease) in working capital	$ 232,324	$(106,858)

EXHIBIT F   Business Enterprise Balance Sheet

SUBURBAN SUPPLY COMPANY

BALANCE SHEET

December 31, 19λ3

(Unaudited)

ASSETS

Current assets

Accounts receivable	$ 9,419.40
NSF checks	174.68
Inventory - at lower of cost or market	54,456.38
Prepaid interest	392.99
Total current assets	$64,443.45

Property and equipment

	Cost	Accumulated Depreciation	Net	
Automobile	$ 6,713.00	$1,998.00	$4,715.00	
Truck	6,054.00	4,038.00	2,016.00	
Improvements	2,234.42	1,184.10	1,050.32	
Equipment	4,788.00	2,300.00	2,488.00	
Total property and equipment	$19,789.42	$9,520.10		$10,269.32
Total assets				$74,712.77

LIABILITIES AND OWNER'S EQUITY

Current liabilities

Bank overdraft	$ 1,124.87
Accounts payable	5,128.48
Note payable - automobile	2,720.46
Bank note payable	34,400.00
Total current liabilities	$43,373.81

Owner's equity

Roger Morgan, January 1, 1983	$26,352.76	
Capital contributed	1,703.12	
Net income	41,543.08	
Withdrawals for the year	(38,260.00)	31,338.96
Total liabilities and owner's equity		$74,712.77

EXHIBIT G   Cash Flow Projection

XYZ Manufacturing Company

Cash Flow Projection

April-December 19X4

	April	May	June	July	Aug.	Sept.	Oct.	Nov.	Dec.
Cash Receipts:	$120,000	$225,000	$234,900	$310,400	$391,000	$437,200	$452,700	$465,500	$461,900
Disbursements:									
Inventory Purchases	114,000	170,900	190,300	197,200	201,200	202,800	187,300	206,800	258,200
Mfg. Labor & O/H	47,300	47,300	47,300	58,100	58,100	58,100	57,700	57,700	57,700
G & A Expenses	26,200	24,700	26,900	28,700	28,700	34,400	29,400	29,400	29,400
Selling Expenses	54,900	45,300	49,100	57,100	59,600	60,000	58,800	61,800	78,300
R & D Expenses	23,000	26,600	21,500	21,500	21,300	20,800	21,300	21,300	20,800
Loan Repayments (Includes Interest):									
SBA & Bank	13,500	13,500	13,500	13,500	13,500	13,500	13,500	13,500	13,500
New Term Loan					7,000	7,000	7,000	7,000	7,000
New Working Capital (Int. Only)		1,700	5,000	6,300	7,100	7,200	6,800	6,000	5,300
Total Disbursements	278,900	330,000	353,600	382,400	396,500	403,800	381,800	403,500	470,200
Cash Excess (Deficit)	(158,900)	(105,000)	(118,700)	(72,000)	(5,500)	33,400	70,900	62,000	(8,300)
Working Capital Loan Requirements:									
Month-Beginning Loan Balance	200,000	358,900	463,900	582,600	654,600	660,100	626,700	555,800	493,800
Additions	158,900	105,000	118,700	72,000	5,500				8,300
Repayments						(33,400)	(70,900)	(62,000)	
Month-End Loan Balance	358,900	463,900	582,600	654,600	660,100	626,700	555,800	493,800	502,100

EXHIBIT H   Pro Forma Income Statement

ABC MANUFACTURING COMPANY

Projected Income Statement, 19_4

	Jan.	Feb.	March	April	May	June	July	Aug.	Sept.	Oct.	Nov.	Dec.	Total
Sales	96135	139649	293295	220000	282592	395012	439902	462682	456582	492772	433172	421427	4133220
Materials/Freight	53117	64937	129068	94600	121515	169855	189158	198953	196330	211892	186264	181214	1796903
Direct Labor	7320	6346	16469	13200	16955	23701	26394	27761	27395	29566	25990	25285	246383
Mfg. O/H & Depr.	19249	18671	38999	21100	27100	37900	42200	44400	43800	47300	41600	40500	422819
Cost of Goods Sold	79686	89954	184536	128900	165570	231456	257752	271114	267525	288758	253854	246999	2466105
Gross Profit	16449	49695	108759	91100	117022	163556	182150	191568	189057	204014	179318	174428	1667115
G&A,P/R, T&I	10116	10830	12856	12800	12800	12800	13300	13300	18300	13300	13300	13300	157002
G&A Facilities Depr.	5636	4623	4952	5000	5000	5000	5000	5000	5000	5000	5000	5000	60211
G&A Costs	6359	6825	6974	9000	7500	9700	9000	9000	9700	9700	9700	9700	103158
Legal & Acctg.	127	3188	1642	1900	1900	1900	1900	1900	1900	1900	1900	1900	22057
Recruiting & Reloc.	391	100	0	0	0	0	2000	2000	2000	2000	2000	2000	12491
Total G&A	22629	25566	26424	28700	27200	29400	31200	31200	36900	31900	31900	31900	354919
Advertising	7437	346	23403	15000	15000	15000	17000	15000	15000	15000	15000	35000	188186
Commissions	4924	9678	16732	13200	16956	23701	26394	27761	27395	29566	25990	25286	247582
Sales P/R, T&I	8068	10821	12908	10856	11744	11744	10784	12574	11679	10784	11679	11678	135320
Sales Costs	4044	1596	7460	12400	5400	5400	5600	5600	5600	5600	5600	5600	69900
Bad Debts/Fees	961	1537	3006	2750	3532	4938	5499	5784	5707	6160	5415	5268	50556
Total Sales Exp.	25434	23978	63509	54206	52632	60782	65277	66719	65381	67110	63684	82832	691544
Research & Dev.	24011	24654	23496	24320	22420	22120	22840	22640	22140	22640	22640	22140	276061
Interest Expense	6768	10569	9000	10000	15000	15000	15000	17000	17000	17000	17000	17000	166337
Other & Int. Inc.	0	0	-12269	0	0	0	0	0	0	0	0	0	-12269
Total Oper. Exp.	78842	84767	110160	117226	117252	127302	134317	137559	141421	138650	135224	153872	1476592
Net Income Before Bonuses and Taxes	-62393	-35072	-1401	-26126	-230	36254	47833	54009	47636	65364	44094	20555	190523
Bonuses	0	0	0	0	0	0	0	1300	4764	6536	4410	2055	19065
Income Taxes	0	0	0	0	0	0	0	0	0	0	0	0	0
Net Income	-62393	-35072	-1401	-26126	-230	36254	47833	52709	42872	58828	39684	18500	171458
YTD Net Income	-62393	-97465	-98866	-124992	-125222	-88968	-41135	11574	54446	113274	152958	171458	

Assumption: 1. Sales are based on an average increase of 14% over 19_3.
2. Material cost is calculated at 43% of sales.
3. Direct labor cost is calculated at 6% of sales.
4. Mfg. O/H includes starting in August depreciation for $300,000 in new equipment of $5,000 per month.
5. All other expenses are from the departmental managers' budgets of 1/_4.

6

Analyzing Financial Information

The study of financial information by the potential lender provides insight into the position and performance of the applicant's business that can be gained in no other way. Therefore, understanding the requirements and techniques for analyzing financial information is of great importance to the loan officer.

Before beginning to analyze the information at hand, the lender must make judgments about two aspects of that information—its adequacy and its quality. Obviously, the lender will never have all possible information about a given borrower's business, and this should not be the lender's objective. Rather, the lender should strive to obtain adequate information that will give him or her an understanding of the borrower's business operation and enable the lender to make a decision on a given loan application. If, for instance, the lender has been asked to make a very short term interim loan for $10,000 pending the collection of a specific account receivable, then the amount of information required may be considerably less than if the lender has been requested to make a $250,000 working capital loan which may be on the lender's books for an extended period of time. Again, if the loan is to be entirely secured by government bonds, the requirement for financial information may be considerably less stringent than in a case where the loan is to be secured by the receivables and inventory of the borrower. Whatever the circumstances surrounding the loan request, a lender should never make a decision on such a request until he or she is satisfied that enough information has been obtained to enable the lender to gain an adequate understanding of the status of the borrower's business. If in doubt, additional information should always be requested.

The better the quality of the information submitted, the easier it is to analyze. Nothing is more frustrating to the analyst than dealing with information that is inconsistently stated, lacking in detail, or presented in a nonconforming format. Many lenders, especially when dealing with small businesses, are much too inclined to accept unsatisfactory information and are too hesitant to demand adequate, concise, and complete information from the potential borrower. Experienced loan officers agree that if adequate information is to be obtained, it must be obtained prior to the time the loan decision is made and the loan funds disbursed. Once the loan proceeds are disbursed, the borrower may become unconcerned and uncooperative. It is especially important that the necessity to submit adequate and acceptable information be impressed upon the new borrower. Borrowers who are made to realize that they must submit good financial information the first time they borrow, will usually continue to perform well in this regard. It is the borrower who has been allowed to develop bad habits by a loan officer who is not demanding enough, who will continue to be a problem as far as submitting acceptable information.

The analysis of financial information should have several objectives. First, it should clearly determine the business' present position and performance. Second, it should determine the direction in which the business is headed, and based on those determinations, it should make an assessment of the business' probable future performance and position. Liquidity, solvency, profitability, and financial efficiency are all factors that should be studied carefully, and trends affecting these factors should be identified. Ultimately, a prediction must be made concerning the future viability and success of the business, based on forecasts of its performance. The documents required for this financial analysis are the balance sheet, income statement, statement of changes in financial position, and projections of future performance, including a cash flow statement and a pro forma income statement.

Balance Sheet Analysis

The balance sheet is a "snapshot" of the condition of a business on a given day. It is a formal listing of all of the assets (property) and all liabilities (claims of creditors against the assets) of the business. The asset side of the balance sheet is a listing of all of the property owned by the business expressed in terms of its estimated value. In studying the listing of assets the analyst should consider two basic questions—the kind of assets the business owns; and how they are valued.

Assets

Assets may generally be classified as current, fixed, intangible, other assets, and deferred charges. Current assets, for statement analysis purposes, consist of cash and those assets which in the normal course of business are expected to be converted into cash within a twelve-month period. Trade accounts receivable, short term notes receivable, and inventory would all normally be considered current assets. Prepaid expenses are often shown as current assets on a financial statement, but for analysis purposes, these should be reclassified as noncurrent assets since they are not normally converted into cash in the normal course of business, and may in fact be nonrecoverable. Fixed assets consist of land, buildings, machinery and equipment, rolling stock, furniture and fixtures, leasehold improvements, etc. These assets generally represent the production, sales and transportation facilities that the company must own in order to operate its business. Intangible assets are those that usually have no physical or tangible being, and which may not be transferable or convertible to cash except through the sale of the business as a whole. In a liquidation they may be of little value, and difficult or impossible to sell. Examples of intangible assets would be good will, unamortized organization expense, patents, subscription lists, trademarks, and proprietory rights. Other assets are those that do not readily fall into one of the other classifications. They may include noncurrent receivables, cash value of life insurance, or investments in securities. Deferred charges include prepaid interest, prepaid taxes, prepaid rent, and prepaid insurance, which although listed as assets, are actually expenses charged to future operating periods. Deferred charges are often not recoverable or refundable, and therefore have little tangible value from an analysis standpoint.

Generally accepted accounting principles require that fixed assets be valued on a basis of cost less accumulated depreciation. Market value, the price for which the asset could readily be sold in the open market, may be either more or less than the valuation arrived at by using generally accepted accounting principles. Obviously, from the standpoint of achieving consistency, it is advantageous to value assets on the basis of cost less accumulated depreciation, as long as the analyst realizes that this may not reflect actual or market value.

The value of cash shown in the balance sheet generally can be verified fairly easily. However, when considering the other assets shown in the statement, the valuation problem becomes more difficult. Accounts receivable may be only partially collectible, and it may be necessary for the analyst to examine an itemized, aged listing of all receivables in order to develop some feel for the collectibility of the business' receivables.

Notes or bills receivable should be examined closely by the analyst. In some instances a business may obtain a note only from a customer who is not paying in a satisfactory manner. In some cases, notes receivable may represent amounts owed to the business by employees or officers. In either case, the collectibility of the note may be questionable.

Inventory may be fresh or a portion of it may be obsolete. If the inventory is perishable, its condition may be questionable. Also, the method used to value inventory, such as the last in, first out (LIFO) method, or the first in, first out (FIFO) method, may significantly affect the statement valuation of the inventory. If a footnote to the statement fails to disclose the valuation method used, the analyst should clarify this by talking to the applicant or the applicant's accountant. Generally, the inventory should be valued at whichever is lower—cost or market value. If it appears that this has not been done, the analyst should proceed with caution. The analyst should also raise the question whether the inventory figure shown in the statement is a result of the actual taking of a physical inventory, whether it was taken from the company's perpetual inventory records, or whether the figure represents a mere estimate of inventory on hand. Further, the analyst should ascertain that all inventory shown in the statement is actually owned by the business and that it does not include inventory received on consignment from others.

The inventory of a manufacturer is usually broken down into three classifications—raw materials, goods in process, and finished goods. Raw materials should be valued at the lower of cost or market. Goods in process are much more difficult to value, since at least from a liquidation standpoint, goods in process may be considerably less saleable than either raw materials or finished goods. Finished goods should generally be valued at cost, including cost of raw materials, labor and other manufacturing costs, provided cost does not exceed probable market value.

In a financial statement prepared in accordance with generally accepted accounting principles, land will be valued at its purchase cost. If that land was purchased many years ago, its current market value may far exceed original cost. Generally accepted accounting principles require that improvements to real estate, such as buildings, storage tanks, improved parking lots, etc., be valued in the balance sheet at cost less accumulated depreciation. Actual market value may be either more or less than the value shown in the balance sheet. A well constructed, well maintained, well located, multipurpose building, such as an office building, may have appreciated significantly in market value since the date of its construction. An obsolete factory building in a poor location may be worth significantly less than the value shown in the balance sheet. On some occasions, in order to increase the value of total assets shown in the balance sheet, a borrower may obtain an appraisal of the real estate, and then substitute appraisal value for depreciated cost value in an unaudited statement. This may have the effect of significantly increasing the value of the real estate, with a corresponding increase in net worth or equity. Such a deviation from generally accepted accounting principles should be shown in a footnote to the statement, but this is not always done. Therefore, the analyst should raise a question about the manner in which the real estate was valued in the balance sheet, and should also obtain information about the probable actual market value of the real estate. A determination of actual market value may involve both a visit to the borrower's premises and a request for an appraisal.

The loan analyst should always be alert for figures in an unauditied balance sheet which may represent the owner's equity in an asset, rather than the value of the asset offset by a liability shown in the liabilities section of the statement. Especially in the case of real estate, some accountants have made it a practice to show equity only in the balance sheet itself, rather than showing the full value of the asset and the offsetting liability. Sometimes the asset valuation and the offsetting liability are shown in an attached schedule, and sometimes this is left to the conjecture of the analyst. Obviously, showing equities only in the balance sheet creates several problems. First, it makes it difficult for the analyst to determine the applicant's total indebtedness. Second, the balance sheet shows an untrue relationship between the amount of the applicant's assets and liabilities. Third, it makes it difficult to determine how many creditors the applicant has, who they are, and the amount owed each creditor. A statement showing equities only is generally unsatisfactory from an analysis standpoint, and at the very least should be reconstructed by the analyst, if the information is available to do this. Preferably, a better statement should be requested from the borrower.

As a preliminary step for statement analysis, the analyst may want to deduct all assets that are considered to be intangible. Examples of intangible assets would be good will, organization expense, subscription lists, patents, trademarks, copyrights, and franchises. The analyst should not automatically assume that intangible assets have no value. A patent or a franchise, for instance, may be readily saleable at a good price. However, for loan analysis purposes, the analyst should deduct the value of most intangible assets, thereby reducing the dollar value of total assets and net worth by a corresponding amount. This generally gives a much more realistic picture of the amount of assets and equity that would actually be available to support the lender's loan.

Liabilities

Liabilities, unlike assets, consist of specific dollar amounts. Therefore, when dealing with liabilities, the problem is to verify the amounts rather than to determine the values. Liabilities are generally divided into two classifications, current and noncurrent. A current liability may be defined as one that is payable on demand or that will be due within the coming twelve-month period. Current liabilities can generally be divided into five sections— accounts payable, notes payable, accrued expenses, accrued taxes, and current portion of long term debt. Accounts payable are payments due to various suppliers of goods and services. The loan analyst should raise a number of questions concerning accounts payable. Who are the company's major suppliers? Are payments being made in a timely manner? In order to answer these questions the analyst will require an itemized, aged listing of all accounts payable. The status of the company's accounts payable and its relationship with its suppliers are often key indicators of the manner in which a company meets its debt obligations. Notes payable represent short term borrowings, usually primarily from banks. Notes payable covering trade obligations to suppliers may indicate that the company is slow in meeting its obligations, since accounts payable are often converted to notes when the creditor becomes concerned about the inclination or ability of the account debtor to pay. The analyst should obtain a listing of all notes payable showing the amount owed each creditor, and what assets are pledged as security. In many instances, a closely held business will borrow from its officers or principal stockholders, and this will be evidenced by a note payable. There is nothing wrong with this practice, but the analyst should be familiar with the circumstances surrounding such a transaction. Accrued expenses are accounts payable for nontrade items, such as utility bills, rent, wages, salaries, and legal fees. Normally, accrued expenses are a relatively small portion of total current liabilities. If accrued expenses seem unusually large, the analyst should inquire further. Accrued taxes include all taxes that have been incurred but not paid, including federal and state income taxes, payroll tax deposits, sales taxes, and real estate taxes. The accrued taxes account should be closely examined by the analyst, since unpaid taxes represent existing or potential liens which may have priority to other creditors. Any evidence that tax payments are delinquent is a red flag which requires further investigation by the analyst.

The final category of item ordinarily found in the current liabilities section of a financial statement consists of the current portion of long term debt, which is that portion of long term indebtedness that becomes due and payable within twelve months. Other items may also be found in the current liabilities section, such as advances or deposits, dividends payable, etc., but these are usually a relatively small portion of total current liabilities, and need be of no great concern to the analyst unless they are for an unusually large amount, in which case further inquiry should be made.

Noncurrent Liabilities (long term debt)

Noncurrent liabilities include real estate mortgage debt, term loans for the purchase of equipment, and debentures or bonds issued by the business. Long term debt is usually associated with the acquisition of a company's fixed assets, such as production facilities, equipment, vehicles, etc. Noncurrent debt is generally not as great a concern to the short term lender as current liabilities. As long as adequate cash flow is available to service noncurrent debt, it generally does not create a problem.

Contingent Liabilities

Another question that should be considered by the loan analyst when examining the applicant's statements is whether contingent liabilities may exist. Contingent liabilities may be defined as indirect or potential liabilities, often indefinite in amount, which may become actual liabilities under certain circumstances. Although contingent liabilities should always be disclosed in a footnote to a balance sheet, or in the balance sheet itself, this is often not done. The borrower may have only a vague awareness of his or her contingent liabilities, which may include the following:

1. Co-obligor of the debts or obligations of others, either as co-maker, cosigner, endorser, or guarantor.
2. Liability for additional taxes on revenue already received, especially federal income taxes.
3. Contingent income tax liability that would result from liquidation of assets at the market value shown in the balance sheet.
4. Pending lawsuits.
5. Accounts or notes sold with recourse.
6. Liability under a lease.
7. Liability on contracts or other agreements, including commodity sales or purchase contracts.
8. Liability incurred in connection with violations of the regulations of various state and federal agencies such as EPA and OSHA.
9. Warranties of quality or performance of goods sold.
10. Unused commercial letters of credit.

Working Capital

Working capital may be defined as the dollar difference between total current assets and current liabilities, and represents a cushion in the current assets. The dollar amount of working capital available is usually less important than the relationship of working capital to other statement items, such as current liabilities, net worth, and cash flow. From a practical standpoint, working capital may be increased in several ways, such as (1) earnings, (2) the sale of new stock by a corporation, or the contribution of capital by individual partners to a partnership, (3) the sale of fixed assets, or (4) long term borrowings.

Conceptually, working capital is increased by one of the following:

1. Increasing current assets.
2. Decreasing current liabilities.
3. Converting short term liabilities to long term liabilities.
4. Converting noncurrent assets to current assets.

Conversely, working capital is decreased by the following:

1. Decreasing current assets.
2. Increasing current liabilities.
3. Converting current assets to noncurrent assets.
4. Paying noncurrent liabilities with cash.
5. Purchasing long term assets with cash or short term borrowings.

Therefore, a borrower cannot increase his or her working capital by borrowing cash on a short term basis, since this results in offsetting increases in current assets (cash) and in current liabilities (notes payable). However, the borrower may increase working capital by borrowing long term, which results in an increase in current assets (cash), and an increase in long term liabilities (term loan payable). The same result may be accomplished by converting short term debt to long term debt, or by selling noncurrent assets, such as equipment, for cash.

A business may have a strong net worth, but if all its equity is in fixed assets such as equipment and real estate, it may have virtually no funds available for its daily operations. The loan analyst must therefore examine a business' working capital position very carefully, to insure that the business will not be entirely dependent upon borrowed funds to cover its short term operating needs.

Analyzing Equity Position

The importance of adequate equity was discussed in chapter 3, but judging "adequacy" can be difficult. Lenders often raise the question, "How much equity is necessary to make a loan safe?"

The amount of equity required to make a loan safe will vary depending on the nature of the business, adequacy of cash flow and collateral, and other factors. Some lenders believe that the owner should have a larger equity in the assets than the creditors. However, in some industries, especially those that are quite seasonal in nature, this rule of thumb may not be readily applicable. In most cases, the workability of a loan is more dependent on repayment capacity and cash flow than on equity. However, the amount of equity available as a cushion against loss and the relationship of equity to total assets and total liabilities are important factors to be considered by the loan analyst.

Conceptually, equity is adequate if it provides a sufficient cushion against potential loss by the creditor. Every lender knows that when a loan runs into trouble, the value of the borrower's assets tends to shrink. Assets may disappear, or their quality may deteriorate. A forced sale of inventory and equipment may bring considerably less than anticipated. Legal and liquidation costs often absorb a sizeable percentage of proceeds. Undisclosed liens may appear. All this will result in the creditor realizing substantially less from the sale of assets than anticipated. The true test of adequacy of equity therefore may be whether it is sufficient to allow full recovery by the lender under the worst conditions. How much equity is required to achieve this is a decision that a lender must make in each individual case, based on the strength of the credit factors and the specific circumstances under which the loan is made. As pointed out previously, the amount of equity shown in the balance sheet and tangible equity may differ considerably, and this must be taken into consideration when making a judgment concerning the safety of a loan.

Income Statement Analysis

The principal indicator of the long term survival and success of a business is its profitability. The continuing, long term ability of a business to meet its obligations is directly tied to its profits. Therefore, every lender must be vitally interested in the profit performance of the businesses with which he or she deals. Income statements contain historical information regarding a business' profit performance. The income statement, which is always compiled for a specific period of time, usually a year, indicates the amount and nature of the business' income, and the amount and nature of the business' total expenses, including non-cash expenses such as depreciation. The final item on the income statement shows the business' profit or loss for that period.

To fully understand the profit performance of a business, the loan analyst needs income statements for at least two-to-three prior years. Information for a shorter period may give a distorted picture of the real profitability of the business. Although interim statements, covering a period shorter than a year, such as a calendar quarter, can be very helpful in monitoring the ongoing performance of a business, such a statement may give a distorted picture of performance, especially if the business is seasonal in nature. The analyst should also ascertain that he or she is working with statements prepared on an accrual basis rather than on a cash basis. A cash basis income statement lists only cash sales and cash expenses for a given period, without taking into consideration changes in inventory, changes in accounts receivable, and accrued expenses. Some businesses, such as farm operations, traditionally file their income tax returns on a cash basis, and therefore it is not uncommon for these businesses to furnish lenders cash basis statements. However, net income measured on a cash basis may give an erroneous impression about the business, since cash basis net income for a given year may vary dramatically from net income measured on an accrual basis. The accrual basis, which gives a more accurate picture of performance, is therefore far more appropriate for measuring business performance.

Depending on whether the entity for which the income statement is prepared is a sole proprietorship, partnership, or corporation, the loan analyst's interpretation of the actual profitability of the business will vary. In the statement of a sole proprietorship, if properly prepared, the net income figure represents the return for management *and labor* of the sole proprietor. In a partnership income statement, the expenses listed may include salaries paid to one or more partners. Interpretation of the income statement of a closely held corporation is more complex. The officers and principal stockholders of such a corporation may be withdrawing the majority of the business' earnings in the form of salaries, bonuses, and fringe benefits. Therefore, in order to develop a realistic understanding of the profit performance of a closely held corporation, it is often necessary for the analyst to consider not only net profits, but also officers' salaries, officers' bonuses, and fringe benefits.

Importance of Credible Projections

As was pointed out in chapter 5, loans are paid off with future revenue and cash flow, not with past profits. Therefore it is not only necessary for the loan analyst to have adequate information about past performance, but also necessary to have credible projections of future performance.

Projections normally come in three forms—pro forma income statements, cash flow projections, and pro forma balance sheets. A pro forma income statement is done in the same format as a regular income statement but uses projections of revenue and expenses rather than actual results for a past period (see Exhibit H in chapter 5). A pro forma income statement may tell the lender a great deal about the probable profit performance of the business, but it will not indicate when borrowings will be needed to cover cash shortfalls, or when excess cash will be available to repay debt. For this, a cash flow projection is required. A cash flow projection summarizes estimates of future cash outlays and cash receipts. It lists all anticipated cash inflows (from all sources) for the planning period. It also lists all anticipated cash outflows including operating and overhead expenses, capital outlays, and repayment commitments on debt. Cash needs and cash inflows are usually estimated on either a monthly or quarterly basis. The net difference between cash inflow and cash outflow each month or quarter will indicate whether borrowings will be required during that period to cover cash shortfalls, or whether a cash excess will be available which may be used to repay short term debt. It is crucial to recognize that only anticipated cash items, both revenue and expenditures, are included in the cash flow projection.

The pro forma balance sheet is a projected balance sheet for the end of a future period, showing the anticipated financial position of a borrower at the end of the planning period. It will show projected leverage, working capital, and debt structure.

Careful examination of these projections by the loan analyst will give a good indication of the future profitability, borrowing needs, repayment ability, and financial position of the borrower, provided that these projections are realistic and achievable. The analyst should always question the soundness and achievability of any projection presented by a borrower. Borrowers sometimes are genuinely overly optimistic about the capability of their business, or a borrower may deliberately "window dress" a projection in an attempt to obtain a loan that the lender otherwise would not make. The best way to test performance projections is to compare them to past performance, taking into consideration any changes in the operation of the business that may result from the use of the loan proceeds. The analyst should always question whether increases in sales volume, profit margins, sales prices, inventory turnover, and receivables turnover are realistic. Conversely, the analyst should question whether percentage decreases in manufacturing costs, general and administrative expenses, and overhead costs are realistic. Is management really capable of achieving those objectives? It will be helpful to the analyst to compare past projections with past performance. If projections prepared by company management have been overly optimistic in the past, there is a strong likelihood that any new projection presented will also be too optimistic. I have observed lenders who, year after year, accept optimistic projections at face value from a borrower who has never achieved the level of performance indicated by his or her projections.

Judging the validity of projections furnished by a new or startup business, which does not have a history of past performance, is one of the most difficult tasks faced by the loan analyst. In this kind of situation it is usually extremely difficult to judge what sales volume can be achieved, since this often depends to a great extent upon public acceptance of a new product, ability of the new company to penetrate the market, effectiveness of the company's pricing strategy, and the intensity of competition. It may also be very difficult to accurately estimate production and overhead costs, and the unforseen costs that are often connected with starting a new business. The loan analyst may find a study of similar companies in the industry and consultation with businesspeople who own similar existing businesses to be very helpful. However, under the best conditions, it remains a very difficult task to accurately assess the future performance of a business that has no track record in the form of historical performance information.

Internal Analysis

It has been pointed out that the prime objective of loan analysis is not only to make a determination of the current position of a business, but also to determine in which direction it is moving, and how rapidly. One means for accomplishing this is through internal comparison, which is the comparison of a business' current position and performance with its past position and performance. By placing current information and past information side by side, it becomes relatively easy to make such comparisons. This is normally accomplished by preparing a spread sheet, such as the one shown in Exhibit I. With balance sheet and income statement information for the three years compiled in this form, it is relatively easy to make some basic observations about trends in the financial position and performance of Southern Material Company, Inc. We can see that over the past two years its cash and receivables have increased, while its inventory increased the first year, and then decreased the second year. We can also see that its total current assets, fixed assets, and total assets have increased significantly. We can also readily observe that, while short term notes payable to banks have decreased significantly, the company during the past year obtained a bank term loan of approximately $160,000. We can also see that current liabilities are little changed over the two-year period, but that the total liabilities have increased. We can further observe that the company's net worth has increased from net earnings by approximately $100,000 during the two-year period.

By examining spread sheet information from the income statement, we can also ascertain that net sales, cost of goods sold, gross profit, operating expenses, general administrative expenses, and profits have all increased. We can also see that no dividends have been paid during the past three years; that there has been an addition to surplus from earnings each year; and that executive salaries have increased from $40,000 to $44,000 during this period. It would be premature for the loan analyst to conclude that the performance of this business has been entirely satisfactory during this time period. However, the analyst can conclude that the sales volume of this business is growing, and that it is profitable. However, making a determination whether growth and profits are adequate will require additional information. Although only a summary of the income statement is shown on the spread sheet, in most instances the loan analyst should compare an itemized current listing of expenses with a similar listing for prior periods.

To develop a further understanding of the changes in the position and performance of this company, the loan analyst should prepare a common size statement. This is a statement in which numbers in the balance sheet have been reduced to a percentage of total assets, and all numbers in the income statement have been reduced to a percentage of net sales. Therefore, in the balance sheet, total assets always equal 100, and in the income statement total sales always equal 100. This procedure enables the analyst to easily identify the changes in the relationships between various statement items. Exhibit J shows the financial statement spread sheet of Southern Material Company, Inc., as shown in the previous exhibit, reduced to a common size basis.

By studying the common size statements for the three years shown, we can draw conclusions that were not obvious when we studied the statements stated in the terms of dollars. We can observe that accounts receivable over the two-year period have increased from 42.8% to 44.5% of total assets, and that during the same period inventory has decreased from 27.6% to 20.9% of total assets. Fixed assets have increased from 22.9% of total assets to 28.1%, and conversely, current assets have decreased from 76.3% to 71.0% of total assets. During the same period total current liabilities have decreased from 43.6% to 34.3% of total assets, but term loans have increased from 0 to 12.0% of total assets. Likewise, total liabilities have increased from 43.6% to 46.3% of total assets, and net worth has decreased from 56.4% to 53.7% of total assets. It is also interesting to note that the trends for the period 1981-82 differ from those for 1982-83.

By futher studying the common size income statement we can learn that cost of goods sold has increased from 62.9% to 63.7% of net sales. We can also observe that operating expenses have increased proportionate to sales while general and administrative expenses have decreased. We can further note that net profit has decreased from 2.9% to 2.4% of net sales during this two-year period. Therefore, while the dollar sales volume and dollar profits of this business are increasing, there are signs that its profit margin may be deteriorating, and this should raise questions in the mind of the loan analyst about the possible future profit trends of this business.

External Analysis

We have illustrated that through internal comparison the loan analyst may compare a company's present position and performance with that of the past, and is thereby able to draw conclusions concerning trends in the company's performance, which will enable him or her to make predictions about its future performance. However, internal analysis tells us nothing about how this company's performance compares to similar companies in the same industry. For example, if the average wholesaler of building materials achieves a profit margin of 4% of net sales, then Southern Material Company's profit margin, ranging from 2.4% to 2.9% over the past two-year period, may be quite unsatisfactory. Conversely, if the average company in this line of business achieves a profit margin of 1.4%, then Southern Material Company's performance may be exceptionally good. The comparison of a company's position and performance with that of a similar company or with that of a group of similar companies is known as external comparison. Material for an external comparison comes primarily from two sources—from the files of other companies of similar nature in the bank's credit department, or from published sources such as Robert Morris Associates' *Annual Statement Studies* and the publications of various trade associations.

Many trade associations today compile information regarding typical balance sheets, income statements, and ratios for their industry. In some instances, data compiled by the United States Department of Commerce can be useful. Dunn and Bradstreet, Inc. compiles statistics for its subscribers that include operating data and ratios on many different types of businesses. Unfortunately, most material from these sources is not available to the user until many months after the statements upon which it is based have been issued, and this may present a problem, especially for an industry in which conditions are changing rapidly.

In making an external comparison, the analyst must be careful that the businesses being compared are similar, since two businesses which appear to be very much alike may prove to be quite different upon further investigation. Two apparently similar businesses may differ greatly in functions performed, in character of the products or services sold, in territory served, in the type of customer served, in investment in fixed assets, and in accounting methods. One manufacturer may start with raw materials and carry on the whole manufacturing process required to convert raw material to a finished product, while another manufacturer of the same product may buy semi-finished components and assemble them. One furniture dealer may operate on a strictly cash and carry basis while another may grant credit and provide delivery service. A given furniture dealer may sell household furnishings to consumers, while another may provide office furniture to commercial businesses. One may sell furniture of the highest quality while the other may sell strictly cut rate items.

A commodities dealer in a Great Plains state may deal strictly in wheat, while a commodities dealer in the Southeast may deal in cotton, peanuts, and tobacco. A hardware store in a wealthy suburban community may have an entirely different type of clientele and inventory than a hardware store in a rural community. One business may have a heavy investment in new buildings and equipment, while a similar business may rent its buildings and have equipment and fixtures that are fully depreciated. In addition, one of these businesses may value its inventory on a "first in—first out" basis, while the other may value its inventory on a "last in—first out" basis, as well as having other variations in accounting practices. Therefore, the loan analyst should proceed with caution whenever making an external comparison, because no one business is entirely like another business or group of businesses.

However, an external comparison can be of great value to the loan analyst in indicating how a business is performing in relation to its peer group within the industry, and in spite of the possible problems involved, this kind of comparison should be made. Exhibit K is an external comparison on a common size basis of the year end 1983 statement of Southern Material Company, Inc. and composite information of wholesalers of building materials of similar size taken from *Annual Statement Studies*.[1] Exhibit L shows the page from *Annual Statement Studies* pertaining to wholesalers of building material. The left half of the page contains current statement information divided into four size categories, based on asset size. The fifth column shows composite information for all 493 businesses upon which information was compiled. On the right half of the page the information for all businesses in the category is shown for the current year and for four previous years. Since the total assets of Southern Material Company, Inc. are $998,000, for the purpose of comparison the 0 to $1,000,000 asset size category (first column on the left) has been used.

By studying the information in Exhibit K, the loan analyst can begin to draw conclusions about how Southern Material Company, Inc. compares to similar companies in the same industry. It can be noted that as of its statement date Southern's cash balances were somewhat less than average. Its trade receivables were significantly higher than average, while its inventory was significantly lower. This may indicate that Southern's trade receivables are of lower than average quality or that its credit policy is more liberal than average. This may also indicate that Southern's inventory is of higher quality and is utilized more efficiently than average. However, these figures may simply indicate that the nature of Southern's business is different from that of the average company, and that the quality of its receivables and inventory is not necessarily better or worse than that of the average company. Southern's fixed assets, totalling 28.1% of total assets, are significantly higher than the RMA average of 16.2%. This greater proportion of investment in fixed assets may be due to a recent investment in new facilities and equipment which is carried in the company's statement at a value near cost, or this may be an indication that Southern is overequipped in comparison to other companies of similar size. It should also be noted by the analyst that Southern has only .9% of its total assets in "all other noncurrent assets," while the RMA average for this category is 6.2%. This may indicate that Southern categorizes some of its non-current assets differently from the average company.

On the liabilities side of the statement, the analyst should note that Southern is much less dependent on short term borrowings than the average company, with 2.9% of Southern's total assets in short term notes compared to the RMA average of 10.7%. Its trade payables and accrued expenses are also somewhat less than average. As a result, its total current liabilities equal 34.3% of total assets compared to the RMA average of 47.8%. The amount of long term debt carried by Southern is 12.0% of total assets compared to the RMA average of 11.0%. With net worth representing 53.7% of total assets compared to the RMA average of 39.2%, it is obvious to the loan analyst that

---

[1]   Annual Statement Studies,© Robert Morris Associates, Philadelphia, 1983.

Southern's equity position is considerably stronger than the average for companies of comparable size.

Several conclusions can also be drawn from a comparison of income data. Southern's cost of sales of 63.7% is significantly less than the RMA average of 75.3%. This may indicate that Southern handles a product mix that allows higher markups, or that it operates in a market that is less competitive than most. Southern's operating expenses of 32.7% are significantly higher than the RMA average of 23.6%. In some instances, this might be indicative of an inefficient, overstaffed operation, or of heavy salary withdrawals by owners. However, in view of the fact that Southern's operating profit of 3.6% is significantly better than the RMA average of 1.0%, the variations from average in the cost of sales and operating expense categories probably indicate that Southern's accounting allocations are somewhat different from that of the average company. Since Southern's profit before taxes is 3.6% compared to .5% for the RMA average, it appears that this company is performing very well from a profitability standpoint.

There are, however, further steps that the loan analyst may take in developing an understanding of the financial position and performance of this company. One of these is ratio analysis, which is an analysis of the changing structure and performance trends of the business.

Ratio Analysis

Ratio analysis is a major tool in the evaluation of financial performance. Ratios express the relationship between various financial statement data. They point out changes in direction and patterns of change that reflect risk, opportunities, and efficiencies. Ratios are indicators of what is happening in the business. They are very useful tools in the evaluation of the position and performance trends of a business, and in projecting future position and performance, but do not draw final conclusions from them. Using balance sheet and income statement information, it is possible to construct a large number of ratios. The task of the loan analyst is to select those that provide the greatest insight, based on the objectives of the analysis.

Many analysts believe that there are five basic ratios which are of prime importance in ratio analysis. These are the (1) current ratio, (2) debt to worth ratio, (3) sales to receivables ratio, (4) cost of sales to inventory ratio, and (5) profitability ratio. Other ratios which may be used from time to time include the quick ratio, total debt to working capital ratio, debt structure ratio, return on assets (ROA) ratio, and fixed asset to worth ratio.

The current ratio is probably the most commonly used of all ratios. It measures the relationship between current assets and current liabilities, and is computed by dividing current assets by current liabilities. The margin of current assets over current liabilities is the cushion for the protection of current creditors. The larger this margin, the stronger the financial position of the company is generally considered to be. Some lenders look for a current ratio of 2.00, and this may be satisfactory in many cases, but what is a satisfactory current ratio depends to a great extent on the nature of the business, and on the strength of the other factors. A current ratio of 2.00 would indicate that the company's current assets could shrink by 50% before current creditors would suffer difficulty. The current ratio addresses only the quantity coverage of current assets over current liabilities, and gives no indication of the quality of the assets from which short term debt payment is to come.

The debt to worth ratio is another important ratio, and indicates the relationship of the owner's equity to the amount of funds the creditors have in the business. The debt to worth ratio is computed by dividing total debt by tangible net worth. This ratio is also called the leverage ratio. It is a key indicator of the extent to which the business relies upon borrowed funds in relation to the funds invested by owners. Generally speaking, the greater the leverage, the greater the risk involved for the creditors. Like the current ratio, the debt to worth ratio is a quantitative ratio, and tells the analyst nothing about the quality or liquidity of the assets shown in the statement.

The sales to receivables ratio attempts to measure the overall quality of the company's receivables by measuring their average age. This is based on the assumption that the older the account receivable, the greater the liklihood that it will become uncollectible. This ratio is sometimes also referred to as the receivables turnover ratio, and is generally stated in one of two ways—as the number of times accounts receivable turn annually, or the number of days the average account was outstanding. To calculate turnover, annual sales are divided by accounts receivable. This gives the number of times receivables have turned over during the year. To convert the turnover ratio into days, either 360 or 365 days are divided by the turnover factor. The result is the number of days the average account receivable has remained on the company's books. Depending on the nature of the business involved, average turnover will vary considerably, and to determine if turnover appears to be satisfactory it will be necessary to compare the turnover ratio of the company being analyzed to industry averages. This ratio can tell the analyst a great deal, not only about the quality of the company's receivables, but also whether or not management is adhering to the company's stated collection policy. The major shortcoming of this ratio as a measurement of receivable quality is that it is completely valid only as of the balance sheet date, since the amount of receivables on the company's books will change daily.

The sales to inventory ratio expresses the relationship between a company's inventory and its net sales. Net sales, however, contain the company's customary markup over the cost of the merchandise sold. For this reason, a more valid ratio is the *cost of sales to inventory ratio*, which excludes the profit element and is therefore a more accurate computation of the relationship between sales and inventory. This ratio is an indicator of the quality of the inventory and of the efficiency with which the company is using the funds it has invested in inventory. This ratio is sometimes also called the inventory turnover ratio, and like the sales to receivables ratio, may be expressed either as the number of times inventory turned during the year, or as the number of days the average inventory item has been on hand. As with the sales to receivables ratio, one of the major shortcomings of the sales to inventory ratio is that it is valid only as of the balance sheet date. The loan analyst should remember that many companies end their fiscal year on or near the date that inventory is at its lowest level for the year.

As pointed out previously, the profitability of a business is a key factor in its success, and therefore the profitability ratio is a very important one. This ratio is also referred to as the return on equity (ROE) ratio, and is generally expressed as a percentage return on equity. However, when computing this ratio for a closely held business, the analyst will need to take into consideration officers' salaries, officers' bonuses, etc. This ratio is a measure of the company's ability to produce earnings, and therefore is an excellent indicator both of the viability of a company and the capability of its management.

The quick ratio, also known as the "acid test," is a refined version of the current ratio, since it measures only cash and accounts receivable against current liabilities. It is therefore an indicator of the coverage of those assets which could be converted to cash very readily against the current liabilities. The total debt to working capital ratio is computed by dividing total debt by the dollar amount of working capital. This ratio is a general indicator of how many dollars will be available to meet the company's debt obligations. The debt structure ratio is computed by dividing current liabilities by total liabilities and focuses attention on that portion of total debt that must be repaid within the coming twelve months.

The return on assets (ROA) ratio is computed by adding net earnings and interest paid and dividing that amount by total assets. Since this is a calculation of the rate of return on all capital (both debt and equity), interest paid must be added back to earnings, since it is the return that creditors earn on debt capital. This ratio is an indicator of the amount of net income generated by each dollar of assets, and is a measure of the efficiency with which the company's assets are used.

The fixed asset to net worth ratio is computed by dividing net fixed assets by tangible net worth. This ratio measures the proportion of the owner's equity which has been invested in fixed assets such as plant and equipment. The analyst should be aware that if the company is leasing a substantial amount of fixed assets, this may deceptively lower the ratio. This ratio is also a measure of liquidity, since a high investment in fixed assets generally has an adverse effect on the company's liquidity position.

Trends

The most important use of ratios in loan analysis is to identify trends. This requires computation of ratios for a number of years and a study of the change in these ratios from year to year. This enables the analyst to readily identify changes in the nature and performance of the business over a period of time. Any deteriorating ratio requires further investigation by the loan analyst. Since all the ratios listed are to some extent related, it is also important that the analyst consider all the ratios, rather than one particular ratio, in developing an understanding of the changes in the business' financial performance.

Exhibit M is a ratio analysis for the years 1981 through 1983 for Southern Material Company, Inc. and a comparison of those ratios to RMA averages. Three figures are shown in the RMA average column; the top figure represents the upper quartile of the companies represented, the middle figure represents the median, and the lower figure represents the lower quartile. By using this kind of format the analyst may observe that Southern's current ratio is improving, and that it is better than the RMA median. Although the trend in the sales to receivable ratio is improving, Southern's receivable turnover is considerably less than even the RMA lower quartile. This situation certainly requires further inquiry by the loan analyst. The cost of sales to inventory ratio is improving, and 1983 turnover is approaching the RMA median. However, turnover in 1981 and 1982 was only slightly better than the lower quartile. In this case, the loan analyst should inquire as to what steps were taken by the company to improve its inventory turnover so significantly. As far as debt to worth ratio goes, Southern, which we have previously observed is a company with strong equity, ranks close to the upper quartile. The loan analyst may also readily observe that Southern's profitability ratio improved in 1983, and falls between the RMA median and upper quartile figures. It is also interesting to note the tremendous difference in profitability performance between the upper quartile and lower quartile companies in this industry group.

Having now concluded his or her preliminary analysis of Southern Material Company, Inc., the loan analyst would probably come to the conclusion that this is a relatively strong, growing, profitable company. Although some weaknesses may exist in the form of a slow receivables turnover and a possible too heavy investment in fixed assets, it appears that the company is a viable, well managed company which has considerable potential for future success.

In this chapter I have examined the basic loan analysis process. However, even though the loan officer has completed an adequate analysis of the financial information presented to him or her, there is still a lot to do before a sound loan can be put on the books. In the following chapters I will examine the remaining steps that must be completed before that can be done.

EXHIBIT I   Credit File, Southern Material Company, Inc., Spread Sheet

SOUTHERN MATERIAL CO., INC.
A Corporation   BUSINESS: Building Materials Supply

ASSETS (Spread in thousands)	12/31/81	12/31/82	12/31/83
Cash	38	42	50
Marketable Securities			
Receivables (Net)	332	372	444
Inventory (Net)	214	234	209
Prepaid Costs	8	8	6
TOTAL CURRENT ASSETS	592	656	709
Fixed Assets (Net)	178	156	280
Deferred Receivables			
Cash Value-Officer's Life Ins.	6	6	9
TOTAL ASSETS	776	818	998

LIABILITIES			
Notes Payable-Banks	82	82	29
Account Payable-Trade	178	172	188
Bank Term Loan (Current Portion)	—	—	40
Miscellaneous Accruals	6	8	7
Taxes (Due and or Accrued)	18	24	29
Notes to Stockholders	54	48	49
TOTAL CURRENT LIABILITIES	338	334	342
Bank Term Loan (Non-Current Por.)	—	—	120
TOTAL LIABILITIES	338	334	462
Capital Stock-Common	200	200	200
Earned Surplus	198	244	296
Capital Surplus	40	40	40
NET WORTH	438	484	536
TOTAL NET WORTH & LIABILITIES	776	818	998

WORKING CAPITAL	254	322	367
Equity Working Capital	254	322	247

NET SALES	1,576	1,728	2,179
COST OF GOODS SOLD	992	1,122	1,389
GROSS PROFIT	584	606	790
Expense-Operating	302	316	462
Gen & Admin. Expense	224	228	250
OPERATING PROFIT	58	62	78
Other Income	2	—	—
NET PROFIT	60	62	78
Federal Taxes	14	18	25
NET PROFIT	46	44	53

Dividends or Withdrawals	0	0	0
Surplus Adjustments			
Debit (Red)			
Credit (Black)		8	
Addition to Surplus	46	44	53
MEMO-Depreciation Incl. in Above Exp.			
Exec. Remuneration	40	40	44
Contingent Liabilities			

EXHIBIT   J   Credit File, Southern Material Company, Inc., Spread Sheet
COMMON SIZE STATEMENT

SOUTHERN MATERIAL CO., INC.
A Corporation   BUSINESS: Building Materials Supply

ASSETS (Spread in thousands)	12/31/81	12/31/82	12/31/83
Cash	4.9	5.1	5.0
Marketable Securities			
Receivables (Net)	42.8	45.5	44.5
Inventory (Net)	27.6	28.6	20.9
Prepaid Costs	1.0	1.0	.6
TOTAL CURRENT ASSETS	76.3	80.2	71.0
Fixed Assets (Net)	22.9	19.1	28.1
Deferred Receivables	—	—	—
Cash Value-Officer's Life Ins.	.8	.7	.9
TOTAL ASSETS	100.0	100.0	100.0

LIABILITIES			
Notes Payable-Banks	10.6	10.0	2.9
Account Payable-Trade	23.0	21.0	18.9
Bank Term Loan (Current Portion)	—	—	4.0
Miscellaneous Accruals	.7	1.0	.7
Taxes (Due and or Accrued)	2.3	2.9	2.9
Notes to Stockholders	7.0	5.9	4.9
TOTAL CURRENT LIABILITIES	43.6	40.8	34.3
Bank Term Loan (Non-Current Por.)	—	—	12.0
TOTAL LIABILITIES	43.6	40.8	46.3
Capital Stock-Common	25.8	24.5	20.0
Earned Surplus	25.5	29.8	29.7
Capital Surplus	5.1	4.9	4.0
NET WORTH	56.4	59.2	53.7
TOTAL NET WORTH & LIABILITIES	100.0	100.0	100.0

WORKING CAPITAL	32.7	39.4	36.8
Equity Working Capital	32.7	39.4	24.7

NET SALES	100.0	100.0	100.0
COST OF GOODS SOLD	62.9	64.9	63.7
GROSS PROFIT	37.1	35.1	36.3
Expense-Operating	19.2	18.3	21.2
Gen & Admin. Expense	14.2	13.2	11.5
OPERATING PROFIT	3.7	3.6	3.6
Other Income	.1	—	—
NET PROFIT	3.8	3.6	3.6
Federal Taxes	.9	1.0	1.2
NET PROFIT	2.9	2.6	2.4

EXHIBIT   K   COMMON SIZE BASE COMPARISON

SOUTHERN MATERIAL CO, INC.

ASSETS	12/31/83	RMA[1] %
Cash and equivalents	5.0	8.6
Accounts and notes receivable	44.5	34.5
Inventory	20.9	31.5
All other current assets	.6	2.3
TOTAL CURRENT ASSETS	71.0	76.9
Fixed assets (net)	28.1	16.2
Intangibles (net)	—	.7
All other non-current assets	.9	6.2
TOTAL ASSETS	100.0	100.0

LIABILITIES		
Notes payable-short term	2.9	10.7
Current maturity-long term debt	4.0	2.9
Accounts and notes payable—trade	18.9	23.8
Accrued expenses	3.6	5.4
All other current liabilities	4.9	4.9
TOTAL CURRENT LIABILITIES	34.3	47.8
Long term debt	12.0	11.0
All other non-current liabilities	—	2.0
NET WORTH	53.7	39.2
TOTAL LIABILITIES AND NET WORTH	100.0	100.0

INCOME DATA		
NET SALES	100.0	100.0
COST OF SALES	63.7	75.3
GROSS PROFIT	36.3	24.7
Operating expenses	32.7	23.6
OPERATING PROFIT	3.6	1.0
All other expenses (net)	—	.5
PROFIT BEFORE TAXES	3.6	.5

---

[1]   Annual Statement Studies, © Robert Morris Associates, Philadelphia, 1983, p. 218, 0−$1,000,000 asset size category.

WHOLESALERS - BUILDING MATERIALS
SIC# 5039

166(6/30-9/30/82)			327(10/1'82-3/31/83)				6/30/78-3/31/79	6/30/79-3/31/80	6/30/80-3/31/81	6/30/81-3/31/82	6/30/82-3/31/83
0-1MM	1-10MM	10-50MM	50-100MM	ALL		ASSET SIZE	ALL	ALL	ALL	ALL	ALL
215	256	22		493		NUMBER OF STATEMENTS	447	466	467	459	493
%	%	%	%	%		ASSETS	%	%	%	%	%
8.6	6.9	4.5		7.5		Cash & Equivalents	7.0	7.1	7.3	6.9	7.5
34.5	33.0	29.0		33.5		Accts. & Notes Rec. - Trade(net)	35.8	34.9	33.4	33.2	33.5
31.5	30.4	27.3		30.7		Inventory	32.4	33.0	33.0	32.9	30.7
2.3	2.4	.8		2.3		All Other Current	1.5	1.7	2.2	2.1	2.3
76.9	72.7	61.6		74.0		Total Current	76.7	76.7	75.9	75.1	74.0
16.2	19.4	26.0		18.3		Fixed Assets (net)	17.4	16.6	16.6	17.8	18.3
.7	.4	.3		.5		Intangibles (net)	.5	.4	.6	.5	.5
6.2	7.5	12.1		7.2		All Other Non-Current	5.4	6.3	6.9	6.6	7.2
100.0	100.0	100.0		100.0		Total	100.0	100.0	100.0	100.0	100.0
						LIABILITIES					
10.7	13.2	22.6		12.5		Notes Payable-Short Term	11.4	10.5	10.6	10.9	12.5
2.9	3.6	2.3		3.2		Cur. Mat.-L/T/D	2.6	2.9	3.0	3.1	3.2
23.8	20.9	14.7		21.9		Accts. & Notes Payable - Trade	23.7	23.6	21.9	21.8	21.9
5.4	4.6	4.3		4.9		Accrued Expenses	6.3	6.4	5.5	5.3	4.9
4.9	2.8	1.2		3.6		All Other Current	3.4	3.8	4.1	3.8	3.6
47.8	44.9	45.1		46.2		Total Current	47.6	47.1	45.1	44.9	46.2
11.0	13.0	9.5		12.0		Long Term Debt	10.7	10.8	10.4	11.1	12.0
2.0	1.2	2.6		1.6		All Other Non-Current	1.8	1.2	1.5	1.4	1.6
39.2	40.8	42.8		40.2		Net Worth	40.0	41.0	43.0	42.6	40.2
100.0	100.0	100.0		100.0		Total Liabilities & Net Worth	100.0	100.0	100.0	100.0	100.0
						INCOME DATA					
100.0	100.0	100.0		100.0		Net Sales	100.0	100.0	100.0	100.0	100.0
75.3	76.5	78.5		76.1		Cost Of Sales	76.5	76.6	75.5	75.8	76.1
24.7	23.5	21.5		23.9		Gross Profit	23.5	23.4	24.5	24.2	23.9
23.6	21.5	16.7		22.2		Operating Expenses	19.3	18.9	20.8	21.7	22.2
1.0	2.0	4.8		1.7		Operating Profit	4.1	4.6	3.7	2.6	1.7
.5	.8	2.7		.7		All Other Expenses (net)	.4	.1	.6	1.0	.7
.5	1.2	2.1		1.0		Profit Before Taxes	3.7	4.4	3.1	1.6	1.0
						RATIOS					
2.6	2.5	2.0		2.5			2.2	2.3	2.4	2.6	2.5
1.6	1.6	1.5		1.6		Current	1.6	1.6	1.7	1.7	1.6
1.2	1.2	1.1		1.2			1.3	1.3	1.3	1.3	1.2
1.6	1.4	1.3		1.4			1.2	1.2	1.3	1.3	1.4
.9	.9	.8		.9		Quick	.9	.9	.9	.9	.9
.6	.6	.5		.6			.7	.7	.6	.6	.6
28 13.0	35 10.3	36 10.1		33 11.1			32 11.4	31 11.6	31 11.6	31 11.7	33 11.1
40 9.2	42 8.6	49 7.4		41 8.8		Sales/Receivables	43 8.4	42 8.7	41 8.9	41 8.9	41 8.8
54 6.7	56 6.5	64 5.7		56 6.5			55 6.6	54 6.8	54 6.8	53 6.9	56 6.5
25 14.4	36 10.1	40 9.2		34 10.7			29 12.7	33 11.0	31 11.7	34 10.7	34 10.7
49 7.5	56 6.5	58 6.3		54 6.7		Cost of Sales/Inventory	51 7.2	54 6.7	55 6.6	56 6.5	54 6.7
89 4.1	83 4.4	83 4.4		85 4.3			79 4.6	81 4.5	87 4.2	87 4.2	85 4.3
5.3	5.4	4.0		5.4			6.7	6.5	5.9	5.9	5.4
11.3	9.9	12.6		10.5		Sales/Working Capital	10.1	9.9	9.3	9.6	10.5
27.0	21.3	30.2		22.3			17.2	18.7	18.2	18.5	22.3
5.2	4.1	8.8		4.8			10.2	10.0	7.6	6.2	4.8
(175) 1.7	(221) 1.8	(17) 1.5		(413) 1.7		EBIT/Interest	(376) 5.1	(388) 4.4	(392) 3.1	(386) 2.1	(413) 1.7
.3	.8	.5		.5			2.5	2.3	1.4	.9	.5
4.7	3.8	11.2		4.4			9.8	9.2	7.1	6.6	4.4
(88) 1.4	(158) 1.7	(18) 5.3		(264) 1.7		Cash Flow/Cur. Mat. L/T/D	(248) 3.7	(260) 3.2	(262) 2.3	(258) 2.1	(264) 1.7
.2	.3	1.1		.3			1.9	1.5	.9	.9	.3
.1	.2	.2		.2			.2	.2	.2	.2	.2
.3	.5	.5		.4		Fixed/Worth	.4	.3	.3	.3	.4
.9	.9	1.2		.9			.7	.6	.6	.8	.9
.8	.7	.8		.7			.9	.8	.7	.6	.7
1.5	1.4	1.1		1.4		Debt/Worth	1.6	1.6	1.4	1.3	1.4
4.0	3.4	4.1		3.7			3.1	3.0	2.9	3.0	3.7
24.9	18.5	16.4		21.2		% Profit Before Taxes/Tangible	43.2	43.4	31.7	26.2	21.2
(196) 9.6	(245) 8.4	(21) 6.6		(462) 8.6		Net Worth	(438) 26.6	(458) 27.2	(463) 17.5	(445) 11.6	(462) 8.6
-5.9	.2	-1.5		-3.9			13.8	14.7	5.8	.0	-3.9
10.1	7.4	8.0		8.3		% Profit Before Taxes/Total	15.5	16.1	12.3	10.8	8.3
2.8	2.9	2.5		2.8		Assets	9.3	10.3	6.7	4.1	2.8
-3.2	-.9	-1.6		-2.3			4.8	5.3	2.1	-.4	-2.3
56.2	36.9	22.3		41.4			55.8	53.5	50.2	43.1	41.4
28.2	17.7	8.2		21.0		Sales/Net Fixed Assets	25.2	25.4	23.8	21.5	21.0
14.5	9.3	4.6		9.8			11.2	12.1	11.8	10.9	9.8
3.7	3.2	2.7		3.3			3.7	3.7	3.5	3.4	3.3
2.8	2.6	2.1		2.7		Sales/Total Assets	2.9	2.9	2.8	2.8	2.7
2.2	2.1	1.2		2.1			2.3	2.2	2.1	2.2	2.1
.6	.7	.9		.6			.5	.5	.6	.6	.6
(191) 1.1	(235) 1.1	(21) 1.8		(447) 1.1		% Depr., Dep., Amort./Sales	(419) .8	(432) .9	(431) 1.0	(413) 1.0	(447) 1.1
1.9	1.7	4.3		1.9			1.3	1.4	1.6	1.6	1.9
.8	.5			.7			.4	.4	.5	.5	.7
(126) 1.4	(131) 1.0			(263) 1.2		% Lease & Rental Exp/Sales	(282) .9	(273) .9	(284) 1.0	(254) 1.1	(263) 1.2
2.5	1.5			2.1			1.6	1.7	1.7	1.8	2.1
3.0	1.3			1.9			1.6	1.8	1.7	1.8	1.9
(107) 4.7	(106) 2.1			(215) 3.3		% Officers' Comp/Sales	(243) 3.0	(225) 2.8	(246) 2.9	(219) 3.1	(215) 3.3
7.3	3.8			5.4			5.0	4.8	4.6	4.8	5.4
338764M	1917467M	844435M		3100666M		Net Sales ($)	2732972M	3530783M	2968270M	2704218M	3100666M
114221M	748854M	454888M		1317963M		Total Assets ($)	985473M	1344683M	1241009M	1048449M	1317963M

©Robert Morris Associates 1983

M = $thousand   MM = $million

See Pages 1 through 12 for Explanation of Ratios and Data

EXHIBIT   M   **Southern Material Company, Inc. Ratio Analysis**

	12/31/81	12/31/82	12/31/83	RMA[1]*
Current	1.75	1.96	2.07	2.6 1.6 1.2
Sales/Receivables	4.75	4.65	4.91	13.0 9.2 6.7
Cost of Sales/Inventory	4.64	4.79	6.65	14.4 7.5 4.1
Debt/Worth	.77	.69	.86	.8 1.5 4.0
Profit Before Taxes/ Net Worth	13.7	12.8	14.6	24.9 9.6 −5.9

*   Top figure indicates upper quartile, middle figure indicates median, and lower figure indicates lower quartile.
[1]   Annual Statement Studies,© Robert Morris Associates, Philadelphia, 1983, page 218, 0−$1,000,000 asset size category.

7

Processing a Loan Request

A loan request is generally initiated by a prospective borrower contacting the loan officer. In the case of a larger company, this may be a very formal meeting, attended by senior management personnel of the company and their accountant. If the applicant is the proprietor or manager of a small business, the initial contact may be very informal. Regardless of the nature of the contact, this is the loan officer's first opportunity to begin developing information about the borrower and his or her business. During the initial and subsequent interviews, the loan officer should have two primary objectives—that of obtaining as much information as possible, and of building a relationship of mutual trust and cooperation with the borrower. If the applicant has had a previous borrowing relationship with the bank, it may be only a matter of updating the bank's credit file. If the applicant has not had a previous borrowing relationship, the loan officer must begin the task of building a comprehensive credit file on the borrower's business.

The Loan Interview

The loan officer should recognize that the loan interview is a primary source of information about the prospective borrower. It is a prime opportunity to observe the applicant's attitudes, assess his or her ability, and begin to establish a working relationship. How easy or how difficult this may be depends on two factors—the extent to which the borrower is prepared to furnish the necessary information, and the expertise of the loan officer. A good business manager generally will come prepared with adequate financial information and a well developed loan request. An inexperienced borrower, or one with marginal management ability, may be totally unprepared to furnish the necessary information. The loan officer may have to give the applicant a list of necessary information to be delivered at a future meeting, or it may require him or her to assist in the actual compilation of that information.

Opinions differ among loan officers as to how much assistance an applicant should be given in preparing financial information. Most loan officers insist that the borrower prepare all the information. Others will offer guidance and advice without actually assisting in the preparation of statements, while some may actually assist in statement preparation. In rare cases, the loan officer may actually prepare the statement based on information furnished verbally by the applicant. Each loan officer must decide which approach he or she prefers, within the policy guidelines of the institution he or she serves. However, if information is to be credible, it generally should be prepared by the borrower. In a number of collection cases where an institution has attempted to prove fraud, courts have ruled that the borrower could not be held accountable for an inaccurate statement prepared by the lender, even though it was predicated on incorrect information furnished by the borrower and had been signed by him or her.

The loan officer should beware of the applicant who appears unwilling to furnish requested information. Even more suspect is the applicant who refuses to furnish the required information based on his or her long association with the bank, his or her personal acquaintance with senior management, or social standing in the community. At the very least, this kind of attitude is indicative of a lack of understanding of financial transactions and questionable management. At worst, it may be a deliberate attempt to hide derogatory information from the bank.

Most experienced loan officers have developed techniques for obtaining a maximum amount of pertinent information from the borrower in a short period of time. Often this is done in a seemingly casual manner, with the borrower being largely unaware that he or she is being interrogated. It is important that the applicant be put at ease, and that a frank and open relationship be established at the earliest possible time. During the initial and subsequent loan interviews, the following basic information should be obtained:

1.   Business Information
    a.   Legal organization—sole proprietorship, partnership or corporation
    b.   Names of affiliates and subsidiaries
    c.   Names and titles of senior management staff
    d.   The company's mission and objectives
    e.   Size, scope, and nature of the business operation
    f.   Principal products or services
    g.   Market served and marketing strategy

      h.   Location of the business' principal offices and facilities
      i.   Number of employees
      j.   Adequacy of equipment and facilities
      k.   Names of major customers
      l.   Names of major suppliers
      m.   Name of the business' accounting firm.

2. Financial Information
      a.   Short financial history of the company
      b.   Recent balance sheet, and one as of most recent fiscal year end.
      c.   Income statement for the past year, and preferably for the past two or three years. If not available in another form, copies of the applicant's income tax returns may suffice.
      d.   Projection of cash flow for at least the coming year.
      e.   Projection of capital needs for at least the next two years.
      f.   Summary of past borrowing history

3. Personal Information (if a closely held company)
      a.   Principals' names and addresses
      b.   Their background, employment history, and experience in the business
      c.   Their attitude toward the business and its finances
      d.   Their ambitions and financial objectives

4. Loan Request
      a.   The entity that will be the borrower
      b.   Amount needed, when, and for what purposes
      c.   Proposed repayment plan, including sources of repayment, and when available
      d.   Collateral available, and whether the business is willing to pledge it

It is unlikely that the loan officer will obtain all the necessary information during the initial interview. An analysis of the information acquired during the initial interview, a visit to the business' premises, and a search of the public records generally will create additional questions that must be answered for the loan officer to fully understand the applicant's situation. This often requires subsequent conferences with the borrower and the submission of additional documentation.

Visit to the Applicant's Premises

An old proverb states, "One picture is worth a thousand words." Similarly, an observant lender can learn a great deal that could never be learned from financial information alone by visiting the borrower's premises. During the visit, the lender should attempt to assess the adequacy of facilities, condition of equipment, and desirability of the business' location. The lender may be able to obtain a physical inventory of equipment (including serial numbers) for collateral purposes, as well as estimated collateral values. Much can also be learned about the quantity, quality, and condition of the business' inventory. The visit also may present an excellent opportunity to examine the borrower's records. The lender may also learn a great deal from the general appearance and state of repair of the borrower's premises, the appearance and attitude of the employees, and the general tone of the operation.

A visit should be made to the business premises of every new applicant. Ideally, a visit should be made at least annually thereafter. It has been my experience that most borrowers welcome the lender's visit. Most good businesspeople are proud of their operations and appreciate the lender's willingness to take the time to make a visit. In those rare cases where the borrower shows resentment or apprehension, the lender should be concerned, not only about his or her working relationship with the borrower, but also whether the borrower is deliberately trying to conceal pertinent information.

Credit Investigations

When processing a loan application, especially from a new customer, a lender should investigate the applicant's past credit performance. A thorough credit investigation can be a key part of the lending process, and should accomplish a twofold purpose: to verify data furnished by the applicant, and to unearth new information which the loan officer may not have been able to obtain from other sources. A thorough credit investigation will use five primary sources of information: credit reporting agencies, other financial institutions, trade sources, public records, and the bank's own records. In the case of an existing borrower, verified information will already exist in the bank's credit files. An updated credit investigation will reveal any changes in the borrower's credit performance. In many banks, the credit department will update information on a regular basis on all businesses that are sizeable borrowers.

Most lenders subscribe to the services of a credit reporting agency such as a local credit bureau. Credit bureaus compile credit information that is available to subscribers for a fee. This information, which is often primarily compiled on consumers, includes both information gleaned from the public records and that obtained from other businesses in the community. Generally, credit bureau information will include an individual's place of residence, employer's name, length of employment, marital status, collection actions, other legal actions such as bankruptcy, names of some creditors, maximum amount owed, and performance rating with each creditor. When dealing with an individual such as a sole proprietor, credit bureau information can be useful in giving a general indication of both the applicant's past performance and past credit difficulties. However, credit bureau information is not always complete and should be considered only a general indicator of the borrower's performance.

When dealing with a commercial business, commercial credit reporting agencies such as Dunn & Bradstreet are usually better sources of information. Dunn & Bradstreet, one of the oldest and best known of the commercial credit reporting agencies, is national in scope, and through its local offices conducts investigations that provide the basis for written reports on individual business firms and for comprehensive published data. Equifax is a large Atlanta based firm which also provides credit and investigative reports to its clients on a nationwide basis. The National Association of Credit Management (NACM) is an association of wholesale and commercial creditors that exchanges credit information and information on credit conditions. Various trade associations also provide credit reports and compile credit ratings within their industry.

When processing a new loan application, most credit institutions make it a practice to check with other financial institutions from which the applicant has obtained credit. This is generally helpful. However, due to such legislation as the Fair Credit Reporting Act, many lending institutions are hesitant to give much information. Generally, basic information will be given concerning the borrower's approximate loan balance, repayment performance, and the handling of his or her checking account, but little else. If the subject's loans have been delinquent, or if there are frequent overdrafts in the checking account, this usually will be disclosed. Other derogatory information, such as knowledge of delinquent accounts with other creditors or of pending legal action, generally will not be divulged. Most lending institutions are fair and cooperative in furnishing credit information, but in rare instances a creditor, hoping to get a bad loan refinanced, may give incomplete and therefore misleading information. Nevertheless, it is prudent practice for a prospective lender to inquire of several institutions that are currently extending credit to the applicant, or have done so in the past. There is one danger in this procedure—it may result in a competitive institution attempting to get the applicant's business. From an ethical standpoint the inquiring institution should always divulge that the subject of the inquiry is a lending prospect. Robert Morris Associates has compiled a "Statement of Principles for the Exchange of Credit Information," which has been widely accepted and adhered to by commercial lenders.

Another method of obtaining information about a business' past performance is to contact its suppliers and other trade creditors. A business that pays its institutional creditors as agreed may be quite careless about paying suppliers. In the case of a business that carries a large purchased inventory, its suppliers may be the largest creditors of the business, and it is essential that they be contacted. As a rule, when a business is having difficulties, the trade creditors are aware of this before the institutional creditors. Therefore, a concerned trade creditor is usually a real danger signal. I have seen cases where trade suppliers were preparing to repossess inventory while the institutional creditors had no inkling that the business was in trouble. Contacting suppliers is also an excellent method of ascertaining whether the applicant has erroneously listed or omitted accounts payable from the financial statement.

A bank sometimes overlooks the fact that its own records may contain a considerable amount of information about a loan applicant. For instance, its Consumer Loan Department may have records of the personal borrowings of a sole proprietor or the principal owner of a business. If the applicant has a deposit account, much can be learned from the average balances carried in that account, and also by studying the nature of the account transactions. If the loan applicant is a customer of the Trust Department, or uses the bank's payroll services, or purchases investments through the bank, additional information can be gleaned from these sources. If the applicant or some of the applicant's management staff is known to members of the bank's staff, this may be an excellent source of information about the applicant's reputation and personal habits. If the bank is fortunate enough to have a central information file, all this information may be readily available to the loan officer. If not, considerable research may be required to reveal all the information available in the bank's own records.

Searching Public Records

Depending on the state in which the business' principal office is located, the Uniform Commercial Code may require central filing, or local filing, or both. Central filings are usually made in the Uniform Commercial Code Division of the Office of the Secretary of State in the state capitol. Local filings are ordinarily made in the office of the County Recorder or County Clerk of the county in which the business' principal office is located. It is usually impractical for a lender to conduct a search of the central records in the Secretary of State's office, and therefore a procedure has been established for requesting search information through the mails. A standard form (UCC-11) requesting either a listing of all financing statements filed and/or copies thereof, may be submitted to the Uniform Commercial Code Division, which will provide the necessary information or copies for a nominal fee. The lender should make sure that the request is submitted under the proper name. Variations in names such as "Jones, Edward J." and "Jones, Edward J. dba Jones Trucking Company" and "Jones Trucking Company by Edward J. Jones" are commonplace in financing statements filed by various creditors, and this may cause difficulty for a lender attempting to perform a records search. Generally, when such variations exist, the office performing the search will notify the lender of those variations, but this cannot always be relied upon to reveal all filings pertinent to a particular loan applicant. There are also a number of companies that are in the business of performing professional searches, which for a fee will generally provide comprehensive information on a more timely basis than is normally provided by the central filing office itself.

Except for those counties in large metropolitan areas, it is generally not difficult for a lender to make a UCC search in the county in which the applicant's business is located. The local filing office, usually that of the County Recorder or County Clerk, maintains an index of UCC filings. By using a document number obtained from the index, the searcher may then locate and examine an actual copy of the form UCC-1. Since a UCC filing is ordinarily effective for five years, the searcher should examine the index for at least the previous five years to make sure that all UCC filings that are still effective are identified. If unfamiliar with the procedures of the county in which a search is being performed, the searcher should inquire as to how continuation statements are indexed. If continuation statements are indexed in the same manner as the original UCC filing, then a search for only the five previous years is necessary. However, in some counties the filing of a continuation statement may be noted in the index according to the date of the original filing. If this system is used, a search for an indefinite period considerably longer than five years may be necessary to identify all filings still in effect. The searcher should exercise caution in this regard.

Additional information is generally available in the public records of a county. In addition to an index of financing statements, the office of the Recorder of Deeds or Registrar of Deeds will generally contain a complete record of all transactions affecting the title to land within the county, which may be categorized as follows:

1. *Deed records* are the records of all conveyances of real estate, and are generally indexed in two ways—under the name of the seller in the Grantor Index and under the name of the buyer in the Grantee Index. Examination of the pertinent index will provide the searcher with a reference number which will enable him or her to locate a copy of the actual deed document in the records library. The use of computers and microfilm or microfiche record systems have greatly facilitated the search process.

2. *Mortgage records*, which are indexed under the name of the borrower in the Mortgagor Index and under that of the lender in the Mortgagee Index, contain a record of all real estate mortgages recorded within the county. Releases of mortgages are generally

also recorded here. By obtaining a reference number from the index, the searcher may locate a copy of the actual document in the records library.

3. *Memoranda of judgments* are filed in the Recorder or Registrar's office. Although lawsuits and other legal actions which may result in a lien or judgment are generally filed in the Circuit Clerk's office, memoranda of judgment, which create a judgment lien against real estate, are filed in the Recorder's Office. These are usually listed in a separate index which will show the amount of judgment and the name of the judgment holder. For further information, it is usually necessary to examine the case file in the Circuit Clerk's office. Since judgments generally are valid for up to seven years, a complete search of this index usually requires searching at least the preceding seven year period.

4. Notices of *federal and state tax liens* are usually also filed in the recorder's or registrar's office. Usually only the date and the amount of lien is shown.

5. *Mechanics' liens* are also recorded here. These are liens filed by suppliers of materials or labor for the construction of improvements to real estate.

All records in the Recorder's or Registrar's office generally are open to the public and may be searched without charge. Copies may be obtained for a fee.

The office of the Circuit Clerk or Clerk of the Court contains all court records and files on court cases, including both civil and criminal actions. The court docket is the major index in which all cases are listed as they are filed. The docket generally shows names of the plantiff and defendant, the type of action, and status or disposition of the case. By referring to the case number shown in the docket, the searcher may locate and examine the actual case file. Familiarity with these sources enables the lender to obtain the basic facts regarding any judgment, lawsuit, or criminal action in which a borrower may be involved.

The Office of the Probate Clerk is generally a separate office in larger counties, and in smaller counties is often a division of the Circuit Clerk's or County Clerk's office. It maintains all records pertaining to the administration of estates. If a will has been filed or an estate probated, a file will have been established, which will ordinarily contain a copy of the will, an inventory of the decedent's property, and a copy of the court order appointing the administrator or executor. These files generally are open to the searcher and are often useful in proving a loan applicant's ownership of inherited property or a claim to a share in an unsettled estate.

If the lender is unable or unwilling to do his or her own searches, most county offices will provide document copies for a fee, but generally will do only very limited searches. In many areas abstract companies will perform not only real estate title searches, but also searches for UCC filings, judgments, etc. However, every lender should have at least one staff member who is adept at performing this kind of search.

Borrower's Objectives and Loan Purpose

When making a loan request, a capable business manager will always have a well defined objective, such as the purchase of new equipment to improve production or efficiency, or to cover a seasonal increase in inventory. The ultimate objective of most business borrowings is to increase profits. When dealing with an unsophisticated business manager, the loan officer may find that the borrower's objectives are less clearcut, and it may require additional effort on the part of the lender to understand the actual objectives of the borrower and the real purpose of the loan. The term "working capital loan" is greatly overworked. This term, when used by a loan applicant, may have a great variety of meanings, and it is therefore necessary for the loan officer to inquire further as to what is really needed or wanted. When a borrower requests a working capital loan, does he or she in fact mean that funds are needed to cover a seasonal or temporary increase in inventory and receivables? Are they needed to pay operating expenses until a progress payment is received on a contract, or to pay delinquent accounts payable? Are the funds necessary to provide funds for a business that is undercapitalized and in which short term borrowings are being substituted for equity, or to replenish the business' cash accounts which have been depleted by operating losses?

Some businesses have a tendency to overequip, and a loan request often is made to finance equipment that is not really needed by the company, and which it often cannot afford. In such a case, a question often exists whether management's true objective is to increase profits, to increase convenience of operation, or to build the public image and prestige of the business.

Borrowers are also often confused about the proper maturity for a given loan, and will request a long term maturity for what is actually a seasonal loan, or suggest an unreasonably short maturity for a loan to finance a major capital purchase. A business will sometimes also request a working capital loan when it is in fact seeking funds to finance an expansion of the size, scope, or facilities of the business. A loan for the expansion of a business should not be viewed by the lender as a working capital loan, since a loan of this type ordinarily must be repaid, not by liquidation of receivables and inventory, but by profits. Managers of an expanding business also have the tendency to want to finance the expansion completely with borrowed funds. In many cases, if the business is to remain on a sound basis, a significant portion of the cost of such expansion should be financed with equity.

Counseling Borrowers

Once the loan officer has gained insight into the borrower's objectives and the real purpose of the loan, he or she should then ask the following questions:

1. Are the borrower's objectives constructive—will the loan in fact contribute to the profitable performance of the business?
2. Will the requested loan achieve the borrower's objectives?
3. Is the structuring of the loan appropriate in view of its purpose?

If the lender believes that the loan request is not sound, that is, that it will not benefit the business, or that the making of the loan will not achieve the desired objective, or that the loan is structured incorrectly, then the loan officer has an obligation to call these facts to the attention of the borrower. Most borrowers appreciate the counsel of their lenders, and are very receptive to suggestions. For example, if the lender believes that a revolving receivables and inventory loan will be of greater benefit to the borrower than a 90-day single pay working capital loan, this should be discussed with the borrower in detail. Or, if an overly heavy short term debt loan can constructively be restructured by refinancing short term debt into a term loan, this again should be pointed out to the borrower. Lenders can significantly assist borrowers by helping them structure debt properly.

Lenders can also assist borrowers by pointing out the importance of adequate equity capital. Lenders are often far too hesitant to recommend that borrowers put more equity in the business, instead of leveraging more and more heavily. In a situation where a business becomes too heavily indebted, this often is as much the lender's fault as the borrower's, due to the lender's failure to insist upon the injection of adequate equity into the business.

I know that some borrowers neither want nor will benefit from counseling by the lender. In such a case, the lender can do nothing except make a sound credit decision. However, the great majority of borrowers can benefit from counseling, and many in fact rely heavily upon the guidance of the lender to help them make sound decisions.

Effect of the Loan on the Business

When a lender makes a loan, this obviously changes the financial structure of the borrower's business. A lender may understand this effect better by preparing pro forma statements for the business. When a lender disburses a loan, the total indebtedness of the business is increased unless all loan proceeds are used to refinance existing debt. Also, unless all proceeds are used to pay existing debt, or a proportionate amount of equity is injected into the business, the loan will cause a deterioration in the business' debt to worth ratio. Exhibit N illustrates the effect on the balance sheet of Southern Material Company, Inc. if a lender were to make a new $96,000 capital term loan and a new $120,000 short term working capital loan. As can be seen from Exhibit N, these loans would significantly change the structure of Southern's balance sheet, and would create a deterioration in both the debt to worth ratio and the current ratio. Whether the current ratio improves or deteriorates as a result of a new loan depends on the term of the loan and the purpose for which the proceeds are used. A long term loan to finance current assets improves the current ratio, while a short term loan to purchase noncurrent assets would cause the current ratio to deteriorate. The format used in Exhibit N gives the loan officer a relatively simple means for estimating the balance sheet structure of the business after the loan proceeds are disbursed.

A pro forma income statement may also be constructed by using a similar format. Exhibit O shows a pro forma income statement for Southern Material Company, Inc. based on assumptions as to how the new loans will affect the sales volume, cost of goods sold, and operating expenses of the company. The procedure obviously requires a certain amount of guesswork, but it does have two advantages. First, it requires company management to forecast how they believe company performance will be affected by the loan, and second, it gives the lender a benchmark against which to measure future actual performance.

Southern Material Company, Inc.

Balance Sheet

	12/31/83	Debit	Credit	Pro-Forma
ASSETS (Spread in thousands)				
Cash	50			50
Receivables (Net)	444	60		504
Inventory (Net)	209	40		249
Prepaid Costs	6			6
TOTAL CURRENT ASSETS	709			809
Fixed Assets (Net)	280	96		376
Cash Value - Officer's Life Ins.	9			9
TOTAL ASSETS	998			1194
LIABILITIES				
Notes Payable-Banks	29		120	149
Account Payable - Trade	188	20		168
Bank Term Loan (Current Portion)	40		24	64
Miscellaneous Accruals	7			7
Taxes (Due and or Accrued)	29			29
Notes to Stockholders	49			49
TOTAL CURRENT LIABILITIES	342			466
Bank Term Loan (Non-Current Por.)	120		72	192
TOTAL LIABILITIES	462			658
Capital Stock - Common	200			200
Earned Surplus	296			296
Capital Surplus	40			40
NET WORTH	536			536
TOTAL NET WORTH & LIABILITIES	998			1194
Current Ratio	2.07			1.74
Debt/Worth Ratio	.86			1.23

Pro forma balance sheet based on the following premises:

(1) New four year term loan in amount of $96,000 for purchase of equipment.

(2) New $120,000 short term working capital loan, $40,000 of which will be used to purchase inventory, $60,000 to carry additional receivables, and $20,000 to reduce payables.

EXHIBIT   O   Southern Material Company, Inc. Pro Forma Income Statement

(In thousands)	yr. ending 12/31/83		Dollar Change	Percentage Change	Pro Forma	
Net Sales	2,179	(100.0)	+653	—	2,832	(100.0)
Cost of Goods Sold	1,390	(63.7)	+414	—	1,804	(63.7)
Gross Profit	789	(36.3)	+239	—	1,028	(36.3)
Operating Costs	462	(21.2)	+110	−1.0	572	(20.2)
G + A Costs	249	(11.5)	+ 68	− .3	317	(11.2)
Net Operating Income	78	(3.6)	+ 61	+1.3	139	(4.9)

Pro forma based on the following assumptions:

1. Increase in annual net sales of 30%.
2. Cost of goods sold to remain at 63.7%.
3. Operating costs to decrease from 21.2% to 20.2% of sales.
4. G + A costs to decrease from 11.5% to 11.2% of sales.

8

Making a Loan Decision

All loan analysis has one primary purpose, that of enabling the lender to make a good loan decision. In this chapter we will discuss the various steps involved in the decision-making process. These include determining whether information is adequate, assembling that information in a meaningful manner, weighing strong factors against weak factors, and ultimately making a decision about the soundness and workability of the loan.

When the lender has accumulated the information available, the next step in the lending process is to organize the information in a meaningful manner, so that it may be analyzed and valid conclusions may be drawn concerning the strengths and weaknesses of the loan application. First, however, the lender should be sure that the information at hand is adequate. *Inadequate information is probably the major cause of bad loan decisions.* Lack of pertinent knowledge about the applicant's overall position and past performance, or faulty projections of future performance, make it virtually impossible for the lender to make a sound decision.

How can the loan officer be sure that adequate information is available? There is no way to be entirely sure, but observing the following rules will be helpful:

1. Use a standard format or checklist in compiling information to be sure that no significant questions are overlooked.
2. Use *all* sources of information that are available to the fullest extent.
3. Compare information obtained from other sources with the information submitted by the borrower to detect any discrepancies. -
4. Discuss with the applicant, and obtain a satisfactory explanation for any apparent omissions, discrepancies, or contradictions in the information provided.

5. Be sure that you as a loan officer feel that you have an in-depth understanding of the applicant's operation. If you do not feel comfortable, it may be wise to proceed very cautiously.

Next, the available financial information must be compiled so that comparisons may be readily made between current and past information and trends identified. This is usually done by means of a financial history or "spread sheet" such as Exhibit I in chapter 6. The spread sheet enables the analyst to identify the changes in each statement item from one balance sheet date to the next. This internal analysis makes it relatively easy to trace the progress (or lack of) of a business over a period of several years.

Third, a decision must be made on the relative strength or weakness of each credit factor, based on the lender's analysis of the available information. Figure 8-1 illustrates how the results of this decision-making process might be compiled in a simple chart.

FIGURE 8-1   Credit factors.

Credit factor	Strong	Above average	Average	Somewhat weak	Unacceptable
Moral character		X			
Managerial ability			X		
Repayment capacity			X		
Financial strength				X	
Security available			X		
Loan purpose		X			

This diagram, of course, is an oversimplification intended to illustrate a thought process more than to suggest an actual form or format. The significant point is that the loan officer must make a decision regarding the relative strength of each factor. Once this is done, the final loan decision is made by weighing the strong factors against the weak factors, and determining, in the lender's judgment, whether the credit factors considered as a whole are sufficiently strong to warrant approval of the loan.

Although the basic process appears to be relatively elementary, every loan officer knows that making a good loan decision is rarely a simple matter. Some of the credit factors, such as character, management ability, and repayment capacity are more significant than others, and therefore must be given greater weight. It is often difficult to judge what degree of weakness in one factor may be offset by strength in another factor. For instance, strong repayment may offset a relatively weak financial position. However, it is unlikely that adequate collateral will offset weak repayment, since few lenders wish to find themselves in a situation where they must sell the security to obtain repayment on the loan. Weak moral character or lack of managerial ability always constitutes a serious flaw, which usually cannot be offset by other strengths. If *any* factor is rated as completely unacceptable, the loan ordinarily should not be made.

An inexperienced loan officer may have difficulty in defining weakness or strength. A lending institution's loan policy will provide some guidelines for making this judgment, as will other sources, such as the *RMA Statement Studies*. A loan officer also may develop a feel for what constitutes critical weakness by studying his or her institution's files on its problem and charge-off loans. Ultimately, however, a certain amount of lending experience is required before a loan officer can begin to develop a feel for what kind and degree of weakness in a loan makes it unworkable. Even greater experience and knowledge is required in structuring a loan in such a way that it can be made acceptable in spite of its weaknesses.

Financial Position

As part of the loan decision-making process four basic aspects of the borrower's financial position must be considered—quality of assets, nature of indebtedness, equity, and leverage.

1.   *Quality of Assets.* A high percentage of the applicant's total assets should be productive (income producing) assets. If not, this may be an indication of a business that is not using its resources well, and a symptom of weak management. The relationship of current assets to noncurrent assets should also be considered. Some types of businesses require a high investment in fixed assets. However, a higher than normal investment in noncurrent assets may indicate an inefficient business operation that is producing inadequate sales volume in relation to total assets, and which may be short on cash flow.

Asset valuations must be realistic. Over-valuation of assets distorts equity position and may indicate that the borrower has an unrealistic attitude toward his or her financial position. Marketability of assets should also be considered. Assets that are highly specialized in nature, or which would be difficult to liquidate, or which may be unsaleable, add little or nothing to the financial strength of the borrower.

2.   *Nature of Indebtedness.* Not only the amount of debt owed, but also its relationship to total assets and equity must be considered. Heavy indebt-

edness in relation to worth is the surest sign of a financially weak business. If the applicant deals with a large number of creditors, this may be an indicator of poor financial planning. Heavy reliance on supplier credit, or debt owed to finance companies, may indicate that the applicant has been unable to obtain bank financing. Another concern of the lender should be the maturity of the borrower's present indebtedness. A heavy short term debt load may indicate that the business is or will be under severe pressure to meet its obligations.

3. *Equity.* Previous reference has been made to the importance of equity. Equity is what the borrower has "at risk," and also represents the lender's cushion against adversity. A borrower who has little capital at risk may be less dedicated to the success of the venture than one who has a larger amount of capital to lose. The need for adequate equity can hardly be over-emphasized as a perogative for both safety and workability in a loan. In spite of this, some lenders continue to finance business ventures without demanding the injection of sufficient equity by owners. Minimal retained earnings may indicate that the business has not been profitable, or that ownership has made heavy withdrawals.

4. *Leverage.* The extent to which a business funds its operations with borrowed capital is a key indicator of its strength or weakness. Heavy reliance on borrowed funds may make it difficult to fund needed expansion. In addition, debt service costs will be a large proportion of operating expenses, and the business may suffer severely when interest rates increase substantially. A heavily leveraged business may also have difficulty borrowing additional funds should an unforeseen need arise.

Repayment Capacity

The borrower's ability to repay is one of the key determinants of the workability of a loan, and repayment ability depends on the borrower's ability to generate sufficient cash to meet obligations. Lack of repayment capacity will inevitably result in delinquency and default. Therefore, it is vital that the lender assess this credit factor accurately.

Any business has four basic sources of cash: earnings, conversion of assets to cash, injections of capital by owners, and borrowed funds. In its normal operations, a business generates cash from two of these sources: earnings and the conversion of current assets (such as its receivables) to cash. The other sources—borrowings or injection of capital—are usually supplementary sources of cash when normal sources prove inadequate.

Every business also sets certain priorities for the use of its available cash. These priorities (in order of highest priority) are generally the payment of operating expenses including management salaries, payment of taxes, withdrawals by owners in a closely held business, and lastly, repayment of debt. Therefore, if the loan is to work as anticipated, the lender must be relatively certain that sufficient cash will be generated not only to repay the debt, but also to pay the other needs of the business, which in the eyes of management, will have priority over the repayment of debt. The lender may also want to obtain a loan agreement that gives the lender a certain amount of control over cash expenditures such as management salaries, dividends, and owner's withdrawals.

The best indicator of a healthy, flourishing business is a history of consistent profitability. Failure to produce adequate profits over a period of time is a major weakness and should be a cause of immediate concern to the lender. This may indicate poor management, marketing problems, poor quality products, or lack of proper planning. The lender should make every effort to determine the cause of the problem and to counsel management in making the changes required to get the business on a profitable basis, since no business can survive for long without profits.

Since loans are repaid not from past profits, but from future cash flow, the lender must also have assurances that future performance will be satisfactory. Therefore, the lender must be concerned with both the business' future profitability and cash flow. To judge the strength of these factors, the lender must have several years' income and expense statements and a credible projection of future performance, including both income and cash flow projections.

Projections must be viewed with a critical eye. The loan officer should be certain that significant items, such as tax payments and payments on other indebtedness, have not been omitted. The achievability of projections should be gauged by comparison to past performance, allowing for any proposed changes in the size or structure of the business. In the case of a new business, for which historical information is not available, the lender must resort to other sources, such as industry averages, to test the credibility of projections. The soundness of projections is a key factor in making a good loan decision, and therefore must be a prime concern of the loan officer.

When processing a request for a capital term loan, the lender's perspective must be somewhat different, for several reasons. First, at least theoretically, capital debt must be repaid from net profits and depreciation charges, rather than from the gross income of the business. Second, the lender must have assurances that the business will operate successfully for a more extended period of time, rather than for one seasonal cycle or one year. Therefore, adequate profits, stability, and continuity of management become more important.

Secured or Unsecured Loan

How does a lender make a decision whether a loan should be made on a secured or unsecured basis? Obviously, most lenders would prefer a secured loan, since this gives the lender collateral to fall back on if repayment fails to materialize. While most loans will be made on a secured basis, from time to time commercial lenders will receive a request for an unsecured loan.

To justify making an unsecured loan, most experienced lenders believe three conditions must exist: strong financial position, strong repayment capacity, and a history of satisfactory performance. Also, the loan ordinarily must be for a relatively short term, since most lenders will extend term credit only on a secured basis.

Therefore, the borrower with a strong equity position, who carries relatively little debt, who has an excellent cash flow, who has performed as agreed in the past, and who needs to borrow a reasonable amount for a short term is the applicant who is eligible for unsecured credit.

Analyzing Collateral Position

If the loan is to be secured, the lender should consider carefully the kind and amount of collateral that is available, and the resulting net collateral position of the lender, not only at the inception of the loan, but also during the entire life of the loan. Net collateral margin, that is, the difference between the net saleable value of the security and the amount required to pay the loan in full, will vary throughout the life of the loan. This fluctuation in net collateral margin may be due to partial payments made on the loan, appreciation or depreciation in the value of collateral, change in market value, loss, destruction, or release of collateral, or the pledge of additional collateral. Because of the possibility that collateral margin may decrease, and because of the costs associated with repossession and sale of collateral, which may run 10% or more of sales proceeds, most lenders require the borrower to pledge collateral having a marketable value substantially in excess of the amount of the loan.

If the collateral is unusually stable in value and easily marketable, as in the case of U.S. Government securities, the lender may feel comfortable with a collateral margin that is quite small, such as 10%. However, when dealing with security such as equipment, vehicles, inventory, or receivables, most lenders will require collateral valued considerably in excess of the amount of the loan. Based on this concept, a lender might establish the following guidelines: that it will loan no more than 80% of the cost of new equipment; no more than 65% of the cost of used equipment; no more than 75% of current accounts receivable; and no more than 50% of inventory. If the collateral is depreciable in nature, such as vehicles or equipment, often the lender will demand periodic partial payments that are at least sufficient to cover the depreciation in market value of the collateral.

Theoretically, anything that has value and can be converted to cash can serve as collateral. Although real estate, equipment, inventory, accounts receivable, contract rights, documents of title, negotiable instruments, and securities are the types of collateral most commonly held by lenders, there are many other kinds of assets that could conceivably be used as security for a loan. Some examples are a license, franchise, antiques, artworks, royalties, commissions, jewelry, or even a seat on a stock exchange. The Uniform Commercial Code creates a very general category of collateral called, "general intangibles," which are defined as any personal property (including things in action) other than goods, accounts, chattel paper, documents, instruments and money.[1] What can be used as collateral is in fact limited only by the imagination of the lender and by the provisions of law, which prohibit the pledging of some kinds of assets, and which in some cases, while not prohibiting the use of a particular kind of asset as security, fail to establish clearcut procedures for perfecting a security interest in that kind of asset.

Assets which lenders generally are prohibited from holding as collateral include individual retirement accounts (IRA's), the borrower's interest in a pension or profit-sharing plan, U.S. savings bonds, Social Security benefits, and assets held in a fiduciary capacity by the debtor. Examples of collateral for which perfection procedures may be ambiguous, or for which there may be considerable variation from one jurisdiction to another, might be a liquor license, a franchise, or a stock exchange seat.

From a practical standpoint, collateral must meet certain basic criteria if it is to be acceptable to a lender. These criteria include: (1) The collateral must be identifiable. If the lender is to enforce its claim, proper identification of the collateral is necessary. (2) The collateral must have value. This is intrinsic to the very concept of collateral. (3) It must be readily saleable. Cash is what is required to pay the lender's claim, and therefore the collateral must be such that it can be converted to cash without great difficulty. (4) It must be in the lender's possession, or its location must be known to the lender. If the lender cannot find the collateral it is of little value. (5) It must be relatively nonperishable. A load of fresh fish in an area where no cold storage facilities are available would have questionable collateral value. (6) The collateral must maintain its value. It must be relatively nondepreciable, and not subject to rapid obsolescence. A piece of equipment that wears out in twelve months is poor collateral for a three-year term loan. A warehouse full of calendars may have considerable value in their current year, but little or no value in the following year.

Collateral Valuations

Proper valuation of collateral is a key factor in making a good loan decision. It is not unusual for a lender who has repossessed and sold collateral

---

[1] UCC 9-106

to find that the net sales proceeds are insufficient to pay off the loan in full. There are three basic reasons for this: (1) the lender initially overestimated the market value of the security, (2) the lender failed to update collateral valuations and demand additional collateral if adequate margin no longer existed, and/or (3) the security depreciated faster than the loan balance was reduced by periodic principal payments.

Many lenders have a tendency to accept without question collateral valuation figures prepared by the borrower, which can hardly be considered an unbiased source. Borrowers tend to be overly optimistic about the value of their assets, and this may result in the lender's initial collateral valuation figures being too high, unless the lender substantiates them from an outside source. In the case of equipment, a professional appraisal is desirable, and at the very least, the equipment to be used as collateral should be examined by the loan officer, and reference made to a published price guide in estimating values. In the case of listed stocks, bonds, or bulk commodities, a valuation can usually be obtained from a published source, such as *The Wall Street Journal*. Inventory may be difficult to value due to perishability, saleability, condition, obsolescence, or problems in getting an accurate count. Accounts receivable present valuation problems due to collectibility, potential disputes as to amount, geographic distribution, etc. However, it appears that most problems with collateral valuations occur because the lender's efforts to obtain realistic valuations have been inadequate, rather than due to any great difficulty in determining realistic values. Many lenders simply do not expend sufficient effort in determining the character, condition, and marketability of the assets they accept as security.

Determining a realistic collateral valuation for an item of collateral is really a two-step process. First, a normal market or book value must be determined by means of an appraisal, listed price quotation, or reference to the records of the borrower. Then, this value must be adjusted downward because the saleable value and net proceeds of collateral tend to shrink when a loan becomes a collection case. There are many reasons for this. Repossessed items may be in poor condition, costs of repossession, reconditioning, and sale may be substantial, and assets sold in a liquidation seldom bring their full market value. Therefore, lenders normally require a collateral margin to protect them against this shrinkage in net proceeds. However, lenders often seem to overestimate the amount of proceeds that can be realized from collateral liquidation, and as a result, fail to demand sufficient collateral to protect their position.

The collateral evaluation form shown in Exhibit P may be helpful in determining both collateral values and collateral margin. First, all the borrower's secured loans are listed. Then all collateral is listed by item or category. Next, a market, book, or appraisal valuation is assigned to each item of collateral, indicating the source of the valuation. The source of the valuation may be the borrower's own financial statement, a published source such as *The Wall Street Journal*, an appraisal, or other source. Then, a percentage factor is applied to that valuation based upon the lender's assessment of what proportion of value could be realized in a liquidation, net of costs of repossession and resale. The resulting net collateral value is then compared to the loan amount and a percentage of collateral coverage computed. Although an imprecise process, it does give the lender a feel for the adequacy of his or her collateral position.

Lenders are often much too lax in updating collateral valuations. The value of some kinds of collateral, such as commodities, can change very rapidly, and in such a case a monthly, or even a weekly, revaluation may be necessary. In the case of securities, a monthly update of values is preferable, and in no case should this be done less than quarterly. If the collateral is receivables or inventory, a monthly valuation, including an aged list of receivables, should be obtained from the borrower. The lender may wish to verify these figures periodically by auditing the borrower's records. If equipment is used as collateral, an annual inspection is usually prudent. I realize that these procedures are time consuming, but they are necessary if the lender is to have meaningful information regarding the amount of exposure on a loan.

With term loans being written for longer maturities, lenders are finding that in many instances the security depreciates in value at a faster rate than the principal balance is reduced by monthly or quarterly payments. This is especially true of vehicle loans written for terms of 48 months or more. Although collateral margin may be adequate at the inception of the loan, a lender forced to make a repossession in the second or third year of the loan may have a substantial deficiency. Strong competition in this area of lending often makes it difficult for a lender to lend a lower percentage of value initially, or to obtain additional security. However, all lenders should be cognizant of the potential problems involved when making the initial loan decision.

Significance of Loan Purpose

It is often difficult for either a borrower or an inexperienced loan officer to understand that the purpose of the loan is a factor in making the loan decision. However, it does not take a great deal of thought to realize that both the borrower and the lender are better off if the loan proceeds are to be used for productive rather than non-productive purposes. If the loan will enable the business to increase its revenue, this obviously will increase repayment capacity and improve the financial position of the business. Therefore, most commercial lenders prefer to make loans for necessary equipment rather than a new car for a company executive; or make an inventory or receivables loan which will allow expansion of the sales volume of the business, rather than to finance a remodeling of the corporate offices. This is not to say that a commercial lender would refuse to finance a company car or new carpeting for the company offices. However, if the business was heavily leveraged, or if repayment was relatively weak, the lender might well request company management to defer these expenditures. Certainly, the borrowing capacity of a business should never be used up to fund the purchase of "wants," until such time as the "needs" of the business have been provided for. For this reason, the working capital needs of a business should normally be given priority over its request for a loan to fund capital expenditures. A failure to establish proper priorities for borrowing is a sign of weak or inexperienced management. By providing proper guidance, the commercial loan officer can aid business management in establishing sound borrowing priorities.

Analyzing a Renewal Request

In the preceding material, we concentrated on the analysis of a new application. In this section, we will deal with handling a projected renewal or renewal request. When dealing with a prospective renewal, the lender should analyze the credit factors in the same manner he or she would analyze a new application. Some reliance may be placed on the lender's prior analysis at the time of the initial loan, but the lender also must be aware that the borrower's position may have changed significantly in the interim. In considering a renewal, several additional questions must be addressed: (1) Was the renewal anticipated when the initial loan was made? (2) Did the lender fail to match maturity of the loan to the date repayment would be available? (3) Has the borrower failed to comply with the repayment agreement? (4) Have unforeseen circumstances changed the amount of repayment or the time that it will be available? (5) Is the renewal justifiable due to unsold inventory on hand, uncollected receivables, or because of capital expenditures funded by the loan?

A renewal for which there is a valid reason is commonly referred to as a *justifiable* renewal. One for which there is no acceptable explanation is known as a *carryover*. If ABC Printing Company did a large printing job for the state government, and they will not receive payment until 90 days after delivery instead of 60 days, as was anticipated at the time the loan was made, then a 30 day renewal of the loan that funded the production costs of the project may be entirely justifiable. Also, if ABC Printing financed the purchase of a new $40,000 printing press as part of its short term working capital loan, then a portion of the working capital loan may be a justifiable renewal, since the company ordinarily could not be expected to pay for a relatively expensive piece of equipment on a very short term basis. However, if ABC Printing Company has collected the funds receivable for this job, and those funds have been spent for other purposes, or if ABC failed to complete the job satisfactorily due to its carelessness, then the requested renewal may well be a carryover. There is no ironclad formula for computing justifiable renewal or carryover. The loan officer, taking into consideration the circumstances of the loan, must determine what constitutes a justifiable renewal. If capital expenditures are financed on a short term basis, then the lender should make sure that the principal reduction at each renewal is sufficient to retire the entire debt in the same period of time for which a term loan for a similar item would ordinarily be written. It is when working capital needs and capital expenditures are combined in one loan that determining the amount of justifiable renewal becomes difficult. For that reason, it may be better for many lenders to write separate loans for working capital purposes and to finance capital expenditures.

Making a Loan Decision

The culmination of the whole analysis process is the loan decision. Relatively few loan decisions are clear cut. Although some loan requests are of such superior quality that they can obviously be approved, and some so unacceptable that there is no question that they should be rejected, most fall in a gray area in which the proper decision is less obvious.

In such a case, the lender must weigh each credit factor carefully, and assess the strength or weakness of that factor. This involves judging the integrity and ability of management, the strength of the applicant's financial position, the capacity of the business to generate adequate profits and cash flow, the adequacy of collateral, and soundness of purpose. Then, all factors must be considered as a group, weighing strengths in some areas against weaknesses in others. Finally, taking into consideration the strengths and weaknesses of the credit factors, loan policy, and the institution's goals and objectives, the lender must make a decision.

The decision should be made in a timely manner, and the applicant should be informed of the decision as promptly as possible. If the application is rejected, the applicant should be told the reason for the lender's decision, at least in general terms. "The loan committee didn't like it," or "We just aren't comfortable with the request," are totally inadequate. "We feel that projected cash flow is too weak to service the additional indebtedness," or "We concluded the proffered security was insufficient," are examples of reasons for rejection which help the borrower understand why the adverse decision was made. If the request is approved, the loan officer should promptly give the borrower a list of the documentation required to close the loan and set a tentative closing date. I recognize that many loans to established customers are handled in a much less formal manner than that described above, but the loan officer should make sure the borrower understands all the terms and requirements of the loan, no matter how routine the transaction may be.

Depending on the policies and procedures of the lending institution, the loan decision may be made by the loan officer, jointly by two loan officers, by a committee of loan officers, or by a loan committee composed of officers and/or outside board members. Regardless of who makes the decision, the decision-making process basically remains the same. When a committee is involved, the loan officer who accepted the request generally is required to present the application to the committee.

Making a Loan Committee Presentation

Many loan officers are hesitant and unsure of their ability to adequately present an application to a loan committee. They also recognize that making such presentations is an important part of the loan officer's job. Failure to make an adequate presentation may result in criticism from management and a loan decision that is detrimental to the best interests of both the bank and the borrowing customer. Therefore, it is imperative that every loan officer develop the ability to make a concise, complete, and professional presentation to a loan committee.

The format and formality of a loan committee presentation is usually dictated by the size, staff organization, and procedures of the lending institution. In a larger institution the process may be very formal. In a small bank, it may be very informal, lacking any structured format. Most institutions have a procedure under which a written summary is used, accompanied by a verbal presentation by the loan officer. After questions and discussion by the committee members, a vote is taken. In some instances, the committee may approve the request subject to a revision of the proposed terms of the loan, or may approve the request for a lesser amount. Whatever the decision, its quality is directly related to the completeness and accuracy of the information presented. Obviously, the loan officer must be knowledgeable and well prepared. It is also very helpful if a consistent, standard format is followed in making a presentation. This will insure that all information is presented in a logical manner, and that no significant fact is overlooked. It will also give the inexperienced loan officer a feeling of confidence. This is important, since hesitancy and lack of self assurance on the part of the loan officer are sometimes interpreted by a loan committee as uncertainty about the quality of a loan request. Here is a suggested format for such a presentation.

1. Information about the applicant
    a. Name and what kind of legal entity
    b. Nature of the business

    c.   Names of management or principals

    d.   How long in business

    e.   How long a customer

2.   Financial overview

    a.   Balance sheet

    b.   Profitability performance

    c.   Performance projections

    d.   Borrowing history and balances outstanding

3.   Overall relationship with the bank

    a.   Compensating balances

    b.   Time deposits

    c.   Other—trust, payroll services, etc.

4.   The loan request

    a.   Amount requested

    b.   Purpose

    c.   Rate and term

    d.   Proposed repayment plan

    e.   Proposed collateral (if secured)

    f.   Guarantors, endorsers, etc.

5.   Analysis of the request

    a.   Strengths

    b.   Weaknesses

    c.   Soundness and workability

6.   Recommendations

    a.   For approval or disapproval

    b.   For approval on a modified basis

EXHIBIT P Collateral Evaluation Form

COLLATERAL EVALUATION

e __August 10, 19X4__   Loan Customer __John J. Borrower__

Customer Contact _____

:URED LOANS:

Loan #	Date	Due	Balance
12460	1/12/82	1/12/86	$ 96,622
16121	3/10/84	9/10/84	142,000
17320	5/27/84	5/25/85	43,420

TOTAL SECURED LOANS $ 282,042

.LATERAL:

Item or Category	Valuation	Source	Factor	Net Collateral Value
100 sh. Dupont Stock	$ 5,600	WSJ	.70	$ 3,920
Manufacturing Equipment	61,000	Price Guide	.60	36,600
R/E Mortgage – Commercial Building	185,000	Appraisal	.80	148,000
1981 Ford F-250 Truck	4,600	NADA	.75	3,450
Inventory	94,000	FIN/STMT	.50	47,000
Accounts Receivable	162,000	FIN/STMT	.70	113,400
Term Life Insurance	200,000	Policy	- 0 -	- 0 -
Certificate of Deposit	20,000	Our Records	1.00	20,000

TOTAL COLLATERAL VALUE $ 372,370

COLLATERAL COVERAGE   132 %

Loan Officer __R. Brown__

Loan Rating _____

117

9

Structuring and Closing the Loan

The most important decision a lender makes is whether or not to approve a given loan request. The lender's second most important decision is how the loan will be structured. A properly structured loan is one that is tailored to the specific needs of the borrower, while also satisfying the credit criteria of the lender. The loan will provide adequate loan funds to the borrower when needed, and its repayment requirements will correspond to the availability of repayment from the normal operation of the borrower's business. A well structured loan is characterized by its workability, while an improperly structured one will be characterized by a continuing need to make adjustments in the loan arrangements, concern on the part of the lender, and dissatisfaction on the part of the borrower.

Five basic elements must be considered to structure a loan properly: interest rate, term and repayment schedule, security, guarantors, and restrictions and controls. All of these elements are generally subject to a certain amount of negotiation between the borrower and the lender. The lender's parameters for negotiation are generally set by the lender's perception of risk, loan policy, and profit objectives. The borrower's parameters for negotiation are generally set by his or her perception of what is an acceptable rate, attitude toward how much security should be pledged, and willingness to accept certain restrictions and controls set by the lender.

Rate is probably subject to more negotiation by borrowers than any other element. The factors to be considered in pricing a loan are discussed in chapter 10.

Proper term and repayment schedules are affected by a number of factors; one factor is loan purpose. A loan to fund a seasonal bulge in inventory and receivables should obviously be for a relatively short term, and should mature at approximately the projected time that inventory and receivables will return to a normal level. A loan for capital expenditures may be written for a considerably longer term, depending on the depreciable life of the asset being purchased, and also depending to some extent on the amount of repayment available to retire capital debt. Therefore, if the cost of a new piece of manufacturing equipment may be repaid easily in two years, two years may be the proper term. If less cash flow is available, then a proper term for that loan may be three to five years. Some types of loan, such as a revolving loan against receivables and inventory, may not have a specific repayment schedule, with the lender more concerned about maintaining a proper collateral margin than the ultimate repayment in full of the loan.

Analysis of the lender's collateral position and the importance of adequate collateral margin were discussed in the previous chapter. However, the specific assets or categories of assets that are to be pledged as collateral for the loan may be subject to negotiation. The lender should always insist that the assets that will provide the repayment—such as inventory and accounts receivable in the case of a retailer, or crops or livestock in the case of a farmer—be pledged as security for the loan. This avoids the problem of another creditor gaining control of the lender's source of repayment. Many lenders make it a practice to perfect a "broad form" or "blanket" security interest covering all or most of the borrower's productive assets, both to strengthen their collateral position, and to prevent another creditor from gaining control of a portion of the productive assets. Reluctance on the part of the borrower to pledge all of the security requested by the lender, or a last minute request to substitute collateral, should be viewed with suspicion by the lender, and the lender's security position should be thoroughly reexamined before proceeding with the loan.

Most lenders will require that the principals of a closely held company or a small business personally guarantee the business borrowings. It is not unusual for the borrower to request that this requirement be waived. The borrower's hesitancy may result from a lack of understanding as to why the guaranty is being requested, and the lender should explain in detail why the request is being made. A guaranty may be important for two reasons—first, to add financial strength, and second, to insure that the principals of the business do not "walk away" if the business gets in trouble. In view of this, the lender's requirement for a guaranty should be waived only in rare cases, and after the lender has ascertained that the loan will have adequate strength and workability without the guaranty.

In some instances, the lender may require certain restrictions and controls over the operation of the borrower's business. This is generally accomplished by means of a loan agreement. The specific terms of such an agreement are usually subject to negotiation between the borrower and the lender. In some instances, lenders may be able to make some concessions regarding the terms of the loan agreement without seriously jeopardizing their ability to adequately control the business. Depending on the circumstances of the loan, lenders should decide which provisions of the loan agreement are key, and concessions should not be made in those areas.

Line of Credit Financing

Many lenders are willing to grant a borrower a line of credit, that is, a commitment to loan funds at any time up to a given maximum amount, until the date that the commitment expires. With a line of credit, the borrower has assurances that funds will be available when they are needed without further negotiations with the lender. Generally, there will be restrictions on the purpose for which the funds drawn under the line of credit may be used. Normally, a line of credit will be set up for working capital purposes, and the borrower may be prohibited from using the funds for capital expenditures. There are a number of advantages to a line of credit arrangement. It eliminates the necessity for the lender to process numerous similar loan applications over a period of time, and it eliminates the necessity for the borrower to draw the funds before they are really needed. In some instances, funds are disbursed as needed, and in other cases they are disbursed in accordance with a specific plan or budget, and the borrower is obligated to use the funds in accordance with the plan. In some instances, funds may also be disbursed at specific intervals, rather than upon the request of the borrower. Depending on the nature of the loan and the financial strength of the borrower, a line of credit commitment may be made for as little as 30 days, or for as long as a year. Most lenders insist on reviewing line of credit arrangements at least annually.

From a mechanical standpoint a line of credit may be handled in one of three ways: by a note executed each time there is a draw, by a master note, or by a revolving note. To stay in close contact with the customer, the lender may wish to have the borrower execute a note each time a draw is made. However, this can be time consuming and inconvenient for both the lender and the borrower. For that reason, many lenders use either a master note or revolving note. With a master note, the funds generally may be disbursed only once. Therefore, if the lender uses a master note, the amount of the note must be the anticipated aggregate total of all dollars to be disbursed during the period. Once all funds on the master note have been disbursed, and additional funds are required, a new note must be executed. This may simplify control and accounting, but it provides less flexibility than the revolving note. Also, as already noted, it requires a note in the amount of the total required disbursements, an amount that may be considerably larger than the anticipated maximum outstanding balance. With a revolving note, the borrower may draw amounts up to the maximum, repay, and then redraw those funds again, repeating the process any number of times, as long as the outstanding balance does not exceed the amount of the note. This system allows great flexibility, but may create control and accounting problems if the lender is not accustomed to handling this type of transaction.

In the case of either a master or revolving note, the note itself may be a standard form, but should have a schedule attached upon which partial disbursements and repayments may be recorded. This schedule not only enables the lender to record the dates and amounts of partial disbursements and payments and the outstanding balance, but also facilitates the computation of interest, which normally is charged only from the date of each disbursement. Since computer programs that will perform these computations are now readily available, this should not present a problem to the lender.

A written agreement between the lender and the borrower should recite the basic terms of the line of credit agreement, such as the fact that the disbursement and usage of the loan proceeds will be governed by a budget or disbursement plan. The agreement should also designate who is authorized to request disbursements, and how disbursements will be handled. Most lenders prefer that the proprietor, a partner, or corporate officer, make disbursement requests, although in some instances a manager or trusted employee may be authorized to do so. Some lenders also require that the request be made in writing, but many will disburse on the basis of a telephone conversation. Most bank lenders will disburse only by a deposit to a checking account. Funds should never be disbursed directly to a third party unless a written authorization is received from the borrower. Exhibit Q contains a sample of a letter agreement between lender and borrower for a revolving loan arrangement.

A lender should not make the mistake of assuming that simply because a line of credit has been committed for a given period of time, no supervision of the loan is necessary during that period. The lender should monitor usage, since heavier than anticipated usage of the line may be a danger signal. The lender should also strive to monitor the purpose for which funds disbursed are used. Before renewing a line of credit commitment, the lender should request complete current financial information, which should be analyzed thoroughly before a new commitment is made.

Split Line Financing

A prospective lender often is requested to refinance existing debt owed to another institutional creditor. The lender's initial reaction may be that it prefers not to refinance existing debt, especially if it has a high loan to deposit ratio or a low legal loan limit. Furthermore, after analyzing the prospective borrower's situation, the lender may be uncomfortable with a loan that exceeds a given dollar amount. This, however, may prove to be a short sighted attitude.

Split line financing may be defined as the financing of an enterprise from two or more sources. Some arrangements that are theoretically split lines are not objectionable. Examples of this might be an account payable to a supplier, or an item of equipment financed through a dealer. Generally, split financing is objectionable if it creates problems of split repayment or split collateral. The financing of operating costs or working capital needs by more than one institutional creditor almost invariably results in problems of split repayment, and if the loan is secured, problems of split collateral. Therefore, a lender generally should finance all the working capital needs of a particular enterprise, or decline to finance any of them. The lender should be especially wary of conflicting security interests in receivables and inventory. As noted previously, a security interest in inventory held by one creditor, while another creditor holds a security interest in receivables, will invariably result in conflict. In the case of equipment financed by another creditor, the lender should ascertain that the third party security interest covers only the item financed, and that the form UCC-1 filed does not contain a blanket provision or after acquired clause covering other assets owned by the debtor.

Even where there is no conflict regarding collateral, there may be several other areas of potential conflict with other creditors, such as:

1. If more funds are required than anticipated, each lender involved may take the position that the others should advance the additional funds.
2. If repayment fails to materialize as anticipated, each creditor may demand the available repayment and expect the other creditors to renew or extend their notes.
3. The various lenders may require the borrower to sign loan agreements or make other requirements that have conflicting provisions.
4. If a problem develops, a creditor may initiate legal action prematurely in the hope of improving its position relative to the other creditors.

Some borrowers are hesitant to deal with only one lender; they maintain that this gives the lender too much control over their operation. Most knowledgeable borrowers, however, recognize the advantages and prefer to develop a good working relationship with one lender. The lender should feel more secure being the sole institutional creditor, even though the size of the loan is larger than if a split financing situation existed.

Loan Agreements

A loan agreement is a written agreement between a lender and borrower which outlines the obligations of each party, makes certain warranties, and usually places certain controls and restrictions on the borrower. Loan agreements originally were used primarily by larger banks in connection with term loans. Most lenders now recognize the benefits of a written agreement in connection with various types of loans, including short term working capital and revolving loans. A loan agreement may accomplish a number of objectives.

1. It sets out in writing the various agreements between the parties, thereby preventing disputes and misunderstandings.
2. It may give the lender a certain degree of control over the debtor's business by requiring or restricting certain actions on the part of the debtor.
3. It clarifies to the borrower exactly what is required.
4. It usually gives the borrower assurances that as long as the terms of the loan agreement are complied with, the lender will provide credit as outlined in the agreement.

Although loan agreements usually are tailored to meet the requirements of a specific situation, most loan agreements contain certain standard provisions, which may be divided into three general categories: warranties, positive covenants, and negative covenants. Exhibit S is an example of a fairly comprehensive loan agreement.

The "warranties" section of the loan agreement normally will contain such provisions as:

1. A warranty that all financial statements submitted to the lender are genuine and fairly represent the financial position of the borrower.
2. A warranty that the borrower has good title to all assets.
3. A warranty that the borrower has complied with all federal, state, and municipal laws and is not involved in litigation.
4. A warranty that the borrower has filed all necessary tax returns and has paid all taxes due.

"Positive covenants" are those things the borrower agrees to do under the provisions of the loan agreement. This section of the agreement generally contains provisions such as:

1. To furnish certain financial information to the lender periodically.
2. To promptly advise the lender of any change which affects the management structure of the borrower.

3. To promptly notify the lender of any probable or pending lawsuit or legal action.
4. To keep its insurable assets insured by financially sound and reputable insurance companies.
5. To keep all assets and properties in good repair and condition.
6. To cooperate with the lender in any field review or audit of the borrower's records the lender may wish to conduct.
7. To advise the lender promptly of any change or event that will materially affect the financial condition or performance of the borrower.
8. To maintain certain balance sheet ratios.
9. To use all loan proceeds for the specific purposes for which the funds were requested.
10. The borrower grants the lender a security interest in the collateral.
11. The borrower agrees to pay any reasonable attorney's fees incurred by the lender in the preparation or review of any documents required in connection with the loan.
12. The borrower agrees, upon request of the lender, to deliver such additional notes, guarantys, security agreements or other documents necessary to complete the loan properly.

"Negative covenants" are those things that the borrower is prohibited from doing during the life of the loan agreement unless the consent of the lender is obtained. This section of the loan agreement may contain provisions such as:

1. The borrower will not sell or lease any of its property or assets, other than in the normal course of business.
2. The borrower will not declare or pay a dividend or make a capital distribution, or purchase or redeem any of its capital stock.
3. The borrower will not repay loans from owners or shareholders.
4. The borrower will not pay any profit sharing or bonuses, or increase the compensation of any officer or director, in excess of an amount agreed to in the loan agreement.
5. The borrower will not obtain loans from any other institutional creditor.
6. The borrower will not consolidate or merge with or into any other business.
7. The borrower will not make capital purchases in excess of a given amount.

The loan agreement also may contain provisions especially tailored to a specific situation. For example:

1. The borrower agrees to sell, within the next 12 months, at public auction, or by any other commercially reasonable means, a commercial property owned by the borrower located at the corner of Oak and Springfield Streets in Center City.
2. The borrower agrees, within 180 days, to divest himself of his interest in a partnership known as Branson Truck Lines, and to apply any and all proceeds from the sale thereof to this loan.
3. The borrower agrees to obtain, as soon as possible, and to assign to the bank, $100,000 of term life insurance.

In summary, we can say that loan agreements are very useful, both in solidifying the terms agreed upon by the lender and the borrower, and in giving the lender a certain amount of control over the operations of the borrower. The agreement should be tailored to fit the specific situation and to meet the requirements of the lender. Most lenders should use loan agreements more frequently.

Closing the Loan

It is extremely important, that before closing the loan, a checklist of all required documentation is prepared. Any oversight in the preparation of complete documentation for the loan may have grave consequences in the future. The loan documentation checklist shown in Exhibit R may assist the loan officer in preparing the required documentation. When setting a closing date, the lender should be certain that all parties whose signatures will be required will be present at the closing. It can be very frustrating to both the lender and the borrower if funds cannot be disbursed at the closing because one party to the loan forgot to attend the closing.

At the closing, the terms of the loan should be reviewed in detail with the borrower to prevent any future misunderstandings. The lender should also allow the borrower to examine all loan documents and should take pains to explain the significance of each loan document. One of the most frequent complaints heard from borrowers is that they did not understand the loan documentation, and that the lender made little effort to explain the security agreement, financing statement, or loan agreement. The lender should be sure that all documents are signed at the closing, since it may be difficult to obtain necessary signatures subsequently. In some cases, such as that of a loan guaranty, the legal enforceability of the document may become questionable if it is signed subsequent to the disbursement of the funds. The lender should also be sure that all necessary fees, such as filing fees, service fees, and credit life premiums are collected at the closing. Generally, loan proceeds will be used to pay these fees.

A well managed loan closing can do a great deal to promote a good working relationship between the lender and the borrower. A borrower who leaves a closing puzzled, or uneasy, or with unanswered questions, will question his or her working relationship with the lender. It certainly behooves the lender to see that every loan closing is handled in a professional manner if a good relationship is to be maintained with the borrower.

EXHIBIT Q   Revolving Credit Line Agreement

REVOLVING CREDIT LINE AGREEMENT

The Commercial Bank of Champaign
P.O. Box 798
Champaign, IL   61820   Date____November 10, 19XX_____

Gentlemen:

Enclosed herewith you will find our Note dated __November 9, 19XX_____ which is
to evidence loans or advances which we may from time to time request you to make to us
and which you may from time to time, in your sole discretion make in amounts which are
not to exceed in the aggregate $ 300,000.00_____.

In consideration of any loan or advance or other financial accommodation you may at any
time make to us, we hereby agree to the following, which shall govern all borrowings presently outstanding and all borrowings which we may further request that you lend to us from
time to time up to an aggregate maximum amount of $ 300,000.00_____ at any one time
outstanding.

In making any loan or advance hereunder you may comply with any telephone, personal or
written request to credit our Account No. 220-006-2_____ at The Commercial Bank of
Champaign by any one of the following persons:

Name	Title
Thomas J. Jones	President
William T. Smith	Treasurer

All borrowings hereunder shall be paid by us at the note maturity, but they may at our
election in any instance be repaid, in whole or in part, at any time prior to maturity
upon advice to you by telephone, in person, or in writing. Upon receipt of such advice,
the payment of a loan will be effected by debiting our Account No 220-006-2_____
at The Commercial Bank of Champaign for the principal amount of such payment.

You shall incur no liability to us in acting upon telephone, personal, or written
instructions which the recipient thereof believed in good faith to have been given by
any authorized officers or individuals.

We understand that your acceptance of this Agreement does not commit you to make any of
the loans or advances contemplated hereunder and that you shall make any such loan or
advance in your sole and absolute discretion. Interest on the borrowings shall be at
the rate stated in the Note and shall be paid ____monthly_____, which shall be billed
by you, and shall be computed on daily balances outstanding on the basis of a 360 day
year. Our Note and this letter will constitute evidence of our indebtedness to you
outstanding hereunder from time to time. This agreement may be terminated at any time by
either of us by verbal or written notice to the other, but such termination shall not
affect our liabilities to you therefore incurred hereunder. Any changes in this agreement
will be made in written form.

You shall not be liable to us for, and we hereby indemnify you against, and agree to hold
you harmless from, any liability or claims (including court costs, reasonable attorneys'
fees and other expenses), which you may incur, in connection with or pursuant to this
Agreement or the Promissory Note.

If this Agreement is satisfactory to you, please indicate your acceptance by signing and
returning to us a copy of this letter provided for that purpose.

Very truly yours,

THE COMMERCIAL BANK OF CHAMPAIGN   ABC Manufacturing Company

By:____Robert C. Brown, V.P.__(title)   By:___Thomas J. Jones, Pres.____(title)

Date:_____November 10, 19XX_____   By:___Wm. T. Smith, Treas._____(title)

EXHIBIT R   Loan Documentation Checklist

LOAN DOCUMENTATION CHECKLIST

Received   Required

1. Financial Information
   □ □   a. Balance sheet dated _____.
   □ □   b. Income statement dated _____.
   □ □ 2. Corporate resolution or partnership authorization.
   □ □ 3. Promissory note.
   □ □ 4. Security agreement.
   □ □ 5. Form UCC-1, ___ copies required.
   □ □ 6. UCC filing fee, $_____ .
   □ □ 7. Appraisal or inspection of collateral.
   8. Guarantor #1:
   □ □   a. Guaranty for $_____.
   □ □   b. Financial statement dated _____.
   Guarantor #2:
   □ □   a. Guaranty for $_____.
   □ □   b. Financial statement dated _____.
   □ □ 9. Casualty insurance binder.
   □ □ 10. Term or credit life insurance = $_____.
   □ □   a. Credit life premium of $_____.
   □ □ 11. Loan agreement.
   □ □ 12. Loan fees of ___ % = $_____.
   13. Documents of title
   □ □   a.
   □ □   b.
   □ □   c.
   □ □ 14. Fee to file title liens, $_____

(If real estate is to be part of the security)

   □ □ 15. Real estate mortgage.
   □ □ 16. Title search or title insurance commitment.
   □ □ 17. Appraisal.
   □ □ 18. Recording and title search fees, $_____.

Summary of Fees:

1. UCC filing fees $_____
2. Credit life premium   _____
3. Loan fees   _____
4. Title lien fees   _____
5. Recording + title search fees   _____
            Total fees required $_____

EXHIBIT S   LOAN AGREEMENT

AGREEMENT made this 21st day of October, 19X4, by and between HI-TEC CORPORATION, a Delaware corporation, hereinafter referred to as "Borrower," and DONALD ROBINS and FRED HUTCHINS, hereinafter referred to as "Guarantors," and THE COMMERCIAL BANK OF CENTER CITY, hereinafter referred to as "the Bank":

WHEREAS, Borrower has applied to the Bank for a financial package, including a ten-year capital term loan in the amount of $766,000, a $500,000 debenture issue under the Small Business Administration's 503 Program, a $360,000 seven-year working capital loan guaranteed by SBA, and a $500,000 interim loan pending issuance of the SBA 503 Program debentures; and

WHEREAS, the Bank is willing to commit said financing package, subject to the terms and conditions hereinafter specified.

THEREFORE the parties agree as follows:

1. *All loans.* This agreement shall apply to each and every loan now or hereafter made by the Bank to the Borrower. Each such loan shall be evidenced by a note signed by the Borrower and the Terms and conditions of each such loan may vary solely according to the requirements of the Bank as the Bank may then require.

2. *Warranty of financial statements.* The Borrower and Guarantors warrant that all submitted and hereafter submitted financial statements representing balance sheets of the Borrower or Guarantors, and related statements of income and retained earnings for the period then ended, have and will present fairly the financial position of the Borrower or the Guarantors, as the case may be, as of the respective dates and the results of operations for the periods indicated, and the stated financial statements are and will be in conformity with generally accepted accounting principles applied on a consistent basis.

3. *Annual financial statements.* The Borrower and Guarantors shall each deliver to the Bank within 90 days after the close of each fiscal year a balance sheet as of the close of such fiscal year and statements of income and retained earnings and sources and applications of funds for the year then ended, prepared in conformity with generally accepted accounting principles, applied on a basis consistent with that of the preceding year or containing disclosure of the effect on financial position or results of operations of any change in the application of accounting principles during the year. Beginning with the Borrower's fiscal year ending in 19X4, the above mentioned financial statements of the Borrower shall be accompanied by a report thereon, containing an opinion, unqualified as to scope limitations imposed by the Borrower, of a firm of independent certified public accountants selected by the Borrower and acceptable to the Bank.

4. *Quarterly financial statements.* The Borrower shall deliver to the Bank within 45 days after the close of each of the first three quarters of each fiscal year of the Borrower the following:

(a) A balance sheet of the Borrower as of the close of each quarter and statements of consolidated income and retained earnings for that portion of the fiscal year-to-date then ended, prepared in conformity with generally accepted accounting principles, applied on a basis consistent with that of the preceding period or containing disclosure of the effect on the financial position or results of operations of any change in the application of

EXHIBIT **S** *(Continued)*

generally accepted accounting principles during the period, and reported on by the President or an authorized financial officer of the Borrower; and

(b)   A written statement by the President or an authorized financial officer of the Borrower at the end of each quarterly period, including the last quarter of each fiscal year, that there existed no conditions or event which constitutes a default in the observance, performance, and fulfillment of any of the covenants, agreements, or conditions contained in this Loan Agreement or in the Notes, of which, after notice by the Bank, or lapse of time, or both, would constitute such default; or a statement specifying the nature and period of existence of any such condition or event.

5.   *Management*. The Borrower will advise the Bank immediately of any change, either having occurred or pending, which affects the management structure of the Borrower.

6.   *Litigation*. The Borrower warrants that it has complied, and will continue to comply with all federal, state, municipal, and other laws, ordinances and regulations applicable to it and its business; that there are no actions, suits, or proceedings pending or threatened against or affecting the Borrower, its officers or directors in law or in equity; that there exists no possibility of any such action, suit, or proceeding; that there exists no ground for any such action, suit or proceeding except as is clearly indicated in the financial statements having been submitted to the Bank. Furthermore, the Borrower warrants that should any such action, suit, or proceeding become possible, or grounds be known, or take place, that the Bank will be notified immediately and that the Borrower's legal counsel will be required to submit to the Bank current opinions regarding status of said action or suit from time to time. Should liability of the Borrower become probable as a result of any such action, suit, or proceeding, then the Borrower shall reserve the full extent of the probable liability.

7.   *Insurance*. The Borrower will keep all of its assets of insurable character insured by financially sound reputable companies acceptable to the Bank against loss or damage by fire and other causes ordinarily included within the term "extended coverage." Such insurance will be in amounts sufficient to prevent the Borrower from becoming the co-insurer within the terms of the insurance policies covering such risks and, in any event, in amounts not less than eighty percent (80%) of the insurable value of the property as established periodically by standard insurance appraisals, or to the full extent of the Bank's interest, whichever is greater. All of such policies covering assets pledged to the Bank shall show the bank "as its interest may appear" as loss payee on Uniform Standard Form No. 107, and shall be subject to the Bank's approval of the form and substance of same. The Borrower will also maintain insurance by financially sound reputable companies acceptable to the Bank and in amounts satisfactory to the Bank against loss or damage from all other hazards, risks, and public liability which are commonly insured against by companies engaged in the same or similar business as the Borrower.

8.   *Taxes*. The Borrower warrants that it has filed and will continue to file, all tax returns which are required to be filed and has paid, and will continue to pay, all taxes which may become due pursuant to said return or pursuant to any assessment related thereto, said filing and payment to be made on or before any required due date, except that prudent and reasonable extensions for the filing or payment of taxes requested by the borrower's independent certified public accountant in the normal course of business will be allowed. Further, no tax liability has been assessed by the

EXHIBIT S *(Continued)*

Internal Revenue Service or any other taxing agency which is materially in excess of that already paid and the Borrower knows of no basis for any such deficiency assessment. The term taxes as used herein shall include all assessments, governmental charges, levies, and similar liabilities.

9.   *Leases.* Without prior written approval of the Bank; Borrower will not sell any of its property or assets, now owned or hereafter acquired, pursuant to any arrangement whether concurrent with such sale or otherwise, whereby it shall, directly or indirectly, lease or agree to lease such property or assets from the purchaser thereof or any other person. The Borrower will not lease to another party any of its assets or property. The Borrower will not create or assume any obligation to make any direct or indirect payment, whether as rent or otherwise, under any lease, rental or other arrangement for the use of real or personal property, or both, except for typewriters, duplicators and other similar general office equipment which will be used in general office work and in normal quantities.

10.   *Payment of loans.* All payments will, at the option of the Bank, apply first to accrued interest and then to principal. Loans made by the Bank to the Borrower may be repaid in full or in part prior to maturity, without penalty. The Borrower will make all payments of principal and interest on loans made under this Loan Agreement promptly as the same become due and said payment will be in immediately available funds to the Bank.

11.   *Nature of business.* The Borrower will conduct the business of the company in the same product and service line as presently engaged. No new product or service which is not substantially of the same general character or line of business as the company is presently engaged will be implemented without the prior written consent of the Bank. The Borrower will not purchase any shares of stock, bonds, or other securities; nor make advances to, loans to, or investment in, nor guarantee any obligation of, endorse any notes of, or in any way become responsible for the obligations of any kind of any person, entity, corporation or firm.

12.   *Protection of assets.* The Borrower will keep all of its assets and properties in good repair, working order, and condition, and from time to time will make all needed and proper repairs, renewals, replacements, extensions, additions, and improvements thereto as may be required for the normal conduct of its business in accordance with prudent management. The Borrower will not pledge, sell, transfer or otherwise obligate or dispose of all or a part of its assets and properties (except through selling those assets usually acquired or produced for resale in the normal course of business) without the consent of the Bank, which will not unreasonably withhold its consent. Should the asset or property be collateral to the Bank then the Bank shall receive the sale proceeds of the property sold. The Borrower will not sell, transfer, pledge or otherwise dispose of its accounts receivable to anyone other than the Bank and/or the Small Business Administration.

13.   *Dividends, profit sharing, compensation.* The Borrower will not declare or pay in cash or in kind any dividend, nor make any distribution with respect to its capital stock, nor redeem or purchase any shares of its capital stock, nor repay loans from owners or shareholders, without prior approval in writing by the Bank, but such approval will not be unreasonably withheld so long as Borrower is not in default of any obligation to the Bank. The Borrower will not pay any profit sharing or bonus, directly or indirectly, to any employee except pursuant to a formal written plan previously approved in writing by the Bank. The Borrower will not increase the compensation of

EXHIBIT   S *(Continued)*

any officer, director, or beneficial owner of the Borrower's capital stock, or spouse of any of the aforementioned over the rate prevailing at the date of this Loan Agreement, without prior approval in writing by the Bank. As long as the Borrower is not in default under any loan with the Bank in this agreement, the Bank will not refuse to consent to increases not in excess of the annual cost of living factor. As used herein the term "compensation" shall include all salaries, bonuses, directors' fees, commissions, retainers, loans, regular drawing accounts, and other personal services.

14.   *Other debt.* The Borrower will not become or remain liable in any manner with respect to indebtedness for money borrowed from others whether by loan, guarantee, endorsement, the issuance of securities or otherwise except to the Bank or unless consented to by the Bank. The Borrower will pay when due all lawful claims for liabilities which, if unpaid, would by law be or become a lien or charge upon the assets or property of the Borrower, or lead to the suspension of the business of the Borrower, and which shall include all claims for amounts due for merchandise, labor, materials, or supplies. Provided, however, nothing herein shall require the Borrower to make any such payment or compliance so long as:

(a)   The Borrower, in good faith, by appropriate proceedings diligently contests its obligations to do so and to the full extent of any probable liability, the Borrower sets aside on its books a reserve as shall be required by generally accepted principles of accountings; except that, if such contest will result in the forfeiture or loss of any asset or property of the Borrower then the Borrower shall pay forthwith any such tax, assessment, charge, levy or claim upon commencement of proceedings to foreclose any lien with respect thereto on any of its assets or property, and further, in respect to this item, the Borrower has submitted a written opinion from legal counsel as to the probable conclusion and outcome of any such action and the extent of the Borrower's liability thereunder.

(b)   They result from any obligations for city, county, or state taxes which are assessed but not yet due.

(c)   They result from any obligation or attachment which is bonded or insured and for which a bond or insurance claim would be honored.

(d)   They result from obligations to vendors, carriers, warehouses, mechanics, laborers and materialmen incurred in the normal course of business for sums not then due, or due less than thirty (30) days, or being contested.

15.   *Licenses, patents, permits.* The Borrower warrants that, to the best of its knowledge, it possesses all necessary licenses, trademarks, trademark rights, trade names, trade name rights, copyrights, permits, certificates, and approvals necessary to conduct its business and that there are no conflicts as to the rights of others in any of the aforementioned.

16.   *Merger, acquisition, sale.* The Borrower will not consolidate or merge with or into any other business, firm or corporation or permit any other business, firm or corporation to merge into it, without prior written approval by the Bank. The acquisition by the Borrower through lease, purchase, or otherwise of all or substantially all of the assets of any business, firm, or corporation shall be deemed a consolidation or merger. The Borrower will not issue or sell any of its shares of stock of any class, nor issue or grant any warrants, options or calls to purchase the same to any other business, firm, or corporation without prior written approval by the Bank. The

EXHIBIT   S *(Continued)*

Borrower will notify the Bank at once upon any stock tender offer or offer to buy any or all of the Borrower's outstanding stock or business ownership. Upon the sale of controlling interest of the Borrower, the Bank may, at the Bank's option, accelerate the maturity of any and all loans of the Borrower, and Borrower will move said loans from the Bank within 60 days.

17.   *Field reviews.* The Borrower agrees that the Bank may require periodic reviews (generally quarterly) of the Borrower's operations, reports, and records, with said reviews to be undertaken by Bank employees or agents who will be allowed free access to all of the Borrower's operations, reports, and records. Provided that Borrower shall be given reasonable notice of such reviews, and they shall be conducted at reasonably convenient times to the officers and employees of the Borrower.

18.   *Rights of Bank.* The rights, powers, and remedies given to the Bank by this Loan Agreement are in addition to all rights, powers, and remedies given to the Bank by virtue of any other agreement, statute, or rule of law. Any forbearance or failure or delay by the Bank in exercising any right, power, or remedy and any single or partial exercise of any right, power, or remedy hereunder shall not preclude further or subsequent exercise thereof. Every right, power, and remedy of the Bank shall continue in full force and effect until such right, power, or remedy is specifically waived, or modified by an instrument in writing executed by an authorized officer of the Bank. A waiver or modification by the Bank of any right, power, or remedy hereunder on any one occasion shall not be construed as a bar, waiver, or modification, to any right, power, or remedy that the Bank would otherwise have had on any future occasion.

19.   *Subsidiaries.* Each reference herein to Borrower shall be deemed to include any and all subsidiaries of the Borrower's business or corporation.

20.   *Separability.* If any provision of this Loan Agreement is held for any reason to be unenforceable, the remainder of this Loan Agreement shall, nevertheless, remain in full force and effect.

21.   *True and complete statements.* The Borrower warrants that none of the material submitted or to be submitted or none of the statements and representations made or to be made have or will contain untrue statements or information, nor have or will contain partial or misleading statements or information. The Borrower further warrants that the Bank may rely upon such statements, representations, and material as accurate and complete information in its determination of the viability and financial strength of the Borrower. The Borrower further agrees to advise the Bank at once of any change or event which will materially alter or impair the performance of the Borrower either financially or in its normal course of business routines.

22.   *Collateral.* The Borrower warrants that it has good title, free and clear of all liens and encumbrances, to all property which it submits to the Bank as collateral securing any loans made under this Loan Agreement. The Borrower hereby authorizes the Bank to sign and file financing statements at any time with respect to any collateral without the signature of the Borrower. The Borrower hereby appoints and grants the Bank Power of Attorney to sign any and all documents necessary to protect the Bank's security interest.

23.   *Bank checking accounts.* The principal checking accounts of Borrower will be maintained with the Bank. Said accounts shall always contain collected demand deposit balances equal to at least ten percent (10%) of the outstanding balance of the

EXHIBIT   S *(Continued)*

Borrower's working capital loan with the Bank, plus demand deposit balances adequate to cover the servicing costs of the Borrower's accounts, as computed by means of the Bank's usual account analysis formula. If at any time Borrower moves its checking accounts from the Bank or ceases to carry in those accounts its principal checking balances, the Borrower will, at the request of the Bank, move all its borrowings from the Bank. This will be done within 120 days after the Bank makes such a request, notwithstanding the fact that the loans involved may have a maturity date later than the removal date established under this provision.

24.   *Capital purchases.* During fiscal years 19X4 and 19X5, the Borrower will not make capital purchases or expenditures, with the exception of those contemplated under the terms of a financing proposal presented to the Bank in September, 19X4, without the consent of the Bank. In years subsequent to 19X5, the Borrower will not make capital expenditures in excess of $25,000 per calendar year without the consent of the Bank.

25.   *Current ratio.* The Borrower will maintain a current ratio of at least 1.2 to 1, and a net worth of at least $400,000.

26.   *Capital term loan.* The Bank has committed to the Borrower a capital term loan in the amount of $766,000 for a ten-year term for the purpose of financing fifty percent (50%) of the cost of land the Borrower is purchasing in Interstate Research Park in Center City, the cost of a building to be constructed upon that land, and the equipment necessary for the Borrower's manufacturing operation. The first year of the loan only monthly payments of interest will be required. Thereafter, monthly payments of principal and interest amortized on a nine-year basis will be required. The interest rate on the loan will be two percent (2%) over The Commercial Bank base loan rate, adjusted on the first day of each calendar quarter. In addition, the Borrower is to pay to the Bank a fee of one and one-half percent (1½%) of the amount of the loan, payable at closing. Security for the loan will be a first real estate mortgage on the real estate being purchased, located at 1401 Congress Drive, Center City, and a first security interest in all equipment, furnishings, and fixtures. The Bank understands that the Small Business Administration will hold a second mortgage on the real estate and a second security interest in the chattel assets to secure the $500,000 of debentures being issued under the SBA 503 Program, and consents to the Borrower granting a second mortgage and a second security interest to the Small Business Administration.

27.   *Working capital loan.* The Bank has committed to the Borrower a working capital loan in the amount of $360,000 for a seven year term at a rate of two percent (2%) over the business prime rate of The Chase Manhattan Bank in New York City, with monthly payments of $7,100, and with rate adjusted on the first day of each calendar quarter. This commitment is made subject to the receipt of a ninety percent (90%) guaranty of this loan from the Small Business Administration, and is to be secured by a first security interest in all receivables and inventory of the Borrower. Borrower consents to pay to the Small Business Administration a guaranty fee of $3,240.

28.   *Interim loan.* The Bank has committed to the Borrower an interim construction loan in the amount of $500,000 for the purpose of financing the acquisition of land located at 1401 Congress Drive, Center City, and for the purpose of paying construction costs for a building to be erected upon that property in accordance with plans and specifications submitted to the Bank. The maturity date of this loan will be March 15, 19X5. Interest rate will be one and one-half percent (1½%) over The Commercial Bank base loan rate, adjusted on the first day of each calendar quarter.

EXHIBIT S *(Continued)*

Construction pay-outs will be made no more often than monthly and upon receipt of contractor's affidavits and partial lien waivers acceptable to the Bank. This loan is to be secured by a mortgage on the real estate. Evidence of adequate builder's risk insurance coverage will be required. This commitment is also subject to receipt from the Small Business Administration of an authorization for the issuance of debentures in the amount of $500,000. and it is agreed that the proceeds of the SBA debentures will be used to pay off the interim loan in full.

29. *Orders.* Prior to the disbursement of any loan funds, the Borrower will present evidence acceptable to the Bank that it has a minimum of $1,000,000 of orders for its products forthcoming from reputable buyers.

30. *Life insurance.* In connection with the aforementioned loans, the Borrower agrees to obtain life insurance in an amount not less than $750,000 upon the life of Donald Robins, and in an amount not less than $750,000 upon the life of Fred Hutchins, and further agrees to assign said insurance policies to the Bank as additional security.

31. *Personal Guaranty.* Donald Robins and Fred Hutchins jointly and severally guarantee all indebtedness of the Borrower to the Bank. As security for said guarantys, Robins and Hutchins agree to deliver to the Bank all certificates of stock in Hi-Tec Corporation owned by them, and further agree to promptly deliver to the Bank certificates acquired in the future.

32. *Sale of stock.* Prior to the disbursement of any loan funds the Borrower will sell sufficient of its common stock to investors to generate additional equity capital in an amount not less than $675,000. The proceeds of the sale of said common stock are to be deposited in a special account at the Bank, and are to be used for the following purposes: to pay in full an existing loan from the Bank in the amount of $65,000; for capital purchases of real estate and equipment in the amount of $266,000; for working capital purposes in the amount of $344,000.

33. *Proceeds.* All loans shall be used for the specific purposes previously outlined by Borrower to the Bank. All indebtedness of the Borrower to the Guarantors shall hereafter be subordinate to the indebtedness of the Borrower to the Bank.

34. *Default.* If Borrower is in default under any terms of this agreement or the loans referred to herein, the Bank may elect to declare all sums owed to it from Borrower immediately due and payable, provided that the Bank has given Borrower at least 30 days written notice of, and opportunity to cure, any such default.

35. *Collateral security agreement.* Borrower agrees that the Bank shall have, and there is hereby created as security for the Borrower's indebtedness to said Bank, now or hereafter owing, a security interest in all production equipment, manufacturing equipment, testing equipment, engineering equipment, office equipment, inventory, accounts receivable, contracts receivable and general intangibles, now owned or hereafter acquired by Borrower, and proceeds thereof.

36. *Attorney fees.* The Borrower shall pay any reasonable attorney fees which the Bank incurs in the preparation or review of this Loan Agreement, or the documents referred to in it, not to exceed $1,000.

37. *Appraisals.* Upon completion of the improvements being constructed by Borrower in Interstate Research Park in Center City, the Borrower will furnish the Bank with an appraisal, by an appraiser satisfactory to the Bank, of the fair market value of the real estate and improvements located thereon.

38. *Further assurances.* On request, the Borrower will execute and deliver to

EXHIBIT   S *(Continued)*

the Bank all notes, guarantees, security agreement, financing statements, mortgages and other documents necessary or convenient to properly complete the loan and perfect the security positions contemplated herein.

    39.   *Successors and assigns.* All convenants, conditions, and terms contained in this Loan Agreement shall inure to the benefit of and bind the respective successors of the parties hereto.

    IN WITNESS WHEREOF each of the parties has caused this agreement to be executed by a duly authorized representative, and each person signing in a representative capacity warrants that he has full power and authority to execute this agreement on behalf of the party for whom he signs this agreement.

HI-TEC CORPORATION

BY _____   _____
                                        Donald Robins, Individually

THE COMMERCIAL BANK

BY _____   _____
                                        Fred Hutchins, Individually

10

Pricing Loans

The proper pricing of loans is a key factor in the profitability of a commercial lending operation. Several decades ago, when money market conditions were very stable, most lenders did not consider loan pricing to be a problem. With one or two minor annual changes in national prime rate, and with little change from year to year in the average annual yield in the bank's investment portfolio, neither pricing nor investment decisions required a great deal of attention on the part of bank management. All this has been drastically changed by the chaotic money market conditions of the past decade. Rapidly changing money market conditions, deregulation of the interest rates paid on deposits, the rapid shift of deposits from non-interest bearing to interest bearing accounts, and greatly intensified competition from non-banking institutions for both deposits and loans, have confronted bank management with a completely new environment for making pricing decisions for both loans and deposits.

Another result of these conditions has been the movement away from the fixed rate loan, which was predominant a decade ago, to the adjustable rate or floating rate loan. Today the great majority of commercial loans are written with either a short maturity or on an adjustable rate basis, which may call for a daily, monthly, or quarterly adjustment in interest rate, which may be tied to a criteria such as national prime rate, a bank's in-house prime rate, or treasury bill rate.

In dealing with the question of what interest rate is the proper rate for a given loan, the commercial lender must consider a number of factors that will affect the pricing of a loan.

Money Market Conditions

Money market conditions affect the bank's cost of funds in several ways. If the bank is dependent on purchased funds in the form of money market certificates, large negotiable CDs, or Fed funds, its cost of funds is directly affected by money market conditions. In addition, the money market determines the attractiveness of alternative investments. For example, if a bank can purchase government bonds yielding 10%, it may be reluctant to make loans unless the rate is substantially higher, in order to compensate for the additional risk and administrative work involved. If the bank is selling loans in the secondary market, it will be further affected, since the rate demanded by the secondary market is closely tied to money market conditions.

Risk

The greater the perceived risk in a loan, the higher the rate generally demanded by the lender to compensate for the additional risk. For this reason, some lenders will accept a lower rate on a loan secured by hard collateral than on an unsecured loan, or one secured by less desirable collateral. This is also why consumer loans, which may involve a relatively high level of risk and a relatively high amount of supervision, normally are written at a somewhat higher rate than commercial loans.

Fixed Rate vs. Adjustable Rate

Generally, the longer the maturity of the loan, or the longer the interval at which rate is adjusted, the higher the rate the lender will demand. This is because the lender is locked in for a longer period of time and has a greater exposure to future changes in money market conditions. As stated earlier, lenders have become quite apprehensive about carrying a loan at a fixed rate for an extended period, since a significant upward movement in market rates may cause a negative margin position. Although a floating or adjustable rate system may appear less desirable from the viewpoint of some borrowers, and may create minor administrative and accounting problems for the lender, it probably represents the fairest means of pricing a loan for both the borrower and lender.

Repayment Term

Generally, the longer the period over which the loan is to be repaid, the higher the rate demanded by the lender. The reason for this is that the lender has a greater exposure to future changes in the borrower's financial status, and the longer the term of the loan, the greater the likelihood that the collateral may depreciate to the point that its value no longer covers the outstanding loan balance. Assuming that an item of equipment has a useful life of six years, then the lender's collateral margin is certainly much more comfortable if the loan is written for a three-year term rather than for a five-year term, and this will be considered when the lender prices the loan.

Compensating Balances

If the borrower is providing some of the money required to fund the loan, the lender's yield is improved. In commercial banks, a borrower's deposits in checking, savings, and time deposit accounts constitute a compensating balance. Obviously, compensating balances upon which the lender is not required to pay interest, such as funds in a non-interest bearing checking account, are of greater value to the lender than funds upon which interest must be paid, as in a NOW account, money market account, or certificate of deposit. Many commercial banks include a provision in their loan agreements which requires that a compensating balance be held in a checking account, usually 10 to 15% of the amount of the loan. Even those banks that do not require specific compensating balances generally consider average collected account balances when calculating rate and yield on a loan.

Operating and Overhead Costs

If the bank is to stay in business it must cover the cost of salaries, rent, utilities, etc. Therefore, it must achieve a profit margin sufficient to cover these costs. In addition, a bank must generate sufficient profit to meet its profitability goals, build capital and reserves, and pay dividends to stockholders.

Competition

In calculating the required loan rate a commercial lender theoretically might use the basic formula shown in the example below:

Cost of funds	9.10%
Operating and overhead costs	2.40%
Loss reserves	.50%
Projected profit margin	2.50%
Required rate	14.50%

Competition will be a major limiting factor on the lender's desired profit margin. The lender may want a 7% profit margin but competitive factors probably will prevent achievement of that level of profit. A lender (or any other businessperson) cannot charge significantly more for the same products and services than its competitors without losing a significant number of customers—and in most communities, commercial lending is intensively competitive. Since savings and loan associations are now capable of making commercial loans, it is likely that competition in this area will increase further.

State Usury Laws

Usury laws may place a ceiling on the allowable rate on certain types of loans. A number of states have usury laws limiting rates on personal or consumer loans. Business loans generally are exempt from these limitations. You should familiarize yourself with the usury statutes of the state in which you operate.

Loan Pricing Formulas

In an attempt to achieve consistency in pricing loans, many banks have devised written formulas for determining the price on a given loan. There are many formulas which vary considerably in approach and complexity. Exhibit T contains an example of a loan pricing formula used by several banks. This formula takes into consideration a number of factors, including the bank's desired return on equity, the cost of the bank's funds, overhead costs, and the borrower's compensating balances.

The formula used as an example makes a number of assumptions: (1) That the bank has equity capital of 8%; (2) That the bank's desired return on equity is the greater of 14% or national prime rate; (3) That the bank is in a 46% Federal income tax bracket; (4) That the bank's overhead cost is 2.4% of the amount of the loan; (5) That the bank's cost of funds is 9.1%; (6) That the bank has 12% reserve requirements.

It is obvious that if a commercial bank is to use this kind of formula it must have knowledge of both its cost of funds and its overhead costs. Until relatively recently, many banks have not generated credible information concerning these costs. Until the proper pricing of loans and services became such a significant factor in the prudent management of a banking operation, many banks had little interest in generating accurate information concerning these costs. However, the great majority of banks now recognize the necessity for this information, and have instituted the cost accounting procedures required to generate adequate information.

It should also be noted that this pricing formula does not take into consideration several factors that may affect the pricing of the loan; the most significant of these is the risk involved. The commercial lender should therefore make an adjustment in the loan rate for the perceived level of risk after calculating the rate by using the formula. Also, like most pricing formulas, this formula assumes that the loan will be made on a floating rate basis. If the loan is to be made on a fixed rate basis, the lender may wish to add a premium to the rate to compensate for that fact. The formula also does not take the competitive factor into consideration. There is obviously no perfect formula. However, a good loan pricing formula can be of great help to a lender in pricing loans in a manner that is fair and equitable to all borrowers, and which will help achieve the lender's profitability goals.

EXHIBIT   T   Commercial Loan Pricing Formula

1. Total loans	$ 500,000
2.˙ % equity capital to support loan	× 8%
3. Equity capital to support loan	40,000
4. % return on equity goal (greater of 14% or National Prime)	14%
5. After tax earning required for goal (#3 × #4)	5,600
6. 1 - Bank's Corporate tax rate (1 − .46)	÷ .54
7. Pre-tax earnings required for goal (#5 ÷ #6)	10,370
8. Plus overhead 2.4% of loan	12,000
9. *Cost of funds ($500,000 × 9.1%)	45,500
10. Less equity capital × rate used in #9 ($40,000 ×9.1%)	(3,640)
11. Interest income required with no compensating balance	64,230
12. Credit given for compensating balances	(12,012)
Compensating balance × rate used in #10 × 88% (150,000 × 9.1% × 88%)	
13, Interest paid by bank on compensating balance	8,000
14. Interest income required with compensating balance	60,218
15. Interest rate required (#14 ÷ #1)	12.04%

*   Greater of marginal or average cost of money.

ANALYSIS OF CUSTOMERS LOANS AND DEPOSITS

Loans	Balance
This request	$100,000
Commercial loans	400,000
Real estate loans	
Subtotal	$500,000

Deposits	Balance	Rate	Interest Expense
D.D.A.	($ 50,000)	—	(—)
Money Market	($ 50,000)	7%	($3,500)
C.D.'s	($ 50,000)	9%	($4,500)
Subtotal	($150,000)		($8,000)

11

Legal Documentation

Every lending institution continuously uses standardized forms and legal documents in connection with its lending activities. In many cases, and especially if he or she is relatively inexperienced, the loan officer may have little understanding of the content or significance of the various forms and documents used in the lending operation. Even some experienced loan officers may have little knowledge of the legal significance of the loan documents they use every day. In this chapter, we will examine in detail the significance and usage of standard provisions found in loan documents, and give special attention to the legal terminology contained in them.

All loan forms should be reviewed and updated periodically. Any change in state law or federal regulations which affects a commericial lending operation should result in the review and revision of the pertinent lending documents. Any deficiency in loan provisions discovered during legal proceedings to collect a loan should result in a review and revision. At the very least, even if these problems do not occur, the lending institution's legal counsel should review all loan forms and documents at least every three years, and any suggested changes should be considered and implemented by management.

Promissory Notes

A promissory note is the primary document used in making a loan. It is a written promise, signed by the borrower, to pay the lender, or a holder in due course, a specified amount of money, either on demand, or at a specified time. It is, in fact, a specialized kind of contract between the borrower and the lender. The borrower's legal relationship with the lender is to a great extent determined by the provisions of two basic documents—the promissory note and the security agreement. Therefore, it is extremely important that these two documents contain the provisions necessary to protect the lender's interest to the greatest extent possible.

A standard note form will usually contain basic terminology similar to the following:

Center City U.S.A.
January 7, 19xx

$100,000.00

Ninety days after date, for value received, the undersigned, jointly and severally, promise to pay to the order of the Center City National Bank One hundred thousand and no/100 dollars, at its office in Center City U.S.A.., with interest from date at the rate of 13.00% per annum, until paid, together with costs and reasonable attorney fees if this note be placed in the hands of an attorney for collection.

"For value received" indicates that consideration has been given. "Consideration" is a legal concept which, in simplest terms, is what a promisor obtains in return for his or her promise. Consideration may consist of a promise to do something the promisee is not otherwise bound to do, or to refrain from doing something he or she is otherwise free to do. A general rule of law is that a contract is unenforceable unless there is consideration, and courts have generally held that the consideration must be adequate. In the case of the promissory note above, the borrower promises to repay a certain amount at a specified time at a stated rate of interest, and the loan proceeds are the consideration he or she receives in exchange for his or her promise.

"Jointly and severally" is a legal term indicating, in a case where there is more than one maker, that all makers are obligated as a group *and* individually for the full amount of the obligation. Since the above is a "joint and several" obligation, the holder at its option, may bring action to collect against all the makers jointly, or against any one of them individually, for the full amount due.

"Together with costs and reasonable attorney fees if this note be placed in the hands of an attorney for collection." The law generally allows the lender to insert a provision in the note requiring the borrower to pay court costs and reasonable attorney fees incurred by the lender in enforcing collection of the note. In most jurisdictions the court will decide if the attorney fees requested by the lender are, in fact, reasonable. Lenders' experience in this regard indicates that although they usually will not be able to collect all attorney fees incurred in a collection case, this note provision usually will enable the lender to recover a significant portion of the fees incurred.

Setoff

Most commercial notes will have a provision similar to the following:

> The said bank or its assigns is hereby authorized to apply upon this note or
> upon any other indebtedness of the undersigned or either of them or each
> and every guarantor and endorser hereof to said bank at its option at any
> time before or after the maturity thereof, any money or other property in
> the possession of said bank or its assigns belonging to the undersigned or
> either of them or each and every guarantor and endorser hereof.

This provision refers to a bank's right of "setoff." It is a well recognized
rule of law that, within certain limits, a bank has a right to set off what the
depositor owes the bank against the amount that the bank owes the depositor.
Although the courts have long upheld the right of setoff, they have also
established that there is a limit to this right. While a bank may exercise this
right against a general deposit, it may not do so against some special deposits.
A special deposit is roughly defined as one that is made for a special purpose,
and is to be used only for that purpose. The courts have held that in accepting a
bona fide special deposit the bank waives any right to use the funds for a
purpose other than the one for which they were deposited. Specifically, the
bank waives the right to use the funds to satisfy a debt owed by the depositor to
the bank. An example of a special deposit might be a bank account established
by court order in settlement of a personal injury suit, or a deposit held in an
escrow account. However, burden of proof that the deposit is a special deposit
usually rests on the debtor, and the bank should consult its legal counsel in a
situation of this kind.

According to the terms of the above provision, the bank may exercise
the right of setoff not only against the maker of the note, but also against any
co-maker, endorser, or guarantor, and may do so at any time regardless of
whether the note has matured, although the bank probably would not exercise
the right of setoff until a default or acceleration had occurred. It should be
noted, that according to the above shown provisions, the right of setoff covers
not only money, but also other property in the possession of the bank. "Other
property" might include securities held in safekeeping, repurchase agreements, or other assets that do not specifically fall under the description of a
deposit. In a number of cases involving setoff, a considerable controversy has
arisen as to what constitutes a deposit and as a result most lenders now include
in their setoff provision the broader language covering deposits and other
property.

Under the Bankruptcy Reform Act of 1978, the right of setoff has been
substantially restricted, and the possibility that a setoff will be declared a
preference has been greatly increased, especially in cases where the funds
were deposited to the debtor's account during the 90-day preference period
preceding the filing of the bankruptcy petition, (see chapter 15). Thus, where

a bankruptcy is involved, a bank may find that it is unable to retain funds taken from the debtor's account by setoff, and that it will be required to deliver those funds to the trustee for distribution to the unsecured creditors.

However, there is no doubt that the right of setoff is an extremely useful remedy and every financial institution should be sure that its legal documents contain adequate setoff provisions.

Waiver Provisions

Most standard note forms also contain a provision similar to the following:

> All parties hereto severally waive presentment for payment, demand, and protest, and hereby consent to any extensions, releases or agreement not to sue of any person in any way liable hereon, or of any collateral securing the same, which rights are expressly reserved for the holder hereof.

These are standard waiver provisions found in practically all note forms, in which the borrower waives certain rights often accorded him or her by statute; these include the requirements for formal presentation for payment, formal demand for payment, due notice of dishonor, or notice to co-makers regarding extension or renewal. These waivers relieve the holder of duties imposed by law which are generally inconvenient and time consuming, and which, if neither waived or performed in a timely manner by the holder, may affect the legal validity of the note. The waiver provisions quoted above further contain the makers' consent in advance to certain actions or accommodations which the holder of the note may wish to take regarding the note, such as release of collateral, or release of a co-maker or guarantor.

Acceleration Provision

Most commercial note forms also contain a provision, commonly known as an "acceleration clause," which allows the holder to advance the maturity of the note if it "deems itself insecure." Obviously, if the loan is delinquent, the lender may declare the full amount due and payable. In addition, the lender may accelerate if another event of default has occurred. Most commercial note forms contain default provisions which identify the actions or omissions of the borrower that will constitute a default. However, the provision referred to above goes considerably further. It permits the creditor to accelerate maturity based on a good faith belief that the debtor's situation is deteriorating and that prospects for repayment are diminished. This particular note provision is sometimes called an "insecurity clause."

The Uniform Commercial Code recognizes the creditor's right to accelerate the maturity of a note.

A term providing that one party or his successor in interest may accelerate payment or performance or require collateral or additional collateral "at will" or "when he deems himself insecure" or words of similar import shall be construed to mean that he shall have the power to do so only if he in good faith believes that the prospect of payment or performance is impaired. The burden of establishing lack of good faith is on the party against whom the power has been exercised.[1]

As noted previously, the Uniform Commercial Code sets a good faith requirement. However, it also places the burden of establishing lack of good faith on the debtor. "Reasonable evidence" that the bank is insecure might include the discovery that the debtor has submitted fraudulent financial information; the filing of law suits by other creditors; the closing of the debtor's business; the filing of a tax lien; or a violation of the debtor's loan agreement with the bank.

The acceleration clause is obviously an extremely useful means for taking immediate legal action when the debtor's situation is deteriorating rapidly. Without an acceleration clause or adequate default provisions in its notes, the bank might find itself unable to take any action until the next maturity of the note, even though it is aware of the deterioration of the debtor's position.

Default Provisions

Most commercial notes contain provisions that define what actions or omissions on the part of the borrower shall constitute a default. The following is an example of the default provisions typically found in such notes:

The undersigned shall be in default hereunder upon the occurrence of any of the following events:

(a)   Default in the performance of any provision of this note

(b)   The death, dissolution or the termination of the existence of any of the undersigned or any guarantor hereof

(c)   Any assignment by any of the undersigned or any guarantor for the benefit of creditors, or any receivership, whether in or out of court, of any of the undersigned or any guarantor

(d)   Any proceedings in bankruptcy or for the relief of debtors or readjustment of debts filed by or against any of the undersigned or any guarantor

(e)   Any failure to pay or perform when due any obligation other than this note

(f)   Any failure to maintain or protect collateral

(g)   Any financial statement, application, or supporting statement fur-

---

[1]   UCC 1-208

nished to the bank by the undersigned shall be found to be false in
any material respect

(h)   The undersigned shall fail to furnish additional security immediately upon call by the bank as provided for hereunder

(i)   In the event the bank shall deem itself insecure

A provision of this type clearly defines what constitutes a default. However, it
should be noted that the final provision allows the bank to deem itself insecure
if some other event detrimental to the bank's position occurs which is not
covered in the previous provisions.

Cognovit Clause
In those states that allow cognovit or "confession of judgment" clauses,
commercial notes will generally contain a clause similar to the following:

> And to secure the payment of said amount the undersigned hereby autho-
> rize, irrevocably, any attorney of any Court of Record to appear for under-
> signed in such Court, in term time, or vacation, after the instrument is due
> by maturity or acceleration, and to confess a judgment without process in
> favor of the holder of this Note for such amount as may appear to be unpaid
> thereon, together with interest costs and reasonable attorneys' fees on
> amount due, admitting the allegations of any complaint filed in connection
> with this note, and to waive and release all errors which may intervene in
> such proceedings, and consent to immediate execution upon said judg-
> ment, hereby ratifying and confirming all that said attorney may do by
> virtue hereof.

The cognovit clause is prohibited in many states, and in some other
states, it remains permissible only in business transactions. Although it undoubtedly has been the subject of some abuse, the cognovit clause gives the
creditor a means for obtaining an immediate judgment, which will encumber
the assets of the debtor, in a case where dissipation or liquidation of assets is an
immediate problem. This procedure enables the creditor to obtain a judgment without a hearing, and without the knowledge or consent of the debtor.
Therefore, the confession of judgment procedure raises constitutional issues
concerning due process rights of the debtor, who has not been given a notice
of the proceedings, and has been deprived of an opportunity to defend the
action. The debtor will usually have a right to file a motion to vacate the entry
of a judgment by confession, but the results will depend on the particular facts
of each case.

A lender should be aware that the use of the confession of judgment
clause may create a problem in a consumer transaction, even where allowed
by statute, due to the fact that the transaction may be subject to the right of
recission under the Federal Truth in Lending Law.

Dealing with Co-Obligors

A co-obligor may be defined as a party who becomes obligated for the payment of the note in addition to the maker. The co-obligor may be either a cosigner (also called a co-maker), an endorser, or a guarantor.

A cosigner signs the note along with the primary borrower, thereby becoming a party to the loan on the same terms as the primary borrower. Although he or she usually receives none of the loan proceeds, the cosigner is a co-borrower who is equally obligated to repay the debt. An endorser, rather than signing the face of the note, obligates himself or herself by signing the back of the note, which usually contains a statement such as, "for value received, I (we) jointly and severally, hereby guarantee the payment of the within note." An endorser is not necessarily bound by the provisions on the face of the note and may be in a position to raise legal defenses not available to the primary borrower. For this reason, most lenders consider an endorsement less desirable than a co-signature. A lender who makes a practice of accepting endorsements should consult legal counsel concerning the potential legal problems involved. A guarantor obligates himself or herself for the debt of the borrower by signing a separate agreement called a loan guaranty agreement. The guarantor is bound, not by terms of the note, but by the provisions of the guaranty agreement.

Generally a co-obligor becomes involved in the loan because the lender is not satisfied with the financial strength of the primary borrower. The primary function of the co-obligor is usually to add financial strength to the loan, and since the lender is relying on the financial strength of the co-obligor, it is just as important that adequate financial information be obtained on the co-obligor as the primary borrower. Any co-obligor should be required to submit complete current financial statements, and these should be updated on an annual basis as long as the co-obligor remains obligated on the loan.

The lender should realize that the entry of a co-obligor into the picture creates a sensitive three-way relationship between the lender, the primary borrower, and the co-obligor. Once that three-way relationship exists, the lender has a twofold obligation toward the co-obligor—to keep the co-obligor fully informed of any significant changes in the status of the loan, and to avoid any action that would be detrimental to the interests of the co-obligor. Lenders have learned that dealing with co-obligors may create problems. It inherently involves a third party in the transaction between the lender and the borrower who may not fully understand the transaction, and who may wish to repudiate the guaranty at a later date. The lender must maintain a line of communication with at least two parties instead of one. Experience indicates that the best co-obligor is one who has a personal interest in the success of the borrower's venture—usually a parent, relative, or business partner. Friends and casual acquaintances usually make undesirable co-obligors if they have no personal or financial interest in the borrower's success or failure.

Since most individual borrowers hold at least a portion of their assets in joint tenancy with their spouses, and since the spouse is often an active participant in the business, lenders often find it advantageous for the spouse to be a co-obligor on a loan. This generally contributes materially to the soundness of the loan. However, the lender should be aware of the legal problems related to requiring the spouse to sign the note, and should be careful to insure that no violation of the Equal Credit Opportunity Act occurs in that regard.

Loan Guaranty Agreements

A loan guaranty agreement is a separate agreement between the lender and a third party in which the third party obligates himself or herself for the debt of the borrower. Since the guarantor is bound only by the terms of the guaranty agreement, a lending institution should be careful that the provisions of its guaranty agreement forms contain the same legal remedies as those in the note. All too often a lending institution will use a very comprehensive note form, while its guaranty agreement form is largely lacking in adequate provisions regarding setoff, default, acceleration, and payment of court costs and attorney fees.

A guaranty may be unlimited, in which case it covers any and all debts of the borrower, whatever their type or amount, and is enforceable until revoked by written notice to the lender. Even if revoked, it remains enforceable as to any existing debt. A limited guaranty is similar to an unlimited guaranty except that it puts a dollar limit on the guarantor's liability. A specific guaranty is applicable only to a certain debt which is specifically described in the agreement. An oral guaranty is of no value since it is invalid under the Statute of Frauds.

Lenders should also be aware of the difference between a guaranty of payment and a guaranty of collection. A guaranty of payment, upon default, allows the lender to proceed directly against the guarantor as a primary obligor, regardless of whether any action has been taken against the primary borrower. A guaranty of collection allows the lender to proceed against the guarantor only after all legal remedies against the borrower have been exhausted. Most lending institutions use a guaranty of payment, and Exhibit U contains an example of such a guaranty. Guarantys of collection are often found on dealer paper purchased by lending institutions. Guarantys are strictly construed by the courts, and therefore should be drawn in explicit and concise terms.

How long is a guaranty effective? Theoretically, until it is revoked in writing. However, the older a guaranty the more vulnerable it is to attack, due to the ongoing relationship between the lender and the primary debtor, which may create conditions that may invalidate the guaranty. Therefore, most prudent lenders will request that a guaranty be re-executed under the following circumstances:

1. When the borrower's loan is increased to an amount that exceeds the dollar limit on the guaranty.
2. If there is a significant change in the character of the loan or the relationship between the borrower and the lender. An example of this would be where a borrower has had only short term working capital loans, and then requests a sizeable term loan for the purchase of equipment.
3. When the guaranty agreement is five or six years old. Although theoretically still effective, most lenders feel that it is prudent to have a guaranty re-executed periodically.

All lenders should be aware of the legal concept known as "impairment of collateral." This involves the principle that any action by the lender that results in the exposure of the guarantor being significantly increased may invalidate the guaranty. An example of this is a loan that was originally secured, and on which the collateral is subsequently released by the lender without the consent of the guarantor. Failure of the lender to perfect the security interest may also be considered impairment of collateral. Therefore, to avoid the possibility of invalidating the guaranty, the lender must be extremely careful that any security interest in collateral is perfected properly, and that collateral is not subsequently released without the consent of the guarantor.

In summary, a guarantor can add a great deal of strength to a loan. However, the lender must recognize that the relationship with the guarantor is a sensitive one, and be careful to avoid any actions that would give the guarantor grounds for claiming that the guaranty is unenforceable.

Hypothecation and Subordination Agreements

A hypothecation agreement is a document with which a third party authorizes a borrower to pledge property owned by that third party, often in the form of negotiable securities, as collateral for the borrower's loan. The third party risks only the property being hypothecated, and has no liability on the loan. The lender must perfect its security interest in the collateral being pledged, either by taking physical possession of the property, or by filing in the appropriate public office. Where securities are involved, the lender also must obtain an assignment of each certificate, either in the form of the owner's endorsement in the transfer section of the certificate, or by having the owner sign a separate stock power or bond power. Obviously, the lender improves its position only to the extent of the value of the collateral being hypothecated and, therefore, must consider both the present and probable future value of the collateral, as well as its marketability.

A subordination agreement is a document signed by a third party creditor agreeing to defer the repayment of indebtedness owed to him or her until such time as the borrower has repaid his or her indebtedness to another creditor. In other words, one creditor agrees to give another creditor priority as to the repayment of its debt, which may be existing or future indebtedness. A creditor may also subordinate its priority interest in collateral by means of a subordination agreement. The creditor to whom the subordination agreement is given in effect steps into the shoes of the creditor granting the subordination as to its priority in the collateral. There are many instances in which a subordination agreement may be useful, such as a case where a stockholder has made a substantial loan to a corporation, or a case where a struggling young businessman has received a loan from his parents or other relatives, who may be willing to subordinate, even if unwilling to guarantee or cosign.

In searching for additional financial strength to support a prospective borrower's loan, a lender normally would prefer a cosignature, guaranty, or endorsement (probably in that order of preference) from a third party who has adequate financial strength. However, there are instances in which a hypothecation or subordination can add necessary strength, and these alternatives should not be overlooked by a resourceful lender.

Collateral Assignments

In simple terms, an assignment may be defined as a transfer of rights relating to money or property from one party to another. On occasion, a lender may require that a borrower assign to it his or her rights in a note, certificate of deposit, negotiable instrument, contract, or lease for collateral purposes. This is usually done by means of a written agreement, either by endorsement upon the instrument itself in the case of a note or other negotiable instrument, or by means of a separate document. An assignment of a note might read as follows:

> For value received, and with (without) recourse, the undersigned does hereby sell, assign and transfer all rights, title and interest to the within note to the Center City National Bank, its successors or assigns, and certifies that there is now owing the amount set forth therein and that the undersigned has the right to assign said instrument.

Upon the execution of the assignment, the assignee (the lender) then has the same right to payment of the note formerly held by the assignor. However, the assignee has the duty of notifying the maker of the note of the assignment. Should the assignee fail to do so, and the debtor, without knowledge of the assignment, makes payment in good faith to the assignor, he or she may be discharged of any further liability. The assignee in such a case would have grounds for legal action against the assignor for the money paid, a course of action which under the circumstances might well be futile.

The term "with recourse" indicates that the assignor remains obligated to the assignee for the performance of the obligation. Therefore, the assignor guarantees payment to the assignee if the maker of the note fails to pay. The term "without recourse" indicates that the assignor makes no such guaranty. Obviously, the lender's position is improved if it can obtain an assignment with recourse.

Since contract sales and purchases of real estate are commonplace, it is not unusual for a lender to require the assignment of a debtor's interest in a contract for the sale of real estate. Either the seller's or buyer's interest may be assigned. In the case of a collateral assignment by the seller, the lender looks to the cash payments the buyer is obligated to make for both security and repayment. In the case of a collateral assignment by the buyer, the lender looks to the equity the buyer gains in the real estate as he or she makes periodic payments to provide additional security. Such an assignment might read as follows:

> In consideration of a loan being made concurrently with this assignment, we hereby assign to the Center City National Bank all of our right and interest as contract purchaser in a certain Agreement for Deed dated October 18, 19xx, wherein George Mason and Anna Mason are sellers, and the undersigned is the buyer, of a tract described as follows---

When an assignment is obtained, notification should be given as soon as practical to the other party to the contract, and a written consent to the assignment should be obtained, if possible. If an escrow agent is involved, notification should also be given to the escrow agent. Perfection of an assignment of an interest in a contract for sale or purchase of real estate may require either the recording of the assignment in the county office where deeds are recorded, or the filing of a Form UCC-1, or both, and the lender should consult legal counsel to insure that the proper filing requirements are met.

Assignment of Life Insurance

Many bank loans are secured by the assignment of life insurance policies, which are considered very acceptable collateral. The bank ordinarily holds the policy in its possession, obtains an assignment form signed by the owners and beneficiaries of the policy, and then has this assignment recorded in the records of the insurance company that issued the policy. Generally, a standard assignment form is used throughout the banking industry, and a copy of this form is shown in Exhibit V. The bank also ordinarily obtains from the life insurance company a statement of the current cash value of the policy.

By obtaining the assignment of the life insurance policy, the bank gains two advantages. First, if the borrower defaults, the bank, theoretically at least, may liquidate the policy for its cash value and apply those proceeds against the loan. Second, if the borrower dies during the term of the loan, the proceeds of the life insurance will be available to pay off the loan. However, several factors should be considered by the bank when a loan secured by an assignment of life insurance becomes a problem loan. The insurance company ordinarily retains the right to use the cash value of the policy to pay any delinquent premiums. Therefore, the bank may find that its collateral in the form of cash value has been diminished by the amount of any unpaid premium. Many major life insurance companies often require the signing of a consent form by the policy owner before they will liquidate the policy and forward the cash value to the assignee. If the bank has the cooperation of the borrower, obtaining a signature on this consent form will generally not present a problem. However, if the borrower is no longer cooperative, it may prove difficult to collect the cash value of a policy. Legal action may be required in some cases to force the debtor to sign the consent form, or to force the insurance company to pay.

The standard assignment form is usually executed in three copies. It normally requires the signatures of both the owner(s) and beneficiaries of the policy. It is generally required that these signatures be notarized. One copy of the signed assignment is then retained by the bank, and two copies are forwarded to the insurance company. The insurance company retains one copy for its file, acknowledges the assignment on the other copy, and returns that copy to the lender. The lender should maintain a tickler file to insure that the acknowledged copy is returned by the insurance company.

In a case where the success of a business is dependent upon the management expertise of one individual, an assignment of life insurance on the life of that individual becomes quite important to the lender, since the business might fail upon the death of that one key individual. Most lenders are far too lax in insisting that key management personnel be covered by life insurance, and that insurance be assigned to the bank.

A borrower may offer to name the lender as beneficiary of his or her life insurance policy rather than to assign the policy to the lender. This is unsatisfactory, since a beneficiary does not have the same rights as an assignee, such as a right of notification of cancellation of the policy. Also, the borrower may change the designated beneficiary at any time without notice to or the consent of previous beneficiaries.

Motor Vehicle Titles

From time to time, a lender may wish to perfect a security interest in an automobile, truck, motor home, recreational vehicle, trailer, mobile home, or other vehicle covered by a certificate of title. The laws regarding liens on vehicles are not found in the Uniform Commercial Code, but generally in a separate section of the state statutes. A designated state office, usually that of the Secretary of State, issues certificates of title, which normally contain the date of issue; the name and address of the owner; names and addresses of lien holders; the title number assigned to the vehicle; the description of the vehicle, including make, model, serial number, body type, number of cylinders, and whether it was purchased new or used.

To perfect a lien, it must be registered with the state office that issues certificates of title. To accomplish this, the existing certificate of title must be surrendered, along with an application for a new certificate of title containing the name and the address of the lien holder (and in some states, the amount of the lien), and showing the date of the lien. A new certificate of title is then issued showing the lien, and this normally is mailed directly to the lien holder. Upon satisfaction of the debt, the lien holder signs a release section on the certificate of title and returns it to the debtor.

A lender should take care to register the lien in every instance. Unless this is done, the vehicle may be subject to the claims of other creditors, even though the lender has possession of the certificate of title. Some lenders have made a practice of holding vehicle titles without registering the lien, a practice sometimes known as a "desk drawer lien." This is dangerous and should be avoided. If the lien is not registered, in most states the owner of the vehicle can file a lost title affidavit, obtain a new certificate of title, and then sell the vehicle or pledge it to another creditor.

In addition to registering the lien, the lender should obtain a security agreement. Recent court decisions indicate that a lender who fails to do so may have difficulty enforcing the lien, especially if a bankruptcy is involved. A lender should also be aware that certain violations of the law, such as those involving transportation of drugs, firearms, or alcohol, may result in the forfeiture of the vehicle to federal or state agencies, resulting in a significant loss to the lender.

Aircraft Financings

The Federal Aviation Act of 1958[2] established special documentation and procedures for perfecting security interests in aircraft. To perfect its interest,

---

[2]   49USC §1403

the secured party is required to file a notice of its lien with the Federal Aviation Administration central office in Oklahoma City. This federal filing system preempts the filing requirements of the Uniform Commercial Code, and therefore it is not necessary to file a Form UCC-1 in addition to the FAA filing, although the secured party may do so if it wishes, as a notification to other creditors.

When perfecting a security interest in an aircraft, the lender should follow the procedure prescribed by the FAA, and FAA prescribed forms must be used. First, the lender should obtain a bill of sale properly executed by the prior owner of the aircraft. Exhibit W shows an example of the required form. Second, an application for aircraft registration should be completed in the purchaser's (borrower's) name. Exhibit X shows an example of the required FAA registration form. Third, an aircraft chattel mortgage form should be executed by the borrower. Exhibit Y shows an example of the FAA prescribed aircraft chattel mortgage form. Lastly, the lender should obtain releases of any prior mortgage or mortgages. All documents filed with the Federal Aeronautics Administratin must bear original ink signatures.

All of the above documents should then be submitted to the FAA, or to one of the private companies that specialize in aircraft records and title searches. Most lenders who finance aircraft retain the services of one of these companies, both to assist in recording the documents and to perform title searches. A title search prior to the closing of the loan is recommended to assure the lender that all previous encumbrances are being released. Another title search subsequent to the filing of the lender's aircraft chattel mortgage will verify that the filing has been made properly. When the documents are received and filed by the FAA, it will stamp recording information on the aircraft chattel mortgage and return it to the lender. It will also return a form to the lender that acknowledges the recording of the security instrument. This form has a second purpose, since it will serve as a release form which the lender must execute and return to the FAA when the aircraft lien is satisfied.

Many lenders have been hesitant to finance aircraft since they are unfamiliar with the procedures. Since most lenders do not have an expert in appraising aircraft on their staff, an outside appraisal is usually necessary. A certain amount of specialized knowledge is also required, such as the fact that all aircraft have two identification numbers, a manufacturer's serial number, and a United States registration number. From the standpoint of identifying and tracing the ownership of the aircraft, the United States registration number is the key number.

Many lenders who do finance aircraft have learned that this is very acceptable business. Most aircraft do not depreciate at a rapid rate, and are usually relatively easy to resell. This type of loan has considerable potential, both from the standpoint of generating net income for the bank and enabling the bank to meet all its customers' financial needs.

EXHIBIT U   Loan Guaranty Agreement with Cognovit

LOAN GUARANTY AGREEMENT

For Value Received, and to enable ___JOHN J. DOE, dba DOE TRANSIT LINES___

of ___CHAMPAIGN, ILLINOIS_____, hereinafter designated as "Debtor," to obtain credit, from time to time, of THE COMMERCIAL BANK OF CHAMPAIGN, we hereby request said Bank to extend to said Debtor such credit as said Bank may deem proper, and we hereby jointly and severally guarantee the full and prompt payment to said Bank when due, whether at maturity, by declaration, demand or otherwise, of any and all indebtedness, liabilities and obligations of every nature and kind of said Debtor to said Bank, and every balance and part thereof, whether now owing or due, or which may hereafter, from time to time, be owing or due, and howsoever heretofore or hereafter created or arising or evidenced to the extent of __Two Hundred Thousand and $\frac{no}{100}$ ----------------------- Dollars__, in aggregate at any one time outstanding, plus such interest as may accrue thereon, whether such indebtedness is now existing or arises hereafter and in addition thereto, all costs, expenses and reasonable attorney's fees at any time paid or incurred in collecting and/or enforcing said indebtedness, liabilities and obligations, and in and about enforcing this instrument (all such indebtedness, interest, costs, fees and expenses, being hereinafter called the "Indebtedness").

Each of the undersigned expressly waives all diligence in collection, and all presentment for payment, demand, protest, notice of protest, and notice of nonpayment, dishonor and default, and of the acceptance of this guaranty, and of any and all extensions of credit hereunder, and all demands and notices of any kind in connection with this guaranty or the Indebtedness.

The granting of credit from time to time by said Bank to said Debtor in excess of the amount of this guaranty and without notice to the undersigned is hereby authorized and shall in no way affect or impair this guaranty.

No renewal or extension of time of payment of the Indebtedness, no release or surrender of any security for the Indebtedness of this guaranty, no release of any person primarily or secondarily liable on the Indebtedness (including any maker, endorser or guarantor), no delay in enforcement of payment of the Indebtedness of this guaranty and no delay or omission in exercising any right or power with respect to the Indebtedness or this guaranty, shall affect the liability of any of the undersigned hereunder and each of the above items is expressly authorized and consented to.

In case of the death, dissolution, liquidation, failure, insolvency or bankruptcy of said Debtor, all of said Indebtedness, to the extent of the amount of this guaranty, shall, at the option of said Bank, become immediately due from, and be forthwith paid by the undersigned to said Bank, the same as though said debts, liabilities and obligations had matured by lapse of time.

The undersigned grant(s) to the Bank a security interest in all property of the undersigned, now or at any time hereafter in the possession of the Bank, to secure the payment of any liability of the undersigned under this guaranty and the Bank shall have the rights and remedies of a secured party under the Uniform Commercial Code, as adopted in Illinois in respect to said property, including without limitation thereto, the right to sell or otherwise dispose of any or all of such property. The Bank may apply or set off any deposit or other indebtedness at any time credited by or due from the Bank to any of the undersigned against any liability of the undersigned under this guaranty, if the Indebtedness is not paid when due. Such deposits or other indebtedness may at all times be held and treated as collateral security for the payment of any liability of the undersigned under this guaranty.

Any and all payments upon the Indebtedness made by the Debtor, or by any of the undersigned, or by any other person, and the proceeds of any and all collateral or security for any of the Indebtedness may be applied by the Bank upon such of the items of the Indebtedness as it may determine.

This guaranty shall be construed according to the laws of the State of Illinois, in which state it shall be performed by the undersigned.

This guaranty shall be binding upon the undersigned jointly and severally, and upon the heirs, legal representatives and assigns of the undersigned, and each of them, respectively, and shall inure to the benefit of said Bank, its successors, legal representatives and assigns.

TO SECURE the payment of said Indebtedness the undersigned hereby authorize, irrevocably, any attorney of any court of record to appear for the undersigned in such court, in term time, or vacation, after payment of any part of the Indebtedness is due under the terms of this guaranty, and to confess a judgment without process in favor of the holder of this guaranty for such amount as may appear due under the terms of this guaranty, together with interest, costs and reasonable attorney's fees in amount due, admitting the allegations of any complaint filed in connection with this guaranty and to waive and release all errors which may intervene in any such proceedings, and consent to immediate execution upon said judgment, hereby ratifying and confirming all that said attorney may do by virtue hereof.

Signed by the undersigned at ___CHAMPAIGN, ILLINOIS_____ this __20th__ day of __January__, 19____.

_____   *Lawrence W. Smith*

_____   *Clement J. Adams*

_____

EXHIBIT V   Collateral Assignment of Life Insurance Policy

DeLANO SERVICE, Inc., Allegan, Mich. Form L-10

FORM APPROVED BY
BANK MANAGEMENT COMMISSION
AMERICAN BANKERS ASSOCIATION

ASSIGNMENT OF LIFE INSURANCE POLICY AS COLLATERAL

A. **For Value Received** the undersigned hereby assign, transfer and set over to ___Center City National Bank___

_____ of _ Center City, Illinois___

its successors and assigns, (herein called the "Assignee") Policy No. _06180092P_____ issued by the

_____Republic National Life Insurance Company_____

(herein called the "Insurer") and any supplementary contracts issued in connection therewith (said policy and contracts being herein called the "Policy"), upon the life of ___John J. Doe_____

of _____Champaign, Illinois_____ and all claims, options, privileges, rights, title and interest therein and thereunder (except as provided in Paragraph C hereof), subject to all the terms and conditions of the Policy and to all superior liens, if any, which the Insurer may have against the Policy. The undersigned by this instrument jointly and severally agree and the Assignee by the acceptance of this assignment agrees to the conditions and provisions herein set forth.

B.   It is expressly agreed that, without detracting from the generality of the foregoing, the following specific rights are included in this assignment and pass by virtue hereof:

1. The sole right to collect from the Insurer the net proceeds of the Policy when it becomes a claim by death or maturity;
2. The sole right to surrender the Policy and receive the surrender value thereof at any time provided by the terms of the Policy and at such other times as the Insurer may allow;
3. The sole right to obtain one or more loans or advances on the Policy, either from the Insurer or, at any time, from other persons, and to pledge or assign the Policy as security for such loans or advances;
4. The sole right to collect and receive all distributions or shares of surplus, dividend deposits or additions to the Policy now or hereafter made or apportioned thereto, and to exercise any and all options contained in the Policy with respect thereto; provided, that unless and until the Assignee shall notify the Insurer in writing to the contrary, the distributions or shares of surplus, dividend deposits and additions shall continue on the plan in force at the time of this assignment; and
5. The sole right to exercise all nonforfeiture rights permitted by the terms of the Policy or allowed by the Insurer and to receive all benefits and advantages derived therefrom.

C.   It is expressly agreed that the following specific rights, so long as the Policy has not been surrendered, are reserved and excluded from this assignment and do not pass by virtue hereof:

1. The right to collect from the Insurer any disability benefit payable in cash that does not reduce the amount of insurance;
2. The right to designate and change the beneficiary;
3. The right to elect any optional mode of settlement permitted by the Policy or allowed by the Insurer;

but the reservation of these rights shall in no way impair the right of the Assignee to surrender the Policy completely with all its incidents or impair any other right of the Assignee hereunder, and any designation or change of beneficiary or election of a mode of settlement shall be made subject to this assignment agrees to the conditions and to the rights of the Assignee hereunder.

D.   This assignment is made and the Policy is to be held as collateral security for any and all liabilities of the undersigned, or any of them, to the Assignee, either now existing or that may hereafter arise in the ordinary course of business between any of the undersigned and the Assignee (all of which liabilities are herein called "Liabilities").

E.   The Assignee covenants and agrees with the undersigned as follows:

1. That any balance of sums received hereunder from the Insurer remaining after payment of the then existing Liabilities, matured or unmatured, shall be paid by the Assignee to the persons entitled thereto under the terms of the policy had this assignment not been executed;
2. That the Assignee will not exercise either the right to surrender the Policy or (except for the purpose of paying premiums) the right to obtain policy loans from the Insurer, until there has been default in any of the Liabilities or a failure to pay any premium when due, nor until twenty days after the Assignee shall have mailed, by first-class mail, to the undersigned at the addresses last supplied in writing to the Assignee specifically referring to this assignment, notice of intention to exercise such right; and
3. That the Assignee will upon request forward without unreasonable delay to the Insurer the Policy for endorsement of any designation or change of beneficiary or any election of an optional mode of settlement.

F.   The Insurer is hereby authorized to recognize the Assignee's claims to rights hereunder without investigating the reason for any action taken by the Assignee, or the validity or the amount of the Liabilities or the existence of any default therein, or the giving of any notice under Paragraph E (2) above or otherwise, or the application to be made by the Assignee of any amounts to be paid to the Assignee. The sole signature of the Assignee shall be sufficient for the exercise of any rights under the Policy assigned hereby and the sole receipt of the Assignee for any sums received shall be a full discharge and release therefor to the Insurer. Checks for all or any part of the sums payable under the Policy and assigned herein, shall be drawn to the exclusive order of the Assignee if, when, and in such amounts as may be, requested by the Assignee.

G.   The Assignee shall be under no obligation to pay any premium, or the principal of or interest on any loans or advances on the Policy whether or not obtained by the Assignee, or any other charges on the Policy, but any such amounts so paid by the Assignee from its own funds, shall become a part of the Liabilities hereby secured, shall be due immediately, and shall draw interest at a rate fixed by the Assignee from time to time not exceeding 6% per annum.

H.   The exercise of any right, option, privilege or power given herein to the Assignee shall be at the option of the Assignee, but (except as restricted by Paragraph E (2) above) the Assignee may exercise any such right, option, privilege or power without notice to, or assent by, or affecting the liability of, or releasing any interest hereby assigned by the undersigned, or any of them.

I.   The Assignee may take or release other security, may release any party primarily or secondarily liable for any of the Liabilities, may grant extensions, renewals or indulgences with respect to the Liabilities, or may apply to the Liabilities in such order as the Assignee shall determine, the proceeds of the Policy hereby assigned or any amount received on account of the Policy by the exercise of any right permitted under this assignment, without resorting or regard to other security.

EXHIBIT   V *(Continued)*

J.   In the event of any conflict between the provisions of this assignment and provisions of the note or other evidence of any Liability, with respect to the Policy or rights of collateral security therein, the provisions of this assignment shall prevail.

K.   Each of the undersigned declares that no proceedings in bankruptcy are pending against him and that his property is not subject to any assignment for the benefit of creditors.

Signed and sealed this _____27th___ day of ____October_____, 19.____

_____   *John J. Doe*_____(L.S.)
            Witness   *Insured or Owner*
_____   1016 W. Lincoln St., Champaign, Illinois 61820
                                                                    Address

_____   *Mary A. Doe*_____(L.S.)
            Witness   *Beneficiary*
                                          1016 W. Lincoln St., Champaign, Illinois 61820
                                                                    Address

EXHIBIT W   Aircraft Bill of Sale

FORM APPROVED:
OMB NO. 04-R0076

UNITED STATES OF AMERICA
DEPARTMENT OF TRANSPORTATION FEDERAL AVIATION ADMINISTRATION

AIRCRAFT BILL OF SALE

FOR AND IN CONSIDERATION OF **$ 1.00**   THE
UNDERSIGNED OWNER(S) OF THE FULL LEGAL
AND BENEFICIAL TITLE OF THE AIRCRAFT DES-
CRIBED AS FOLLOWS:

UNITED STATES
REGISTRATION NUMBER **N** 172GH

AIRCRAFT MANUFACTURER & MODEL
Piper PA 23320T Turbo Aztec F

AIRCRAFT SERIAL No.
27-6845073

DOES THIS 28th   DAY OF Jan.   19

HEREBY SELL, GRANT, TRANSFER AND

DELIVER ALL RIGHTS, TITLE, AND INTERESTS

IN AND TO SUCH AIRCRAFT UNTO:

Do Not Write In This Block
FOR FAA USE ONLY

NAME AND ADDRESS
(IF INDIVIDUAL(S), GIVE LAST NAME, FIRST NAME, AND MIDDLE INITIAL.)

PURCHASER

Doe, John J.
1016 W. Lincoln St.
Champaign, Illinois   61820

DEALER CERTIFICATE NUMBER

AND TO   his   EXECUTORS, ADMINISTRATORS, AND ASSIGNS TO HAVE AND TO HOLD
SINGULARLY THE SAID AIRCRAFT FOREVER, AND WARRANTS THE TITLE THEREOF.

IN TESTIMONY WHEREOF my HAVE SET   HAND AND SEAL THIS 28 DAY OF Jan 19

NAME (S) OF SELLER (TYPED OR PRINTED)	SIGNATURE (S) (IN INK) (IF EXECUTED FOR CO-OWNERSHIP, ALL MUST SIGN.)	TITLE (TYPED OR PRINTED)
Owen C. Black	*Owen C. Black*	Owner

SELLER

ACKNOWLEDGMENT (NOT REQUIRED FOR PURPOSES OF FAA RECORDING; HOWEVER, MAY BE REQUIRED
BY LOCAL LAW FOR VALIDITY OF THE INSTRUMENT.)

ORIGINAL: TO FAA

AC FORM 8050-2 (8-76) (0052-629-0002)

EXHIBIT X   Aircraft Registration Application

FORM APPROVED OMB NO. 04-R0076

UNITED STATES OF AMERICA DEPARTMENT OF TRANSPORTATION FEDERAL AVIATION ADMINISTRATION-MIKE MONRONEY AERONAUTICAL CENTER AIRCRAFT REGISTRATION APPLICATION	CERT. ISSUE DATE

UNITED STATES REGISTRATION NUMBER **N** 172GH	
AIRCRAFT MANUFACTURER & MODEL Piper PA 23320T Turbo Aztec F	
AIRCRAFT SERIAL No. 27-6845073	FOR FAA USE ONLY

TYPE OF REGISTRATION (Check one box)

☒ 1. Individual   ☐ 2. Partnership   ☐ 3. Corporation   ☐ 4. Co-Owner   ☐ 5. Gov't.

NAME OF APPLICANT (Person(s) shown on evidence of ownership. If individual, give last name, first name, and middle initial.)

DOE, JOHN J.

ADDRESS (Permanent mailing address for first applicant listed.)

Number and street: ___1016 W. LINCOLN ST.___

Rural Route: P.O. Box:

CITY CHAMPAIGN	STATE ILLINOIS	ZIP CODE 61820

☐   **CHECK HERE IF YOU ARE ONLY REPORTING A CHANGE OF ADDRESS**

ATTENTION! Read the following statement before signing this application.

A false or dishonest answer to any question in this application may be grounds for punishment by fine and/or imprisonment (U.S. Code, Title 18, Sec. 1001).

CERTIFICATION

I/WE CERTIFY:

(1) That the above aircraft is owned by the undersigned applicant, who is:
Check one as appropriate

a. ☒ A citizen of the United States;

b. ☐ A resident alien, with alien registration (Form 1-151 or Form 1-551) No. _____

c. ☐ A foreign-owned corporation organized and doing business under the laws of (state or possession) _____, and said aircraft is based and primarily used in the United States. Records of flight hours are available for inspection at _____

(2) That the aircraft is not registered under the laws of any foreign country; and
(3) That legal evidence of ownership is attached or has been filed with the Federal Aviation Administration.

NOTE: If executed for co-ownership all applicants must sign. Use reverse side if necessary.

	SIGNATURE *John J. Doe*	TITLE OWNER	DATE 28 Jan
EACH PART OF THIS APPLICATION MUST BE SIGNED IN INK.	SIGNATURE	TITLE	DATE
	SIGNATURE	TITLE	DATE

NOTE:	Pending receipt of the Certificate of Aircraft Registration, the aircraft may be operated for a period not in excess of 90 days, during which time the PINK copy of this application must be carried in the aircraft.

EXHIBIT Y Aircraft Chattel Mortgage

This mortgage, made this 28th day of January , 19   by and between John J. Doe

whose address is *(Number, street, city, zone, and State)*   1016 West Lincoln St., Champaign, Illinois 61820

hereinafter called the MORTGAGOR, and Center City National Bank

whose address is *(Number, street, city, zone, and State)*   123 Main St., Center City, Illinois 61111

hereinafter called the MORTGAGEE,

WITNESSETH: That the said mortgagor, being justly indebted unto the said mortgagee in the sum of Eighty Eight Thousand and no/100

dollars ($ 88,000.00) as evidenced by a promissory note referred to herein, grants, bargains, sells, and mortgages to the said mortgagee, his heirs, administrators, successors, and assigns, the following described aircraft:

Aircraft make and model Piper PA 23320T Turbo Aztec F   FAA registration number N172GH

Manufacturer's serial number 27-6845073

Together with all equipment and accessories attached thereto or used in connection therewith including the following:

all of which are included in the term aircraft as used herein.

The above described aircraft is hereby mortgaged to the mortgagee for the purpose of securing in the order named:

First: The payment of all indebtedness evidenced by and according to the terms of that certain promissory note, hereinbelow described, and all renewals and extensions thereof:

Note bearing date of Jan. 24   19   executed by the mortgagor and payable to the order of Center City National Bank

in the aggregate principal sum of $ 88,000.00   with interest thereon at the

rate of 16.00   per centum per annum, from date, payable in installments as follows:

The principal and interest of said note is payable in   60   installments of $ 2161.40   each on the 1st day

of each successive month beginning with the   1st   day of March   19X4 .

The last payment of $ 2161.40   is due on the   1st   day of February   19X9

Second: The prompt and faithful discharge and performance of each agreement of the mortgagor herein contained made with or for the benefit of the mortgagee in connection with the indebtedness to secure which this instrument is executed, and the repayment of any sums expended or advanced by the mortgagee for the maintenance or preservation of the property mortgaged hereby or in enforcing his rights hereunder.

Said mortgagor hereby declares and hereby warrants to the said mortgagee that he is the absolute owner of the legal and beneficial title to the said aircraft and in possession thereof, and that the same is free and clear of all liens, encumbrances, and adverse claims whatsoever, except as follows: *(If no liens other than this mortgage indicate "None".)*

None

The following space is for the inclusion of any special provisions which the parties hereto are desirous of making a part of this mortgage.

Provided, however, that if the mortgagor, his heirs, administrators, successors, or assigns shall pay said note and the interest thereon in accordance with the terms thereof and shall keep and perform all and singular the terms, covenants, and agreements in this mortgage, then this mortgage shall be null and void.

Time is of the essence of this mortgage. It is hereby agreed that if default be made in the payment of any part of the principal or interest of the promissory note secured hereby at the time and in the manner therein specified, or if any breach be made of any obligation or promise of the mortgagor herein contained or secured hereby, or if any or all of the property covered hereby be hereafter sold, leased, transferred, mortgaged, or otherwise encumbered without the written consent of the mortgagee first had and obtained, or in the event of the seizure of the aircraft under execution or other legal process, or if for any other reason the mortgagee may deem himself insecure, then the whole principal sum unpaid upon said promissory note, with the interest accrued thereon, or advanced under the terms of this mortgage, or secured thereby, and the interest thereon, shall immediately become due and payable at the option of the mortgagee. *(Any other causes of default should be listed below:)*

Upon default, mortgagee may at once proceed to foreclose this mortgage in any manner provided by law, or he may at his option, and he is hereby empowered so to do, with or without a foreclosure action, enter upon the premises where the said aircraft may be and take possession thereof; and remove and sell and dispose of the same at public or private sale, and from the proceeds of such sale retain all costs and charges incurred by him in the taking or sale of said aircraft, including any reasonable attorney's fees incurred; also all sums due him on said promissory note, under any provisions thereof, or advanced under the terms of this mortgage, and interest thereon, or due or owing to the said mortgagee, under any provisions of this mortgage, or secured hereby, with the interest thereon, and any surplus of such proceeds remaining shall be paid to the mortgagor, or whoever may be lawfully entitled to receive the same. If a deficiency occurs, the mortgagor agrees to pay such deficiency forthwith.

Said mortgagee or his agent may bid and purchase at any sale made under this mortgage or herein authorized, or at any sale made upon foreclosure of this mortgage.

IN WITNESS WHEREOF, the mortgagor has hereunto set   hand and seal on the day and year first above written.

Name of mortgagor   **John J. Doe**

Signature(s) *(in ink)*   *John J. Doe*
(If executed for co-ownership, all must sign)

Title   **Owner**
(If signed for a corporation, partnership, owner, or agent)

ACKNOWLEDGMENT BY MORTGAGOR

State of   **Illinois**

County of   **Lincoln**

(SEAL)

On this **28th** day of **January**, 19**44**, before me personally appeared the above-named mortgagor, to me known to be the person described in and who executed the foregoing chattel mortgage, and acknowledged that he executed the same as his free act and deed, and, if said chattel mortgage be that of a corporation swore that he was duly authorized to execute the same. Given under my hand and official seal the day and year written above.

(SEAL)

My commission expires   **Jan. 3, 19X5**

Samuel P. Adams
(Signature of notary public *(in ink)*)

ASSIGNMENT BY MORTGAGEE

For value received, the undersigned mortgagee does hereby sell, assign, and transfer all his right, title and interest in and to the foregoing

note and chattel mortgage, and the aircraft covered thereby, unto

whose address is *(Number, street, city, zone, and State)*

and hereby authorizes the said   to do every act, and thing necessary to collect and discharge the same. The undersigned mortgagee warrants and agrees to defend the title of said aircraft hereby conveyed against all lawful claims and demands except the rights of the maker. The undersigned mortgagee warrants that he is the owner of a valid security interest in the said aircraft. *(A guaranty clause or any other provisions which the parties hereto are desirous of making a part of this assignment should be included in the following space.)*

Dated this   day of   , 19 .

Name of mortgagee (assignor)

Signature(s) *(in ink)*
(If executed for co-ownership, all must sign)

Title
(If signed for a corporation, partnership, owner, or agent)

ACKNOWLEDGMENT BY MORTGAGEE (ASSIGNOR)

State of

County of

(SEAL)

On this   day of   , 19 , before me personally appeared the above-named mortgagee, to me known to be the person described in and who executed the foregoing assignment, and acknowledged that he executed the same as his free act and deed, and, if said assignment be that of a corporation swore that he was duly authorized to execute the same. Given under my hand and official seal the day and year written above.

My commission expires

(Signature of notary public *(in ink)*)

12

The Uniform Commercial Code

James W. Evans and Robert H. Behrens

Secured Transactions

The Uniform Commercial Code is the body of law that governs the great majority of commercial transactions in the United States today. The Code has been adopted in 49 states: Louisiana is the only exception. Both the National Conference of Commissioners on Uniform State Laws and the American Law Institute had advocated a uniform body of law governing commercial transactions since the 1940s. In 1961 a permanent editorial board was created, which keeps the Code up to date with appropriate amendments. When the 1962 Official Text was adopted by the various states, it replaced a sizeable body of previous law, including the Uniform Stock Transfer Act, the Uniform Trust Receipts Act, the Uniform Conditional Sales Act, and various other state statutes covering chattel mortgages, negotiable instruments, and the sale and transfer of goods.

One of the purposes of the Uniform Commercial Code was to create a uniform body of law for the entire country. Unfortunately, over the past 20 years the Code, as it exists in the various states, has become less uniform than the original drafters intended. In 1972 a new Official Text, which revised a number of key provisions in the code, was issued. Some 30 states, including the large mercantile centers of California, Illinois, New York, Ohio, and Texas, adopted the 1972 version of the Code, while the remaining states continue to operate under the 1962 version. In addition, there were minor amendments to the Code in 1966 and 1977 which some states have adopted. Most state legislatures have had a tendency to tinker with the Code by adding

James W. Evans is a partner in the law firm of Evans & Froelich in Champaign, Illinois, where he specializes in banking, real estate and commercial litigation. He holds a B.A. degree from Beloit College and an L.L.B. from the University of Illinois College of Law. Mr. Evans lectures extensively for various banking organizations in the area of secured lending and bankruptcy law.

nonconforming amendments to some sections of the Code. The result is that while most of the major concepts and provisions of the Code remain intact, there are significant variations in some Code provisions from state to state, and the lender must be familiar with the particular Code provisions of his or her state.

Citations of the Uniform Commercial Code are made in a standardized format, such as "UCC 9-312." The first numeral indicates which article of the code is being cited. There are a total of 11 articles in the Code. The second number indicates which part of that article is being cited, and the final two numerals indicate the specific section.

The Code is quite comprehensive in the variety of commercial transactions it covers, and the reader may best gain a perspective of the broad coverage of the Uniform Commercial Code by perusing a listing of the titles of the various articles, and their parts.

Article   1:   General Provisions
      Part 1:   Short Title, Construction, Application and Subject Matter of the Act
      Part 2:   General Definitions and Principles of Interpretation
Article   2:   Sales
      Part 1:   Short Title, General Construction and Subject Matter
      Part 2:   Form, Formation and Readjustment of Contract
      Part 3:   General Obligation and Construction of Contract
      Part 4:   Title, Creditors, and Good Faith Purchasers
      Part 5:   Performance
      Part 6:   Breach, Repudiation and Excuse
      Part 7:   Remedies
Article   3:   Commercial Paper
      Part 1:   Short Title, Form and Interpretation
      Part 2:   Transfer and Negotiation
      Part 3:   Rights of a Holder
      Part 4:   Liability of Parties
      Part 5:   Presentment, Notice of Dishonor and Protest
      Part 6:   Discharge
      Part 7:   Advice of International Sight Draft
Article   4:   Bank Deposits and Collections
      Part 1:   General Provisions and Definitions
      Part 2:   Collection of Items: Depository and Collecting Banks
      Part 3:   Collection of Items: Payor Banks
      Part 4:   Relationship Between Payor Bank and Its Customer
      Part 5:   Collection of Documentary Drafts
Article   5:   Letters of Credit
Article   6:   Bulk Transfers
Article   7:   Warehouse Receipts, Bills of Lading and Other Documents of Title
      Part 1:   General
      Part 2:   Warehouse Receipts: Special Provisions
      Part 3:   Bills of Lading: Special Provisions
      Part 4:   Warehouse Receipts and Bills of Lading: General Obligations
      Part 5:   Warehouse Receipts and Bills of Lading: Negotiation and Transfer
      Part 6:   Warehouse Receipts and Bills of Lading: Miscellaneous Provisions

Articles 3,4,5,7, and 9 are obviously of special interest to the banker. A bank's principal operations activities are governed by Article 4, and most loan transactions are subject to the provisions of Article 9.

Article 9 of the Uniform Commercial Code

Article 9 primarily covers security interests in personal property and fixtures (items of personal property that are attached to real estate). It therefore governs most secured loan transactions, and it is imperative that the lender understand these rules of the game prescribed by Article 9. Article 9 establishes a new concept, that of a "security interest," which replaces such pre-code security devices as the "chattel mortgage," "conditional sale," "trust receipt," and "factor's lien." A security interest may be defined as an interest in personal property or fixtures that secure payment or performance of an obligation.[1] The basic document which creates a security interest is called a security agreement. Lenders usually refer to a security interest as a "lien." This is correct, but the lender must recognize the difference between a consensual lien and non-consensual liens, which arise by statute or judicial proceedings. A security interest is established with the consent of the debtor and based on an agreement between the debtor and the secured party. A security interest may be created to secure a loan made by a lender, to secure a seller of goods on credit, or to secure the performance of some other kind of obligation.

Excluded Transactions

It has been noted that Article 9 covers only personal property and fixtures, and therefore loan transactions where the security is a mortgage or

---

[1]   UCC 1-201(37)

trust deed on real estate are not covered by Article 9. UCC 9-104 specifically excludes certain types of transactions:

(a) A security interest subject to any statute of the United States, to the extent that such statute governs the rights of parties to and third parties affected by transactions in particular types of property. Examples of this would be ship mortgages and aircraft liens, which are covered by federal statutes.

(b) A landlord's lien.

(c) A lien given by statute or other rule of law for services or materials, except as provided in UCC 9-310 on priority of such liens. An example would be a mechanic's lien.

(d) A transfer of a claim for wages, salary or other compensation of an employee.

(e) A transfer by a government or governmental subdivision or agency.

(f) The sale of accounts or chattel paper as part of a sale of the business out of which they arose, or an assignment of accounts or chattel paper which is for the purpose of collection only, or a transfer of a right to payment under a contract to an assignee who is also to do the performance under the contract, or a transfer of a single account to an assignee in whole or in partial satisfaction of a preexisting indebtedness.

(g) A transfer of an interest in or claim in or under any policy of insurance, except as provided with respect to proceeds and priorities in proceeds in Sections 9-306 and 9-312. Loans secured by the assignment of life insurance are therefore not covered by Article 9.

(h) A right represented by a judgment, other than a judgment taken on a right to payment which was collateral.

(i) Any right of setoff.

(j) Except to the extent that provision is made for fixtures in Section 9-313, the creation or transfer of an interest in or lien on real estate, including a lease or rents thereunder.

(k) A transfer in whole or in part of any claim arising out of tort (a tort is a civil injury).

(l) A transfer of an interest in any deposit account, except as provided with respect to proceeds and priorities in proceeds in sections 9-306 and 9-312.[2]

After-Acquired Property, Future Advances, and Proceeds

Article 9 allows the commercial lender much more flexibility than previously existed under pre-code law. For instance, the lender is no longer

[2]   UCC 9-104

required to relate specific items of collateral to a specific note, as was required under the old chattel mortgage procedure. In addition, the lender has several valuable options available to it that did not exist under pre-code law. One of these pertains to having the security interest cover after-acquired property of the debtor. UCC 9-204 (1) states that, except as provided in Sub-section 2, (which pertains to consumer goods), a security agreement may provide that any obligations covered by the security agreement are to be secured by after-acquired collateral. In other words, the debtor may grant to the secured party a security interest not only in the property he or she owns today, but also in property of the same type acquired by the debtor at some unspecified future date. This is true even though some other creditor may have advanced the funds for the purchase of those after-acquired assets, unless that third party creditor has perfected a purchase money security interest, which will be discussed in a subsequent section. If the secured party intends to cover after-acquired property, that must be clearly stated in an after-acquired property clause included in both the security agreement and the financing statement.

Another benefit available to the lender relates to having future loan advances covered by a preexisting security agreement. UCC 9-204 (3) states that obligations covered by a security agreement may include future advances or other value, whether or not the advances or value are given pursuant to a commitment. Therefore, the security interest created at the time of a loan transaction may cover not only that transaction, but any number of future loan transactions, even though no future loans were committed at the time of the original transaction. Since the coverage of future advances is not automatic, a "future advances clause" must be contained in the security agreement. Most standard form security agreements contain a clause covering "all present and future debts" or "all indebtedness and obligations whatsoever of the debtor to the secured party, whether direct or indirect, absolute or contingent, or due or to become due, and whether now existing or hereafter arising."

It is obvious that the lender who uses both the after-acquired property clause and the future advances clause in loan documentation greatly enhances its security position. These two clauses also enable the lender to establish and maintain a "floating lien" in receivables and inventory. Since most loans secured by receivables and inventory involve multiple disbursements, and are revolving in nature, with receivables and inventory constantly turning over, the lender would have severe problems in maintaining its security position in the absence of the after-acquired property and future advances clauses. By utilizing these Code provisions, the lender is able to secure successive disbursements with a continuing security interest in receivables and inventory, which are in a constant state of flux.

The Code also provides the lender with increased protection and flexibility in dealing with proceeds. Proceeds may be defined as whatever is received upon the sale, exchange, collection or other disposition of collateral or proceeds. Money, checks, deposit accounts, and the like are cash proceeds. All other proceeds are non-cash proceeds.[3] The Code makes it clear that a security interest continues in any identifiable proceeds of the sale of collateral. Under the 1962 version of the Code, a security interest is continuously perfected in proceeds from the disposition of collateral for ten days after receipt of the proceeds by the debtor, but this perfected status lapses unless the financing statement covering the original collateral also specifically covered proceeds, or a new security interest in those proceeds is perfected before expiration of the ten-day period. Under the 1962 Code, the form UCC-1 contained a proceeds box which had to be checked if proceeds were to be covered. This problem of checking the proceeds box was eliminated in the 1972 version of the Code, which automatically extends the security interest to proceeds without the necessity of mentioning proceeds in the UCC-1. Since, in the case of a loan secured by receivables and inventory, the collateral is constantly being converted to proceeds, this extension of the security interest to proceeds is essential. Also, in a situation where the debtor is liquidating collateral without the consent of the lender, the existence of this proceeds provision facilitates recovery by the lender.

Classification of Collateral

Under the provisions of the Code, a wide variety of personal assets may be used for collateral. To deal with the great variation in the kinds of collateral in which a security interest may be established, the Code classifies all collateral into certain categories. It is crucial that the lender understand these categories, since the procedure for establishing and perfecting a security interest varies depending upon the category into which the collateral fits. In order to comprehend the operation of the Code, it is necessary to develop an understanding of this classification system. The principal classifications are as follows:

1.   *Goods*. Goods include all things which are moveable at the time the security interest attaches, or which are fixtures, but does not include money, documents, instruments, accounts, chattel paper, general intangibles, or minerals or the like before extraction. Goods also includes standing timber, the unborn young of animals, and growing crops.[4]

---

[3]   UCC 9-306(1)
[4]   UCC 9-105(h)

(a) *Consumer goods*. These are goods used or bought for use primarily for personal, family, or household purposes.[5]

(b) *Equipment*. Equipment is goods used or bought for use primarily in business (including farming or a profession) or by a debtor who is a nonprofit organization, or a governmental subdivision or agency, or if the goods are not included in the definitions of inventory, farm products, or consumer goods.[6]

(c) *Inventory*. Inventory is goods held by a person who holds them for sale *or lease* or to be furnished under contracts of service, or if he has so furnished them, or if they are raw materials, work in process or materials used or consumed in a business.[7]

(d) *Farm products*. Farm products are crops or livestock or supplies used or produced in farming operations, or if they are products of crops or livestock in their unmanufactured states (such as ginned cotton, wool clip, maple syrup, milk, and eggs), and if they are in possession of a debtor engaged in raising, fattening, grazing, or other farming operations. If goods are farm products they are neither inventory nor equipment.[8]

The category into which goods fall is determined by the manner in which they will be used by the debtor. Therefore, identical goods used for different purposes may fall into different categories. For example, a boat held by a dealer for resale would be inventory, while the same boat used by a commercial fisherman would be equipment, or if used by a consumer as a pleasure craft, it would be consumer goods. Similarly, grain held by a farmer would be farm products, while grain held by a grain elevator would be inventory. An automobile driven by a car dealer as a business vehicle would be equipment, while a similar automobile held for resale would be inventory. A third similar automobile driven by the car dealer's family for their personal use would be consumer goods. These examples illustrate that the lender must ascertain the intended use of the goods to determine which procedures for perfecting a security interest are applicable.

2. *Instruments*. An instrument is a negotiable instrument or a security, or any other writing which evidences a right to the payment of money and is not itself a security agreement or lease, and is of a type which is in ordinary course of business transferred by delivery with any

---

[5] UCC 9-109(1)
[6] UCC 9-109(2)
[7] UCC 9-109(4)
[8] UCC 9-109(3)

necessary endorsement or assignment.[9] A negotiatable instrument is further defined by the Code as a draft, check, certificate of deposit, or note, which is signed by the maker or drawer, contains an unconditional promise or order to pay a sum certain in money and no other promise, order, obligation or power given by the maker or drawer, and which is payable on demand or at a definite time, and which is payable to order or to bearer.[10] A security is an instrument that is issued in bearer or registered form, and which is commonly dealt in on securities exchanges or markets, or commonly recognized in any area in which it is issued or dealt in as a medium for investment, and is either one of a class or series, or by its terms is divisible into a class or series of instruments, and evidences a share, participation, or other interest in property or in an enterprise, or evidences an obligation of the issuer.[11]

3. *Documents.* A document of title is a bill of lading, dock warrant, dock receipt, warehouse receipt, or order for the delivery of goods, and also any other document which in the regular course of business or financing is treated as adequately evidencing that the person in possession of it is entitled to receive, hold, and dispose of the document and the goods it covers. To be a document of title, a document must purport to be issued by, or addressed to a bailee, and purport to cover goods in the bailee's possession, which are either identified, or are fungible portions of an identified mass.[12]

4. *Chattel Paper.* Chattel paper is a writing or writings which evidence both a monetary obligation and a security interest in or a lease of specific goods.[13] The agreement lenders generally refer to as "dealer paper" falls into this category.

5. *Accounts and Contract Rights.* These are rights which differ from the other categories of collateral in that they are not tangible, nor are they physically represented by a document or instrument. The Code defines an account as any right to payment for goods sold or leased, or for services rendered, which is not evidenced by an instrument or chattel paper, whether or not it has been earned by performance. A contract right may be described as any right to payment under a contract not yet earned by performance and not evidenced by an instrument or chattel paper.

6. *General Intangibles.* General intangibles are described as any personal property (including things in action) other than goods, accounts,

---

[9]   UCC 9-105(i)
[10]   UCC 3-104(1)
[11]   UCC 8-102(1)
[12]   UCC 1-201(15)
[13]   UCC 9-105(b)

chattel paper, documents, instruments, and money.[14] Without doubt, general intangibles is the least understood category of collateral. This seems to be a catch-all category which covers any item of collateral that does not readily fit into any other category. Royalties, liquor licenses, patents, copyrights, blueprints, tax refunds, or the proceeds from a pending lawsuit are all examples of assets that might be classified as general intangibles.

The Security Agreement

The underlying basis for all secured transactions is the concept of attachment, which means that the lender or secured party has obtained enforceable rights to certain collateral. Under Article 9, a security interest cannot be effective until it "attaches," and three specific events must occur to have attachment. First, the debtor must have executed a written security agreement which establishes the legal relationship between the debtor and secured party. Second, consideration must have been given at that time by the secured party, and third, the debtor must have rights in the collateral.[15]

The Code defines a security agreement as an agreement between the debtor and the secured party which creates or provides for a security interest.[16] The requirements for a valid security agreement are as follows:

1.   It must be in writing and must be signed by the debtor, except in situations where the collateral is in the possession of the secured party.

2.   It must contain a "granting" clause in which the debtor gives to the secured party a security interest in the collateral to secure payment or performance of an obligation.

3.   It must contain a description of the collateral. There has been a great deal of controversy as to what constitutes a sufficient description. The Code states that any description of personal property or real estate is sufficient whether or not it is specific, if it reasonably identifies what is described.[17]

4.   It must contain a recital of the obligations secured by the collateral. The scope of the obligation may be very limited, as in a situation involving one specific note, or it may be very broad, as where the collateral secures "all and any obligations of the debtor of any kind to the secured party, whether direct or indirect, absolute or contingent, now existing or hereafter arising."

[14]   UCC 9-106
[15]   UCC 9-203(1)
[16]   UCC 9-105(1)
[17]   UCC 9-110

5.   Although not required by the Code, the security agreement will usually contain various covenants and warranties by the debtor, such as:

(a)   The place of the debtor's residence and the location at which the collateral will be kept.

(b)   That the debtor is the sole owner of the collateral and that it is free and clear of any prior security interests, liens or encumbrances.

(c)   That the debtor will not sell or otherwise transfer the collateral or the proceeds thereof without the consent of the lender.

(d)   That the debtor will not change the intended use of the collateral without notice to or consent from the lender.

(e)   That the debtor will maintain adequate casualty insurance coverage on the collateral, with a loss payable clause in favor of the lender.

(f)   That the debtor will pay promptly all taxes and assessments levied upon the collateral.

6.   Also, a security agreement will usually contain a comprehensive list of default provisions, similar to those found in most promissory notes. Default provisions were discussed in chapter 11, and Exhibit Z contains an example of a standard form security agreement.

Collateral Descriptions

Collateral descriptions are the cause of more problems and litigation than any other aspect of Article 9. UCC 9-110 simply states that any description of personal property or real estate is sufficient whether or not it is specific, if it reasonably identifies what is described. A great deal of discussion by lenders, attorneys, and judges has centered around what is sufficient and what is reasonable. There is no doubt that a defective description can cause severe problems for the lender, and a description that is incorrect will simply invalidate a security interest. Collateral that is correctly described, except for a wrong serial number, or other minor irregularity, may be lost to a competing creditor who raises the issue.

Is a specific and detailed description preferable? Not necessarily. An overly detailed description may be too narrow in scope and compounds the risk of error. Is a very broad and generic description such as "all personal property" or "all assets of the borrower" acceptable? Probably not. The courts have generally rejected descriptions of this nature as being too broad in scope. A preferable description is one that is neither overly specific nor overly broad. However, judicial decisions concerning collateral descriptions vary considerably between jurisdictions, and it is essential for the lender to consult with legal counsel when dealing with descriptions of collateral in secured transactions.

The Code states that the financing statement must contain a statement indicating the types, or describing the items of collateral.[18] This seems to imply that the description in the financing statement may be more general in nature than that set forth in the security agreement. However, a distinguished expert in the field, Professor Barkley Clark of the University of Kansas School of Law, recommends that the lender avoid a sharp discrepancy between descriptions in the security agreement and financing statement.[19] Based on these guidelines, it would appear that a collateral description such as "all manufacturing equipment" would be adequate in most cases. Judicial decisions are mixed on the adequacy of the term "equipment" alone, but it would appear that terms such as manufacturing equipment, farm equipment, etc. are usually acceptable. The lender should also remember that if after-acquired property is to be covered, that fact must be clearly stated in the collateral description, such as "all inventory and receivables now owned or hereafter acquired."

If the lender intends to obtain a security interest in basically all of the assets of a business, terminology such as the following is often used: "All equipment now owned or hereafter acquired, including but not limited to, manufacturing equipment, delivery equipment, warehouse equipment, and office equipment; office, warehouse, and plant furnishings and fixtures; all inventory, contracts, and accounts receivable now owned or hereafter acquired; all general intangibles; all proceeds from the sale, liquidation or disposition of any of the foregoing items."

The important thing for the lender to remember is that the description of collateral should not be treated casually, and that the use of canned descriptions can be risky. Prior to the execution of the security agreement and financing statement by the debtor, the collateral description should be carefully reviewed by the loan officer to insure that it contains a correct listing of the collateral, and that it is properly described.

Perfection and Priority

Although the lender may have enforceable rights in collateral because attachment has occurred, those rights will be ineffective against competing third party creditors unless the lender's security interest has been perfected. In other words, in the absence of third party creditors, the lender may, upon default under the terms of a security agreement, repossess and liquidate the

---

[18]   UCC 9-402(1)

[19]   Clark, Barkley, The Law of Secured Transactions Under the Uniform Commercial Code, 1980, Warren Gorham & Lamont, Inc., Boston, p. 2-48.

collateral in which its security interest has attached, even though its security interest has never been perfected. Of course, the possible existence of third party creditors makes perfection absolutely essential if the lender is to establish its priority and avoid losing the collateral to a competing claimant.

The Code states that a security interest is perfected when it has attached and when all the applicable steps required for perfection have been taken.[20] As the terms of the security agreement determine the relationship between the debtor and the secured party, so perfection establishes the legal relationship between the secured party and any third party creditors who may have a claim against the same collateral. Perfection may be accomplished in three ways: by attachment alone, by taking possession of the collateral, or by filing a financing statement. The method to be used depends on the category of collateral involved.

1.   *Perfection by Attachment Alone*. When certain categories of collateral are involved, perfection may occur upon attachment. In other words, the secured party need not take possession or make a public filing to perfect its interest. This creates a secret lien and third party creditors have no way of determining that the security interest exists. The following are examples of transactions where perfection occurs by attachment alone:

(a)   A purchase money security interest in consumer goods (except for fixtures and titled vehicles) is probably the most notable example of a transaction where perfection is by attachment alone. The Code exempts this kind of transaction from the filing requirement.[21]

(b)   In those states operating under the 1972 version of the Code, an assignment of the debtor's beneficial interest in a trust or a decedent's estate is exempted from the filing rule.[22] This is especially significant in states like Illinois and Florida, where there is widespread use of land trusts.

(c)   The 1962 version of the Code exempts a purchase money security interest in farm equipment (except for fixtures and titled vehicles) from the filing requirement, provided the purchase price is $2500 or less.[23]

(d)   A filing is not required to perfect a security interest in instruments or documents of title for 21 days from the time of attachment, to the extent that it arises for new value given under a written

---

[20]   UCC 9-303(1)
[21]   UCC 9-302(1)(d)
[22]   UCC 9-302(1)(c) (1972 Code)
[23]   UCC 9-302(1)(c) (1962 Code)

security agreement.[24] This exemption covers those situations where the debtor must have temporary possession of the collateral to arrange proper transfer and delivery. In addition, a security interest remains perfected for 21 days in an instrument or document of title when the secured party turns over to the debtor the collateral for the purpose of shipment, sale, or exchange.[25] Section 9-302 of the Code identifies several other situations in which perfection may occur by attachment alone. The interested reader should consult that section of the Code for more information regarding these exceptions.

2. *Perfection by Possession*. The second method for perfecting a security interest is that of taking possession of the collateral. UCC 9-305 states that a security interest in letters of credit and advices of credit, goods, instruments, money, negotiable documents, or chattel paper may be perfected by the secured party's taking possession of the collateral. In the case of some collateral, possession is the only acceptable means of perfecting, and a security interest in money or instruments (other than instruments that constitute part of chattel paper) generally can be perfected only when the secured party takes possession.[26] Some categories of collateral, such as negotiable documents, goods, and chattel paper, can be perfected either by taking possession or by filing. A security interest in accounts receivable and general intangibles cannot be perfected by taking possession and, in the case of this kind of collateral, a filing must be made to perfect. It is not absolutely necessary for the secured party to hold possession. If collateral other than goods covered by a negotiable document is held by a bailee such as a warehouseman or by an escrow agent, the secured party is deemed to have possession from the time the bailee or escrow agent receives notification of the secured party's interest. The fundamental concept involved appears to be that the debtor must lose control of the collateral in order for the secured party to perfect by possession.

3. *Perfection by Filing*. The third method of perfecting the secured party's interest in collateral is by filing a financing statement. This filing must be made either centrally or locally. Central filings are generally made in a state office, usually that of the Secretary of State. Local filings are usually made in the office of the County Registrar, Recorder of Deeds, or County Clerk. Where the secured party is required to file depends on the type of collateral and on which version of Section 9-401

---

[24]   UCC 9-302(1)(b)
[25]   UCC 9-304(5)
[26]   UCC 9-304(1)

the state involved has adopted, and upon specific filing rules adopted by the particular state. Obviously, variations in filing requirements abound, and lenders must therefore be completely familiar with the filing requirements of their particular state.

The three alternative versions of Section 9-401 are:

1.   The first alternative requires central filing in all cases except those involving property closely related to real estate, such as fixtures, timber, or minerals. When property closely related to real estate is involved, a filing is required in the local office where a mortgage would be recorded. Eight states have adopted this alternative, although variations exist between states.[27]

2.   The second alternative requires central filing for all categories of property, with three notable exceptions:

  (a)   Equipment used in farming operations, or farm products, or accounts or general intangibles arising from or relating to, the sale of farm products by a farmer.[28]

  (b)   Consumer goods.[28]

  (c)   Timber to be cut, or minerals or the like (including oil and gas), or the collateral is goods which are or are to become fixtures.[29]

It is interesting to note that under rule 2(a), if the collateral is farm equipment, a local filing is generally required, whereas if the collateral is equipment used in a business, a central filing would be necessary. This alternative has been adopted with variations in 24 states.[30]

3.   The third alternative is similar to the second alternative, except that in some cases a dual filing is required. Generally, such an additional local filing is required if the debtor has a place of business in only one county. An additional local filing may also be required if the debtor has no place of business in the state but resides in that state. The remaining sixteen states[31] have adopted this alternative, except for Louisiana, which has not adopted Article 9 of the Code, and Nebraska, which has its own unique filing requirements. Interestingly, the District of Columbia also has not adopted any of these alternatives.

---

[27]   Connecticut, Delaware, Georgia, Hawaii, Iowa, Maine, Oregon and Utah.

[28]   UCC 9-401(1)(a)

[29]   UCC 9-401(1)(b)

[30]   Alabama, Alaska, Arizona, California, Colorado, Florida, Idaho, Illinois, Indiana, Kansas, Michigan, Minnesota, Montana, New Jersey, New Mexico, North Dakota, Oklahoma, Rhode Island, South Carolina, South Dakota, Tennessee, Texas, Washington, Wisconsin.

[31]   Arkansas, Kentucky, Maryland, Massachusetts, Mississippi, Missouri, Nevada, New Hampshire, New York, North Carolina, Ohio, Pennsylvania, Vermont, Virginia, West Virginia and Wyoming.

The Financing Statement

The financing statement, commonly referred to as a UCC-1, is the standard form used for a Uniform Commercial Code filing. A nonstandard form may be used as long as it contains all the necessary information and if the secured party is willing to pay the higher fee usually charged for filing nonstandard forms. A copy of the security agreement will suffice as a financing statement if it contains the necessary information and is signed by the debtor, although it is not recommended procedure.[32]

UCC 9-402 requires that the following information be contained in the financing statement:

1. The debtor's name. If the debtor is an individual the name should be shown with the last name first, then the first name and middle initial. It is extremely important that the debtor's name be shown correctly, since an error or misspelling could result in a misfiling and the possibility that the filing is invalid. If the debtor is a partnership, it should be identified by the partnership name, rather than by the names of the individual partners. If the debtor is a corporation, the correct corporate name as shown in the corporate charter should be used in the financing statement. Extreme caution should be used in dealing with trade or assumed business names, to avoid a filing which is seriously misleading.

2. The mailing address of the debtor must be shown, and should be sufficiently complete so that a records search would reveal the location of the debtor.

3. The secured party's name and address must be shown. The secured party's address is essential, as it enables a third party to contact the secured party for information concerning the nature of the security interest disclosed in the UCC-1.

4. The financing statement must be signed. Under the 1962 version of the Code, both the signatures of the debtor and secured party are required, while under the 1972 version only the debtor's signature is required. In the case of a sole proprietor, that individual should execute the UCC-1. With a partnership, a partner with authority should execute the financing statement. The signature of an authorized officer should be obtained on financing statements obtained from corporations. The signature on a financing statement need not be acknowledged, witnessed, or notarized.

5. The financing statement must contain a statement indicating the types or describing the items of collateral. Collateral descriptions have been previously discussed, and the lender should be reminded that

---

[32] UCC 9-402(1)

third parties are entitled to rely on the accuracy of the description which is filed on the public record.

6.   If the collateral is crops, growing timber, or fixtures, the financing statement must contain a description of the real estate. In the case of fixtures, a *legal* description of the real estate is generally required. A defective financing statement will probably not be cured by a security agreement which contains the proper real estate description. Exhibit AA contains an example of the standard form UCC-1.

Filing—When and Where

When should a financing statement be filed? Generally, from the lender's viewpoint, the sooner the better. Many lenders are surprised to learn that a financing statement may be filed before a security agreement is made, or a security interest otherwise attaches.[33] In other words, provided the debtor is willing to sign the UCC-1, the lender may file even before a loan commitment is made. Under the "first to file, first in priority rule", it is obviously to the lender's advantage to file as early as possible, even though a loan has not actually been made.

The requirements for either central or local filing, or both, have been discusssed previously. However, the secured party must still make a decision as to the state in which the filing should be made. The general rule is that the filing must be made in the jurisdiction in which the collateral is kept, and if different, then also in the jurisdiction where the debtor has his or her residence, or in the case of a business, the jurisdiction in which the chief executive offices of the business are located. Therefore, if a business has sales offices in Michigan, Indiana, and Illinois, but its home office is in Michigan, then a central filing should be made in the state of Michigan. If collateral is to be kept in all three states, then the lender should file centrally in Illinois and Indiana as well as in Michigan. A lender should always remember that an additional filing is probably cheap insurance and, if there is any doubt that another filing is necessary in an additional jurisdiction, then a filing should always be made.

If a local filing is necessary, a filing should first be made in the county of the debtor's residence or in the county where the principal offices of the business are located. In addition, if the lender knows that collateral is to be kept in another county, a filing generally should also be made in that county. The Code specifically requires that a filing be made in any county in which crops, timber, minerals, or fixtures to be used as collateral are located.

Even though a filing is made in the wrong place or not in enough places, perfection may still have occurred. The Code states that a filing which is made

[33]   UCC 9-402(1)

in good faith in an improper place or not in all of the places required, is nevertheless effective with regard to any collateral as to which the filing complied with the requirements of the Code, and is also effective with regard to collateral covered by the financing statement against any person who has knowledge of the contents of such financing statement.[34] However, a prudent lender will certainly take precautions to file properly rather than rely on the uncertain relief provided by this provision.

Change of Name by Debtor

What if the debtor changes its name subsequent to the filing? Section 9-402 (7) of the 1972 version of the Code states that where the debtor so changes his or her name, or an organization changes its name, identity, or corporate structure, that a filed financing statement becomes seriously misleading, the filing is not effective to perfect a security interest in collateral acquired by the debtor more than four months after the change, unless a new appropriate financing statement is filed before the expiration of that time. A filed financing statement remains effective with respect to collateral transferred by the debtor even though the secured party knows of or consents to the transfer.[35] It should be noted that for collateral that does not turn over, such as equipment, a change in name does not affect the original filing. However, in the case of collateral such as inventory and receivables, which do turn over, perfection would last four months after the name change unless an amended filing was made. The 1962 version of the Code does not contain UCC 9-402 (7), but court decisions in those states that retained the 1962 version indicate that the secured party generally has a duty to refile under the new name.

Change of Address by Debtor

What if the debtor's address changes subsequent to the filing? Generally, a change in the mailing address or place of residence, or place of business of the debtor within the same state subsequent to the filing has no effect on the original filing.[36] However, some states have adopted another version of Section 9-401, under which the original filing becomes unperfected four months after a change in the debtor's residence to another county in the same state. Therefore, in this regard, the lender must be familiar with the specific requirements of the code in the state(s) in which filing(s) must be made.

---

[34]   UCC 9-401(2)
[35]   UCC 9-402(7)
[36]   UCC 9-401(3)

Removal of Collateral by Debtor

What if the debtor moves the collateral to another state? Generally, the Code provides that a security interest perfected in one state continues to be perfected for four months after the debtor removes the collateral to another state. At the end of the four-month period, the security interest becomes unperfected unless the secured party files in the state to which the collateral has been moved.[37] This rule is applicable even though the collateral has been moved without the knowledge of the secured party and in violation of the security agreement. Obviously, it is to the secured party's advantage to be aware of the location of the collateral at all times, and not to rely solely on representations of the debtor. There is no substitute for on-site inspections of collateral conducted at regular intervals, even if conducted without the knowledge of the debtor.

Security Interests in Crops and Other Farm Products

As previously indicated, "farm products" is one of the categories of goods established by the Code. It should be emphasized that crops, both harvested and growing, are included in this category. A description in the security agreement and financing statement of "all crops growing or to be grown" would undoubtedly cover growing crops. However, there may be some question whether the grain produced would be covered once the crops were harvested. Therefore, a description of "all farm products, including but not limited to growing and harvested crops and grain, wherever stored, produced or grown, together with all documents of title pertaining thereto," would be preferable. This expanded description also attempts to deal with the problem of grain or produce stored under a warehouse receipt.

The Code also requires that both the security agreement and financing statement covering crops must contain a description of the real estate.[38] Generally, a legal description of the real estate is not required, but the description must be adequate enough that a reasonable person could locate the real estate. A few states have passed nonconforming amendments to the Code which require that the actual legal description be used. With the exception of those states, a description of the real estate such as "the John Jones farm located 4 miles north and 3 miles east of Center City, in Lincoln County, Illinois" should be sufficient. However, caution should be exercised in determining the type of real estate description that will be acceptable in the lender's jurisdiction.

The 1962 version of the Code contains a provision that generally prohibits a security interest in crops planted more than one year after the security

[37]   UCC 9-103(1)(d)
[38]   UCC 9-402(1)

agreement is executed.[39] Therefore, in those states operating under the 1962 Code, a security agreement is generally valid as to crops for only one year, and a lender is required to obtain a new security agreement every year to cover successive crops. However, the one year limit does not apply to the financing statement, which remains valid for five years from the date it is filed. In the 1972 version of the Code, this troublesome section was eliminated and a lender in states which have adopted the 1972 version may cover successive crops with only one security agreement and financing statement.

In recent years, a number of states have passed nonconforming amendments to the Code which require a lender to give notification in writing of its security interest in farm products to prospective buyers in the "normal course of business"—such as grain elevators, livestock commission merchants, etc. In these states, perfection by filing is effective for all parties except prospective buyers in the normal course of business and, in order to make the security interest effective against these parties, the lender must follow the prescribed notification procedures. Therefore, the lender must be familiar with all of the statutory requirements of its state when dealing with security interests in farm products. Failure to comply with such notification provisions may result in the lender losing its collateral to a third party despite having a perfected security interest in the property.

Special Category Security Interests

There are several unique categories of security interests that enable the lender to achieve a "super priority" over the holder of any previously perfected security interest in the same collateral. This exalted status is not achieved automatically; it is the result of the lender's compliance with a number of special rules. These special category security interests are as follows:

1. *Purchase money security interest in collateral other than inventory.* The Code defines a purchase money security interest (PMSI) as one taken or retained by the seller of the collateral to secure all or part of its price, or one taken by a person who by making advances or incurring an obligation gives value to enable the debtor to acquire rights in or the use of collateral, if such value is in fact so used.[40] The concept of the purchase money security interest was devised to facilitate sales transactions. It enables the seller of goods or the lender who finances the purchase of goods to acquire a first security position in the goods being purchased, even though under normal Code rules another creditor whose documentation contained an after-acquired clause and who had

---

[39]   UCC 9-204(4)(a) (1962 Code)
[40]   UCC 9-107

previously perfected his or her security interest would have had first priority to that collateral. Obviously, it is essential for the seller on credit or financer of goods to perfect a purchase money security interest. To accomplish this, there must be compliance with two special rules. First, the secured party must provide the purchase funds for the goods. In most cases, it will be obvious that a seller has complied with this rule. However, it may be more difficult for a lender to prove that it actually supplied the purchase funds and, for this reason, many lenders make it a practice to disburse the loan proceeds by means of a joint check to both the borrower and the supplier of the goods being purchased. The second rule is that the secured party must perfect by filing within ten days of the date the debtor receives possession of the goods. During the past few years, several state legislatures have passed amendments to the Code extending this time period to twenty days. It should be noted that the time clock begins to run on the date the *debtor receives possession*, and not on the date the purchase order is signed, or on the date the loan proceeds are disbursed. This date may often be difficult to identify and this fact has resulted in considerable litigation. The cautious lender will file at the earliest possible moment to eliminate any unnecessary time problems.

2.   *Purchase money security interest in inventory*. A lender or supplier must take several additional steps to perfect a purchase money security interest in inventory. The financer of inventory does not have the ten-day period in which to perfect, but must perfect by filing prior to the time the debtor receives possession. In other words, the filing *must* be made before the debtor receives delivery of the inventory. The supplier or lender must also give notification *in writing* to the holder of a previously perfected competing security interest in after-acquired inventory. The holder of the competing security interest must have received the written notification within five years before the debtor receives possession of the inventory. Finally, the notification must state that the holder of the purchase money security interest in inventory "has or expects to acquire a purchase money security interest in inventory of the debtor, describing such inventory by item or type."[41] Exhibit BB is an example of such a notification letter.

Suppliers of inventory on consignment are required to comply with rules similar to those for suppliers or financers of inventory. In fact, the consignment seller is treated exactly like the inventory financer by the Code. The consignor must file a financing statement before delivering the goods and give written notification to any competing inventory

---

[41]   UCC 9-312(3)

financers who have previous filings on record.[42] As in the case of purchased inventory, the holder of the security interest must receive the notification within five years before the consignee receives possession of the goods.

3. *Purchase money security interest in fixtures.* The Code defines fixtures as goods when they become so related to particular real estate that an interest in them arises under real estate law.[43] In other words, fixtures are personal property that become permanently affixed to real estate. By complying fully with the special rules for fixtures, a lender may achieve priority over an existing mortgage or other encumbrance on the real estate to which the fixture becomes attached.

These rules are as follows:

(a) The security interest must be a purchase money interest.

(b) A fixture filing of a financing statement covering goods that are to become fixtures must be filed in the office where a mortgage on the real estate would be filed or recorded, usually that of the Recorder or Registrar of Deeds.

(c) The financing statement must contain a description of the real estate. Under the 1962 version of the Code there is no requirement that this be a legal description, and a reasonable (but non-legal) description may suffice. Under the 1972 version of the code, the *legal* description of the real estate to which the fixtures are to become attached must be shown in the financing statement. In a number of states the financing statement must also show the name of the record owner of the real estate, if that is different from the debtor. Under the 1972 version of the Code, the filing officer is also required to cross index the fixture filing under the name of the debtor as if he or she were the mortgagor in a real estate mortgage.

(d) The financing statement generally must show upon its face that it is a "fixtures filing."

(e) The filing must be made prior to the time that the fixtures become attached to the real estate.

The lender should be familiar with the particular rules of his or her state concerning fixture filings.

4. *Accessions.* An accession may be defined as an item of personal property that becomes attached to other personal property. A security interest in goods (an accession) which attaches before the goods are installed in or affixed to other goods takes priority as to the goods

---

[42] UCC 9-114
[43] UCC 9-313(1)(a)

installed or affixed over the claims of all persons to the whole.[44] There are major exceptions to this rule. A security interest in an accession does not take priority over a subsequent purchaser for value of any interest in the whole, or a creditor with a lien on the whole subsequently obtained by judicial proceedings, or a creditor with a prior perfected security interest in the whole to the extent that he or she makes subsequent advances, if the subsequent purchase is made, the lien by judicial proceedings obtained, or the subsequent advance under the prior perfected security interest is made or contracted for *without knowledge of the security interest and before it is perfected*.[45] In the event of a default, a secured party with an interest in an accession which has priority over the claims of all persons who have an interest in the whole, may remove his or her collateral from the whole, but he or she must reimburse any encumbrancer or owner of the whole who is not the debtor, and who has not otherwise agreed, for the cost of repair of any physical injury, but not for any diminution in value of the whole caused by the absence of the goods removed or by any necessity for replacing them.[46] It should be noted that a security interest in accessions is similar to a security interest in fixtures, in that the security interest must have attached prior to installation of the accession for the secured party to have a priority position.

5. *Special Category Security Interest in Crops*. In UCC 9-312 (2), the Code creates a special type of security interest, which is intended to permit the heavily indebted farmer to finance production costs of the next year's crop. It gives priority to the so-called "seed money" lender to the extent that the funds are used for current crop production costs. This particular section of the Code often confuses agricultural lenders, who fail to realize that UCC 9-312 (2) has nothing to do with obtaining a security interest in crops under normal circumstances. Section 9-312 (2) provides that where future crops are collateral under an earlier security agreement, a subsequent lender who fully complies with the rules established by this section will achieve a priority position superior to that of the previously perfected security interest, to the extent that the lender furnished funds to produce the crop. These rules are as follows:

(a) The lender must give "new value," that is, disburse new funds as opposed to a renewal.
(b) The funds must be advanced for the specific purpose of producing the crop.

44   UCC 9-314(1)
45   UCC 9-314(3)
46   UCC 9-314(4)

(c) The funds must be advanced within three months prior to planting.

(d) The seed money lender prevails only to the extent that the obligation secured by any competing security interest in crops was due more than six months before the new crop is planted.

This final requirement is very significant and, from a practical standpoint, it appears that very few transactions would fit the exact circumstances required by UCC 9-312 (2). Although most lenders will never make a 9-312 (2)loan, they should be familiar with its provisions to avoid any confusion with routine procedures for crop financing.

Sale or Disposition of Collateral by the Debtor

The Code states that a security interest generally continues in collateral notwithstanding sale, exchange, or other disposition thereof (by the debtor), unless the disposition was authorized by the secured party in the security agreement or otherwise.[47] The security interest also continues in any identifiable proceeds from the sale or disposition, including collections received by the debtor if the collateral has been sold on credit. Therefore, in some instances, the lender's security interest may continue in the collateral even though it has been sold to a third party—unless the third party is a purchaser in the "ordinary course of business." Generally, this means that the secured party may repossess the collateral from the third party purchaser even though the debtor has been paid in full for the collateral.

In situations involving the unauthorized disposition or conversion of collateral by the debtor, the lender may proceed against both the debtor and the third party to recover the collateral, the proceeds from disposition or conversion, or both. Also, it should be noted that the debtor and third party purchaser may be liable to the lender for punitive damages and attorney fees that arise from the conversion of the collateral. In many states, a debtor commits a criminal offense if he or she disposes of collateral and fails to pay the secured party the amount due under the security agreement. Interestingly, the debtor who converts collateral may be unable to obtain a bankruptcy discharge for that particular debt—at least to the extent of the value of the collateral that was converted.

As previously indicated, the exception to the usual conversion situation involves a buyer in the "ordinary course of business." A buyer in the ordinary course of business is defined by the Code as a person who in good faith and without knowledge that the sale to him or her is a violation of the ownership rights or security interest of a third party in the goods, buys in ordinary course

---

[47] UCC 9-306(2)

from a person *in the business of selling goods of that kind.*[48] Section 9-307 of the Code specifically provides for the protection of buyers in the ordinary course of business in order to facilitate normal commercial transactions. As a result of 9-307, the individual who buys a television set from an appliance store or the contractor who buys an item of construction equipment from a dealer, may take possession of those goods without the fear that the lender who financed the dealer's inventory may ultimately repossess the goods. Section 9-307 (1) states that a buyer in the ordinary course of business, other than a person buying farm products from a person engaged in farming operations, takes possession free of a security interest created by his or her seller even though the security interest is perfected, and even though the buyer knows of its existence. Therefore, when a dealer sells inventory in the normal course of business, any security interest held by an inventory lender is cut off at the point of sale and the lender has no recourse against the purchaser. It should be noted that farm products being sold by a farmer are specifically excepted from 9-307, and a buyer of farm products in the ordinary course of business may take those products subject to a security interest created by the farmer.

In this context, it is essential that the lender realize that the *only* security interest that is cut off by a sale in the ordinary course of business is one created by the seller. Therefore, if a dealer has granted a security interest to an inventory financer, that security interest is clearly cut off. However, if the dealer is selling an item of equipment which is subject to a security interest created by a former owner, that security interest will remain intact despite a sale in the ordinary course of business. Obviously, this situation usually arises where a debtor sells or trades an item of used equipment to a dealer in violation of the lender's security agreement and the dealer subsequently resells that item of equipment to an innocent third party. Since this sale does not cut off the original security interest, the lender may repossess the equipment and initiate legal action for conversion against both the dealer and the third party purchaser.

Assignment, Amendment, Continuation, and Termination

A secured party's interest in the collateral may be transferred to a third party by means of an assignment. This assignment may be disclosed in the proper section of the initial financing statement or it may be accomplished by filing a subsequent written statement of assignment executed by the secured party of record.[49] This is usually accomplished by filing a form UCC-3.

A financing statement may also be amended by filing a supplemental statement signed by both the debtor and the secured party. An amendment

---

[48]   UCC 1-201(9)
[49]   UCC 9-405

does not extend the period of effectiveness of the original financing statement. If an amendment adds collateral, it is effective as to the added collateral only from the filing date of the amendment.[50] An amendment may also be made to correct an error in description, or to note a change in address.

A form UCC-3 may also be used for a partial release of collateral. The collateral to be released should be described in detail in the UCC-3. The amendment or partial release must then be filed in the same filing office(s) as the original financing statement and must refer to the original financing statement.

A financing statement which does not contain a stated maturity date is effective for five years from the date of filing. In those states that have the 1962 version of the Code, if the financing statement contains a stated maturity date of less than five years, it remains effective until 60 days after the maturity date.[51] When a financing statement expires, the security interest it covers becomes unperfected and the creditor may lose its previously established priority position.

The Code provides for an extension of the expiration date of a financing statement by means of a form called a continuation statement. The secured party may file a continuation statement within six months prior to the statutory five-year expiration date and, if the filing is to remain perfected, the continuation statement must be filed no later than the expiration date. Therefore, the lender has a six-month "window" during which the filing of the continuation statement must be made if it is to be effective. If the financing statement contains a stated maturity date, then the continuation statement must be filed within six months prior to, or within sixty days after the maturity date (1962 Code). The signature of the debtor is not required on a continuation statement. However, it must contain the signature of the secured party, identify the original financing statement by file number, and state that the original filing is still effective. Upon the timely filing of a continuation statement, the effectiveness of the original financing statement is extended five years from the last date to which the original filing was effective.[52]

Most lenders have found that a tickler file is an absolute necessity for scheduling the timely filing of continuation statements. In most transactions it is essential for the lender to preserve his or her priority as of the date of the original filing. Even though it might be possible for the lender to file a new financing statement signed by the debtor, its priority would then be established as of the date of the new filing. Any other secured creditor or lien holder who had perfected in the ensuing five-year period would then have a priority superior to that of the lender who had allowed his or her original filing to

---

[50]   UCC 9-402(4)
[51]   UCC 9-403(2) (1962 Code)
[52]   UCC 9-403(3)

expire. Also, a lapsed perfection may create a preference problem in bankruptcy, which will enable the trustee to treat the lender as an unsecured creditor.

When the debtor no longer has any loans outstanding and has no commitment for further advances, he or she may request by written demand that the secured party terminate the financing statement. Upon receipt of such a request, the secured party is obligated to furnish the debtor a form terminating the financing statement. This form is called a termination statement, and upon proper filing in the office(s) in which the financing statement was filed, the secured party's interest is extinguished. If the secured party fails to provide a termination statement to the debtor within ten days after proper demand is made, the secured party is liable for damages to the debtor. In the case of a financing statement covering consumer goods, the rule is somewhat different. In such a case, the secured party is required to furnish a termination statement to the debtor within one month after there is no longer a secured obligation, or within 10 days of written demand by the debtor.

EXHIBIT Z   Security Agreement

UNIFORM COMMERCIAL CODE — SECURITY AGREEMENT

MNO Industries, Inc. .... 1663 S. Second St., Center City, IL 61111 and
    Name   Address

_____
        Name   Address

hereinafter called "DEBTOR," hereby grants, FOR VALUE RECEIVED, to
    Center City National Bank .... 123 Main Street, Center City, Illinois 61111
        Name   Address

hereinafter called "SECURED PARTY" a security interest in the following described property and all additions and accessions
thereto (herein collectively called "the Collateral"):

**All equipment now owned or hereafter acquired, including but not limited to manufacturing
equipment, delivery equipment, warehouse equipment, office equipment, office, warehouse and
plant furnishings and fixtures; all inventory, contracts and accounts receivable now owned or
hereafter acquired; all general intangibles; all proceeds from the sale, liquidation, or
disposition of any of the foregoing items.**

This security interest is given to secure the payment of any and all indebtednesses and liabilities whatsoever of the DEBTOR
to the SECURED PARTY, whether direct or indirect, absolute or contingent, or due or to become due, and whether now existing
or hereafter arising, and together with all costs and expenses of SECURED PARTY in respect to the indebtedness or the Collateral (all herein collectively called the "Obligations."

The DEBTOR hereby warrants and agrees:

1. That except for the security interest granted hereby, DEBTOR is, or to the extent that this agreement states that the
Collateral is to be acquired after the date hereof, will be, the sole owner of the Collateral, free from any other lien, encumbrance, or
security interest and that DEBTOR will defend the collateral against all claims and demands of all persons at any time claiming
the same or any interest therein;

2. That if checked here ☐, the Collateral is used primarily for personal, family, or household purposes; that if checked here ☐,
the Collateral is used primarily in farming operations;

3. The Collateral will be kept at the place where the DEBTOR resides unless otherwise stated herein, and shall not be moved
unless written consent is first obtained from the SECURED PARTY.

4. That if any or all of the Collateral has been or is to be attached to real estate, DEBTOR shall furnish SECURED PARTY
with a disclaimer signed by all persons having an interest in the real estate, disclaiming any interest in the Collateral prior to the
interest of the SECURED PARTY. The description of the real estate is:

                                        N/A

_____
located in the .... of .... , County of .... , Illinois.

5. That if any or all of the Collateral is crops, the description of the real estate upon which the crops are to be grown is:

                                        N/A

_____
in .... County, Illinois.

6. That no Financing Statement covering said Collateral or any proceeds thereof is on file in any public office; that at the
request of SECURED PARTY, DEBTOR will join with SECURED PARTY in executing one or more Financing Statements
pursuant to the Uniform Commercial Code in form satisfactory to SECURED PARTY and will pay the cost of filing the same
in all public offices whenever filing is deemed by SECURED PARTY to be necessary or desirable;

7. That DEBTOR will not sell or otherwise transfer the Collateral or any interest therein and will not permit any other lien
or security interest to be attached thereto without the written consent of SECURED PARTY.

8. That DEBTOR shall keep the Collateral insured with a reputable insurance company satisfactory to SECURED PARTY
against physical damage for no less than the total amount owed to SECURED PARTY. Insurance policies shall be payable to
SECURED PARTY as its interest may appear. SECURED PARTY may cancel the insurance at any time and receive the return premium, if any. If DEBTOR fails to procure insurance, SECURED PARTY has the option, but is not obligated, to do so
at DEBTOR's expense.

9. That DEBTOR shall promptly pay when due all taxes and assessments that may be levied against the Collateral. If
DEBTOR fails to do so, SECURED PARTY has the option, but is not obligated, to make payment at DEBTOR's expense.

10. SECURED PARTY has the option, but is not obligated, to pay and discharge other liens, encumbrances or security
interests upon the Collateral.

11. That any amounts paid by SECURED PARTY pursuant to paragraphs 8, 9, and 10 above shall become additional obligations secured by this security agreement, and shall bear interest at the highest legal rate allowable by Illinois Statutes from the
dates of any such advances until repaid.

In case any of the following events shall happen or occur, DEBTOR shall be in default:

(a) Failure or neglect to comply with any of the terms, provisions, warranties or covenants of this Security Agreement; or

(b) Failure to pay any of the Obligations when due at any original or renewed or extended maturity; or

(c) If the Collateral or any part thereof ceases to be personal property; or

(d) Any warranty, representation or statement made or furnished to SECURED PARTY by or on behalf of DEBTOR shall
be or prove to have been false when made or furnished; or

(e) Any loss, theft, substantial damage, destruction, or encumbrance to or of any of the Collateral or the voluntary or involuntary transfer of any of the Collateral by way of sale, creation of a security interest, attachment, levy, garnishment or other judicial
process; or

(f) Death, dissolution, termination of existence, insolvency, business failure, assignment for the benefit of creditors of or by, or
the commencement of any proceedings under any bankruptcy or insolvency laws or laws for the relief of debtors, by or against,
DEBTOR (or if more than one any of them) or any guarantor or surety for any Debtor, or the appointment of a receiver, trustee,
court appointee, or otherwise, for any part of the property of any of them; or

(g) If at any time SECURED PARTY feels insecure.

Upon any default and at any time or from time to time thereafter, the SECURED PARTY may at its option and without
notice or demand declare any one or more of the Obligations immediately due and payable, notwithstanding any provisions in
any thereof to the contrary and shall have all of the rights and remedies of a secured party under the Uniform Commercial Code
(Ill. Rev. Stat. Ch. 26). Unless the Collateral is perishable or threatens to decline speedily in value or is of a type customarily sold
on a recognized market, the SECURED PARTY will give the DEBTOR reasonable notice of the time and place of any public
sale thereof or of the time after which intended disposition is to be made. The requirement of reasonable notice shall be met if such
notice is mailed, postage prepaid, to the DEBTOR at the address given herein or if none to any address in the SECURED
PARTY's files, at least five days before the time of sale or other disposition. Expenses of retaking, holding, preparing for sale, selling or the like shall include SECURED PARTY's reasonable attorneys' fees and legal expenses.

No default shall be waived by SECURED PARTY except in writing and no waiver of any default shall operate as a waiver
of any other default or of the same default on a future occasion. All rights of SECURED PARTY hereunder shall be cumulative
and shall inure to the benefit of itself, its successors and assigns; and all obligations of DEBTOR shall bind legal representatives
and successors.

If there is more than one DEBTOR, all undertakings, warranties and covenants made by the DEBTOR and all rights, powers
and authorities given to or conferred on the SECURED PARTY shall be made or given jointly and severally.

IN WITNESS WHEREOF, this Security Agreement has been executed and delivered in **Center City, Illinois** ,
Illinois, by the DEBTOR on the .... 18th .... day of .... **October** .... , A.D. 19 ....

                                                        MNO Industries, Inc.
                                                                Debtor

Center City National Bank   By *Harold C. Bush*   Vice President
        Secured Party   Debtor

BY *Robert C. Brown, V.P.*   BY *Mary Q Harris*   Secretary

EXHIBIT AA   Form UCC-1

STATE OF ILLINOIS
UNIFORM COMMERCIAL CODE — FINANCING STATEMENT — FORM UCC-1

INSTRUCTIONS:
1. PLEASE TYPE this form. Fold only along perforation for mailing.
2. Remove Secured Party and Debtor copies and send other 3 copies with interleaved carbon paper to the filing officer. Enclose filing fee.
3. If the space provided for any item(s) on the form is inadequate the item(s) should be continued on additional sheets, preferably 5″ x 8″ or 8″ x 10″. Only one copy of such additional sheets need be presented to the filing officer with a set of three copies of the financing statement. Long schedules of collateral, indentures, etc., may be on any size paper that is convenient for the secured party.

This STATEMENT is presented to a filing officer for filing pursuant to the Uniform Commercial Code.

Debtor(s) (Last Name First) and address(es)	Secured Party(ies) and address(es)	For Filing Officer (Date, Time, Number; and Filing Office)
MNO Industries, Inc. 1663 S. Second Street Center City, Illinois 61111	Center City National Bank 123 Main Street Center City, Illinois 61111	

1. This financing statement covers the following types (or items) of property:

All equipment now owned or hereafter acquired, including but not limited to, manufacturing equipment, delivery equipment, warehouse equipment, office equipment, office, warehouse and plant furnishings and fixtures; all inventory, contracts and accounts receivable now owned or hereafter acquired; all general intangibles; all proceeds from the sale, liquidation, or disposition of any of the foregoing items.

ASSIGNEE OF SECURED PARTY

2. ☐ Products of Collateral are also covered.

———— Additional sheets presented.
———— Filed with Office of Secretary of State of Illinois.
———— Debtor is a transmitting utility as defined in UCC §9-105.

MNO Industries, Inc.
By: *Eugene C. Connor*   President
        Signature of (Debtor)
                        (Secured Party)*

*Signature of Debtor Required in Most Cases:
Signature of Secured Party in Cases Covered By UCC §9-402 (2)

(1) FILING OFFICER COPY—ALPHABETICAL

This form of financing statement is approved by the Secretary of State.

STANDARD FORM — UNIFORM COMMERCIAL CODE — FORM UCC-1 — REV. 7-75

EXHIBIT   BB   Notification Letter re Purchase Money Security Interest in
Inventory

XYZ Manufacturing Company
16164 South State Street
Chicago, Illinois 62704

UCC Notification Letter

October 24, 19 4

Center City National Bank
123 Main Street
Center City, Illinois 61111

Re: Acme Retail Stores, Inc., debtor

Gentlemen:

This is to advise you pursuant to Section 9-312(3) of the
Uniform Commercial Code that XYZ Manufacturing Company has or ex
to acquire a purchase money security interest in inventory (incl
but not limited to electrical appliances, water heaters, air con
ditioners, furnaces, humidifiers, dehumidifiers and heat pumps)
from time to time to the above listed debtor, and in proceeds of
such inventory.

Please acknowledge receipt of this notice by signing and
returning one copy in the enclosed self addressed envelope.

XYZ Manufacturing Company

By: ___*A. J. Belmont*___
              VICE PRESIDENT

Receipt Acknowledged:

_____

By _____

13

Credit Files and Monitoring Loan Performance

A lending institution's credit files are the written documentation of its overall relationship with the borrower. Good files are absolutely essential for a good lending operation. The quality of the decision that a loan officer makes often depends, to a great extent, on the completeness and accuracy of the credit file. A good credit file should contain the following key items:

1. A general history and background information on the borrower.
2. Current financial information.
3. A financial history of the borrower.
4. Information concerning loan purpose.
5. The repayment agreement.
6. Projections of future performance and operating budgets.
7. A narrative containing specific information on loan transactions with the borrower.
8. Copies of all correspondence relating to the borrower.

These items make an adequate file that not only enables the officer servicing the loan to do a better job, but also allows other officers who may be unfamiliar with the loan to service it. It also provides adequate information for the bank examiner or auditor to make a decision regarding the acceptability of the loan.

An adequate file should meet four requirements:

1. It should contain sufficient financial information to enable the loan officer to make a determination of the financial strength of the borrower and to readily ascertain trends in the borrower's financial status.
2. It should outline the terms of the loan agreement with the customer in detail, and set out the repayment agreement in full.

3. It should enable the user to make an assessment of the past performance of the borrower.
4. It should outline all existing or potential weaknesses in the loan in detail.

A lender may have two credit files on each borrower—one an active file containing material covering the past two or three years, and the other an inactive file containing older items. Generally, a separate active file should be kept for each borrower, although a consolidated file containing the records of several closely affiliated borrowers may be advantageous in some cases. Each file should contain several basic types of material, including the following:

1. *Financial statements.* A current financial statement, including balance sheet and income statement, should be obtained from the borrower at least annually, and these should be filed in chronological order in an accessible portion of the file. In addition, a spread sheet (loan history) should be included in this section of the file, usually as a cover sheet for the various statements. A spread sheet allows the compilation, in columnar form, of basic information from statements of various dates, and greatly facilitates the comparison of information and identification of trends.

2. *Supporting schedules.* A current inventory of equipment, an aged listing of receivables, schedules of insurance coverage, etc., should be placed in the credit file.

3. *Projections.* The file should contain current cash flow projections (including capital needs), operating budgets, and income projections.

4. *Agreements.* All agreements with the borrower should be recorded in the file, either in the form of a formal loan agreement or, at the very least, as a memorandum written by the loan officer. It is especially important that the repayment agreement be outlined clearly and specifically.

5. *Narrative comments.* The loan officer periodically should record in the file any information pertinent to the loan, as well as his or her assessment of the current status of the loan. The narrative portion of the file should contain background information on the borrower and historical information on the status and performance of the borrower's business. Many lenders make it a practice to insert an annual summary of the overall status of the loan in the narrative portion of the credit file. This is usually done at the time the borrower's annual financial statements are received and analyzed. The narrative portion of the file should consist of either a series of memoranda, or a narrative sheet containing a series of comments in chronological order. See Exhibit CC for a sample narrative sheet.

6. *Loan analysis information.* The bank's credit department generally has the duty of analyzing the financial information in the loan file. In those banks that do not have a credit department, either the loan officer, a loan

review officer, or a qualified staff employee should perform this function. This analysis, including ratios and the analyst's comments, should be recorded in the credit file on a systematic basis, and should clearly outline any weaknesses or potential problems in the loan.

7. *Security documents.* Negotiable collateral, and some items of non-negotiable collateral, such as life insurance policies, generally should be kept in a collateral file or vault. However, nonnegotiable collateral, such as security agreements, may be kept in the credit file where it is readily accessible to the loan officer.

8. *Correspondence and miscellaneous.* Copies of all correspondence to and from the borrower, and to and from others regarding the borrower, should be placed in the credit file, as should other items of pertinent information, such as searches of the public records, records of credit inquiries, and newspaper clippings.

For a credit file to be of maximum usefulness, it must be kept up to date. It also must be organized in a logical manner, with the documents in each section usually filed chronologically, with the most recent document on top. This normally requires a file folder in which documents may be fastened down, rather than a pocket type file into which material is simply inserted.

Credit files must also be readily accessible and easily located. This normally requires alphabetical filing by name of borrower. If a borrower operates under more than one name, a card file which cross-references names is quite helpful. Color coding by loan type, either by using file jackets of different colors or colored tabs on standard jackets, also may be useful. For example, with this kind of system, commercial loan files might be brown, agricultural loan files green, and real estate loan files blue.

Finally, if a credit file is to be beneficial, it must be used. The loan officer should consider the file his or her basic working tool, and no loan decision made or transaction completed without consulting it. Better use of loan files may be the quickest and surest way for a lender to improve both loan decisions and the quality of service provided to borrowers.

Central Information Files

The advent of the computer has made it feasible for even a relatively small bank to have a central information file. A central information file may be defined as a centralized summary of a financial institution's overall relationship with each customer. By accessing the central information file (CIF), the user can quickly determine the extent to which a given customer is using the bank's services. A comprehensive central information file may contain information regarding commercial loans, mortgage loans, demand deposit accounts, savings accounts, time deposits, data processing services, payroll services, trust services, profit sharing and pension accounts, and consumer loans to principals of the business. It enables the loan officer to obtain a much better perspective of the borrowing customer's overall relationship with the bank, and thereby achieve a better understanding of the quality and profitability of a certain account. It can also alert the loan officer to problems that other departments of the bank may have had with that particular customer. Although some banks have been hesitant to establish a central information file due to the time and cost involved, its advantages to both the lending departments and other departments of the banks should not be overlooked by bank management.

Monitoring Loan Performance

As well as making good initial loan decisions and structuring loans properly, a lending institution's success depends on the manner in which it monitors its loans. Even the best loans require a certain amount of supervision. Each loan should be examined periodically to insure that it is working as anticipated, that the borrower is complying with the loan agreements, that the necessary current information is being received, and that the status of the loan has not deteriorated. Identifying signs of deterioration at an early date is a prime objective of good loan supervision. In this section, we will examine techniques for adequate supervision.

Even though the loan officer has accumulated a significant amount of information while processing the loan request, he or she must recognize that in order to monitor the loan properly, there must be a continuous inflow of information. This may include interim statements, observations made during a visit to the business premises, information from public records or trade sources, information gained from contact with the borrower, from examination of the borrower's accounts, and from other sources. Whether the overall inflow of information is adequate to enable the creditor to monitor performance properly depends on the amount of information received, and on the size, complexity, and degree of risk involved in the loan. A lender *must* have sufficient inflow of information to enable detection of any significant change in loan status.

In order to benefit from the continuous inflow of new information, a lender must also analyze it on a continuous basis. This analysis should include computation of ratios and trends, comparison of new information with facts previously recorded, and an assessment of how this new information affects the overall status of the loan.

The monitoring of compliance with the repayment agreement is a key step in this continuous analysis. If there is an apparent breakdown in performance, a timely followup by the lender is required to determine if there is a problem. For instance, if ABC Manufacturing Company anticipated collecting a large receivable in early September, the proceeds of which were to be used to reduce the balance of its working capital loan, then the lender's monitoring of the repayment plan should result in a "red flag" if those proceeds have not been received by mid-October. The lender also should monitor the borrower's adherence to other agreements made in connection with the loan. If ABC Manufacturing Company has agreed that it will make no significant capital purchases, and information from the public records reveals a recent UCC filing on a large piece of equipment by a dealer, or perusal of the company's checking account shows a sizeable check written to a dealer, then the lender should consider the possibility that the loan agreement has been violated.

As part of the monitoring process, a prudent lender also will periodically attempt to verify the location, condition, and current value of the collateral. The necessity for periodic physical inspections of the borrower's premises, equipment, and inventory cannot be overstressed.

Another important aspect of loan supervision is the monitoring of periodic disbursements against a line of credit or loan commitment to ascertain that these funds are used for the purposes intended. Diversion or misuse of loan proceeds is just as serious a problem as diversion of pledged repayment, but lenders generally seem less sensitive to the misuse of proceeds than to the diversion of repayment. Bank lenders have a simple means of monitoring the use of proceeds—examine the checks that clear the borrower's account—but it appears that this is seldom done. Unusually heavy use of a line of credit or disbursement of loan funds significantly ahead of schedule constitutes a red flag. For example, if Consolidated Retail Stores' cash flow projection indicates that it will need to borrow funds to build up its Christmas inventory in September, but those funds are requested in June, then the lender certainly should question the reason for such a significant deviation from the cash flow projection.

Changes in economic conditions also may seriously affect the status of a loan, and any significant change in prices, costs, availability of raw materials, etc., should be taken into consideration when a lender reviews the status of a loan. Significant changes in the price of inputs or in demand for the finished product may require revision of both the cash flow projection and repayment plan of the business.

There is no doubt, however, that the real key to a successful program of loan supervision is to maintain a line of communication with the borrower. A periodic visit to the business' premises, an occasional discussion over coffee, or a few pertinent questions asked during a chance meeting on the street, all contribute to keeping lines of communication open. The most important ingredient in achieving this is the borrower's knowledge that the lender can be depended upon, even in times of adversity.

The rules for good loan supervision can be summarized as follows:

1. Recognize the need for a continuous inflow of pertinent information during the life of the loan.
2. Analyze that information properly, and use it to assess the current status of the loan.
3. Monitor loan disbursements and compliance with the repayment agreement.
4. Make periodic visits to the premises of the borrower.
5. Maintain open lines of communication with the borrower at all times.

EXHIBIT CC   Loan Narrative Sheet

Name Southern Material Company, Inc.

Date _____ Amount of Original Loan $ _____

MEMO DATE	REMARKS
5/3/X3	After a number of calls by officers of this Bank we are acquiring the account business of Southern Material Company. Business was started by Mr. Runkel 14 years ago. He has operated it in a conservative manner and the business has consistently had satisfactory, if not spectacular profits. He is now considering purchasing a used "redi mix" concrete plant to replace his existing plant which is in poor condition. He did not feel his tentative request for a term loan was properly handled by his former bank, one reason for moving his business to this Bank. The business carries heavy receivables, which necessitates up to $300,000 seasonal working capital borrowings. Some 40% of his business is done with 5 large contractors, all of whom are slow to pay, although apparently sound financially. Runkel personally has a strong financial position, partially thru inheritance. He is well respected in the community and appears to manage the business well. Runkel owns 72% of the company and other members of the family own another 16%. John Black, Loan Officer
5/10/X3	Committed a $300,000 working capital line to be secured by re- ceivables and inventory. We are not requiring a remittance account to be set up, but he will submit a monthly listing of receivables. In no case is our loan balance to exceed 70% of current receivables. Receivables reach a high of about $760,000 in August, and a low of about $300,000 in February. He should be able to clear this line in January and February of each year. We are encouraging him to take discounts on his payables, even if it means increasing his bank loan balance. This line will be additionally secured by the personal guaranty of Mr. and Mrs. Runkel. He is still looking for a used concrete plant. John Black
8/10/X3	Visited the Southern Material Plant. Discussed our Bank's payroll service with Mr. Runkel. Loan now at a $290,000 balance and seems to be working well. Spent some time talking to John Lutton, office manager, and Mr. Runkel's back-up management. Appears to be a very aggressive, capable individual. John Black
10/28/X3	Mr. Runkel visited the Bank to discuss his capital needs for the coming year. He must replace the concrete plant and feels that at least two of his large trucks should be replaced also. Probable cost will be $200-240,000. He was also concerned about several slow accounts. We advised him to consult his attorney and file mechanic's liens. Sam Adams, Loan Officer
1/22/X4	We are renewing a $54,000 balance on the receivables loan. Line did not clear as anticipated due to slow collections. We are ad- vising Mr. Runkel in the revision and strengthening of his credit and collection policies. He realized that their past practices have been weak and is concerned about improving performance. Charged-off $24,400 bad debt and probably has another $20,000 that should be charged-off. His statement shows profits of $44,000 after taking out $40,000 of executive salary. The company is buying a good used concrete plant at a cost of $180,000. We are loaning $160,000 on a 4-year term basis, with annual principal payments of $40,000 due each January. Loan is to be secured by a security interest in the equipment being purchased and by Runkel's guaranty. We are making an exception to our policy by loaning somewhat more than the usual 80% of purchase cost. In view of the strong finan- cial position, we feel this is justified. John Black
7/12/X4	Made annual visit to the Southern Material Company plant. They state their new credit policy is working satisfactorily. Sales are about $300,000 ahead of last year. John Black
1/7/X5	Receivables loan has a balance of $28,000. Mr. Runkel feels there will be no difficulty in clearing the loan balance in full and is making the $40,000 term loan payment. *1944* was the first year they surpassed $2,000,000 net sales. We have committed a 3 year term loan for the purchase of **2** new trucks, with the amount not to exceed $60,000. John Black

14

Dealing with the
Problem Loan

Every lending institution finds itself, from time to time, with loans in its portfolio for which the risk of loss is greater than anticipated when the loan was made, or in which the risk is greater than a lender would ordinarily willingly assume. This may be due to a poor credit decision at the time the loan was made, to adverse economic conditions, to the mismanagement or misrepresentation of the borrower, or to certain uncontrollable factors, such as the death of the borrower. A loan of this type is commonly referred to as a problem loan.

A problem loan is one in which there is a major breakdown in the repayment agreement, resulting in an undue delay in collection, in which it appears that legal action may be required to effect collection, or in which there appears to be a potential loss. It is a loan that requires special attention on the part of the lender if it is to be collected in full within a reasonable period of time after its maturity. If the lender is to avoid undue losses, it must identify problem loans promptly. Otherwise there may be no possibility of solving the problem before the situation deteriorates to the point where there is no alternative but to take the loss. In addition, if proper corrective measures are to be taken, the type, cause, and magnitude of the problem must be identified.

The quality of most institutions' commercial loan portfolio has deteriorated during the past five-years. This is evidenced by higher delinquency rates, higher charge-off percentages, and a greater incidence of business bankruptcies. A major cause of these problems has been a period of high inflation, resulting in rapidly increasing operating and labor costs and interest rates that reached unprecedented high levels, with national prime rate exceeding 20%. This has been followed by a period of recession during which many of the nation's basic industries, such as the steel, automobile, and farm equipment industries, have encountered serious problems. In addition, the nation's agricultural sector, plagued by surpluses and diminishing export demand, has also experienced financial difficulties. See Figure 14-1 for information on commercial banks' charge-off experience during the years 1980, 1981, and 1982. The increase in charge-off percentages in the commercial and industrial and farm loan categories is especially noteworthy.

Lenders have always experienced problems with some types of borrowers, such as startup companies, highly leveraged businesses, and those serving a volatile market. However, during the past several years, lenders have begun to experience severe problems with businesses that they had formerly considered to be well established and stable. In addition, many lenders feel that the provisions of the Bankruptcy Reform Act of 1978 have made it much more attractive for businesses to file bankruptcy. As a result, most lenders have become much more concerned about the quality of their loan portfolio and about developing specialized expertise in dealing with problem loans.

Danger Signals

Loans do not deteriorate suddenly and without warning. In almost every instance where a loan is deteriorating, there are warning signs that give an indication that trouble is imminent. If the lender is to identify emerging problems in a timely manner, it constantly must scrutinize the loans in its portfolio to identify those key factors that indicate loan deterioration.

The following is a list of some of the danger signals that might alert an observant loan officer to the fact that loan problems may be developing, or that a potential problem exists.

1. Delinquency
2. Unanticipated request for a renewal or extension.
3. Failure of the borrower to make full and accurate disclosure of financial information, especially in listing debts
4. Adverse financial trends
5. Overly optimistic estimates of the business' profitability and cash flow
6. Failure to provide requested information
7. A borrower who wants to expand the business operation too rapidly, and who believes increasing sales volume will solve all the business' problems
8. A borrower who expects an immediate decision and is always in a hurry.
9. History of past financial problems, bankruptcy, or collection cases
10. Judgments, tax liens, mechanic's liens

FIGURE 14-1   Net Charge-Offs by Loan Type
All Reporting Banks, All Federal Reserve Districts

	1983	1982	1981	1980
Real Estate	.12	.11	.06	.11
Financial Institutions	.04	.01	NA	.14
Securities	.03	.06	.05	NA
Farming	1.47	.81	.38	.45
Commercial and Industrial	1.02	.90	.48	.47
Individuals	.64	.89	.87	1.07
All Others	.18	.24	.11	.20
Total Loans	.58	.56	.36	.44

Source: Table 11—Reported loan and charge-off experience by type of loan, Report on Domestic and International Loan Charge-offs, Robert Morris Associates, Philadelphia, 1980, 1981, 1982, and 1983

11. A borrower who is rated "slow" by other creditors
12. Disappearance or depreciation of collateral
13. An antagonistic attitude toward other creditors
14. Hesitancy in explaining the purpose of the loan
15. Appearance of undisclosed creditors and/or numerous inquiries from other creditors
16. A borrower who purchases before arranging financing
17. Involvement in financial ventures, other than the borrower's primary business, that are described only in vague terms, or which appear to be speculative in nature, or which may involve undisclosed contingent liability
18. A borrower whose business is located outside the lender's normal business area
19. Hesitancy in allowing the lender to visit the business operation
20. A borrower who deals with numerous creditors
21. Frequent overdrafts on the business checking account
22. Cancellation of life or casualty insurance
23. Marital or family problems
24. Unusual or erratic behavior
25. Extended illness or death of a proprietor or principal of the business
26. Damage from storm, fire, flood, or other natural disaster
27. A specialized operation vulnerable to a downturn in the economy

Delinquency

Delinquency generally is considered a significant indicator of a potential loan problem. However, the mere fact that a loan is delinquent tells us little about the problems that may exist. To identify the nature of the problem, the cause of the delinquency must be determined. To determine the cause of the delinquency, it is necessary for the lender to contact the borrower promptly and discuss the matter. It may also be necessary to examine the borrower's financial statements, inventory records, list of accounts receivable, and other financial information. If delinquency is an indication of the borrower's unwillingness or inability to pay, there may be serious trouble and the loan may be past salvaging. If the delinquency results from slower than anticipated sale of inventory or collection of receivables, or from an unforseen delay in moving produce to market in the case of an agricultural loan, then the problem may be minor. However, if the delinquency is a result of the diversion of sales proceeds that were pledged for repayment on the loan, the lender has considerable reason to feel concern, and should take immediate steps to determine the seriousness of the situation.

It should be recognized that an unanticipated request for an extension or renewal prior to or at maturity may also be an indication of a breakdown of the repayment agreement which may be as serious as a delinquency. The reason for any request of this nature should be examined carefully to insure that it is justified by a change in circumstances, and that it is not merely an attempt to obscure the fact that the borrower has not complied with the repayment agreement. A loan that has been renewed or extended without justification may be a more serious problem than the loan that is delinquent. A delinquent loan at least, is usually under the surveillance of a loan officer, whereas the loan that has recently been renewed may be largely ignored.

The lender who fails to make the maturity date of the loan coincide with the date at which repayment will be available may, in fact, force a loan into delinquency. If little or no reduction in the principal balance of a loan is aniticipated at its maturity, this should be understood by all parties and clearly recorded in the credit file. Renewing or extending a loan is perfectly proper as long as the renewal or extension is anticipated or justified by circumstances. It is the renewal or extension that is unanticipated, unexplained, or unjustified that should cause concern.

We therefore may conclude that *one of the key factors in identification of a problem loan is the existence of a material breakdown in the repayment agreement*. Therefore, the real importance of a delinquency, or an unjustified request for renewal, is that it may indicate a breakdown in the repayment agreement.

Adverse Trends

Almost every commercial loan is based to a great extent on the financial status of the borrower. Evidence of significant deterioration in the debtor's financial status is almost a sure sign that a problem is developing. Comparative analysis of a series of financial statements must be made to identify adverse trends. If this comparative analysis is to be readily accomplished, it is necessary that a financial history of the loan, in the form of a spread sheet showing several years' history of both balance sheet and income statement information, be maintained. If it appears that an adverse trend is developing, the lender may need more frequent statements from the borrower, which should be examined in detail to monitor the trend. The lender should be aware that even though an adverse trend is not apparent, it nevertheless may exist. There simply may not be enough information, or it may be fraudulent, or the lender may be misinterpreting the available information.

Once an adverse trend has been identified, it then behooves the lender to take immediate steps to determine the seriousness of the situation. Every effort should be made to determine whether the adverse trend reflects a temporary setback, poor financial decisions, deteriorating market conditions, or some basic and possibly fatal weakness in the management of the business.

Fraudulent Information

It is not unusual for unaudited financial statements to omit certain items or contain erroneous information. As a rule, this results either from an oversight or the borrower's lack of understanding of proper procedures for completing a statement. In some instances, the misrepresentation is deliberate and constitutes an attempt to induce the lender to make a loan which otherwise would not be made. This may be a desperate borrower's attempt to obtain funds for which there is a dire need and which he or she intends to repay, even though it may be impossible to do so, or it may represent a calculated attempt to defraud the lender. If fraud exists and funds have been disbursed, it is likely that the lender will suffer a loss.

Fraudulent information is extremely hard to detect. Discrepancies in a financial statement may be discovered either by comparing the current statement to prior statements given by the borrower, or by verifying this information from other sources. Once a discrepancy is found, it usually is very difficult to determine whether it represents error, misunderstanding, or fraud. If additional discrepancies are found, the probability of deliberate misrepresentation is significantly increased. If the lender concludes that the information is fraudulent, then obviously a serious problem exists, and immediate aggressive steps should be taken both to determine the magnitude of the fraud and to protect the lender's interest.

The discovery of error or misrepresentation in financial statement information often reveals the existence of an undisclosed creditor. As soon as the lender becomes aware of an undisclosed creditor, immediate measures should be taken to ascertain the extent of the borrower's involvement with that creditor, including the amount and term of the debt, collateral held, and the repayment agreement. The existence of one undisclosed creditor always raises the possibility that other undisclosed creditors may exist, and this situation merits a thorough credit investigation. While an erroneous financial statement reflects on the financial management ability and sense of responsibility of the borrower, it does not of itself necessarily indicate a serious loan problem. However, if deliberate misrepresentation or the existence of undisclosed creditors is discovered, the lender must take immediate and aggressive corrective action to avoid a loss.

Loss of Debtor Cooperation

A relationship of cooperation, frankness, and mutual trust between the borrower and the lender contributes materially to the strength, quality, and workability of a loan. Deterioration of this working relationship and loss of the debtor's cooperation is detrimental to the quality of the loan and usually is indicative of a developing loan problem. Loss of debtor cooperation may be evidenced by failure to provide financial information, or hesitancy to discuss the business' financial situation. Failure to provide financial statements, or providing poorer quality statements, may indicate an attempt to hide a deteriorating financial position or loans from other sources. Whatever the reason, hesitancy or failure of the debtor to provide adequate financial information when requested is a red flag.

In some cases, the borrower's change of attitude toward the lender may be the only evidence of loss of cooperation. A competent loan officer should be able to detect such changes in attitude, and should investigate further as a result.

Disappearance or Depreciation of Collateral

Lenders generally consider secured loans to be of higher quality than unsecured loans, since the lender holds security that can be converted into cash to pay the loan. However, a number of problems arise with secured loans. To begin with, when a bank has a security interest in property which is not in its possession, the loan is truly secured only if that property can be located, repossessed, and sold for an amount sufficient to pay the loan.

Vehicles and construction equipment are examples of easily transportable items which often are used as collateral. When acquiring a security interest, the lender should obtain a complete description and should verify that description by a physical inspection of the equipment or vehicle. During the term of the loan, the lender should find out the location of the collateral and periodically make physical inspections. Failure to locate collateral should cause immediate concern. Is the equipment merely being used in another location, is it leased to someone else, or has it been sold or traded for other equipment? If the latter is the case, it may be difficult to locate and repossess the collateral. Also, the lender may have to contend with the claim of a third party purchaser of the equipment and the equipment trade may result in the borrower owing a sizeable debt to another creditor.

Disappearance of inventory, whether it consists of raw materials or finished products, results in an immediate twofold problem for the creditor. Not only has the collateral disappeared, but also the source of repayment. This situation almost invariably involves dishonesty on the part of the borrower and should be considered extremely serious.

In loans where cash value of life insurance is used as security, the insurance company normally retains the right to use the cash value of the policy to extend its life in case of nonpayment of a premium. This may materially depreciate the amount of the cash value assigned to the lender. The cancellation of casualty insurance covering collateral, or of life insurance assigned to the lender, should be a cause for immediate concern. This is often the first indication the lender receives that the borrower is experiencing cash flow problems. Depending upon the amount of perceived exposure, the lender may decide to pay the necessary premium to keep the insurance in force, and add that amount to the principal balance of the borrower's loan. The provisions of most promissory notes and security agreements allow a lender to do this.

Other Factors

Several other factors may indicate loan deterioration. Most of these are not controllable, or only partially controllable, by the borrower. These include marital problems, mental or emotional problems, illness or death of the borrower, acts of God, and vulnerability to adverse trends in the economy.

Marital problems may cause deterioration in the quality of a loan for a number of reasons, including loss of control of family finances, and a general increase in personal spending. If both husband and wife are obligated on the note, the bank may find itself dealing with two debtors who are unwilling to cooperate either with each other or with the bank, with each maintaining that the debt is really the obligation of the other. In addition, a debtor's financial position may be weakened by legal costs and a property settlement if a divorce occurs. Repayment capacity may be weakened by alimony and child support payments. Not all borrowers who have marital difficulties become collection problems, but when marital difficulties occur, the possibility of a collection problem is increased.

Many lenders are becoming increasingly concerned about situations involving mental or emotional problems on the part of the borrower. Alcoholism or drug use may be the primary symptom of the problem, which may result from the inability of the borrower to cope with the stresses of modern day life. Mental or emotional problems may be evidenced by erratic behavior, impulsive and imprudent business decisions, depression, abrupt changes in attitude, and emotional outbursts. A debtor suffering severe problems of this kind may become involved in speculative financial schemes, increase personal spending, sell collateral, make unnecessary and imprudent purchases, and become involved in disputes with associates, employees, and the lender. Counseling the debtor may have little or no effect. Business associates, trusted employees, and friends may be unable to influence the debtor's behavior. In some instances, contact by the bank with the borrower's family or business associates may be helpful, but this obviously must be done with the greatest discretion. In some instances, the bank will have to make a decision to collect the loan, and if the borrower is a long term and valued customer, this can be an extremely difficult decision.

The death or extended illness of a borrower may also cause serious problems, especially in cases where back-up management is weak or entirely lacking. The borrower's business may cease to be profitable for lack of management. Labor costs may increase, there may be heavy medical and funeral costs, and liquidation of the debtor's business may become a necessity. In order to protect itself from these problems, the bank should encourage, and in some cases require, that the borrower have adequate life and medical insurance coverage.

Some loans may become problem loans due to an act of God or natural disaster such as fire, flood, hail, or windstorm. These may result in destruction of the borrower's facilities, equipment, and inventory, creating both a loss of current income and the necessity for sizeable capital outlay to reconstruct facilities and reacquire equipment and inventory. Adequate hazard and business interruption insurance coverage is important, both to the debtor and the lender, but there are some hazards that cannot be covered by insurance. For the creditor to be adequately protected against loss from a natural disaster, it is necessary that the borrower have both adequate hazard insurance coverage, and adequate financial strength to enable him or her to repay the loan from other sources, or to reestablish the business.

It is essential that the lender consider the effect that a downturn in the economy may have on the borrower. If vulnerability to economic adversity is high, due to the nature of the business, then financial position and collateral assume much greater importance in providing safety in the loan.

Another concern of the lender is the borrower who becomes involved in a financial venture that has little connection with the borrower's primary business, and which the lender may not fully understand. The borrower may describe such a venture in vague terms, and since such ventures are sometimes speculative in nature, and often involve an undisclosed contingent liability, the lender should require full disclosure of the nature of such a venture. If an investment in another legal entity is involved, full financial information on that entity should be obtained by the lender.

Another danger signal often overlooked by a bank is a continuing overdraft problem in the borrower's account, or a significant decrease in balances and activity in the borrower's account. This may be an indication that the borrower is having cash flow problems, or that deposit accounts have been established elsewhere, and that the borrower may be engaging in financial transactions of which his or her primary lender has no knowledge.

Techniques for Early Identification

It is important for the lender to be able to identify problem loans early so that corrective action can be taken before the situation becomes irretrievable. The necessity for continuing analysis of the financial information in the lender's credit files cannot be overemphasized. Information submitted by the borrower also should be verified by searches of the public records, contact with other creditors, and examination of the records of the borrower. Verification of information is always important, but especially where discrepancy or deterioration exists it becomes important to obtain the greatest possible amount of verified information.

Continuous supervision of a loan is just as important as continuous analysis. The lender's loan agreement and repayment agreement with the debtor should be reviewed periodically, and steps should be taken to ascertain that these agreements are being complied with. Any apparent breakdown in repayment should be investigated immediately. A good loan officer stays in contact with the borrower and arranges periodic conferences for the review of the borrower's overall financial position and progress. It is essential that the loan officer be well informed concerning the debtor's cash flow, anticipated borrowing needs, and the general condition of the business.

In summary, early identification of a problem loan starts with continuous monitoring of the borrower's business. It also requires open lines of communication with the borrower, and periodic updating, verification, and analysis of financial information. Finally, the lender must have the ability to identify and correctly interpret the danger signals.

Determining the Magnitude of the Problem

Once a lender has recognized the likelihood that a problem loan exists, immediate steps should be taken to determine the seriousness of the problem. The type of corrective action that the lender should take will depend upon its collateral position, the availability of repayment, the extent of the debtor's involvement with other creditors, and the attitude of the debtor. To determine the magnitude of the problem, these key factors must be analyzed.

The bank's best source of information on the debtor will be its own credit files, which should be immediately reviewed by one or more loan officers. This detailed examination often reveals pertinent facts which were previously overlooked. If the lender holds collateral, its value should be verified. If the bank has a security interest in collateral not in its possession, its location, condition, and value should be ascertained. The lender also should verify that previous filings under the Uniform Commercial Code are proper. An estimate should be made of the availability of repayment from liquidation of collateral or other saleable assets, and from the debtor's normal cash flow. In the case of a serious problem loan, this may prove to be very difficult. An immediate search of the public records should be made to determine whether any financing statements, liens, or judgments have been filed against the debtor by other creditors.

After the lender has accumulated as much current information as possible, the next step is direct contact with the debtor. If the owner or management of the business is honest and responsible, it is likely that the lender's concern will be welcomed, and that there will be a complete willingness to engage in a frank discussion of the situation. The debtor sometimes does not recognize that trouble is developing and the counsel of the bank is required to help management recognize its difficulties. Even though management recognizes that it is in trouble, it simply may avoid facing that fact until forced to do so. Some businesspeople, recognizing that they are in difficulty, become so fearful of their creditors that they will go to great lengths to avoid any discussion. Lastly, there is the businessperson who is either irresponsible or dishonest and who has no intention of cooperating with the creditors in any way.

If the lender can obtain the debtor's full cooperation, it increases considerably the chances of correcting the situation without a charge-off and the financial ruin of the borrower. By discussion with the debtor and review of the business' records, the lender can usually assist in identifying the cause of the difficulty. The problem then becomes one of correcting the situation.

Depending on the results of the conference with the borrower, the lender may decide to contact the other creditors involved. This can be helpful, but also can be dangerous. If the lender has any reason to doubt the debtor's truthfulness, contacting the other creditors may be almost a necessity. Contact with other creditors should consist of a request for factual information including the amount owed, terms of the loan, and security held. Generally, this is on an exchange-of-information basis, where the other creditor expects to learn as much as is disclosed to the inquirer. The greatest danger is that any show of concern by the lender may precipitate legal action by a third party creditor which might be derogatory to the lender's position. For the most part, it simply becomes a question of weighing the possibility of precipitating action by another creditor against the need for verified information, and the lender must make a decision based upon the available facts.

Identifying the Cause of the Problem

The major causes of problems with commercial and business loans can be divided into four general categories—mismanagement, economic decline, other adversity, and fraud. In many loans, combinations of these factors are involved. Studies by Robert Morris Associates indicate that mismanagement is the most common cause of business failures. Mismanagement refers to the inability of the management to handle the business' affairs and finances in a sound and prudent manner. Economic decline refers to deterioration in market prices and other cyclical changes in the economic climate which contribute to the deterioration of the business' financial situation. Other adversity includes factors beyond the borrower's control, such as weather, natural disaster, illness, and death. Fraud refers to problems caused by misrepresentations by the borrower regarding the business' financial status, the purpose of the loan, or ability to repay.

Identification of the cause of a problem loan is rarely a simple task, and in many cases, identifying the various factors involved many be complex and difficult. I have seen loans in which weak management was the major cause of the problem, but when the borrower's problems caused by mismanagement became severe enough, fraud was resorted to in a misguided attempt to stay in business. In other cases, weak management, aggravated by a change in economic conditions, may be the major cause. At any rate, whatever the situation, the lender must identify the problem and its causes as best it can, and then take those measures necessary to keep the situation under control until the problem is either corrected or the loan is collected.

Supervision of the Problem Loan

When a lender comes to the realization that a problem loan exists, ordinarily there is no immediate way to solve the problem. Therefore, the lender, for a period of time, is forced to live with the loan. As stated previously, it is very important for the lender to contact the debtor and get as much information as possible about the situation. This is the first step in supervision of the problem loan. It is essential that the lender make a correct assessment of the debtor's attitude if the loan is to be handled properly. The debtor's willingness to discuss his or her financial situation with the lender and to make the business' records available for inspection are excellent indicators of attitude. However, the true measure of attitude lies in the debtor's willingness to participate in a program of correction that typically entails some hardship. The debtor may temporarily lose full control of the business' affairs, be required to reduce expenses, and postpone desired capital expenditures. It may be necessary to liquidate business assets against management's wishes. If management's attitude is one of true cooperation, it will consent to necessary but unpleasant actions requested by the lender.

The bank's conference with the debtor should achieve one other objective, that of making the bank's position clear. At this time, it is unlikely that the bank will have a final or firm decision regarding its ultimate attitude toward the loan. During the initial conference, the borrower should be given as much information as possible concerning the actions the bank will or will not condone. Management should be told what records and reports will be required, and the steps it will be expected to take concerning the immediate management of the business. It should be stressed again that many honest borrowers become quite fearful of their creditors when they realize a problem exists, and that the creditor is aware of the problem. Therefore, if the bank expects the debtor's cooperation, it usually is necessary to give assurances that the bank wishes to cooperate with the debtor. It should be pointed out that it is advantageous to both parties to find a solution.

The importance of the proper handling of this initial contact with the debtor cannot be overemphasized, since it will significantly affect the bank's working relationship with the debtor during the stressful period to come. The bank must hope to achieve a twofold effect. It must be forceful enough to convince the debtor that the situation is serious and that positive steps for correction must be taken immediately. It also must be reasonable and conciliatory enough so that the debtor will believe that all is not lost, and that cooperating with the bank to institute a plan for correction may be beneficial. In no case should the bank make unrealistic demands for immediate payment, nor, except where obvious fraud or gross misrepresentation exists, should it threaten legal action at this time.

A Plan for Correction

If the lender and borrower are to correct a problem loan, then the problem must be identified and a solution must be found. Achieving a workable solution rarely is easy, and in some cases, it is impossible. Where no workable solution can be found, the lender has no alternative but to collect the loan, either through the voluntary liquidation of assets by the debtor, or by a forced liquidation through legal action. However, in many cases, through close supervision, patience, and prudent handling by the creditor, and through the cooperation, sacrifice, and hard work of the borrower, a sound plan for correction can be achieved. Ideally, this plan will result in the eventual repayment of the loan from the normal cash flow of the borrower's business operation, without liquidation of those assets necessary for the continued operation of the business.

The benefits that accrue to the debtor, if the plan for correction is successful, are obvious. There are also significant benefits to the lender in addition to the avoidance of a charge off if the plan is successful. If the bank can help the borrower solve his or her problems and become a successful business-person, it will have a loyal customer for many years to come. The bank ordinarily gains the goodwill of the customer, as well as that of the business community. Certainly, almost any individual or business would prefer to deal with an institution that is known for its concern for the welfare of its customers and its readiness to serve them, rather than one known for its harsh treatment of delinquent borrowers.

Protection of the lender's position must be the prime consideration in the formulation of any plan for correction. Every loan officer has an obligation to keep his or her institution's loan portfolio sound, and to avoid losses to the greatest extent possible. Therefore, for the plan for correction to be accept-able, it must not be derogatory to the bank's interests, and ideally should improve its position. The plan should identify all sources of repayment, the amount of repayment anticipated from those sources, and the estimated time at which it will be available. It should specifically set out any plan for reorganization or recapitalization of the business, along with the methods to be used in accomplishing this. The plan further should outline the steps to be taken to strengthen the management of the business, the extent to which the bank is to participate in management, and the manner in which, and intervals at which, the results of these changes are to be reported to the bank. The plan for correction also should contain any agreement with the debtor for the pledging of additional security, the sale of assets, or any other major changes to be made in the debtor's financial structure. It further should outline any commitment on the part of the bank for loan extensions or renewals, and the circumstances under which the bank will extend new credit. Lastly, and very importantly, the plan for the correction should set goals and a timetable for their achievement.

Any plan for correction ordinarily entails a certain amount of sacrifice by the debtor through concerted effort to improve his or her position. For an individual borrower, the plan for correction may entail an effort to increase family income, consolidate debts, and reduce family spending. For a business borrower, the plan for correction may entail a change in management, either an expansion or a reduction in the scope of the business, stringent reductions in operating expenses and management salaries, and a reduction in work force. It may also involve the sale of equipment not essential to the operation of the business, elimination of management perogatives, and other steps which management may find quite distasteful. If the problem is serious, the plan may involve the orderly liquidation of the business.

Once the plan of correction has been established and agreed upon by the bank and the debtor, implementation becomes the problem. If the plan is to work, it will require constant supervision by the bank, frequent reports from the debtor, open lines of communication between the debtor and bank, and a great deal of concern and hard work on the part of both parties.

Additional Collateral or Sale of Assets

As soon as a loan is classified as a problem loan, the lender should strive to improve its position through the acquisition of additional collateral. The debtor's financial statements and other information in the lender's files should be examined to determine the availability of additional collateral. In many cases, the lender will find that all assets not pledged to it are pledged to other creditors. However, this is not invariably so, and a search for additional available assets may be rewarding. For example, a borrower may own a vehicle to which it has clear title, or marketable securities, savings accounts, or cash value of life insurance which could be pledged. The creditor should not overlook the possibility that the individual borrower may have parents or other close relatives who may be willing to guarantee or cosign until the debtor can resolve his or her financial problems.

If the debtor is a contract buyer or seller of real estate, the lender should consider the possibility that an assignment of the debtor's interest in the contract for purchase or sale of real estate may have some collateral value. An assignment of the buyer's interest in a purchase contract provides the creditor with a claim on the buyer's equity in the property, subject to any rights of the seller. An assignment of a seller's interest in a sales contract generally gives the creditor a claim to the periodic payments made by the purchaser to the seller.

If the real estate in which the creditor is attempting to perfect an interest is the personal residence of the borrower, the creditor should be sure to comply with the requirements of the Consumer Credit Protection Act and Federal Regulation Z. Recent court decisions indicate that any lender that fails to comply with Regulation Z or to observe the borrower's right to rescind the transaction is in jeopardy of court action brought by the debtor, especially where the loan becomes a collection case.

The debtor's financial statement also should be examined to determine if there are assets that are marketable and can be converted to cash without seriously affecting the debtor's business operation.

The creditor should remain aware that any additional collateral obtained, or the sales proceeds of assets sold, may be lost if the debtor files bankruptcy within three months of the date that the creditor obtained the collateral or sales proceeds. This possibility of losing additional collateral or proceeds acquired after the loan gets in trouble, through a preference, represents a strong argument for adequately collateralizing the loan at its inception, rather than attempting to do so when the loan is in trouble. However, even if the lender loses the additional collateral, it is no worse off than before, and the chances are relatively good that it will be able to retain any additional collateral acquired.

Extensions and Renewals

The lender may seek to solve the borrower's problem of inadequate cash flow to meet loan obligations through the extension of loan maturity. An extension or renewal should be considered only after a thorough examination of a cash flow projection, and only if there is adequate evidence that repayment will actually materialize at a later time. Any renewal or extension should be for a short period of time, and at each maturity the lender should carefully reexamine its position before granting additional renewals or extensions.

There are several dangers involved in granting an extension or renewal. The debtor may feel relieved of pressure from the lender, and may reduce efforts to repay the debt, or divert available cash to the payment of other debts that are more pressing. At times, a lender is tempted to grant an extension or renewal because it presents a means for avoiding the problem at hand, or because it defers a difficult decision—that of collecting the loan. Also, loans in a current status are often scrutinized less closely by top management and supervisory authorities than those in a delinquent status. Thus, a renewal or extension may have the effect of lessening the lender's supervision of the loan. Another point to be considered is that the lender usually is on firmer legal ground in instituting legal action on a delinquent loan than on a loan that is in a current status. If the lender is considering legal action to collect the loan, under no circumstances should it consent to an extension or renewal, nor imply to the debtor that it is willing to do so. A renewed or extended problem loan may well be a poorer loan from the lender's standpoint than one that is in a delinquent status, unless there is a sound, realistic basis for the renewal or extension.

Analysis of Results

The results of any correction program should be carefully and regularly analyzed by the lender. Although improvement in the borrower's situation is usually a slow process, further deterioration can take place very rapidly. If not recognized quickly, the lender will likely find itself with a charge-off. A number of things should be taken into consideration in the analysis of the results of the program of correction. The borrower's actual performance should be compared to the projections submitted to the lender. Any sizeable deviation from the business' cash flow projection should be examined thoroughly and the reason for the deviation established. Consideration should be given both to the borrower's reduction of debt to the lender, and to the change in overall debt position. If the borrower is merely reducing one debt by increasing another, it is obvious that there is no improvement in overall position. Interim profit and loss statements should be examined closely and compared with both budget and past performance. Through a conference with the borrower and by an examination of the business' records, the lender should establish that it is conforming to the terms of the program of correction. The debtor's attitude also should be assessed periodically to determine that it remains constructive and cooperative.

If the lender's analysis and observations indicate that the program of correction is working well, it may then be only a matter of time and supervision for the problem to be corrected. If the debtor's progress is far short of what was anticipated, or if there is no progress at all, the lender has three alternatives—altering the present program for correction, instituting an entirely new program, or collecting the loan.

Collecting the Problem Loan

Every institution from time to time finds it necessary to initiate action to collect a loan. This is rarely an easy decision, and in most cases is made only after much consideration. In most problem loans, the decision to collect is made quite some time after the loan is recognized as a problem. There usually are lengthy negotiations with the debtor, attempts to improve the lender's position, and efforts to institute a program of correction. Legal action to collect the loan ordinarily is taken only after all these measures have proved ineffective. There are two instances in which a creditor undoubtedly would wish to institute legal action to collect immediately. One of these would be a case involving fraud, and the other a case in which the debtor had dissipated the business' assets to an extent that collectibility of the loan had become very questionable.

The case of the honest debtor who simply cannot pay immediately is difficult to handle and probably creates the greatest amount of soul-searching for the loan officer. This debtor generally readily admits owing the debt, and often has legitimate reasons why payment cannot be made, such as marketing problems, unforeseen operating losses, or the like. In spite of the fact that the loan officer may sympathize with the debtor, he or she often must face the fact that the loan is a collection case, and that the lending institution's interests must be protected by taking legal action.

Even though the debtor is honest, the situation may well have deteriorated to the point where the loan is wholly or partially uncollectible. In this
case, legal action should be considered only in the light of the probable results
it will produce. If the debtor's assets have been totally dissipated, legal action
may fail to result in a recovery of any kind. Thus, in addition to having
a charge-off, the lender may be required to pay heavy court costs and attorney fees. However, there are occasions upon which the lender should still
consider bringing a suit, based upon what may be discovered through supplementary proceedings in the nature of citations and various discovery procedures, such as depositions or motions to produce records. There have been
instances, once legal action was taken, where the claim was collected, even
though to all outward appearances it seemed that the debtor was completely
insolvent.

Judgment should be obtained with all possible speed in the case of
fraud. In many instances, by the time the creditor realizes that a problem
exists, it is too late to make any kind of recovery. Numerous other creditors
usually will be involved, and collateral and other assets will be extremely hard
to locate.

Many lenders' note forms contain an acceleration clause which gives the
lender the opportunity to declare the note immediately due and payable when
it learns that the debtor's situation is deteriorating. Without a clause of this
nature in the note, the lender might find itself unable to take any action until
the next maturity of the debtor's note, even though the deterioration of the
debtor's position is evident. The statutes generally require the lender to have
reasonable evidence of a possible deterioration of the debtor's position and a
"good faith belief" that it is insecure in order to exercise the acceleration
clause. In practice, the acceleration clause has proven to be an extremely
useful means for taking immediate legal action where the situation is deteriorating rapidly.

Once the lender has decided to collect the loan, demand of payment in
the manner required by the terms of the note should be made upon the
debtor. If verbal demand is made, it should be followed by a letter outlining
the terms of the lender's demand. The demand for payment should make it
clear that the lender is willing to accept nothing less than payment in full, and
should give the debtor a reasonable deadline to accomplish this. Depending
upon the circumstances, a reasonable deadline might be as little as a few days
or as long as several months. It should be made clear to the debtor that the
lender expects payment as soon as possible, and that procrastination or
stalling on the part of the debtor will not be tolerated. In making demand for
payment, the lender should be careful not to waive any rights, and may wish to
consult its attorney prior to taking this action.

If the lender is accelerating the maturity of the loan, the debtor should be informed in general terms of the reason the lender has deemed itself insecure. It should be made clear to the debtor that the maturity date of the loan has been advanced to the present date. In addition to verbal communication with the debtor, the lender should make sure that the debtor is given a proper legal notice of the acceleration, preferably by registered letter. If the lender anticipates any difficulty or controversy, any conference with the debtor should be conducted by two representatives of the lender, or by a loan officer and the lending institution's attorney, rather than by a single officer. This will provide a substantiating witness to the conversation. Once demand for payment has been made on the debtor, the lender must then consider itself and the debtor to be adversaries. This should be communicated to the debtor to prevent a subsequent accusation of lack of good faith on the part of the lender. All the lender's actions in the further handling of the loan should be documented carefully and substantiated in the credit file.

It should be emphasized that in the majority of cases the debtor will continue to cooperate with the lender, even after he or she realizes that the loan must be paid in full. It is natural for the debtor to feel a certain amount of resentment toward the lender, but in most cases, the debtor will recognize that he or she is legally and morally obligated to pay the debt and will make a sincere effort to do so. The lender should make every effort to retain the debtor's cooperation, and to counsel and assist him or her in every way possible in refinancing, liquidating assets, or other methods to raise the funds to pay off the loan. The best collection officers are those who are capable of retaining the debtor's cooperation to the extent that the loan is paid without controversy, dispute, or court action, rather than those who institute immediate legal action.

15

Collections and Bankruptcy

Part 5 of Article 9 of the Uniform Commercial Code is titled "Default," and addresses the rights of the secured party when a default occurs. However, the Uniform Commercial Code does not define a default. Rather, what constitutes a default is determined by the provisions of the promissory note and security agreement.

Once a default occurs under the provisions of the note and/or security agreement, and it becomes apparent to the lender that there is no feasible way to cure that default by instituting a plan of correction, the lender must then consider the various available alternatives for proceeding to collect the loan. If the loan has not matured, the first step in the collection process may be for the lender to "deem itself insecure," and accelerate the maturity of the note to the present date. Then, the secured party must consider the various options for further action. These may include the following:

1.   Attempting to convince the debtor to voluntarily liquidate the business' assets. Assets sold in a voluntary sale often bring a higher price than assets sold in a foreclosure, and the debtor avoids the stigma of a foreclosure sale. The secured party avoids both the costs and legal pitfalls involved in the repossession and resale of collateral. Of all the options available to the secured party, the voluntary liquidation is undoubtedly the most beneficial in most instances, provided the secured party can obtain full cooperation of the debtor.

2.   Another alternative available to the secured party is to take no legal action at all and simply charge off the full amount of the loan. If all of the assets of the debtor have been dissipated, and it appears that legal action may be fruitless, then the lender may choose to take no action at all, rather than incurring substantial legal fees and court costs in an action that would be futile. However, the secured party should not give up too easily. There have

been instances, once legal action was taken, where the lender, by means of citation proceedings and motions to produce records, was able to discover formerly undisclosed assets, and as a result was able to collect the claim, even though it appeared the debtor was insolvent.

3.   In some instances, the lender may join with the other creditors in the formation of a creditors committee. This ordinarily requires the cooperation of the debtor, and usually consists of an arrangement under which the creditors appoint a trustee to whom the debtor voluntarily assigns his or her assets. The trustee then liquidates these assets in an orderly manner and divides the proceeds among the various creditors. The creditors committee approach is usually not feasible unless all the major creditors are in agreement, and it often becomes a necessity to buy out the interest of the minor creditors who are unwilling to agree to the creditors committee arrangement. In many or most instances the debtor may prefer filing bankruptcy to cooperating with a creditors committee, due to the protection provided the debtor by the bankruptcy court.

4.   In some instances it may be advantageous to the lender to petition the court for the formation of an equity receivership. This is another form of liquidation, one that is usually considered to be just short of bankruptcy. An equity receivership is set up under court supervision and is often sought in a case where a concern is solvent in an accounting sense, that is, the value of the assets exceeds the liabilities, but the firm is illiquid and cannot generate sufficient cash flow to meet liabilities as they become due. To assure that some of the creditors do not attempt to collect their claim ahead of those who are trying to take a helpful and constructive attitude, an equity receivership may be requested.

An equity receivership can be helpful to the debtor. It relieves the troubled business from harassment by creditors, and buys time for the resolution of its problems. It also gives the creditors assurance of fair treatment relative to the other creditors, and provides an opportunity to assess the business' chance of survival. An equity receivership usually entails an injunction against creditors interfering with the operation of the business, while the receiver attempts to get as much cash as possible out of the business to pay the creditors. At best, an equity receivership will result in a reorganization of the business, and at worst, it entails an orderly liquidation and distribution of the proceeds to the creditors. Again, the debtor may prefer to file for bankruptcy than to become involved in an equity receivership.

5.   The debtor may offer a composition settlement, that is an offer of something less than face value (such as 50%) of the debt owed in return for a full discharge of the indebtedness. When considering the offer of a composition settlement, the secured party must consider the possibility of collecting the loan in full through legal action, as well as the legal costs involved in doing

so. In some cases, the lender may come to the conclusion that it is advantageous to accept the composition settlement, rather than go through the costly and time consuming process of lengthy litigation.

6.   The lender may initiate legal action to obtain a judgment against the debtor. Judgments are discussed in another section of this chapter.

7.   The lender may initiate legal action against co-makers, endorsers, or guarantors for collection of the loan. The provisions of most standard promissory note forms and guaranty of payment forms allow the lender to move directly against a co-obligor without taking legal action against the primary debtor. In a situation where the debtor is insolvent, and where the co-obligor has assets, action against the co-obligor is often the most attractive option available to the lender. The co-obligor, of course, is generally also liable for any deficiency that may exist after the lender has collected as much as possible from the primary debtor.

8.   The lender may proceed to collect the loan by the sale of collateral held by it, or by the repossession and resale of collateral in the possession of the debtor. If the self-help repossession cannot be accomplished, then the lender may also seek court assistance by means of a replevin action.

9.   The lender and other creditors may force the debtor into involuntary bankruptcy. Most lenders do not consider this an attractive alternative for the collection of the debt, since most prefer to collect the debt outside of a bankruptcy. However, in rare cases, where a large number of secured creditors are involved, and there are numerous disputes concerning priority to collateral, this alternative might be considered.

Judgments

Upon default by a debtor the creditor may bring legal action for judgment. A judgment, whether obtained by confession or through court action, becomes a lien upon the personal property and real estate of the debtor. Perfected security interests and mortgage liens in existence at the time the judgment is entered take priority over that judgment. The judgment, however, has priority over any security interests and mortgages subsequently filed or recorded. Through a writ of execution and levy, the judgment creditor may have the sheriff of the county in which the debtor resides take possession of the debtor's property, either real or personal, and have it sold in satisfaction of the judgment debt. A judgment becomes a lien upon the personal property of the debtor at the time it is entered, and upon the real property of the debtor at the time a certified copy or memorandum of the judgment is filed in the office of the Recorder of Deeds in the county in which the real estate is located. In most states, a judgment is effective as a lien against the debtor for a period of seven years from the time it is entered, and it may be revived for additional seven-year periods.

A secured creditor has the option of obtaining a judgment, or enforcing the security interest by exercising the remedies provided in Part 5 of Article 9. UCC 9-501(1) clearly states that when a debtor is in default the secured party may reduce his or her claim to judgment, foreclose or otherwise enforce the security interest by any available judicial procedure. In some instances, there are significant advantages to the secured lender in obtaining a judgment, rather than pursuing the remedies provided in the Code. If it appears that a self-help repossession may be difficult, due to a potential breach of the peace, or that due to its nature the collateral may be difficult to assemble and move, it may be preferable from the the secured party's standpoint to obtain a judgment and a court order for the debtor to assemble and deliver the collateral to the secured party. This approach also enables the secured lender to avoid many of the legal pitfalls involved in repossession or replevin. Also, if the value of the collateral is insufficient to cover the debt, and if it appears that the debtor has additional unencumbered assets, the judgment becomes a lien upon those additional unencumbered assets, and thereby strengthens the lender's collateral position.

Obtaining a judgment is a means for an unsecured lender to secure its claim, provided that the debtor owns unencumbered assets. However, all too often, by the time an unsecured creditor obtains a judgment, there will be few if any remaining assets available to secure its claim. In addition, the lender should be aware that any judgment obtained within 90 days of the date the debtor files bankruptcy will be set aside as a preference.

In those states where the statutes allow cognovit or confession of judgment, and where most banks use commercial note forms containing a cognovit or confession of judgment clause, a judgment can be obtained quickly by having the bank's attorney take the note before a circuit judge, prove that the note is in default, show that the note contains a confession of judgment clause, and request the judge to enter a judgment against the debtor. All this may be done *without either the knowledge or consent of the debtor.* There is considerable controversy over whether the confession of judgment clause violates the debtor's right of due process. For this reason, confession of judgment has been eliminated by statute in many states, and it appears likely that it will soon be eliminated in some other states in which it is still legal. Even in those states where the cognovit clause is legal, the courts will generally refuse to enter a judgment by confession in a consumer case.

If the creditor does not have the remedy of confession of judgment, it must then file a suit for judgment in circuit court. The suit is filed, placed on the court docket, a time set for a hearing, and proper notice given the debtor. At the hearing the creditor presents his or her evidence and arguments as to why the judgment should be entered, and the debtor has the opportunity to present evidence and arguments in his or her defense if he or she wishes to do so. If the creditor prevails, the court then makes its decision, and a judgment is entered.

It then becomes the duty of the creditor's attorney to take the proper steps to enforce the court decree and see to it that the judgment is satisfied. The vigor with which the creditor's attorney seeks enforcement of the judgment is a critical factor in determining the results obtained from the action. The first step in the enforcement process is ordinarily that of filing a memorandum of judgment in the office of the County Recorder, since this is required for the judgment to become a lien upon the real estate of the debtor. The attorney may then have a writ of execution issued ordering the sheriff to seize either real or personal property of the debtor to be sold in satisfaction of the judgment. In some cases, the attorney will request a supplementary proceeding, also known as a citation proceeding. By means of a citation proceeding, the debtor may be brought to court to be interrogated to discover assets, ordered to make payment, or deliver up property, or do other things leading to the satisfaction of the judgment. The court has broad powers to issue orders for just payment of the judgment, except that these orders may not violate the exemption laws. A third party may also be brought to court through a citation proceeding and ordered to deliver up property or funds held by the third party which belong to the debtor.

A judgment is ordinarily entered in an amount consisting of the total of the principal and interest due as of that date, plus court costs and fees of the attorney of the creditor, if the note or instrument so provides. Thereafter, the creditor may no longer charge interest at the rate stated on the note but may charge interest on the full amount of the judgment at a rate set by law. Generally, this statutory interest rate will be significantly less than the rate normally charged on commercial loans. The judgment ordinarily remains on record until paid in full, at which time the creditor must furnish a satisfaction of judgment form which must be recorded to clear the judgment from the records. Under certain circumstances, however, the creditor may wish to furnish partial satisfactions from time to time, to facilitate liquidation of the debtor's property.

During court proceedings on a suit for judgment, the debtor may present a great variety of reasons why he or she should not have to pay the debt. These may include allegations that the amount owed is incorrect, that the obligation is not due, that someone else is the primary obligor, or that the lender misrepresented the terms of the loan. In addition, the debtor may allege that there has been a violation of the Federal Truth in Lending Law or the Equal Credit Opportunity Act (especially where the lender has obtained a cosignature or guaranty from the spouse), or that the actions of the bank's officers were malicious or otherwise improper. If the bank has made the loan on a proper basis and adequately documented its actions, it ordinarily will be able to defend itself against this kind of attack.

If judgment is by confession, the debtor may bring suit to set aside the judgment. If the bank is seeking to repossess collateral held by the debtor, the debtor may seek an injunction or restraining order to prevent the bank from doing so. All these defensive actions by the debtor will probably not prevent the bank from ultimately collecting its loan if the debtor has sufficient assets to pay. However, these defensive actions by the debtor can be time consuming and costly to the creditor, as well as frustrating, due to the inordinate delays and postponements which are typical of this type of court action.

Repossession of Collateral

If the collateral is in the possession of the secured party, repossession obviously does not present a problem. However, at least a portion of the collateral securing most business loans consists of tangible property in possession of the debtor. The Code states that unless otherwise agreed, a secured party has on default the right to take possession of collateral. In taking possession the secured party may proceed without judicial process if this can be done without breach of the peace, or may proceed by action.[1] Therefore, the Code establishes a fairly simple basic rule—the secured party may make a self-help repossession provided no "breach of the peace" occurs.

If the security agreement provides, the secured party may require the debtor to assemble the collateral and make it available to the secured party at a place to be designated by the secured party, which is reasonably convenient to both parties. Without removal a secured party may render equipment unusable, and may dispose of collateral on the debtor's premises under Section 9-504.[1] Therefore, the creditor is not required by law to remove the collateral from the borrower's premises, but from a practical standpoint, removal may be a necessity in order to remove the collateral from the debtor's control.

The rules established by the Code generally also apply to vehicles as far as their repossession and disposition is concerned, although here the creditor has the additional problem of dealing with the certificate of title, upon which the creditor's lien must be properly registered. Upon resale of a vehicle, the law outlines the procedure for obtaining the issuance of a new title.

Repossessed vehicles and equipment often are found to be in poor condition. Businesses that are in financial difficulty may neglect routine maintenance and repairs. It is also common to find equipment stripped of accessories and attachments. Hard use by uncaring operators may result in significant deterioration in condition. For these reasons, the secured party

[1]   UCC 9-503

may find that the saleable value of repossessed equipment and vehicles is substantially less than anticipated. In preparing the collateral for resale, the lender may repair and recondition it, as long as this is done in a commercially reasonable manner.

A "self-help" repossession is one in which the secured party acts on its own behalf, without the involvement of "state action." This means that the repossession is made without the involvement of any public official, such as the county sheriff. The courts have consistently held that a properly conducted self-help repossession does not create a violation of the Fourteenth Amendment rights of the debtor.

The major restriction on a self-help repossession is that it must not "breach the peace." There has been considerable litigation as to what constitutes a breach of the peace. If the collateral cannot be taken without violence, or the threat of violence, the secured creditor must refrain from making the repossession. Obviously, a repossession involving physical violence or forcible entry into the premises of the borrower would involve a breach of the peace. An unauthorized entry into a closed building, or a verbal confrontation with the debtor probably constitutes a breach. However, repossession of a motor vehicle parked in a driveway, public street, or parking lot, and not involving a confrontation, has almost invariably been upheld as a proper self-help repossession. A bank contemplating a repossession should consult its legal counsel regarding what actions are permissible, and what may be construed as a breach of the peace in its particular jurisdiction.

Replevin

What is the secured party's position if a self-help repossession cannot be accomplished? In the past, the creditor ordinarily obtained a writ of replevin—which is a court order to a judicial officer to take possession of property and return it to the party having a rightful claim to it. Therefore, the creditor obtained a writ of replevin and an officer of the court, usually the sheriff, proceeded to take possession of the collateral and deliver it to the creditor. However, in 1972 the United States Supreme Court struck down two prejudgment replevin statutes, because in each case the statute did not provide for a hearing prior to the officer's taking possession of the property. The Supreme Court ruled that this failure to hold a hearing violated the due process requirement of the Fourteenth Amendment to the United States Constitution. The Court's decision in the landmark case of *Fuentes* vs *Shevin*[2] caused widespread concern and repercussions throughout the lending industry. Even though the *Fuentes* vs *Shevin* decision and similar decisions involved consumer loans, many commercial lenders became hesitant to make

[2] *Fuentes* vs *Shevin* 92SCt983(1972)

a self-help repossession or to obtain a writ of replevin. Subsequent court rulings have made it clear that a self-help repossession in either a commercial or consumer case is permissible so long as the lender does not breach the peace. As far as replevin is concerned, court decisions now generally mandate that the court order for repossession involve a modicum of "due process" in order to comply with the requirements of the Fourteenth Amendment. As a result, many states have modified their replevin procedures to require a prior notice to the debtor, and "probable cause" hearing before a judge prior to the replevin. However, statutes regarding repossession and replevin vary from state to state, and therefore a lender should be familiar with the particular statutes of its state.

Resale of Collateral

A secured party after default, may sell, lease or otherwise dispose of any or all of the collateral in its then condition or following any commercially reasonable preparation or processing.[3] The secured party may dispose of the collateral by either private or public sale, but in every instance, the time, place, and terms of the sale must be commercially reasonable. Unless the collateral is perishable, threatens to decline rapidly in value, or is of a type customarily sold on a recognized market, reasonable notification of the time after which a private sale or intended disposition is to be made shall be sent to the debtor. Such notification should be in written form and should be mailed to the debtor at his or her last known address. In the case of consumer goods, only notification to the debtor is required. In other cases, notification must also be sent to any other secured party from whom the secured party has received written notice of a claim of an interest in the collateral.[4]

The secured party may buy the collateral at a public sale, or if the collateral is of a type customarily sold in a recognized market, or for which widely distributed standard price quotations are available, then the secured party may buy it at a private sale.[5]

If the collateral is consumer goods, and if the debtor has paid 60% of the cash price in the case of a purchase money security interest, or 60% of the loan in the case of another security interest, a secured party who has taken possession must dispose of the collateral within 90 days after he or she takes possession or the debtor may recover damages for conversion.[6] At any time before the secured party has disposed of the collateral, the debtor may redeem it by paying the full amount of the obligation, plus the secured party's

---

[3]   UCC 9-504(1)
[4]   UCC 9-504(3)
[5]   UCC 9-504(3)
[6]   UCC 9-505(1)

reasonable expenses of repossession and preparing the collateral for sale, plus court costs and attorney fees as provided in the security agreement.[7]

UCC 9-504 requires that the proceeds from the sale of the collateral be applied in the following manner:

1. The reasonable expenses of repossession, preparation, and resale, and to the extent provided in the security agreement and not prohibited by law, reasonable attorney's fees and legal costs incurred by the secured party.
2. Satisfaction of the indebtedness secured by the security interest under which the disposition is made.
3. The satisfaction of indebtedness secured by any subordinate security interests in the collateral if written notification of demand therefor is received before distribution of the proceeds is completed.[8]

The secured party must account to the debtor for any surplus, and unless otherwise agreed, the debtor is generally liable for any deficiency. However, if the underlying transaction was a sale of accounts or chattel paper, the debtor is entitled to any surplus, or is liable for any deficiency, only if the security agreement so provides.[9]

A secured party repossessing and reselling collateral should exercise caution to be sure that all of the requirements of the Code are complied with, since failure to comply fully may make the secured party liable to the debtor for damages. However, the fact that a better price could have been obtained by a sale at a different time or in a different method from that selected by the secured party is not of itself sufficient to establish that the sale was not made in a commercially reasonable manner, or that the provisions of the Code regarding resale of collateral have been violated.[10]

Bankruptcy

Commercial lenders are becoming involved in bankruptcy proceedings with increasing frequency, and therefore every competent loan officer should be familiar with the provisions of federal bankruptcy law, and the manner in which its provisions are implemented. Article 1, Section VIII of the United States Constitution empowers Congress to establish uniform laws relating to bankruptcy. The Bankruptcy Reform Act of 1978 (Public Law 95-958), which

---

[7]   UCC 9-506
[8]   UCC 9-504(1)
[9]   UCC 9-504(2)
[10] UCC 9-507(2)

became effective October 1, 1979, repealed existing bankruptcy law, instituted significant changes in procedures, and expanded the jurisdiction of the bankruptcy court. The new code is a vast departure from the old act, and one that is much more consumer oriented.

The purpose of federal bankruptcy law is twofold—to bring relief to debtors hopelessly buried in debt, and to equitably divide among their creditors their nonexempt assets. Any natural person, corporation, general or limited partnership, with the exception of railroad, insurance, banking, or building and loan corporations may elect to file bankruptcy. A debtor may take bankruptcy any number of times, but a period of six years must elapse between filings (except for Chapter 11 and 13 filings) if the debtor is to obtain a new discharge. There are two basic types of bankruptcy—voluntary bankruptcy, in which the debtor voluntarily files a petition, and involuntary bankruptcy, in which the debtor is forced into bankruptcy by his or her creditors. The bankruptcy act is intended for the relief of the poor but honest debtor, who is overwhelmed by his or her debts. Almost any lender would agree that an honest debtor, hopelessly buried in insurmountable debt, should have the means of relief provided by the code. However, many creditors feel that there are abuses of the bankruptcy act, especially by businesses seeking to relieve themselves of obligations incurred in a fraudulent manner, and by individuals seeking to relieve themselves of relatively small amounts of debt, which could be readily repaid by hard work and prudent financial management.

The Bankruptcy Reform Act introduced new rules pertaining to individual repayment plans, preferences, exemptions, setoffs, stays of creditor action, and reaffirmation. Under the new code, the structure of the bankruptcy courts has also changed. The bankruptcy court has become an adjunct, rather than a subsidiary of, the United States District Court, with its judge no longer accountable to the U.S. District judge. Its powers are significantly expanded, and the bankruptcy court has all powers possessed by a court of equity or law, with exclusive jurisdiction of the property of the bankrupt debtor wherever located. Bankruptcy judges are now appointed by the President of the United States with the consent of the Senate, for 14-year terms, at an annual salary of $50,000. The operation of the bankruptcy court is also funded to a greater extent with tax dollars, rather than fees from the bankrupt estate, as has been done in the past.

The ultimate goal of any bankruptcy proceeding is for the debtor to obtain a discharge. A discharge means that all debts listed in the petition of the debtor as obligations to be discharged, with the exception of those to which there is an objection, or those which have been reaffirmed, become unenforceable. The debts still exist, but the creditors are prohibited from taking any further action to collect.

Almost anyone may file a petition for bankruptcy. Some people believe that the debtor must be insolvent to be able to file for bankruptcy, but this is not true. A person whose assets exceed their liabilities may file, as may a person earning a high income. Some lenders maintain that there is only one test—that the debtor must have the required $60 filing fee and transportation to the nearest bankruptcy court.

Liquidation under Chapter 7

Chapter 7 covers liquidation or straight bankruptcy, which may be commenced by a voluntary petition by the debtor, or within some limitations, by an involuntary petition filed by creditors. However, involuntary bankruptcies are relatively rare. Under the code, a joint petition may be filed by a husband and wife under Chapter 7 or Chapter 13, although an individual cannot compel his or her spouse to join in a joint petition.

In a Chapter 7 bankruptcy, a trustee is appointed who administers the estate. The trustee plays a very important role in a Chapter 7 bankruptcy, and has two primary functions—that of preserving to the debtor his or her exempt property, and to administer the bankrupt estate for the benefit of the unsecured creditors. Under the old bankruptcy act, a secured creditor was entitled to the proceeds of the collateral in which it had a perfected security interest. Under the new code, a change of considerable significance to lenders has been implemented. The debtor may now elect to keep the collateral and pay the lender its value, *as determined by the bankruptcy court*. In many instances, this may result in a deficiency that will become an unsecured claim.

In a Chapter 7 bankruptcy, only the debtor's assets and liabilities as of the date the petition is filed are considered. The debtor's income, or ability to earn future income, or prospects of acquiring future assets through gift or inheritances are not taken into consideration. This has led to what lenders called horror stories—stories of high salaried individuals who have taken bankruptcy, primarily to obtain the discharge of sizeable unsecured debt, even though it appeared they had the resources to repay that debt over a period of time.

Shortly after a petition for bankruptcy is filed, all the creditors listed in that petition will receive a notice of the bankruptcy. This notice acts as a "stay order" against the creditor, and the creditor may take no further action against the debtor, or his or her property, except through the bankruptcy court. Once the notice is received, the lender may not set off against the debtor's accounts, repossess collateral, liquidate collateral already repossessed, or take any similar action without the permission of the bankruptcy court.

The first meeting of creditors will be scheduled for approximately 30 to 60 days after the petition is filed. There will be a first meeting of creditors, regardless of whether the bankruptcy is a Chapter 7, 11, or 13. It is very important for the lender and its attorney to attend the first meeting of creditors, for two reasons. First, the bank's attorney will have the opportunity to examine the debtor under oath. Debtors are often unprepared for this examination, and may disclose information quite useful to the bank. The bank may be able to learn the location of collateral, its condition, whether it is covered by insurance, the disposition of proceeds of collateral that has been sold, and many other interesting facts. Second, the bank may request that the trustee abandon collateral to the bank. Once the collateral is abandoned to the creditor, the creditor may proceed to repossess it even though the stay order is still effective as to everything else. If the bank does not request an abandonment of collateral at the first meeting of creditors, it may be required to petition for abandonment in written form and support that request with affidavits and other evidence that proves that the debtor has no equity in the collateral.

Redemption and Reaffirmation

A redemption is a cash purchase of the collateral by the debtor from the court. The debtor may file a petition with the court requesting that he or she be allowed to redeem collateral at a certain value. The court will generally hold a valuation hearing at which both the creditor holding the security interest in the collateral and the debtor may present evidence concerning the fair market value of the collateral. The bankruptcy judge will then determine the fair market value of the collateral and the debtor may redeem that collateral by paying that amount to the court. The secured party will be required to release its security interest in that collateral. Obviously, it is to the secured party's advantage to be well prepared to substantiate its valuations of the collateral at the valuation hearing.

Under the old bankruptcy act, a bankrupt would sometimes make an arrangement with a creditor to reaffirm a debt discharged in bankruptcy because he or she was desirous of retaining a good working relationship with certain of his or her creditors. Under the new code, any reaffirmation must be approved by the court. Under Section 524 of the code, reaffirmation is essentially prohibited unless it is entered into by the debtor prior to discharge, and is not rescinded within 30 days. The court will generally give its approval only if the reaffirmation will not impose an undue hardship on the debtor and deems it to be in the debtor's best interest. Also, the court will generally only approve the reaffirmation for the value of the collateral, rather than for the amount of the debt owed. A reaffirmation may also be made in one other instance—in settlement of a dischargeability complaint. If, subsequent to the discharge, a debtor offers voluntary payments to a creditor, the bankruptcy court will not require the creditor to refuse the payments, but these voluntary payments do not constitute a reaffirmation, and may be discontinued by the debtor at any time.

Chapter 13—the Plan

Under Chapter 13, an individual or small business having unsecured debts of less than $100,000 and secured debts of less than $350,000 may file and develop, under court supervision and protection, a plan for the full or partial repayment of the bankrupt's debts over a period of three years, which in some cases may be extended to five years. During the repayment period, creditors are prohibited from harassing the debtor or attempting to collect the debt. They must receive payments only under the plan. Chapter 13 is completely voluntary, and a debtor may not be forced into a Chapter 13 proceeding by his or her creditors. Chapter 13, under the old act, was called the "wage earner plan." However, its coverage has been greatly expanded under the new code, and small businesses and farmers are now eligible to file under Chapter 13. Basically, Chapter 13 is intended for any individual earning regular income.

A Chapter 13 proceeding is almost the converse of a Chapter 7 proceeding. Whereas in a Chapter 7 bankruptcy, the debtor gives up all his or her nonexempt property, in a Chapter 13, the debtor will retain all or most of his or her property. Rather than receiving proceeds from the liquidation of the assets of the debtor, under a Chapter 13 proceeding the creditors will receive payments from the future income of the debtor.

The commencement of a Chapter 13 action operates as a stay of all creditor actions, such as legal action, repossession, or setoff, against the debtor or his or her property, in the same manner as in Chapter 7 bankruptcy. In addition, in the case of consumer debt, creditors are prohibited from proceeding in any manner against a co-maker, guarantor, or endorser who is liable on the debt along with the bankrupt. Since creditors have made a practice of instituting collection proceedings against co-obligors when the primary debtor files bankruptcy, this change in the law has caused considerable concern among lenders. Since this stay against co-obligors occurs only in the case of a Chapter 13 bankruptcy, it appears that many debtors who otherwise would have filed a straight bankruptcy, may be inclined to file under Chapter 13 to protect relatives or associates who are co-obligors. The stay against co-obligors, however, does not apply to those who guarantee an obligation in the normal course of business, such as a dealer who sells paper with recourse.

Under Chapter 13, the debtor has great flexibility in formulating the repayment plan, although the plan must be submitted in good faith. The plan may provide for the payment of claims only out of future income, or out of a combination of future income and a liquidation of some of the debtor's assets. The plan may call for modification of the rights of secured or unsecured creditors, other than a creditor secured by an interest in real property that is the debtor's residence. It may also provide for the curing or waiving of any default and the assumption or rejection of executory contracts or unexpired leases. Obviously, the debtor is given a great deal of latitude in proposing his or her repayment plan.

After notice, the court must hold a confirmation hearing, where any interested party may object. However, contrary to prior law, consent of the unsecured creditors is not required. The code does provide that under the repayment plan the unsecured creditors must not receive less than they would receive in a liquidation. Attorneys often use the slang expressions "nickel plan" or "dime plan" in connection with Chapter 13 plans. These expressions refer to the fact that the unsecured creditors would receive either 5% or 10% of the total amount owed during the repayment period. If, in fact, it appears that the unsecured creditors would have received nothing in a Chapter 7 bankruptcy, then a "nickel plan" or "dime plan" submitted in a Chapter 13 proceeding will probably be acceptable to the court. Other requirements that must be met for the court to confirm the plan are that it must comply with Chapter 13, the requisite fees must be paid, and the debtor, in the court's judgment, must be able to make the required payments. In addition, the secured creditors must either accept the plan, and retain the liens securing their claims, or receive the property securing their claims.

After confirmation of the plan, the trustee collects the payments required by the plan from the debtor and distributes those payments to the creditors. After performance under the plan, the court grants the debtor a discharge of all debts provided for under the plan. If a problem arises, the court may modify the plan by reducing the amount of the required payments, or extending the time of performance. If this is not deemed practical, and the creditors have received at least what they would have in a straight bankruptcy under a Chapter 7, then the court may grant the debtor a discharge notwithstanding his or her incomplete performance.

A Chapter 13 bankruptcy involves several other areas of concern for the lender. In addition to the fact that the lender may be hampered by the stay as to co-obligors, many lenders are concerned by the fact that it is very difficult to file an objection to a Chapter 13 proceeding on the basis of fraud. Also, the so-called "7-year" rule does not apply to a Chapter 13 bankruptcy. While the code requires that six years must elapse before a debtor who has previously filed a Chapter 7 bankruptcy can file again, this rule does not apply to Chapter 13 bankruptcies. For example, a debtor could file for a Chapter 7 bankruptcy in 1984, and then for a Chapter 13 bankruptcy in 1987.

As a result of these rules, a debtor who would have ordinarily filed a Chapter 7 bankruptcy may file a Chapter 13 in order to protect co-obligors, or because he or she has committed fraud, or because less than six years has elapsed since he or she has filed a Chapter 7 bankruptcy.

Reorganization under Chapter 11

Chapter 11 establishes a procedure under which a business may postpone the payment of its debts and continue in operation under the supervision of the court, pending the submission of a reorganization plan. Sole proprietor-ships, partnerships, or corporations may file under Chapter 11. In most cases, the court will allow the debtor to continue in possession of the business. This involves the concept of "debtor in possession," under which the debtor is allowed to retain possession of all assets and continue to operate the business.

Once a Chapter 11 petition has been filed, the debtor is given a period of time, usually at least 120 days, during which the debtor has an exclusive right to formulate and file a reorganization plan with the court, and request its confirmation. In some instances this time period is extended to 150 or 180 days. During that period of time the debtor and the debtor's attorney are generally in control of the situation and there may be very little a secured creditor can do to protect its position. If the plan is confirmed, it binds all creditors, even those that did not consent to it.

There generally is no trustee appointed in a Chapter 11 bankruptcy. In rare instances a trustee or receiver may be appointed, but this will be done only by the bankruptcy judge on good cause shown. The fact that there is usually no trustee with whom the creditors can deal can be very frustrating to the creditors involved. A creditors' committee, usually consisting of the largest unsecured creditors, is usually appointed by the bankruptcy court to represent the interests of the unsecured creditors. I have observed that creditors committees are generally ineffective.

The plan of reorganization for the business is not limited to a specific time period but may cover as much as five years or more. The plan usually involves a restructuring of the business that may require a refinancing, a write-down of debts, release of collateral and other steps quite unsatisfactory to the creditors. In some instances a Chapter 11 proceeding may result in a rehabilitation of the business. However, in many Chapter 11 proceedings a satisfactory plan is never filed and it is ultimately converted into a Chapter 7 liquidation. If the reorganization is successful, the debtor and the creditors may ultimately benefit. If it is not, then liquidation has simply been delayed by a period of months, during which time the creditors have been stayed from any collection action, and the debtor has remained in possession of the assets and continued to operate the business.

Exemptions

By law, certain property of the debtor is exempt from the claims of either the creditors or the trustee in bankruptcy. The exemptions available to the debtor, as set forth in Chapter 5, Section 522, were substantially liberal-ized under the Bankruptcy Reform Act of 1978. The debtor may elect to take exemptions available to him or her under state law, or he or she may elect to take the federal exemptions. Under the code, the federal exemptions include a $7500 exemption in real estate or personal property (such as a mobile home) used as a residence; a $1200 interest in a motor vehicle; a $200 interest in each item of household goods; $500 of personal jewelry; $4,000 of dividends, interest or cash value life insurance; $750 of implements, tools, or professional books; and a $400 "wild card" exemption that can apply to anything. Furthermore, the code specifies that waivers of these exemptions as to a lien arising from a nonpossessory, nonpurchase money security interest in household and personal goods can be avoided. Also, bankruptcy court rulings indicate that an exemption not fully utilized in one category may pour over into another category. In the case of a husband and wife filing a joint bankruptcy, each may claim the above exemptions.

The code authorizes state legislatures to preempt the federal exemptions by specific legislative action. If such action is taken, residents of that state must then take the exemptions allowed by state law rather than the federal exemptions. In some states these exemptions are less liberal than the federal exemptions; other states have exemptions that would appear to be even more generous than the federal exemptions.

In those states that have not specifically preempted the federal exemptions, the debtor may choose either the state or federal exemptions. In some states couples filing bankruptcy may take both exemptions, with the husband claiming one, and the wife the other type of exemption.

Preferences

Under the code a debtor is presumed to have been insolvent for a period of ninety days preceding the actual filing of the bankruptcy petition. Therefore, any transfer of property to a creditor by the bankrupt within ninety days of the bankruptcy adjudication may be deemed a preference. A preference may consist of the payment of money to a creditor, granting a lien or security interest, or the outright transfer of property to a creditor. Obviously, a preference depletes the estate of the bankrupt as far as the unsecured creditors are concerned, although the bankrupt will not be denied a discharge for having made such transfers.

The trustee may set aside preferential transfers, and any creditor having received a preference may be required to return the money or property to the trustee for inclusion in the bankrupt's estate. However, purchase money transactions are generally excepted from the rules of preference. The trustee may also set aside fraudulent conveyances by the debtor, that is, those made with the intent of hindering, delaying, or defrauding creditors, or by a debtor who does not intend to meet his or her maturing obligations.

Under the old bankruptcy act, the preference period was 120 days. Under Section 547 of the new code, this was reduced to 90 days. However, in the case of an insider, the preference period is extended to one year. Insiders are relatives, partners, corporate officers and directors, and persons "in control" of the debtor. This raises a potential problem for the lender who in effect takes over the management of the debtor's business once it gets into trouble, and who may be declared an insider if the debtor files bankruptcy.

Being declared an insider would be detrimental to the lender's position, and will make lenders more cautious than they have been in the past about actively participating in the management of a troubled business on a day by day basis.

It appears that under the new code many more transactions will be declared preferences than under previous law, and that bankruptcy courts and unsecured creditors will aggressively seek the return of payments made during the preference period. Under the old law, the trustee had to establish that the debtor was insolvent, and that the creditor had grounds for believing that he or she was insolvent. The new code presumes that the debtor was insolvent 90 days prior to filing, regardless of whether this was true. Therefore, the trustee has no such burden of proof under the code.

Under Section 68 of the old act, banks were permitted the right of setoff against the accounts of the debtor. Under the new code the right of setoff has been substantially restricted. The setoff must occur prior to receipt of the initial notice of the bankruptcy, which acts as a stay order, and freezes the account. Many setoffs will undoubtedly be declared preferences even if made prior to the receipt of notice, particularly in cases where the funds were deposited to the account during the preference period.

An unsecured loan paid off in the 90-day period prior to the filing of bankruptcy may be declared a preference under certain conditions. In such a case, the lender would be required to deliver the funds used to pay off the loan to the trustee, even though the lender had returned the paid note to the debtor. A secured creditor probably does not have such a problem since secured creditors generally are not subject to the rules concerning preferences. However, if a creditor holds collateral that has increased in value during the preference period, the increase may belong to the trustee rather than to the creditor. Since any transaction that is declared a preference increases the amount of funds available to the unsecured creditors, it is likely that any unsecured creditors who have received payments during the preference period will be challenged not only by the trustee, but also by the other unsecured creditors.

In the past, some unsecured creditors have not filed a claim if it appeared that the estate of the bankrupt had insufficient assets to allow payments to be made to unsecured creditors. Under the code, it would appear prudent for every unsecured creditor to file a claim, due to the probability that some transactions will be declared preferences.

Priority of Claims

The bankruptcy code sets up five classes of claims that are entitled to priority in the distribution of the bankrupt's estate. These are:

1. Administrative costs, including fees for the trustee and the attorney of the bankrupt, and other court costs and fees.

2. Wage claims up to a maximum of $600 earned within three months of the filing of the petition.
3. Costs and expenses incurred by creditors in successfully opposing a discharge or having it set aside.
4. Federal, state, and local tax claims.
5. Debts having priority under federal law and rent claims entitled to priority under state law.

Creditors with perfected security interests have priority over unsecured creditors to the extent of the value of their security. Unsecured claims have the lowest priority, and the unsecured creditors will get a pro rata share of those funds remaining, if any, after claims that have a higher priority are paid.

Nondischargeable Debts

It should be noted that a discharge will not relieve the bankrupt of certain obligations. Alimony and child support payments are not dischargeable in either a Chapter 7, 11, or 13 proceeding. All taxes, including federal and state income tax, social security taxes, employee withholding, or local real estate taxes, are generally nondischargeable. Other nondischargeable debt includes claims that are not provable, such as certain tort claims, and criminal fines and penalties. In addition, the bankrupt may not discharge a liability for obtaining money or property under false pretenses, for willful injury to the person or property of another, or for fraud or embezzlement by the bankrupt. The bankrupt is also not relieved of debt omitted from his or her schedules, provided the creditor was not aware of the bankruptcy proceedings.

Objections to Discharge or Dischargeability

Under certain circumstances a creditor or the trustee may file an objection to discharge or dischargeability in bankruptcy. An objection to discharge seeks to bar the whole bankruptcy. An objection to dischargeability seeks only to bar the discharge of one particular debt. In most instances, it is more advantageous for a creditor to object to the dischargeability of its claim, rather than to object to discharge.

Grounds to objecting to or denying discharge or dischargeability are as follows:

1. Commission of a criminal bankruptcy offense. This would include concealment of assets from the trustee, making a false oath or account, destroying or tampering with the bankrupt's records, and withholding documents or records of the bankrupt from an officer of the court.
2. Failure to keep or preserve adequate books or records showing the condition of the bankrupt and his or her business transactions.

3. Obtaining money or property on credit by false financial statement.
4. A fraudulent conveyance of property or the concealment of assets prior to filing the bankruptcy petition.
5. In the case of a Chapter 7 bankruptcy, a discharge in bankruptcy during the six-year period preceding the filing of the present petition.
6. Refusal to obey a lawful order of the court or to answer a material question approved by the court.
7. Failure to satisfactorily explain any loss or deficiency of assets.

The grounds most commonly used by creditors in objecting to discharge or dischargeability in bankruptcy is that the bankrupt obtained credit through the use of a false financial statement. To succeed in an action of this type, the creditor must prove the statement is false, and also must *prove that it relied upon the false statement*. The creditor may have considerable difficulty proving reliance upon the false statement if the date of the financial statement is significantly prior to or subsequent to the date of the loan transaction. If the creditor has previously dealt with the bankrupt, it may have to satisfy the court that its reliance was upon the financial statement tendered by the bankrupt, and not upon the history of the creditor's past dealings with the borrower. Filing an objection to discharge or to dischargeability in bankruptcy and proving its validity can be a time consuming and costly process. For that reason, many creditors hesitate to take this action unless the amount of the loan is substantial and they have reason to believe their position is legally sound. Many creditors feel that the bankruptcy courts are too sympathetic to the debtor, and that an unfair burden of proof is placed upon the creditor.

16

Business Development Programs

Banking is an extremely competitive business. Commercial banks, savings and loan associations, credit unions, brokerage firms, and money market funds are in direct competition with one another. To make matters worse, during the past several years the commercial banker has seen many nonfinancial businesses which are largely unregulated begin to provide financial services that have traditionally been provided by commercial banks.

This intensely competitive environment has made most banks realize that if they are to retain their share of the market, they must go on the offensive. The result has been that banks have become much more customer oriented, constantly searching for better ways to provide improved services to their customers. It has also made the average bank realize that it needs a business development program. Generally, such a business development program is centered around a formal calling program in which all of the bank's officers are usually requested to participate. Since the bank's commercial loan officers are usually quite familiar with the business community, they are almost inevitably vitally involved in the bank's calling program.

With greatly increased emphasis on business development, the role that the commercial loan officer is expected to play in the bank's calling program is becoming more prominent, and will continue to do so in the future. In spite of this, many commercial loan officers feel that their business development and calling responsibilities are the most difficult and least understood segment of their job descriptions.

What should be the objectives of a calling program?

1. The most important function of a call program is to retain the loyalty and goodwill of the bank's present customers. Banks that neglect their present customers will find that they lose a significant proportion of them. It is human nature for customers to enjoy attention from their bankers, and if neglected by

their own banks, those customers become prime prospects for competitor banks that are willing to call on those customers.

2.   Another important function of a good call program is to bring new business into the bank. In order to achieve growth, or even to hold its own, a bank must bring in a significant number of new customers each year. A good calling program can significantly increase the number of new customers brought into the bank.

3.   Another key function of a good calling program is to acquaint the bank's customers with new services available due to deregulation, and to cross-sell services to the bank's present customers. The more services a customer uses, the closer the relationship with the bank will be, and the less the chance that customer will leave. In many instances an account that has been only marginally profitable can be turned into a highly profitable account by encouraging the customer to use additional services.

Cross-Selling Services

The ability to cross-sell its services is certainly one of the greatest needs and biggest weaknesses in the average commercial bank. Every employee of the bank, from the tellers to the chief executive officer, can be an effective salesperson of the bank's services. If so, then why do most banks do such a poor job of cross-selling? The principal reason is probably that most personnel have a lack of product knowledge outside of their own area of responsibility. This problem can be solved through an intensive training program. Another problem is that most employees feel that they do not know how to sell. This also can be solved by a training program. Lastly, employees often are not properly motivated, and receive little encouragement from management.

All of these obstacles can be overcome through an organized cross-selling program. Research has revealed that the average bank has about 100 different services to sell, and yet the average customer uses only two or three of those services. It therefore appears that cross-selling its services is a fertile field which is readily available to every bank, and represents an excellent opportunity to increase profits.

Organizing a Business Development Program

Banks seem to have difficulty organizing and implementing successful business development programs, often in spite of numerous attempts to do so. Experience indicates that an effective program must be formalized, with a written plan of action, and it must entail a controlled and organized effort. An aggressive program will involve the bank's officers, directors, and staff members. Every officer should have a mandatory quota of calls, usually a minimum of one a week, and performance goals. Generally, an officer can best call on those with whom he or she is familiar, or has something in common. Therefore, most effective call programs allow the officer to choose the customers and prospects upon which he or she will call. The officer is usually allowed a great deal of flexibility in scheduling, technique, and approach, as long as the requisite number of calls are made each week. A good call program should be both simple and flexible, since the program usually must be revised as market conditions change. Reporting requirements should be enforced, but should be kept simple. Many banks feel that about three-fourths of all calls should be made on existing customers to cross-sell services and to keep them satisfied, and the remaining one-fourth should be prospect calls.

Making a Successful Call

To make an effective call, the calling officer must know as much as possible about the customer or prospect upon whom he or she is calling. If the call is to be made on a customer, then the calling officer should be familiar with the nature of the customer's business, account balances, loan arrangements, and the extent to which the customer uses other services, such as trust services. Nothing is more embarrassing for a calling officer than to suggest to a customer that he or she consider using one of the bank's services, such as trust services, and then be informed that those services are already extensively being used. This is not only embarrassing, but also leads the customer to doubt the knowledge and capability of the calling officer.

If a prospect is to be called upon, information may be available from a number of sources, such as Dunn & Bradstreet, the local Chamber of Commerce, or a search of the public records. A bank customer who is in the same type of business or industry often can give helpful information about a prospect. In fact, the bank's present customers are its best source of referrals for prospects. Some calling officers will telephone the receptionist or secretary at the business upon which they plan to call, and will request such basic information as the nature of the company's business and the name of its chief executive officer. At the very least, an officer calling on a prospect should have some information, such as the nature of the business, the name of the company's chief executive officer and financial officer, an approximation of its sales volume and territory, and an educated guess of what banking services the company may require.

Many calling officers feel that the best way to achieve an effective call is to get the prospect to talk about himself or herself and the business operation. This gives the prospect an opportunity to talk about his or her achievements and provides the calling officer an opportunity to learn valuable information about the business. All too often, calling officers are so busy telling the prospect about the advantages of doing business with their bank that the prospect never really gets a chance to talk.

Most good calling officers use a soft sell approach to sell themselves and their institution. The prospect should not be overwhelmed with statistics. Most business people are more concerned about the competence of the bank's personnel and its attitude toward its customers than they are in statistical information about the bank. A good calling officer also will ask for the prospect's business. Many officers, largely due to fear of rejection, hesitate to ask the prospect to establish a relationship with the bank. If the prospect is satisfied with his or her current bank, to ask for only a small portion of the business is a good technique.

Experienced calling officers recognize that the prospect's business is rarely obtained on the first call. It usually takes a period of time to develop a good relationship with the prospect, and this is largely done by means of repeat calls. Persistence definitely pays dividends. Inexperienced calling officers fail to recognize this, and often give up on a prospect too soon, thereby losing any opportunity to obtain his or her business.

A good calling program requires a good record keeping system. After a call has been made, all information obtained by the calling officer, such as company performance statistics, names of key personnel, data concerning banking needs, and observations about the prospect's attitude and ability should be recorded on a call report and retained. This information should be made available to the next calling officer, and a tickler system should be set up to assure timely followup efforts.

After the initial call has been made, a decision must also be made as to whether or not the prospect is viable and worthy of continued solicitation. In some cases, the bank may reach the conclusion that because of the prospect's financial condition, the kind of banking services required, or its close ties with another institution, such as interlocking ownership or common directors, that it will not be worthwhile to continue making calls. To identify and then follow up on the most promising prospects can greatly enhance the results of a call program.

In summary, a good business development program is vital to a bank's continued growth and prosperity. The bank's commercial loan officers should be vitally involved in such a program and should recognize that effective calling is one of their very important functions.

17

Small Business Administration Loans

The Small Business Administration (SBA) is an agency of the United States Government which was created by the Small Business Act of 1953. The SBA's best known function is that of providing guaranteed, direct, or immediate participation loans to small business concerns to finance the construction of plant facilities, acquire equipment and machinery, and provide working capital. Since 1976, farming enterprises have been considered small businesses. The agency also provides disaster loans for victims of floods, civil disorders, or other catastrophies, to enable individuals and businesses to repair, rebuild or replace homes, business facilities or other property. The SBA is also authorized to make special loans to handicapped individuals and to non-profit organizations that employ the handicapped in the production of goods or services. Under its Pollution Control Financing Program, which was initiated in 1977, the SBA helps small businesses obtain long term financing of pollution control equipment by means of 100% guarantys of loans, leases, or other contracts, which may be integrated into taxable or tax exempt bond issues. The agency also has a program for the guaranty to surety companies for up to 90% of losses incurred on surety bonds issued to small contractors. In this chapter we will cover only SBA's Section 7(a) program, under which over 80% of all SBA approved business loans have been granted, and SBA's Section 503 program, which is a relatively new program for the long term financing of hard assets for business firms.

Many lenders are not aware that SBA has many programs other than its loan programs. It works closely with purchasing agencies of the federal government and with large contracting firms to develop policies and procedures that will increase the number of contracts that go to small businesses. SBA maintains a computerized small business source referral system which provides qualified sources for supplies and services for the federal government and for government sponsored projects. It also cooperates closely with various government agencies to insure that small businesses have an opportunity to procure a fair share of government property, such as timber, strategic materials, and mineral leases, that is going to be sold to the private sector. The SBA also sponsors seminars and conferences, and publishes and distributes information concerning the management problems of small businesses. It conducts management workshops and courses for beginning or prospective business managers, and enlists the volunteer aid of retired and active executives to assist small businesses in solving their management problems.

The principal objective of the Minority Small Business Capital Ownership Development Program is to encourage and assist members of minority groups to establish their own businesses. It works closely with private industry, financial institutions, and local community groups to substantially increase the number of minority owned and operated businesses. SBA's Business Development Program, which was established under the provisions of Section 8(a) of the Small Business Act, is intended to assist in the expansion and development of small business concerns owned and managed by eligible socially and economically disadvantaged persons. SBA's Chief Counsel for Advocacy is the government's principal advocate of small business who promotes the position of small businesses with federal, state, and local government agencies and maintains liason with trade and professional organizations. The Office of Advocacy also evaluates the impact on small businesses of legislative proposals and other public policy issues by preparing policy papers and conducting research. The Veteran's Affairs Program has been set up to assist in establishing and improving programs of financial and management assistance to small businesses owned or controlled by veterans.

Lender Participation in SBA's Loan Programs

Over 10,000 commercial banks have participated in SBA's various business loan programs, but relatively few banks participate actively, since at year end 1981 only 700 banks had 25 or more SBA loans in their portfolios. Over 80% of all SBA approved loans have been under the Section 7(a) program, and the great majority of these loans have been made by commercial banks with a guaranty by SBA. Less than 10% of all loans made under the 7(a) program have been direct loans by SBA. In calendar year 1983, SBA guaranteed approximately 2.5 billion dollars of loans for businesses, and it is estimated that there is a total of approximately 10.7 billion dollars of outstanding SBA loans. However, it is also estimated that this amount constitutes less than 8% of all small business loans held by commercial banks. Any bank may participate in SBA's Guaranteed Loan Program by executing SBA Form #750, Loan Guaranty Agreement (Deferred Participation). This form outlines the terms and conditions under which the bank may participate in the program.

In February 1979 the SBA also established a Certified Lenders Program under which selected lenders are allowed to do most of the credit analysis ordinarily done by SBA, which results in a much more timely credit decision on the borrower's application. Lenders are selected for the program on the basis of their past and present SBA loan volume, SBA's loss experience with loans generated by that lender, and overall working relationship with the lender. Under the Certified Lenders Program, the lender must determine that the loan application package is complete and must perform an analysis of eligibility, statement ratios, repayment ability, management skill, collateral adequacy, past credit history of the applicant, moral character, etc. When the lender's credit analysis is completed, the application is submitted to the appropriate SBA office, and SBA is committed to make a credit decision on the application in no more than three working days. Lenders are certified for a two-year period, after which time their performance is reviewed, and a recertification decision is made by SBA. To date, approximately 500 lenders have been certified in this program, and it is SBA's stated goal to continue to expand the scope of this program. Lending institutions considering participation in the Certified Lenders Program should be aware that under the program the participating bank obtains a guaranty of *collection*, and not a guaranty of *payment*, as is the case with most Section 7(a) loans. The difference between a guaranty of collection and of payment is discussed in chapter 11.

Early in 1983 the Small Business Administration implemented a new experimental program, called the Preferred Lenders Program. Under this program the lender is responsible not only for analyzing the application, but also for the approval decision on the loan with no final review by SBA. SBA examiners do audit the participating bank's loan portfolio on a quarterly basis. To date, approximately 35 banks have been approved for the Preferred Lenders Program. Under this program the lender receives a 75% SBA loan guaranty, rather than the usual 90% guaranty under the Section 7(a) program. Also, preferred lenders have greater responsibility and authority in loan administration and in collateral liquidation if the loan defaults.

In June 1983, the federal government's General Accounting Office published a report which was quite critical of the Certified Lenders Program and recommended that both it and the Preferred Lenders Program be terminated. The GAO's principal criticisms were that the lenders' credit analyses were very poor in many cases, that loan application packages were often incomplete, and that information provided by lenders was unreliable. GAO's conclusion was that commercial lenders are generally inexperienced in making the type of credit analysis required for SBA loans, due to the fact that most SBA applications are significantly different in character from the usual request handled by commercial lenders. Although conceding that some problems have existed with the Certified Lenders Program, SBA disagreed with the GAO recommendations, and has expressed its intention to expand both the Certified Lenders Program and the Preferred Lenders Program.

SBA Section 7(a) Loan Guaranty Program

The great majority of SBA loans are made under the Section 7(a) Loan Guaranty Program, and this is the type of SBA loan with which lending institutions are the most familiar. Under this program, loan proceeds may be used for working capital, equipment purchases, real estate acquisition, or new construction. The maximum maturity of a 7(a) loan cannot exceed 25 years, but SBA generally limits working capital loans to a seven-year term, and equipment loans to the life expectancy of the equipment being acquired. SBA will guarantee 90% of a loan that is not in excess of $100,000 with the exception of some cases where debt refinancing is involved. On a loan in excess of $100,000, the agency will guarantee between 70% and 90% of the loan, except in cases where debt refinancing is involved. If a portion of the loan is being used to refinance existing debt, no more than 80% of that debt can be guaranteed. SBA has relatively strict criteria as to what debt is eligible to be refinanced.

Generally, SBA credit requirements are similar to those of commercial lenders. An SBA guaranty is usually sought by a commercial lender when that lender cannot adequately collateralize the loan, or a longer maturity is required than what the lender would ordinarily be willing to extend. The maximum amount that SBA can guarantee under the 7(a) program is $500,000. This means that a lender may obtain a 90% guaranty on a loan in a maximum amount of about $555,000.

SBA's general eligibility requirements are as follows:

1.   The applicant must be of good character and have sufficient business experience and managerial knowledge to operate the business successfully. SBA considers the ability of the borrower to be a key factor.
2.   The applicant must have sufficient equity in the business to insure personal commitment. SBA usually requires that the applicant have sufficient funds to provide about a 20% equity for the project being financed.
3.   The borrower must have adequate collateral to secure the loan. However, this does not mean that the collateral available must be sufficient to fully cover the amount of the loan.
4.   The business must demonstrate sufficient repayment capacity to repay the SBA loan and its other obligations from cash flow and profits. Repayment capacity is another key factor, and the projections of future performance that must accompany the SBA application must clearly

indicate that the business will have the capacity to repay its obligations.
5.   The applicant must meet SBA's definition of a small business, which is one that is independently owned and operated, is not dominant in its field, and that meets certain size standards. Size standards vary, depending on the type of business involved, but generally, in order to qualify, a retail or service business must have annual sales of no more than two million dollars, and a wholesaler's annual sales of not over nine and one-half million dollars. An agricultural business may have annual sales of no more than one million dollars. In the case of a manufacturing firm, size criteria is based on number of employees rather than on annual sales. In most instances, the firm must have no more than 250 employees to qualify. The size standards apply in aggregate to the business and any affiliates. SBA defines an affiliate as a business over which the applicant has an element of control via management agreement, contractual arrangement, or stock ownership. It should be pointed out that there are exceptions to these size standards, and prior to making a decision concerning the eligibility of a specific business, the commercial lender should consult with an SBA representative.

Ineligible Loan Requests

All loans made by SBA must meet guidelines established by Congress and the SBA. Certain kinds of loan requests are not eligible for SBA guarantee under existing guidelines.

1.   A request would be denied if that loan would be readily available on reasonable terms from private financing sources, or where funds would be readily available from the resources of the owner, partners, or stockholders of the business. A project that might be financed from the disposal, at a fair market price, of assets not required for the conduct of the business would also be ineligible.
2.   A loan for the primary purpose of paying off existing institutional debt, for the payment of dividends to stockholders or distribution of profits to partners, or for the repayment of subordinated debt, or to replenish working capital funds that were used for any of these purposes, would be ineligible. However, as mentioned previously, under some circumstances SBA will refinance existing debt, especially where doing so will be of significant benefit to the borrower, and where the existing creditor is not in a position to sustain a loss.
3.   Loans for speculative purposes are ineligible.
4.   Loans to newspapers, book publishers, magazine publishers, or similar enterprises that require an editorial content are ineligible. However, cable television companies and radio stations are eligible.

5. A loan to an applicant whose income is derived from gambling activities is ineligible. However, businesses earning less than one-third of their gross income from the sale of official state lottery tickets under a state license are eligible.

6. Loans to companies in the business of lending or investing are ineligible.

7. Loans to religious organizations are ineligible.

8. Loans to nonprofit organizations are ineligible under the Section 7(a) program, but such organizations may be eligible under other SBA programs, depending on the circumstances.

Interest Rate

The interest rate charged by the participating lender must be legal under the laws of the state in which that lender operates, and may not be higher than the rate of interest charged by local lending institutions for similar loans. The interest rate also may not exceed a maximum rate set by SBA for guaranteed loans. Under current guidelines, the maximum interest rate charged by a lender may be no more than 2.25% over the lowest prime rate published in the Wall Street Journal for loans of up to 7 years maturity, and no more than 2.75% over the lowest prime rate for loans with maturities of more than 7 years.

The lender may charge a variable or floating rate which must be tied to an acceptable criteria and be adjusted periodically to reflect movements in that criteria. The lowest prime rate published in the Wall Street Journal is an acceptable criteria which is used by most lenders. The rate may be adjusted no more than quarterly and the loan must stay at the initial rate for at least one full calendar quarter before an adjustment takes place. The difference between the loan rate and prime rate is referred to by SBA as the spread. Whenever an adjustment in rate is made, the Small Business Administration must be advised of that adjustment within ten days.

The lender must pay the Small Business Administration a one time guaranty fee for each loan approved. This fee amounts to one percent of the total amount guaranteed and must be paid within 90 days of the date of the loan approval. The fee may be passed along to the borrower after the first disbursement has been made on the loan. The borrower should always be informed in advance if he or she is going to be required to pay the guaranty fee.

Section 7(a) Application

A prospective borrower who wishes to apply for an SBA 7(a) guaranteed loan should obtain a forms packet from a commercial lender. Most commercial banks carry a supply of forms packets which may be obtained free of charge by a potential applicant. SBA Form 4 is the application for a business loan. The front of the form summarizes information about the business, its ownership, the amount and purpose of the loan, and the available collateral. The back of the form contains instructions for assembling the various exhibits that must accompany the application. The application and all exhibits must be signed and dated. If the business is a sole proprietorship the signature of the proprietor is required, and if it is a partnership, a partner must sign. In the case of a corporation, the signature of the president, attested by the corporate secretary, is generally required.

The exhibits that must accompany the application are as follows:

1.   A personal History Statement (SBA Form 912) must be submitted by the proprietor if the business is a proprietorship, and by each partner in the case of a partnership. If the business is a corporation, then each corporate officer, director, and any stockholder that holds 20% or more of the voting stock must submit a personal history statement. All others who have management authority (including hired managers), also must submit a Form 912.

2.   A signed current Personal Financial Statement (SBA Form 413) must be submitted for each stockholder with 20% or greater ownership, and for every corporate officer, partner, or proprietor.

3.   A balance sheet, income and expense statement, and reconciliation of net worth for the business must be submitted for the past three years. In addition, a balance sheet, income and expense statement, reconciliation of net worth and aged listing of accounts receivable and payable dated within the past 90 days must be submitted. Earnings projections for the coming year must also be submitted. This material should be considered the heart of the application, and should be prepared with care, and in detail.

4.   A narrative providing a brief history of the business, including a paragraph describing the expected benefits to be received from the loan, must be submitted.

5.   A narrative providing a description of the educational, technical, and business background for all people who will be involved in the management of the company must be included.

6.   A list of all cosigners and/or guarantors for the loan should be submitted, including name, address, and personal balance sheet, if not included elsewhere.

7.   If machinery or equipment is to be purchased with the loan proceeds, a list of that equipment and its cost must be included.

8.   If any principal of the business has been involved in bankruptcy or insolvency proceedings, a narrative describing those proceedings must be included.

9.   If the business is involved in pending lawsuits or litigation, a narrative must be provided describing the circumstances.

10.   If any principal of the business, or any member of his or her family is employed by the Small Business Administration, or any other federal agency, or by the participating lender, a statement must be included providing the details of such employment.

11.   If the business which is applying for the SBA guaranteed loan has subsidiaries or affiliates, a statement must be included providing their names and describing their relationship with the applicant business. A current balance sheet and operating statement for each subsidiary or affiliate must also be included.

12.   If the applicant company purchases from, sells to, or uses the services of any business in which a principal of the company has a significant financial interest, the details of that relationship must be disclosed.

13.   If the business is a franchise, a copy of the franchise agreement and a copy of the Federal Trade Commission disclosure statement supplied by the franchiser must be included.

14.   A Financial Privacy Act notice must be signed by the applicant(s) and guarantor(s), and a copy furnished to each applicant and guarantor in compliance with the Right to Financial Privacy Act of 1978.[1]

In the case of a construction loan, three additional exhibits must be included:

15.   Information showing the estimated cost of the project and a statement of the source of any additional funds.

16.   An Applicant's Agreement of Compliance (SBA Form 601) certifying that the contractor will not discriminate on the basis of race, color, religion, sex, handicap, or national origin signed by the applicant and the contractor. Form 601 is required if the cost of the improvement to be constructed is in excess of $10,000.

17.   Copies of preliminary construction plans and specifications. Final plans generally must be submitted prior to disbursement of the loan.

When the applicant has completed the application and all exhibits, the original and one copy should be submitted to the participating lender. As a rule, a certain amount of negotiation will take place between the lender and the applicant concerning rate, term, guarantys, and collateral. The lender will also examine the application to make sure that it complies with all SBA requirements, and that all necessary information has been submitted. The request is then approved by the lender in much the same manner as any other loan request.

---

[1]   12 U.S.C. Section 3413(h)

Prior to submitting the original application to SBA, the lender must complete SBA Form 4-I, the Lender's Application for Guaranty or Participation. A sample of Form 4-I is shown in Exhibit DD. On the front of the form the lender must list all the particulars of the loan, including the terms and conditions set by the lender, and the form must be signed by an authorized officer of the lending institution. On the back of the form, the lender is required to spread balance sheet information and prepare a pro forma balance sheet. Information concerning sales, depreciation, income taxes, officer compensation, and net profit for the past three years must also be compiled. Lastly, the lender must prepare a written narrative commenting on trends, debt to worth ratio and current ratio. Repayment capacity and management skill of the applicant must also be analyzed. Adequacy of collateral and the lender's credit experience with the applicant must be covered, and a schedule of insurance requirements, standby agreements, and other requirements must be shown.

The lender is also required to prepare and submit a Flood Insurance Certification certifying whether or not the property is located in an FIA special flood hazard area. The loan application cannot be processed by SBA unless this form is submitted.

Closing the SBA Loan

Upon approval of the application by SBA, SBA Form 529B, Authorization and Loan Agreement, will be returned to the lender along with a packet of closing documents. Form 529B contains all the terms and conditions set by SBA and a listing of the required collateral, and should be read very carefully by both the participating lender and the applicant. At closing, it must be signed by the applicant. When all necessary documents have been accepted and signed by the applicant, loan proceeds may be disbursed. Generally, only working capital funds may be disbursed directly to the applicant. Joint checks should be written to the applicant and suppliers or contractors for the purchase of equipment, construction payments, etc.

Immediately after closing the loan, a conformed copy of the note, the Compensation Agreement, and the Settlement Sheet must be forwarded to SBA.

The first disbursement of the loan must be made not later than six months, and no disbursement can be made later than twelve months, from the date of the Authorization, except with the written consent of SBA. Each time a loan disbursement is made a Settlement Sheet (SBA Form 1050) must be completed and submitted to SBA. This form must show the name of each payee to whom funds were disbursed and the amount and purpose of each payment. Two copies of Form 1050 must be submitted to SBA immediately after each disbursement, a copy must be given to the borrower, and another

Small Business Administration Loans   249

copy retained by the lender. There is usually no limit to the number of partial disbursements that may be made. All loan proceeds must be used strictly in accordance with the Authorization.

The participating lender is also required to make a quarterly report to SBA of all guaranteed loans in its portfolio, showing the outstanding balance of each loan and indicating whether or not the loan is in a current status.

Additional Processing Requirements for Certified Lenders

For those banks that are participating in the Certified Lenders Program, there are additional processing requirements to be fulfilled:

1. A complete credit analysis must be performed and submitted to SBA.
2. An appraisal of the collateral must be included.
3. A credit report from an independent credit reporting agency must be included.
4. Both SBA Form 4-I and the envelope containing the loan application must be conspicuously marked "CLP" in red ink.
5. The lending institution must determine by visual observation the applicant's minority code, if applicable, and this information must be entered on Form 4-I.
6. The lender must send the Forms 912 (Personal History Statement) submitted with the application directly to SBA in Washington, D.C., marked "CLP" in red ink.
7. The lender must submit a statement assessing the applicant's moral character.

Servicing the Loan

It is the lender's responsibility to service, supervise, and monitor the SBA guaranteed loan. The lender should establish and maintain a credit file on the loan in the same manner as on any other commercial loan. As discussed previously, disbursement of proceeds should be supervised closely by the lender. Periodic financial information should be obtained and analyzed to identify trends and potential problems. Any significant adverse change in the status or performance of the business should be brought to SBA's attention. The participating lender should also ascertain that all provisions of the loan agreement are complied with, especially those pertaining to compensation of principals, payment of dividends, or purchases of fixed assets. Repayment performance must obviously also be monitored, and any delinquency, even of short duration, should be investigated promptly. A tickler file should be established to identify UCC continuation dates, insurance expiration dates, financial statement due dates, etc. The participating lender should also maintain open lines of communication with the borrower and make periodic visits to the business itself to inspect the collateral and observe the operation of the business.

SBA's Section 503 Program

The Small Business Administration's Certified Development Company Program, also known as the Section 503 Program, was enacted on July 2, 1980 as an amendment to the Small Business Investment Act of 1958. The program's purpose is to encourage the economic development of communities by stimulating the growth and expansion of small businesses. The function of the program is to facilitate the long term financing of fixed assets, and is intended to fill the gap that exists for small and medium-size businesses in obtaining long term credit. In many instances there are few readily available sources of long term credit, particularly in economically depressed areas. The creation of new jobs is also a prime objective, and the number of new jobs that will be created by a project is a prime criteria for approval of a Section 503 loan.

The Certified Development Company

The Section 503 program calls for the organization of certified development companies which may operate on a local, regional, or statewide basis, and which act as an intermediary between the borrower and SBA. The Certified Development Company (CDC) may be organized as a private nonprofit corporation or a for-profit stock corporation. The company must have a minimum of 25 members or stockholders, and must designate a specific geographic area of operation, which may be statewide or smaller. Membership in the company must include representation from at least two of the following four groups—local government, business organizations, private lending institutions, and community organizations. The CDC must have a professional staff with the capacity to assist potential borrowers in the preparation of a loan application and to package, process, close, and service loans. The CDC must be able to provide professional accounting and legal services to small business applicants. These services may be furnished either by the CDC's membership or on a contractual basis, subject to SBA approval, by qualified professional individuals or firms. The CDC must have a board of directors of at least five persons who meet at least bimonthly, and no member of the board may be an officer, principal, or owner of a small business receiving assistance. No member or shareholder of the Certified Development Company may own more than 10% of the total outstanding stock of the company. The CDC must maintain a place of business open to the public during business hours and must be listed under a separate number in the telephone directory. In order to maintain its certification, a CDC must provide financial assistance to at least one small business concern each fiscal year.

Certified Development Companies are authorized to sell debentures pertaining to an identifiable small business project with a 100% SBA guaranty. Proceeds of the sale of each debenture may be used to finance up to 40% of the total cost of the acquisition of land and buildings, construction and renovation, lease holding improvements, and machinery and equipment. The Small Business Administration sells the debentures to the Federal Financing Bank, and acts as agent for the Certified Development Company for the purpose of such a sale. The Federal Financing Bank is an agency of the federal government created under the provisions of the Federal Financing Bank Act of 1973. The interest rate on each debenture is determined by the Federal Financing Bank at the time of each sale, based on the cost of like term funds to the bank.

Eligibility Requirements

With a few exceptions, any for-profit business is eligible for the Section 503 program provided that its net worth is not in excess of six million dollars, and its net profit after taxes has averaged less than two million dollars during each of the previous two years. If it is a manufacturing firm, the business must have no more than a prescribed number of employees based on SBA size standards. Generally, the project must include the acquisition of real estate and real estate improvements. If the project is for the financing of equipment alone, the term of debenture will be limited to the useful life of the equipment being purchased.

The business must also be able to satisfy SBA that its management is capable of conducting the affairs of the business in a prudent and profitable manner. In addition, its projections of future performance must indicate that the business will be capable of producing adequate cash flow and profits to service its obligations, and that a significant number of new permanent jobs will be created, or that existing jobs will be retained which otherwise would have been lost.

Some types of businesses are ineligible for a Section 503 loan. These include nonprofit organizations, print media such as newspapers and magazines, lending institutions such as banks and finance companies, gambling facilities, recreational facilities that are not open to the public, and projects involving rental or investment real estate.

Structuring the Loan Package

Every 503 project must be a joint venture between SBA and a private sector commercial lender. The applicant must obtain a commitment from a commercial lender to finance fifty percent of the cost of the project. The term of the commercial loan must be at least half that of the SBA debentures, and must also be for at least ten years. As collateral, the commercial lender may take a first security interest and/or first mortgage in the assets being purchased. Since they are in a position to make a loan for fifty percent of the cost of the assets and achieve a first priority security position, most lenders feel that such a loan is acceptable from a safety standpoint, although its term may be somewhat longer than a commercial lender would ordinarily consider.

Except for the fact that the maturity of the commercial loan must conform to SBA standards, the applicant and the commercial lender have considerable freedom to negotiate the other terms of the loan. The loan must be made at an interest rate that is legal and reasonable. The SBA will permit renegotiable rate loans with early call options as long as the rate renegotiation formula is established in advance. The formula must be tied to national prime rate, with 2.75% over national prime being the maximum allowable rate. The lender may request personal guarantys, subordination agreements, assignments of life insurance, etc. SBA prohibits the use of tax exempt revenue bonds to finance the commercial lender's portion of the project.

The proceeds of the SBA 503 loan may be used to finance up to forty percent of the project, with a maximum of $500,000. Therefore, if a project totals $1,250,000, it is eligible for a $500,000 Section 503 loan. Projects for a larger amount are eligible, but in such a case only $500,000 of SBA debentures may be issued. The minimum debenture issue is $10,000. The Section 503 loan will be secured by a second security interest and/or second mortgage in the assets being purchased. Personal guarantys of the principals of the business and an assignment of life insurance on the lives of those principals generally will also be required.

The remaining ten percent of the cost of the project is generally equity provided by the applicant. However, in some cases the Certified Development Company may inject these funds as an additional loan to the applicant, or the funds may come from a state or locally sponsored loan program.

The Loan Application

The application for a Section 503 loan is quite similar to that for a Section 7(a) loan. There are, however, several additional requirements. A pro forma balance sheet and projected operating statement for at least two years must be included, while the 7(a) application requires only a one-year projection. A commitment letter from a commercial lending institution for the term loan must also be included. This letter must state the terms and conditions of the institution's loan and the reason it will not finance the entire project. Further, if the improvements being financed are to be constructed, then a commitment for an interim construction loan must also be included. The proceeds of the 503 debenture will not be disbursed until the project is complete. Preliminary plans and specifications and estimates of the cost of new construction, equipment and machinery must also be included. In the case of owned real estate, an appraisal report must be obtained. If the real estate is to be leased or purchased, then a copy of the proposed lease or purchase agreement must be provided. A statement explaining the source of the ten percent injection of funds (usually equity) must also be furnished.

When the application is completed it must be submitted to the CDC for processing. The Certified Development Company staff will examine the application to make sure that all necessary information has been included, and will analyze the request to determine its feasibility. When the applicaiton is processed it is presented to the Board or Loan Committee of the CDC for final approval. This presentation may be made either by the staff or by the applicant. Most CDCs allow the applicant, his or her attorney and/or accountant to make the presentation. If the Board of the CDC approves the application, it is then forwarded to SBA for final approval.

Closing the 503 Loan

When the project is complete, SBA will request the Federal Financing Bank to issue and sell the necessary debenture. This is generally done only once per month. Proceeds of the debenture sale are transferred to the Central Fiscal Agent (a large New York bank) and when all necessary documentation has been signed, the funds are wire transferred to the participating commercial lender. The Central Fiscal Agent normally will charge a .25% initiation fee and the local CDC usually charges a 1.5% initiation fee. Annual servicing fees are also usually charged—the Federal Financing Bank, .125%; the Central Fiscal Agent, .125%; and the local CDC, .50% of the outstanding debenture balance. The rate to be paid by the borrower on the Section 503 loan is established at the time the debentures are sold. The debenture rate will generally be slightly above the rate on U.S. Treasury Bonds of similar maturity. This rate will usually be at least 2% below current commercial rates for a loan of similar maturity. At closing, a reserve account for at least two monthly payments is usually established. Payments on the 503 debenture are generally made monthly, and must be wire transferred to the Central Fiscal Agent.

Form Approved
OMB No. 3245-0016

2 SBA Office Code	U.S. SMALL BUSINESS ADMINISTRATION LENDER'S APPLICATION FOR GUARANTY OR PARTICIPATION (Numbers in circles or squares are SBA codes only)		SBA Loan Number 1

Name of Applicant

30   Johnson Manufacturing Company, a corporation

WE PROPOSE TO MAKE A (Check One)

		Lenders Share	SBA Share	Term of Loan		Monthly Payment
X	Guaranteed Loan	10 %	90 %	Seven Years		$ 3960.00
	Immediate Participation Loan (Lender to make and service)	Lenders Share %	SBA Share %	Lenders Interest Rate % Per Annum		Payment Beginning one Months from Date of Note

Amount of Loan $ 260,000.00

If Interest Rate is to be Variable

Base Rate: New York prime	Spread: 2%	Rate Adjustment ☒ Quarterly ☐ Other (Specify)	Base Rate Source Wall Street Journal

TERMS AND CONDITIONS OF LENDER *(Attach additional sheets if more space is needed.)*

1. Loan to be secured by a purchase money security interest in the equipment being purchased, and a second security interest in all equipment, fixtures, furnishings, inventory, accounts and contracts receivable; also a second mortgage on the company's real estate on Bingham Road.

2. Loan to be personally guaranteed by the company's principals, Ralph Johnson and George Downing.

3. Johnson and Downing will each assign no less than $250,000 of life insurance.

4. Johnson to inject $20,000 additional equity into the corporation.

5. Downing to give a second mortgage on his personal residence to secure his guaranty.

I approve this application to SBA subject to the terms and conditions outlined above. Without the participation of SBA to the extent applied for we would not be willing to make this loan, and in our opinion the financial assistance applied for is not otherwise available on reasonable terms. I certify that none of the Lender's employees, officers, directors or substantial stockholders (more than 10%) have a financial interest in the applicant.

Signature: *Robert C. Brown*	Title: Vice President	Date: June 7, 1984

Name of Lender		Telephone (Inc A/C)	Financial Institution I.D. Code
40 Center City National Bank		217-166-4321	41 A160764

Street Address	City	State	Zip
42 1234 Main Street	43 Center City	44 IL	45 61111

FOR SBA USE ONLY

Loan Officers Recommendation		
	☐ Approve	☐ Decline State Reason(s)

Signature:	Title:	Date:

Other Recommendation, if Required		3
	☐ Approve	☐ Decline State Reason(s)

Signature:	Title:	Date:

THIS BLOCK TO BE COMPLETED BY SBA OFFICIAL TAKING FINAL ACTION

☐ Approve	☐ Decline State Reason(s)

Signature:	Title:	Date:

BUSINESS LOANS ONLY

4 Program Struct. Code	6 MTY (MOS)	9 SMR	46 No. of Employees	47 Franchise Code	48 New Bus 1-No 2-Yes	49 Women 1-No 2-Yes	50 Viet Vet. 1-No 2-Yes	51 Organ. Code 1-Indiv. 2-Part. 3-Corp.
10 City Code	11 State Code	12 Loan Type (1) Dir. (4) IPSBA (3) IPBK (7) Guar	52 SIC Code	53 Location 1-Urban 2-Rural	54 EOL Family Income (5 Only) 5	55 Poll. Code	56	
13 Sub Program Code	14 County Code	15						

SBA LOAN PAY OFFS: LIST ALL SBA LOANS BEING REFUNDED

			15a Loan Number cc 11-20	15b Loan Type cc 21 (1) Direct (2) Part. (3) Guar.	15c Loan Status cc 22 (1) Curr. (4) C/D (2) P/D (5) Liq. (3) Del.	15d Amount $
Loan Amount Approved 16 SBA	% Participation 19	Interest Rate 21 %	cc 29-38	cc 39 (1) Direct (2) Part. (3) Guar.	cc 40 (1) Curr. (4) C/D (2) P/D (5) Liq. (3) Del.	$
17 Bank	20	22 %	cc 11-20	cc 21 (1) Direct (2) Part. (3) Guar.	cc 22 (1) Curr. (4) C/D (2) P/D (5) Liq. (3) Del.	$
18 Total						

23 Minority Code	24 O/S SBA Loan 1-No 2-Yes	25 Const. Cont. Amt. $	IF MORE THAN 3 LOANS ARE PAID OFF ENTER TOTAL OF REMAINING LOANS (16) $
26 New Construction 1-No 2-Yes	27 Real Collateral 1-No 2-Yes	28	**PRIOR SBA LOANS: LIST LOAN NUMBERS OF ALL PRIOR SBA LOANS TO BORROWER**
29	31 Soc. Sec. No.		17a cc 11-20 17b cc 21-30 17c cc 31-40
33 Employer ID No.		35 Borrower Alpha Code	

SBA Form 4-1 (9-81) REF SOP 50 10 1   PREVIOUS EDITIONS ARE OBSOLETE

INSTRUCTIONS: The information requested below must be supplied with the application package.

FINANCIAL SPREAD

BALANCE SHEET	As of 4/30/84	Fiscal Year Ends	AUDITED ☐	UNAUDITED ☒
		DEBIT	CREDIT	PRO FORMA
Assets				
Cash	$ 15,110.	$ 20,000*	$	$ 35,110.
Accounts Rec.	160,422.	80,000.		240,422.
Inventory	120,301.	40,000.		160,301.
Other	18,208.			18,208.
Total Current Assets	314,041.			454,041.
Fixed Assets	236,384.	140,000.		376,384.
Other Assets	21,200.			21,200.
Total Assets	$ 571,625.	$	$	$ 851,625.
Liabilities & Net Worth				
Accounts Payable	$ 59,370.	$	$	$ 59,370.
Notes Payable	140,000.			140,000.
Taxes	9,360.			9,360.
Other	7,880.			7,880.
SBA	--		37,140.	37,140.
Total Current Liabilities	$ 216,610.	$	$	$ 253,750.
Notes Payable	$ 192,360.	$	$	$ 192,360.
SBA			222,860.	222,860.
Other	6,340.			6,340.
Total Liabilities	$ 415,310.	$	$	$ 675,310.
Net Worth	$ 156,315.	$	$ 20,000*	$ 176,315.
Total Liab. & Net Worth	$ 571,625.	$	$	$ 851,625.

Profit & Loss (in 1000's)	1981 YEAR	1982 YEAR	1983 YEAR	4 mos.YEAR 1984
Sales	$ 219	$ 512	$ 840	$ 343
Depreciation	7	21	29	11
Income Taxes	0	6	32	9
W/D Officer Comp.	42	60	83	30
Net Profit After Tax/Deprec.	$ (12)	$ 22	$ 60	$ 27

PRO FORMA SCHEDULE OF FIXED OBLIGATIONS

	YEAR 1	YEAR 2	YEAR 3	YEAR 4
	$ 79200	$ 79200	$ 74750	$ 72840

Lender should comment on the following (Continue on separate sheet if needed):   * Injection of equity
1. Balance sheet and ratio analysis - comment on trends, debt to worth and current ratio.
2. Lenders analysis of repayment ability.
3. Management skill of the applicant.
4. Collateral offered and lien position, and analysis of collateral adequacy.
5. Lenders credit experience with the applicant.
6. Schedule of insurance requirements, standby agreements and other requirements.

Lenders Analysis:

Current ratio = 1.45 at present, 1.79 on a pro-forma basis.
Debt to worth ratio = 2.66 at present, 3.83 on a pro-forma basis.

 This young company, which started its operations in 1981, has had an excellent growth pattern. It produces a quality product for which there is a growing demand. Profits are increasing on a consistent basis. Purchase of the new equipment will significantly improve its production efficiency. It's projections should be readily achievable, and indicate that profits and cash flow should be very adequate to service the company's debt obligations. As a result of this loan working capital position will improve. The business' obvious weakness is its heavily leveraged position, with a pro-forma debt/worth ratio of 3.83. We will have a first security interest in $140,000 of equipment to be purchased with the loan proceeds. There will be an equity of approximately $200,000 in inventory and receivables over and above the amount owed on the company's working capital loan and what is owed to secured suppliers. There is an equity of about $30,000 in the company's real estate, and about $20,000 equity in Downing's personal residence. We therefore have gross collateral value of about $390,000. Assuming a liquidation value of 60%, we have collateral coverage of about 90%.

 Johnson is an experienced engineer, and Downing has a strong background in business and finance. They have managed the firm in a very competent manner. The firm has been a customer of the bank since its inception and has always performed as agreed. Evidence of adequate casualty and liability insurance will be required.

18

Commercial Letters of Credit

A commercial letter of credit is another kind of credit accommodation that a commercial bank may provide to its customers. A letter of credit is a document, usually in letter form, in which the issuing bank, at the request of and in accordance with instructions of its customer, agrees to reimburse a third party (the beneficiary) upon their compliance with the terms and conditions of the letter of credit. Letters of credit, which have been in use in international trade for thousands of years, are one of the oldest kinds of commercial instruments. Although originally they were used primarily in international transactions, letters of credit are now also quite commonly used in domestic transactions.

In a transaction where a seller is unwilling to extend open account credit due to the perceived risk involved, or a lack of knowledge of the buyer's financial status, and the buyer is unwilling to pay cash in advance, a letter of credit is an excellent means for protecting both the buyer and the seller. Since the bank is substituting its own credit standing for that of the buyer by issuing the letter of credit, the seller no longer needs to rely solely on the ability of the buyer to make payment, but may look to the bank. The buyer, in turn, has assurances that the payment will not be made until the seller has complied with the terms and conditions contained in the letter. For example, the letter may require that the goods be shipped, and the bill of lading be attached to the sight draft by which the seller draws funds against the letter of credit. Generally, under a sight draft arrangement, the seller forwards all required documents, which may include bills of lading, invoices, insurance certificates, etc. along with a draft drawn at sight on the buyer through his or her bank to the buyer's bank, with instructions that the documents can be released to the buyer only upon payment of the draft.

Commercial letters of credit are governed by the provisions of Article 5 of the Uniform Commercial Code and by the "Uniform Customs and Practice for Documentary Credits" contained in International Chamber of Commerce

Publication No. 290. The Uniform Commercial Code defines a letter of credit as an engagement by a bank or other person made at the request of a customer and of a kind within the scope of Section 5-102 that the issuer will honor drafts or other demands for payment, upon compliance with the conditions specified in the credit.[1] Section 5-102 of the UCC further defines a letter of credit as (a) a credit issued by a bank if the credit requires a documentary draft or a documentary demand for payment; or (b) a credit issued by a person other than a bank if the credit requires that the draft or demand for payment be accompanied by a document of title; or (c) a credit issued by a bank or other person if the credit is not within (a) or (b) above, but conspicuously states that it is a letter of credit or is conspicuously so entitled.

A documentary draft is a draft, honor of which is conditioned upon the presentation of a document or documents. An issuer is a bank or other person issuing a letter of credit. A beneficiary is a person who is entitled under the terms of the letter of credit to draw or demand payment. A customer is a buyer or other person who causes an issuer to issue a letter of credit. An advising bank is a bank that gives notification of the issuance of a credit by another bank. A confirming bank is a bank that engages either that it will itself honor a credit already issued by another bank, or that such a credit will be honored by the issuer or a third bank.[2]

Standby Letters of Credit

In most cases it is the intent of the parties that the letter of credit be used as a vehicle for payment to the seller of goods. However, in some instances a letter of credit may be issued as a guaranty of performance. This kind of letter of credit is known as a standby letter of credit. A standby letter of credit generally is never drawn against unless there is a default on the part of the party for whose account the letter was issued. This default may be in the repayment of money borrowed, or in payment of invoices for goods purchased within a specified time period, or in performance under a contract. Standby letters of credit are sometimes also used to assure timely delivery of goods or the quality of goods and services provided. A standby letter of credit is generally payable upon presentation of a draft accompanied by a statement indicating that the customer has failed to perform according to the underlying contract or agreement. This signed statement may be provided either by the beneficiary or by an independent third party, depending on the requirements of the letter of credit. It should be noted, however, that the letter of credit itself is not an unconditional guaranty of payment. The letter only assures payment to the beneficiary if the terms and conditions of the letter of credit are complied with in full.

[1]   UCC 5-103(1)(a)
[2]   UCC 5-103(1)

Letters of credit may be either revocable or irrevocable in form.[3] A revocable letter of credit may be modified or cancelled by the issuing bank at any time without notice to or consent of the beneficiary. Since a revocable letter of credit does not give the beneficiary full assurance of payment, this form of letter is rarely used. An irrevocable letter of credit cannot be amended or cancelled without the full consent of all parties concerned.[4] Therefore, almost all commercial letters of credit are the irrevocable form, and constitute an absolute promise to pay by the issuing bank, provided the terms and conditions of the letter have been complied with by the beneficiary. Any letter of credit should clearly indicate whether it is revocable or irrevocable, but in the absence of such indication, the letter will be deemed to be revocable.

Since all letters of credit are governed by the Uniform Commercial Code and by ICC Publication No. 290, every commercial bank that issues letters of credit should have copies of these publications in its files, and the officers handling letters of credit should be familiar with their rules and provisions. Although Article 5 of the Uniform Commercial Code is the primary law in the United States pertaining to letters of credit, the parties involved may agree to make the letter subject to the provisions of Publication 290, especially if an international transaction is involved. In that case, those provisions prevail. ICC Publication No. 290 will be superseded by ICC Publication No. 400 effective October, 1984.

Every letter of credit should contain an expiration date after which the letter is null and void. When the designated expiration date falls on a day on which banks are closed, such as a weekend or national holiday, the expiration date will be automatically extended until the next business day.

In addition to stipulating an expiration date, a letter of credit should also stipulate a specific period of time after the date of issuance of the bills of lading or other shipping documents during which presentation of documents for payment, acceptance, or negotiation must be made. If no such period of time is stipulated in the letter of credit, a bank generally may refuse documents presented later than 21 days after the date of issuance of the bills of lading or other shipping documents.

The UCC requires that a credit must be in writing, conspicuously state that it is a letter of credit, and be signed by the issuer. A confirmation must also be in writing and signed by the confirming bank. As long as these requirements are met, no particular form of phrasing is required for a letter of credit.[5] Also, contrary to most contract law, no consideration is necessary to establish a letter of credit or to enlarge or otherwise modify its terms.[6] Terms

[3]   UCC 5-103(1)(a)
[4]   UCC 5-106(2)
[5]   UCC 5-104(1)
[6]   UCC 5-105

that are ambiguous should be avoided in a letter of credit, and therefore such terms as qualified, adequate, or well known should not be used.

A letter of credit may also be transferable or non-transferable. A transferable letter is one under which the beneficiary has the right to transfer the letter to a third party. A letter of credit is transferable only if it is expressly designated as being transferable by the issuing bank.[7] A transferable letter generally can be transferred only once. Transferable letters are ordinarily used only in a case where the original beneficiary acts as a middle man or broker between the seller of the merchandise and the buyer. Even though the letter of credit is not transferable, this does not affect the beneficiary's right to assign the proceeds of the letter of credit in accordance with the provisions of applicable law. The assignment of the proceeds of a letter of credit is governed by the provisions of Article 9 of the Uniform Commercial Code, as if the assignment were an assignment of an account, except that certain provisions of UCC 5-116(2) must be complied with for the security interest to become perfected. These include a requirement that the letter of credit be delivered to the assignee, and a requirement that notice of the assignment, signed by the beneficiary, be given to the issuer.

Even though no funds are disbursed at the time the letter of credit is issued, the lender should be fully cognizant that it is an extension of credit. Therefore, a decision to issue a letter of credit should be made in much the same manner as a decision to make a loan, unless the amount of the letter is covered by a cash deposit from the customer. A fee, usually in the range of one to two percent, is ordinarily charged for the issuance of the letter. Since the lender must be prepared to disburse funds at any time, it must have assurance that the funds can be recovered from the party for whose account the letter was issued (the customer). In some cases, a bank may require a segregated cash deposit to cover potential disbursements. In other cases, the bank may require the party for whose account the letter is issued to sign a promissory note which will be disbursed when funds are drawn against the letter. Whatever procedures are employed, the bank must always be in a position to recover the funds drawn against the letter of credit. Since an outstanding letter of credit is a contingent liability of the bank, the bank must account for all outstanding letters. For this reason, letters of credit are numbered consecutively as they are issued, and a register is maintained of all outstanding letters of credit.

While international letters of credit remain pretty much the exclusive domain of the larger city banks, many smaller banks issue domestic letters of credit. Some small banks have been hesitant to issue commercial letters of credit, primarily because they do not fully understand the pertinent rules and

---

[7] UCC 5-116(1)

procedures. However, letters of credit can be an excellent means for accommodating the needs of a customer, and can also be an excellent source of fee income. The same care must be taken in issuing the letter as in making a loan, and the bank must fully understand its obligations under the letter.

Exhibit EE is an example of a policy for the issuance of irrevocable domestic letters of credit which may be suitable for a smaller bank, and Exhibit FF is an example of a domestic irrevocable letter of credit.

EXHIBIT EE   POLICY FOR ISSUANCE OF IRREVOCABLE DOMESTIC AND STANDBY LETTERS OF CREDIT

I. *General*

The bank from time to time issues Irrevocable Letters of Credit for the account of its customers. The purpose of this policy is to standardize eligibility criteria, procedures, and charges for issuance of Irrevocable Letters of Credit.

An international letter of credit is one that involves a business transaction in which the beneficiary is in a foreign country. The bank will not issue international letters of credit, but when required, will make arrangements with one of its large city correspondent banks to issue a letter for the account of its customer.

A domestic letter of credit is one that involves a business transaction in which the beneficiary is located in the United States. A standby letter of credit is one that is issued to guarantee the performance of an obligation. The bank will actively issue domestic and standby letters of credit.

II. *Eligibility Criteria*

A. The applicant should be an established account customer of the bank, and must be creditworthy.

B. An Irrevocable Letter of Credit is an extension of credit. Therefore, any applicant for a Letter must furnish one of the following:

(1) A cash deposit covering the amount of the Letter.

(2) A promissory note covering the amount of the Letter. A complete financial statement and other necessary financial information indicating the applicant is creditworthy shall be obtained in the same manner as required for a loan. In some instances, collateral may be required, and if so, the bank's security interest in the collateral shall be perfected in the same manner as for a loan.

III. *Limitations and Guidelines*

A. No Letter shall be issued in an amount in excess of the legal lending limit of the bank. If the applicant has an outstanding line of credit, which, when added to the amount of the Letter, creates a total obligation exceeding the bank's legal lending limit, contingent arrangements to sell an overline to another bank must be made.

B. Any Letter of Credit in excess of the loan officers' lending authority shall be approved by the Loan Committee. To make this determination, all the customer's outstanding loans and letters of credit shall be aggregated.

C. No Letter shall be issued for a term in excess of five years.

IV. *Procedures*

A. Upon receipt of a request for a Letter, a determination should be made by the officer processing the request that the applicant is eligible under Section II.

B. If the Letter is to be secured by a cash deposit, it should be accepted and a receipt issued. The deposit may be in the form of a DDA account, savings account, or time deposit which must be assigned to the bank.

C. If the Letter is covered by a promissory note, financial information shall be obtained as outlined in Section IIB(2), and a note in an amount equal to

EXHIBIT   EE(*Continued*)

the amount of the letter signed by the applicant and processed in the same manner as a loan.

In each case a credit decision must be made as though the transaction were a loan. The note should have a maturity date not later than 30 days after the expiration date of the Letter.

In those instances where collateral is required to make the transaction acceptable from a credit standpoint, the collateral will be handled in the same manner as though the transaction were a loan. Generally, the collateral should have a value at least 30% in excess of the amount of the Letter.

D.   The Letter shall then be issued in a form conforming to Article 5 of the Uniform Commercial Code and the Uniform Customs and Practice for Documentary Credits of the International Chamber of Commerce Publication No. 290 in an original and three copies. The Letter must be signed by an authorized officer and the original and one copy delivered to the applicant. One file copy shall be placed in the Register File, and the other in the applicant's credit file, if applicable. An entry must then be made in the Register File as described in Section VI, and a number assigned to the Letter. This number shall be prominently shown on the face of the Letter.

V.   *Fees*

A.   A fee equal to one percent of the amount of the Letter shall be charged for the issuance of a Letter.

B.   If the Letter has a maturity date in excess of one year, on each one year anniversary of the issue date of the Letter the customer shall be billed an additional fee of one percent of the amount of the Letter. If remaining maturity is less than one year as of the billing date, the fee shall be prorated on the basis of remaining term in months vs. 12 months.

C.   If the fee, as computed in Section V(A) or V(B) amounts to less than $50.00, a minimum fee of $50.00 shall be charged.

D.   In rare instances, the officer issuing the Letter may reduce the fee for preferred customers, but in all cases an amount equal to the minimum fee shall be charged.

VI.   *Register File*

A.   A Register File shall be maintained, in which all Letters shall be recorded. Based on a list kept in the Register File, a consecutive number shall be assigned each Letter as it is issued.

B.   All pertinent information, including number, date of issue, amount, name of beneficiary, name of purchaser and expiration date, shall be recorded in the Register File.

C.   Upon the expiration date of a Letter, a notation to that effect shall be made in the Register File.

D.   A copy of each Letter issued shall be permanently filed in the Register File.

EXHIBIT   FF   DOMESTIC IRREVOCABLE LETTER OF CREDIT

CENTER CITY NATIONAL BANK
123 Main Street Center City, Illinois 61111
Telephone A.C. 217 352-052-0561

COMMERCIAL IRREVOCABLE LETTER OF CREDIT #472

December 23, 19X4

Amalgamated Metals, Inc.
3270 Park Avenue
New York, NY 10017

Gentlemen:

We hereby authorize you to draw on the Center City National Bank, Center City, Illinois for the account of ABC Manufacturing Company, 1480 State Street, Center City, Illinois, up to an aggregate amount of One Hundred Forty Thousand and 00/100 Dollars ($140,000.00) available by your drafts at sight. Your drafts must be accompanied by a copy of an invoice and a bill of lading for 6.445 inch aluminum discs as described in ABC's purchase order #6875. All drafts hereunder must be marked "Drawn under Center City National Bank Letter of Credit #472 dated December 23, 19X4."

The amount of each draft drawn under this credit must be endorsed hereon, and the presentation of each draft, if negotiated, shall be a warranty by the negotiating bank that such endorsement has been made and that documents have been forwarded as herein requested. All payments under this letter of credit will be made by wire transfer to Northern Trust Company, Chicago.

We hereby engage with the drawers, endorsers, and bona fide holders of drafts drawn under and in compliance with the terms of this credit that the same will be duly honored on due presentation and delivery of documents as specified if presented to this bank on or before June 1, 19X5.

Except as expressly provided herein, this credit is subject to the Uniform Customs and Practice for Documentary Credits (1974 revision), The International Chamber of Commerce Publication #290.

Very truly yours,

CENTER CITY NATIONAL BANK

Robert H. Brown
Vice President

RHB:cp

19

Introduction to Equipment Leasing

J. L. Bennion

As cyclical swings in the economy have become shorter and less predictable, businesses have felt increased pressure to control costs and effect good cash management. Decisions regarding methods of financing capital equipment may be predicated more on return on investment and the useful life of the equipment than on the cost of borrowing. Leasing of capital equipment (personal property) has become an alternative that, subject to certain conditions, provides a form of financing that reduces cash outflow and improves short term profits.

When short term cost of money exceeds long term cost, cash is at a premium and a 100% financing and a reduction of payment size to avoid negative cash flow becomes more attractive. Equipment leasing serves a variety of needs of businesses, but none so great as the need to preserve cash and reduce the drain on capital reserves.

Leasing offers advantages to both the lessor (owner) and the lessee (customer). The lessor is able to shelter taxable income and obtain a rate of return which is usually higher than that for a comparable commercial loan. The lessee benefits from updated equipment while keeping his or her funds and credit lines available for other uses. Lease payments are generally fully deductible for tax purposes, and are at a fixed rate. The lessee is also often able to obtain cash from the sale of equipment being replaced by the leased equipment.

Equipment leasing revolves around the lease agreement that spells out the responsibilities of the owner (lessor) and the duties and liabilities of the

Jan L. (J. L.) Bennion is a Senior Vice President of First Lease and Equipment Consulting Corporation where she is in charge of Marketing for the Western Region. She has twelve years experience in banking and has specialized in equipment leasing. Ms. Bennion has a BA from the University of Utah and has had extensive post graduate work in marketing and equipment leasing.

user (lessee) of the equipment. The basic issue of who is the owner and who retains ownership rights often becomes confused when the terms of the lease agreement bend too far in favor of either the lessee or the lessor. This major issue of whether the owner has legal, tax, or actual ownership has given rise over the past two decades to a multitude of rules, regulations, and controls from a variety of regulatory agencies.

There are a few basic differences from traditional lending and these need to be examined. The *lessor is the owner* of the equipment. To be the owner of the equipment sounds like a simple task, when in fact many responsibilities and requirements, and in most instances, risks, are associated with asset ownership. These risks and responsibilities of asset ownership will be discussed as we compare the equipment lease to a loan.

Asset ownership also means the retention of all rights, title, and interest in the equipment unless transferred to the lessee by the use of the lease documentation. Simply stated, that means the owner of the equipment is responsible for all equipment issues including, but not limited to, taxes, insurance, product liability, [1] equipment use, equipment maintenance, and equipment value. How the lease documentation deals with these many responsibilities and duties dramatically impacts how the regulatory agencies deal with the question of who retains the rights of ownership.

Any major discussion of equipment leasing first requires the separation of equipment leasing into a tax or a non-tax motivated lease. During the 1950s, when equipment leasing began its current popularity, the term "true leasing" was developed to identify a tax motivated lease. A tax motivated lease is a lease in which the owner of the equipment (lessor) retains the rights, title, and interest in the equipment. The user of the equipment (lessee) is allowed to take possession of the equipment for a predetermined period of time and use the equiment for the purpose for which it was originally intended. A "non-true lease" is a lease in which the legal title of the equipment remains with the lessor, but the tax considerations, (i.e., the right, interest, and benefits of the equipment) rest with the lessee. Only the legal title remains with the lessor. Typically, at the end of the lease term, the title is passed to the lessee for a nominal prestated amount. The Internal Revenue Service (IRS) states that the difference between a true lease and a non-true lease is a function of the *substance of the lease agreement* and *the intent of the parties involved* instead of the *form of the lease agreement*. An example would be an attempt to disguise a conditional or installment sales contract by labeling it a lease.

One of the basic issues a banker has to come to grips with when dealing

---

[1]   Product Liability—the issue of liability that an owner (lessor) has when the product does not live up to the performance standards promised by the vendor; or the possibility of a claim from the misuse of the equipment by a third party; or the question of liability from an accident or destruction of property by the equipment.

with an equipment lease is that the asset ownership nature of a true equipment lease means that all payments from a lessee must be considered revenue and are totally taxable. A commercial loan is repaid with principal and interest. Only the interest portion is considered income and is taxable. The rental payments on an equipment lease are offset for income tax purposes by depreciation and Investment Tax Credit (ITC).[2] This basic difference needs to be understood to clarify that an equipment lease and the value that it represents must be dealt with and accounted for differently from a traditional loan.

Due to its unique nature and the variety of equipment that may be involved, the terms of the lease may vary considerably, depending on the circumstances. For example, mobile equipment that transfers cargo from one state to another requires documentation different from a lease dealing with stationary equipment in a manufacturing facility. Also, there is a difference in lease documentation for income producing and non-income producing equipment. The lessor must deal with multi-use and single use property, domestic or international use, and a variety of other distinctions. A bank lessor must develop the viewpoint that equipment in an equipment lease is significantly different from collateral in a traditional loan.

The total amount of leasing business a bank can do is limited. A bank must remember that the annual volume of true leases it should put in its portfolio is limited by the amount of shelter necessary to offset the tax liability (tax appetite) that would ordinarily be paid by the bank. Usually, tax liability is difficult to determine early in the year; therefore, the bank's leasing department needs to be well informed as to the bank's tax position at all times during the year.

Now that the basics are covered, let's consider the lease itself. For a complete understanding of a lease, it is necessary to begin with the pricing. How does the lessor determine how much the customer should pay to achieve the required yield (interest) from the transaction? The lessor must recognize that all payments from the customer will be considered revenue and will be offset for income tax purposes by the values that are retained from asset ownership. Those values are (1) the right to depreciate the equipment; (2) the value of ITC (ITC can be passed to the customer and in that case would have no value to the lessor) and (3) the value of the equipment at the end of the agreed lease term.

Once the concept of lease revenue is understood, it then becomes clear

---

[2]   Investment Tax Credit (ITC)—a credit allowed under federal tax law that reduces taxes payable by a specified percentage of the cost of equipment purchased during the taxable period.

that the amount of payments made in any one year represents taxable income. Therefore, a lease that commences in February may have eleven monthly rental payments (revenue) the first year, whereas a lease that commences in November may have only two payments the first year. Therefore, taxable income in the first year of the equipment lease may vary dramatically depending on the date monthly payments commence.

Depreciation benefits under the Accelerated Cost Recovery System (ACRS)[3] allow for 15% of the original equipment cost to be deducted in the first year of ownership, 22% for year two, and 21% for years three, four, and five on a five-year asset. In addition, the Investment Tax Credit (ITC) allows the first owner/user of the equipment to reduce his or her *federal tax liability* by as much as 10% of the original equipment cost in the first year, provided the asset is depreciated over a term no shorter than five years. For terms shorter than five years, ITC is allowed at the rate of 2% for each year of depreciation. The value of the equipment at lease termination (residual value) needs to be determined to establish the residual assumption that is priced into the lease, since the bank expects to receive a cash inflow at the end of the lease term from selling the equipment either to the user or someone else. That value is unknown until then, but it must be estimated to price the lease. The prudent banker will make a conservative estimate of residual value.

Pricing the value of depreciation, ITC, and the estimated value of the equipment at lease termination into an equipment lease results in the customer's payments being reduced, and the resulting effective rate is called an implicit rate. The implicit rate paid by the customer and the value of the variables discussed above are combined to compute the bank's total yield.

To illustrate how this yield is comparable to the interest rate in a traditional loan, the value of the yield components in an equipment lease must be dealt with in an *after-tax* environment. For example, an 18% pretax interest rate can be expressed as a 9.72% after-tax return (after 46% federal income taxes are paid). Figure 19-1 shows how cash flow and yield analysis of an equipment lease can be used to compute return on investment in the same manner as interest is calculated on a traditional loan. The presentation of cash flows on this equipment lease shows that the outstanding balance and the 9.72% after-tax return (18.00% pre-tax return) can be compared to any conventional loan with identical repayment terms.

Another way to explain the value of the variables in an equipment lease

---

[3]   Accelerated Cost Recovery System—This system allows businesses to claim tax deductions for certain capital expenditures, and thus recover a large part of the original cost. ACRS generally replaces the ADR class life system in use for assets placed in service after 1980.

FIGURE 19-1   Equipment Lease Yield and Cash Flow Analysis

Assumptions:

Equipment Cost:	$1,000,000
Lease Term:	5 years
Monthly Payments:	60 (in advance)
Federal Tax Rate:	46%
Investment Tax Credit:	10%
Depreciation:	5 year accelerated (95%)[1]
Tax Method:	Accrual
Bank Yield:	18%
Customer Cost:	5.7%
Delivery Date:	Dec. 1, 1983

	+ Rent Revenue	Equipment − Cost	Pretax Cash Flow	Taxes[3] Paid	After Tax Cash Flow
1983	19,102	(1,000,000)	(980,898)	156,763	(824,135)
1984	229,221		229,221	(9,302)	219,919
1985	229,221		229,221	(13,672)	215,549
1986	229,221		229,221	(13,672)	215,549
1987	229,221		229,221	(13,672)	215,549
1988	310,119[2]		310,119	(142,655)	167,464

	After Tax Cash Flow	After Tax Return @ 9.72%		Reduction in Balance	After Tax Cash Cost
1983	—	—		—	824,135
1984	219,919	− 73,607	=	146,312	677,823
1985	215,549	− 58,889	=	156,660	521,163
1986	215,549	− 42,964	=	172,585	348,578
1987	215,549	− 25,420	=	190,129	158,449
1988	167,464	− 9,015	=	158,449	0

[1]   IRS regulations require that, if the full ITC is taken, cost basis for depreciation purposes must be reduced by one-half that amount.

[2]   Includes sale of the equipment at residual value of 10%.

[3]   "Taxes paid" shows effect of depreciation and ITC write off.

is to break down that portion of the pretax yield that is identifiable to each variable. Thus, we have:

Customer Effective Rate	5.70%
Investment Tax Credit (10%)	7.68%
Accelerated Depreciation (ACRS)	1.03%
Equipment Value at Termination (10%)	3.59%
Total yield to the bank	18.00%

To show how the variables in the equipment lease may take on different values, it is important to understand that the delivery date of the equipment is also a variable because the number of rental payments received in any tax year affects the total revenue to be taxed in that year. Depreciation and investment tax credit normally have a constant value the first year regardless of when the equipment is delivered. The later in the year the lease is closed, the shorter the time the bank has had its funds invested in the lease relative to the amount of ITC and depreciation. Therefore, the later in the tax year the lease transaction is closed, the lower the revenue, and the greater the tax savings to the bank for that tax year. The following example illustrates how the time of year at which the lease transaction is closed affects the bank's total yield.

	Jan.	June	Dec.
Customer Rate	5.70	5.70	5.70
ITC 10%	6.20	6.81	7.68
ACRS	.01	.42	1.03
Residual 10%	3.14	3.35	3.59
Total bank yield	15.05	16.28	18.00

The value of the variables in an equipment lease can vary dramatically between lending institutions when their state tax rates and/or equipment residual assumptions[4] are different, even though the customer is provided the same effective rate (implicit rate). As long as he or she receives the same rate, the customer is probably impartial as to which lending institution he or she leases the equipment from because the impact to him or her is constant. The lending institution must consider that for each 1% of state tax rate, its yield is increased by 9 basis points,[5] which the bank may either retain or pass along to the customer as a reduction in his or her implicit rate. Also, for each 5% of additional assumed residual value, the yield is increased by 158 basis points. Therefore, if two banks are competing for the customer's business and are located in different states with different state tax rates, and they assume different residual values, then even though each bank expects to receive an 18% yield, the rates quoted to the customer will vary because of the different value of the variables selected by each bank. This may result in major differences in the quoted lease rates, whereas if the customer had requested

---

[4]   Residual Assumption—The assumed value of equipment at the conclusion of the lease term.
[5]   Basis Points—Each 1% of the interest rate is divided into 100 points so that a 3/4 of 1% interest can be expressed as 75 basis points. Nine basis points added to 15.05% would yield 15.14%.

interest rates on a commercial loan, the variances from one lending institution to another would probably have been minimal.

Now that we understand the impact of pricing on an equipment lease, we can begin to discuss the lease itself and how its terms are controlled by the various regulatory agencies.

Regulation of Bank Leasing Activities

National banks must follow the rules issued in 1963 by the Comptroller of the Currency in 12CFR Section 7.3400 regarding bank ownership of property, and Interpretive Ruling 7.3400 issued April 10, 1979. These rules apply to national banks. However, the Federal Reserve Board's Regulation Y should be reviewed by those banks offering equipment leasing under the Bank Holding Company Act, and there are many variances in rules and regulations from state to state for state banks. A bank interested in starting a leasing operation should contact the pertinent regulatory agency to obtain a copy of current regulations. The rules issued by the Comptroller of the Currency have been the standard by which the other regulatory agencies have addressed the issue of bank leasing, and therefore many of these regulations are similar.

The basic elements of the Comptroller's rulings are as follows:

1. A national bank may engage in leasing , acting as lessor, as long as its leases are net, full payout leases. (The bank must look to the original user of the equipment as the only source of revenue besides the tax advantages and the value of the equipment at termination to meet the full payout nature of this test.)

   a. A net lease is a lease under which the bank will not provide or be obligated to provide for maintenance, taxes, repair or replacement, insurance, or licensing of the equipment it leases to others.

   b. A full payout lease is a lease that provides the lessor a return both of its full investment and of the cost of financing the equipment over the term of the lease. The full payout will include cash flows from lease payments, tax benefits; and residual value.

2. The residual value (value of equipment at the end of the lease term) should be conservatively estimated and must not exceed 25% of the cost of the equipment in any case, unless the residual value is guaranteed by a responsible unrelated third party.

3. With respect to the legal lending limit of a bank, leases must be treated just like any other extensions of credit.

4. The bank can lease equipment only in response to a customer's request. For example, the bank cannot select the equipment or direct the

potential lessee's attention to a piece of equipment. The inventorying of equipment is not consistent with the nature of this authority.

Rules for state banks vary from state to state, but most follow the Comptroller's guidelines fairly closely. Both the Comptroller of the Currency and the Federal Reserve Board's Regulation Y require that the lease be the "functional equivalent of an extension of credit to the lessee."

The Federal Reserve Board's Regulation Y is essentially the same as the Comptroller's rulings with the following exceptions:

1. The maximum lease term is 40 years.
2. The maximum residual value which can be assumed is 20%.

The major concern of bank regulators is to ensure that the bank, when engaging in equipment lease activities, does not become responsible for risks outside the normal range of lending. A bank has authority to engage in money lending which is the extension of credit where the only potential loss is the principal and interest, which is therefore a definable risk. Equipment leasing provides additional risks which are not easy to define.

What is the liability of the owner of the equipment when the equipment has been involved in injury to persons or property?

What liability does the owner of the equipment have for the proper performance of the equipment under the terms of the purchase order?

What liability does the owner of the equipment have when that equipment has been used in some unlawful manner?

What liability does the owner have if necessary repossession expenses due to a default are greater than the value of the asset?

What liability does the owner have if the salesman for the vendor has promised additional compensation or reduced terms not included in lease documentation?

These potential problems and difficulties illustrate that the problems presented by equipment leasing vary dramatically from those normally related to a standard commercial loan. The various regulatory agencies are only beginning to grapple with some of these problems, and changes in rules and regulations are inevitable.

The IRS and other taxing authorities believe that the true ownership nature of a lease forces the owner to become a renter of equipment, and therefore the revenue rulings provided for guidance in tax matters begin to conflict with the basic premise of how a bank conducts its leasing activity.

The tax implications of leasing have been a most difficult subject in the past and are currently undergoing modification and change. Lacking any direct Congressional action, the IRS has established rules that define the true owner of an asset, thereby ensuring that only the true owner gets the tax deductions. These rules tended to be a definition of what a prudent owner would be expected to do, or contract for, when engaged in leasing his or her asset to another party. Each subsequent tax act in recent years has sought to define the tax side of leasing, but due to the variety of interested parties involved, additional changes are expected in the future. While many changes are expected, the basic issues of ownership will remain intact, and the following section discusses the current rules. However, you should obtain information regarding current tax guidelines before entering into an equipment lease.

A lease *will not* be considered a true lease if it meets any one of the following requirements: (1) a portion of the lease payments made is specifically applied to equity in the asset on behalf of the lessee; (2) ownership of the equipment automatically passes to the lessee after payment of a specific number of lease payments; (3) the amount paid by the lessee for a short term lease represents an extraordinarily large part of what would be required to purchase the equipment; (4) the rental payments are substantially higher than the current fair rental value; (5) the transaction contains a nominally priced purchase option; (6) a portion of the lease payment is characterized as interest or is readily recognizable as the equivalent of interest.

If a transaction is a leveraged lease, that is, one where the lessor has borrowed part of the funds necessary to acquire title to the equipment on a non-recourse basis, and the lease meets the following requirements, it *will be* considered a true lease.

1. Throughout the term of the lease, the lessor's minimum equity investment is 20% of the cost of the equipment.
2. The residual value at the end of the lease is estimated to be 20% or greater, and the estimated useful life of the asset extends at least 20% beyond the initial lease term.
3. The terms of the lease agreement do not allow the lessee to purchase the equipment at a price less than its fair market value.
4. The lessor has not executed an option for a third party to buy the equipment at the end of the lease term at a fixed price.
5. The lessee has not furnished any part of the cost of the equipment or the cost of subsequent improvements thereon (aside from normal maintenance).
6. The lessee has not provided or guaranteed any of the debt in the leveraged lease.
7. The lessor has demonstrated that it expects to make a profit on the lease transaction, apart from the tax benefits.
8. Generally, uneven lease payments are not allowed unless those payments remain within certain established limits.

These two sets of rules which describe what is and what is not a true lease have become blended in the past few years. Some leasing rules were modified by the Economic Recovery and Tax Act (ERTA) of 1981 and were further modified by the Tax Equity and Fiscal Responsibility Act (TEFRA) of 1982, and then were set aside until January of 1988 by the Tax Reform Act of 1984. In 1988 these additional rules will apply.

1. Both the lessor and the lessee must agree that the transaction is a lease and agree to treat the lessor as owner of the property for tax purposes.
2. The lessor must be a corporation.
3. A purchase option is allowed provided that purchase option at lease termination is for an amount greater than 10% of the original cost of the equipment.
4. The term of the lease (including extensions) is no longer than the greater of (a) 90% of the useful life of the equipment or (b) 150% of the present ADR class life of the equipment.

A special exception was made for agricultural equipment leasing, allowing use of these rules immediately provided the equipment is to be used in farming. This exception allows a standard lease without the requirement of spreading the ITC over the term of the lease, provided that the equipment cost is no more than $150,000.

Much could be written about the frequently changing tax implications of a commercial equipment lease, and you should check the current tax situation before proceeding with an equipment lease.

Insurance Considerations

Another basic difference between leasing and lending is the problem of insurance. Investors, regardless of the kind of investment or the circumstances, will attempt to guarantee the safety and security of their funds. In the field of leasing, there are some risks against which the lessor can do little to protect itself. However, some risks can be covered by insurance, and proper insurance coverage can make the overall risks involved in a lease much more acceptable for both the lessor and lessee.

Two basic types of insurance protection are involved in the leasing field. The first concerns protection for the asset itself, while the other concerns protection of the lessee and lessor against direct or contingent liability that stems from the use and operation of the leased asset. The risks we deal with in the area of insurance concern losses if certain events, such as fire, theft, or accident occur. As a result of these occurrences, assets can be partially or totally destroyed, or an injury done to a third party, creating a major financial setback for the lessor and/or lessee. Insurance specialists readily agree that most businessmen are either uninformed or confused about insurance and its function within their business. Many businesses frequently carry either too much or too little coverage.

For the lessor in an equipment lease, the insurance coverage required differs significantly from that required in the case of an installment or commercial loan. One important function of insurance in a lease agreement is to protect the lessor's interest since it is the owner of the asset. As the owner of the equipment, the lessor may become involved in legal action resulting from damage by the equipment to property or persons. Insurance coverage must be obtained at the beginning of the lease period and carried throughout the entire term of the lease. It is the lessee's responsibility to carry the insurance and the lessor's responsibility to make sure that it is maintained throughout the term of the lease. If the lessor fails to obtain the proper endorsements on the insurance certificate and the equipment is involved in a property or personal accident, the lessor's attorney fees and court costs may easily wipe out any profit that would have been realized from the transaction, even though the lessor's potential liability as a non-operator may be minor.

The master lease document should require that the lessee maintain and pay for the insurance throughout the entire lease term. It is usually necessary to supplement the master lease document with an acceptance supplement that specifies the exact insurance limits required. Also, it is essential that the lease not be funded until evidence of proper insurance coverage is obtained.

There are two basic categories of required insurance: liability coverage and physical damage coverage.

Liability Coverage
This is the type of coverage that protects the insured against injury and/or damage claims from another party. General liability coverage of leased equipment is like an individual's comprehensive automobile policy. It protects the insured party from financial disaster in case of an accident. For most equipment leases it is recommended that there be at least $250,000 bodily injury coverage for each occurrence, $500,000 bodily injury coverage for each aggregate, and $50,000 property damage coverage. The term "each occurrence" means the insurance company will pay a certain amount each time a claim is made, and the term "each aggregate" means the total amount an insurance company will pay if more than one claim is filed. For example, if a John Deere tractor injures a person, the most the insurance company will be responsible for is $250,000 on the one occurrence, "per occurrence". If the tractor hits two or more people, the insurance company will pay a total maximum of $500,000, "per aggregate." Any equipment that is mobile,

manually operated, or referred to as heavy equipment should have this basic coverage as a minimum. On stationary equipment such as computers, telephone systems, or other items that impose little possibility of physical harm, the recommended limits are $250,000 bodily injury coverage for each occurrence, $300,000 bodily injury coverage for each aggregate and $50,000 property damage.

If a lessee's liability limits are $300,000 bodily injury coverage per aggregate and the lessor wants $500,000 coverage per aggregate the customer's insurance agent should be contacted and it should be explained that there is a $200,000 gap between the customer's policy and the lessor's insurance requirements. The agent then has two options. The first is to supply the lessor with an umbrella policy, which is an excess liability policy that provides coverage over and above the aggregate portion of the general liability policy. The other option, of course, is to have the lessee's limits of liability raised. It is not always an easy task to get the umbrella policy added or to have the limits of liability coverage raised because of the additional expense to the customer. However, the lessor as owner of the equipment, must insist that the customer maintain proper insurance coverage to adequately protect the lessor's interests.

When initiating a leasing program, a bank should consult its insurance agent to ensure that the provisions of the bank's umbrella policy also provide adequate protection.

Physical Damage Coverage

The other form of insurance that should be required is physical damage coverage. Physical damage insurance covers such losses as fire, theft, vandalism, casualty losses, and other occurrences that may cause damage to the equipment. In regard to casualty losses specifically, the stipulated loss value schedule, which is part of the lease documentation, is provided to indicate the minimum amount necessary for the lessor to be made whole. To be made whole, the lessor must be able to recover the loss of ITC, depreciation, and residual benefits. In most cases, the stipulated loss value will be sufficient to accomplish this. However, in cases where the equipment appreciates in value, rather than depreciates, it is important to evaluate the policy periodically to assure that the existing coverage takes into account the current market value of the asset.

At the beginning of the lease, insurance coverage is normally obtained for the actual cost of the equipment. Throughout the term of the lease, the amount of coverage required by the acceptance supplement depends on the market value of the equipment. As the owner of the equipment, it is important to the lessor that the equipment be insured for its market value rather than the lease balance. For instance, if a leased airplane has an original cost of five million dollars, physical damage coverage of five million dollars should be required at the time the lease commences. If one year into the lease term the value of the airplane has increased to six million dollars, coverage should be increased in case the aircraft ever had to be replaced. Therefore, physical damage coverage must be evaluated periodically throughout the term of the lease. Since most policies are issued on an annual basis, policy renewal time is an excellent time to review these coverages.

Special Endorsements

The coverages discussed in the previous sections are very straight forward. It is also essential for the lessor to be named an insured party along with the lessee on both liability and physical damage policies with respect to the leased equipment. This is accomplished by obtaining an *additional insured endorsement* for liability coverage and a *loss payee clause* for physical damage coverage. By obtaining these two very important endorsements, several things will occur in the event of a claim. In the event of a liability claim, the lessee's insurance company will be required to defend all insured parties in any legal action. Therefore, the additional insured endorsement will save the lessor the legal expense of defending itself.

Second, in the event of a physical damage claim, the loss payee clause requires the insurance company to issue the check jointly to the lessee and the lessor for any repairs, or for the replacement in the event of total destruction of the equipment. Therefore, since the lessor's endorsement will be required on the check, it has a significant degree of control of the funds. The amount paid may or may not equal the stipulated loss value in the lease documentation. If it does not, the lessee is responsible for making up the difference. If repairs are needed, the lessor should require proof that the repairs have been made before endorsing and releasing the check from the insurance company to the lessee. The proof may be in the form of photographs or an on-site inspection.

Insurance Problems

There are a variety of problems associated with equipment leasing and insurance. The most common is that many insurance agents are unfamiliar with equipment leasing and fail to understand the need for additional insured and loss payee clauses. Most agents are familiar with the loss payable clause since it is required in connection with most traditional installment or mortgage loans, but many may be unfamiliar with the fact that the lessor must be named as an additional insured in a lease transaction. Also, most insurance companies are beginning to request an additional 10% premium for additional insured endorsements.

Insurance limits are another problem. The lessor will find that some lessees will not have sufficient liability limits on their current policy, and this will necessitate a request that this policy limit be increased before the lease can be closed. This, of course, means an increase in the lessee's premium, and this can be a sensitive issue. As explained before, the lessor must evaluate each specific situation to determine what limit and assocated risk it is willing to accept with regard to insurance coverage.

It is also important that the lessee be fully protected to the greatest extent possible against loss related to leased assets. There have been cases where lessees were not adequately covered for losses incurred when their leased assets were destroyed. Besides having to pay for an asset that no longer generated any benefits, they also had to invest additional dollars in replacing the asset.

Summary

Leasing affords benefits to both lessor and lessee provided the multitude of rules and regulations are complied with and the risks, rewards, and responsibilities are clearly understood. This chapter on equipment leasing is intended only as an introduction to the complex subject of equipment leasing.

Once understood, leasing provides an alternative solution for many problems facing businesses today. The study of equipment leasing has provided many bankers with an opportunity to expand their understanding of a customer's needs by providing a new way to view the complex art of financing.

Equipment leasing is an ever changing product that requires constant attention and training. As the economic cycles of the next decade dictate modification, change, and adaptability on the part of commercial lenders, equipment leasing will be a key portion of a modern package of financial services.

20

Financing a Start-up Business

From the time it is established until it becomes a mature business, a company generally progresses through a number of identifiable stages of development. During each stage it exhibits certain characteristics, which create unique challenges, opportunities, and problems for both company management and the lender. Management experts use various terms to identify these developmental stages; I will use start-up, survival, success, expansion, and maturity.

The start-up stage, when it first opens its doors and attempts to carve a niche for itself in the marketplace, is obviously a crucial time in the life of a business. The business' principal objectives at this stage usually include obtaining customers, developing products and services, raising sufficient funds to meet cash demands, and assembling the necessary (if minimal) employee staff and production facilities. Funding is usually based on a combination of equity and loans, with heavy dependence on borrowed funds.

A business in the survival stage is usually generating enough cash flow to stay in business, but accelerating growth generally continues to create funding problems. At the survival stage the business is beginning to become profitable, but it must commit a sizeable percentage of its resources to market penetration and to broadening and improving product lines.

In the success stage, the business has become securely established, and its prime objectives are expansion on a sound and controlled basis, development of a professional management staff, and insuring that basic financial, marketing, and production systems are in place. Profitability and market share are usually well established at this stage.

The expansion stage is characterized by rapid growth and its attendant problems. Funding of growth is a major concern and the business is trending toward a more heavily leveraged position. Management is generally becoming more decentralized, with less direct involvement of owners and founders.

The final stage, maturity, is characterized by consolidation of the financial gains that resulted from rapid growth. The business becomes more interested in maintaining its market share than growth, and achieving maximum operating efficiency becomes more important. Borrowing needs generally lessen significantly.

The commercial lender is faced with problems and challenges that will vary depending on the stage of the business' development. In most instances, the greatest challenges for the lender occur during a business' start-up stage.

The Lender's Challenge—A Start-up Business

One of the greatest challenges encountered by a commercial loan officer is that of financing a start-up business. There are a number of reasons why financing a new business presents problems for the loan officer. There is no history of past performance on which to base predictions of future performance. New businesses often require a high degree of leverage, and the ability of management may be untested. If the product or service being offered is new or unique, it is usually difficult to assess its acceptance in the marketplace. Problems may arise in getting a new product into production, especially if a precision process or a high degree of quality control is required. It may be difficult to accurately estimate construction costs of facilities and the acquisition cost of machinery, equipment, furnishings, and fixtures. Building a competent managerial team, and adequately training production workers may be costly and time consuming. In a new business operation, unforeseen problems frequently arise in spite of the best planning, which may require time, money, and managerial resourcefulness to solve. All of these reasons make the commercial loan officer's job of financing a new business a challenging one. The following case study is intended to illustrate some of the challenges and problems that may be encountered in financing this kind of business.

Hi-Tec Corporation

Hi-Tec Corporation was formed in 1978 by John Amherst and Fred Hutchins, for the purpose of perfecting an improved process for diamond turning rigid information storage disks for computers, and to build a production facility for such disks using the new process. Amherst was a businessman, and Hutchins was a highly skilled engineer who had done the research and development work on the new diamond turning process. The company established modest offices and a laboratory in Milwaukee, where Hutchins continued to do his research and development. Although research continued to progress in a fairly satisfactory manner, it soon became apparent that the company was undercapitalized and that its financial needs had been grossly underestimated. Several new stockholders, primarily friends and relatives of Amherst, contributed some additional capital in the form of both equity and loans, but this injection of funds fell far short of meeting the company's needs. Soon after, Amherst developed serious health problems, and the company began to flounder.

In November, 1980, the company was approached by Donald Robins, a successful businessman from Center City, who had developed a small communications company which recently had been sold to a large national corporation. Since the sale Robins had actively been seeking an opportunity to invest in a small company with growth potential. Robins entered into lengthy negotiations with both Amherst and Hutchins, and as a result of those negotiations, Robins acquired the 40% of the company owned by Amherst in February, 1981. Donald Robins was named president of the company, and immediately began to formulate plans for the acquisition of additional capital to fund the company's research and development activities. Five investors, all former business associates of Robins, agreed to invest $20,000 each in the company. Based on the injection of $100,000 of new equity, Robins applied for a working capital loan at several area banks, but found that the banks had little interest in accepting an application for a loan, because the company was not an operating company, had no income, and the diamond turning process was not yet perfected. With Robins being paid no salary, and living from his savings, and with Hutchins drawing only the minimum salary necessary to pay his living expenses, the company managed to continue its research and development work.

In February, 1982, Hutchins and Robins felt that the diamond turning process had been perfected, and that the company should construct a prototype machine for implementing the process. Greatly in need of additional working capital, Robins approached the Commercial Bank of Center City, a bank with which Robins had a long-term working relationship, and which had financed his previous business venture. After listening to Robins' presentation, the bank agreed to make a $65,000 loan to pay the cost of constructing a prototype manufacturing machine. This loan was based primarily upon the personal guaranty of Robins, and upon the bank's previous satisfactory business experience with him. The bank also perfected a blanket security interest in all equipment, furnishings, fixtures, and leasehold improvements of the company.

In early July, 1982, the manufacturing machine was completed and prototype disks were being produced on a test basis. Sample disks sent to independent testing laboratories proved to be of high quality, and because of the exceptionally smooth finish produced by the diamond turning process, test results showed that the information storage capacity of the disks was approximately 30% in excess of most disks of the same type available on the market.

The company also commissioned a market study by a reputable firm which indicated that the total market for rigid disks, which were rapidly replacing the floppy disk, was growing by 30% per year. The market survey also indicated that production was growing at a less rapid rate than the market, and that although several other companies were utilizing a diamond turning process rather than the standard sandstone turning process, all of these companies were having significant problems in maintaining quality. Correspondence with five national firms that were users of large numbers of rigid disks indicated that all of these companies would be interested in purchasing the production of Hi-Tec Corporation if the company could consistently produce a large volume of high quality disks. Several of these companies indicated that their present suppliers were having difficulty in meeting delivery schedules.

With this information in hand, Donald Robins and Fred Hutchins now approached the Commercial Bank with a request for a financing package which would enable them to construct a production facility, hire and train a managerial and production staff, and pay operating costs until such time as cash flow became sufficient to cover their costs. The balance sheet that the company presented to the bank was as follows:

FIGURE 20-1   Hi-Tec Corporation, Balance Sheet, July 31, 1982

ASSETS

CURRENT ASSETS		
Cash	$ 5,386.	
Prepaid Expenses	3,502.	
Inventory (raw material)	17,860.	
Total Current Assets		$ 26,748.
FIXED ASSETS (at cost)		
Equipment	$ 138,300.	
Vehicles	7,400.	
Furniture and Fixtures	4,786.	
Total Fixed Assets		$150,486.
TOTAL ASSETS		$177,234.

(*Continued*)

FIGURE 20-1   *(Continued)*

LIABILITIES AND STOCKHOLDERS' EQUITY

CURRENT LIABILITIES

Payroll Taxes Payable	$ 3,748.	
Notes Payable	65,000.	
Notes Payable-Shareholders	8,818.	
Total Current Liabilities		$ 77,566.

STOCKHOLDERS' EQUITY

Common Stock	$ 253,400.	
Paid in Capital	59,607.	
Net Income (Loss)	(213,339.)	
Total Stockholders' Equity		$ 99,668.
TOTAL LIABILITIES AND STOCKHOLDERS' EQUITY		$177,234.

The company also presented a year-to-date income and expense statement as follows:

FIGURE 20-2   **Hi-Tec Corporation, Income and Expenses, January 1 – July 31, 1982**

INCOME		$-0-
EXPENSES		
Salaries	$63,370.	
Payroll Taxes	6,364.	
Travel	19,215.	
Machine Tools and Supplies	16,861.	
Consulting Fees	8,731.	
Legal Fees	8,372.	
Interest	4,520.	
Telephone	4,066.	
Insurance	4,062.	
Office Rent	2,836.	
Market Surveys	1,630.	
Office Supplies	1,096.	
Accounting	750.	
Maintenance and Repairs	727.	
Equipment Rental	564.	
Freight Charges	509.	
Postage	292.	
Licenses and Fees	32.	
Utilities	416.	
Subscriptions and Publications	12.	
Miscellaneous	125.	
Total Expenses		$ 144,550.
Net Income (Loss)		$(144,550.)

Loan officer Bob Brown, to whom the Hi-Tec Corporation application had been assigned, spent considerable time discussing the history and status of the company with Robins and Hutchins. If the company was to become a successful business, it was obvious that a production facility had to be built as soon as possible. Brown requested that the company prepare an itemized listing of its needs, a detailed cash flow projection for the first year of operation, a summary projection of its income and expenses for the following two years, and a timetable for getting into production. Mr. Brown also observed that in view of the apparent substantial cash needs and the company's weak financial position, it was unlikely that the total project could be funded by borrowed funds, and that it would almost surely become necessary for the company to raise additional equity if the project were to be feasible. Robins felt that a minimum of one-half million dollars of additional equity could be raised, and assured Mr. Brown that he would immediately begin to explore this alternative. The company had recently hired David Patterson, a man experienced in accounting, personnel management, and with a background in high technology manufacturing. Mr. Patterson was assigned the task of preparing the necessary projections. Loan officer Brown also indicated that he would review the various U.S. Small Business Administration programs to see if these could be of benefit in this situation. He further requested that the results of the market survey done by the company be submitted to him.

Approximately one week later Robins and Patterson returned to the bank with a proposal that Hi-Tec Corporation build a 15,000 square foot manufacturing facility in Center City on a tract of land to be purchased in an industrial park at the northwest edge of the city. The company had looked at several existing facilities, but felt that the cost of renovating these facilities would be prohibitive. Also, since the production process was very sensitive to vibration, the location of the production facility had to be several hundred yards from any railroad or heavily traveled highway. They had engaged in discussions with a local contractor who assured them he could build their facility in about 90 days. They had also retained an architect to do preliminary drawings of the building. They further proposed that the facility contain a total of eight production machines, all of which would be custom built by the company itself. They proposed moving their prototype machine from Milwaukee as soon as the building was completed, and getting it into production. Thereafter, as additional machines were built, they would be brought into production one at a time, until all machines were into full production. As soon as all eight machines were performing satisfactorily from a quality control standpoint, the company would then go to a double work shift, and subsequently to three work shifts per day. The company's projections indicated that all of this could be accomplished within six months of the date the building was completed and ready for occupancy.

FIGURE 20-3   Hi-Tech Corporation, Projection of Total Funds Needed

CAPITAL NEEDS:

Land	$ 80,000.
Building	420,000.
Equipment	974,600.
Office furniture	17,000.
Vehicles	40,000.
Total	$1,531,600.

WORKING CAPITAL NEEDS:

Initial inventory (raw material)	$ 40,000.
Working capital needs—	
September 1982 thru April 1983	664,000.
Total	$ 704,000.
TOTAL NEEDS:	$2,235,600.

The company also submitted a Pro Forma Cash Flow Statement for the coming 13-month period.

Dave Patterson explained that the Pro Forma Cash Flow projection was based on the following assumptions:

1.   That the building would be completed by late December, 1982.

2.   That one machine would be production in mid-January, 1983, and that thereafter additional machines would be phased into production until all eight machines were in production in April, 1983. In May production would move to a two-shift status, and in August to a three-shift status.

3.   That there would be an injection of approximately $200,000 new equity capital by the stockholders in December, 1982.

4.   That all equipment purchases would be completed in May, 1983.

5.   That the company would begin to develop considerable cash flow in May from the collection of accounts receivable from product manufactured and shipped in March and April, 1983.

6.   As a result of growing production and collections, the business' operating income would begin to exceed its cash expenses in June 1983.

7.   In July, with rapidly increasing cash flow, the business would begin paying $50,000 per month principal on its indebtedness.

FIGURE 20-4 Hi-Tech Corporation, Pro Forma Cash Flow Statement

	Sept. 1982	Oct. 1982	Nov. 1982	Dec. 1982	Jan. 1983	Feb. 1983	Mar. 1983	April 1983	May 1983	June 1983	July 1983	Aug. 1983	Sept. 1983
CASH IN:													
Beginning Cash	$ 2,386	$ 2,337	$ 3,390	$ 3,128	$ 57,977	$ 99,226	$ 35,413	$ 1,286	$ 1,502	$ 19,220	$ 21,105	$ 75,864	$ 25,863
Operating Income	-0-	-0-	-0-	-0-	-0-	-0-	-0-	-0-	102,876	134,534	237,409	237,409	316,546
Loan or Equity Funds	275,000	543,500	459,000	200,000	193,000	88,000	147,000	268,000	127,100	-0-	-0-	-0-	-0-
Total Cash In	$277,386	$545,837	$462,390	$203,128	$250,977	$187,226	$182,413	$269,286	$231,478	$153,754	$258,514	$313,273	$342,409
CASH OUT:													
Inventory Purchases	-0-	-0-	$ 6,600	$ 13,200	$ 19,800	$ 14,862	$ 14,862	$ 14,863	$ 29,725	$ 29,725	$ 29,725	$ 74,312	$ 74,312
Debt Repayment	-0-	$ 65,000	-0-	-0-	-0-	-0-	-0-	-0-	-0-	-0-	50,000	50,000	50,000
Capital Expenditures	$217,444	428,842	392,057	83,146	83,146	88,146	79,609	79,609	79,609	-0-	-0-	-0-	-0-
Operating Expenses	57,605	48,605	60,605	48,805	48,805	48,805	86,656	173,312	102,924	102,924	102,925	163,098	163,098
Total Cash Out	$275,049	$542,447	$459,262	$145,151	$151,751	$151,813	$181,127	$267,784	$212,258	$132,649	$182,650	$287,410	$287,410
Ending Cash	$ 2,337	$ 3,390	$ 3,128	$ 57,977	$ 99,226	$ 35,413	$ 1,286	$ 1,502	$ 19,220	$ 21,105	$ 75,864	$ 25,863	$ 54,999

In analyzing the information submitted to him, and endeavoring to determine the feasibility of the project, loan officer Brown identified the following strengths and weaknesses:

Weaknesses

1.   The company's financial position was very weak in relation to its capital needs. (Equity of $99,668 vs. capital and working capital needs of $2,235,600.)

2.   To date the company had generated no income. Even though its projections indicated it would be quite profitable once it was in full production, there was no history of successful past performance to provide credibility to these projections.

3.   The company had produced only a small quantity of prototype disks, and it was far from certain that it could mass produce these disks and maintain the necessary high quality.

4.   Even if the stockholders injected $200,000 of new equity, the company would still be in a very heavily leveraged position.

5.   The company had not yet assembled a complete management team, nor did it have a trained production staff.

6.   Since management was inexperienced in the construction of a manufacturing facility, it seemed likely that significant cost overruns might occur.

7.   Much of the required equipment would be specialized or custom built. If the company failed, the price at which the equipment could be sold was questionable.

8.   Fred Hutchins alone had complete engineering knowledge of the diamond turning process and the skill to fine tune the required production equipment. Therefore, his disability or death would seriously impede the company's ability to get into successful production.

Strengths

1.   The bank believed Donald Robins to be a capable business manager, and had a very satisfactory business relationship with him. His past performance had proven him to be a man of integrity.

2.   The independent tests showed the prototype disks to be of high quality, exceeding normal industry standards.

3.   The market study indicated that the market for high quality rigid disks was growing very rapidly, and that current industry production would not meet demand for the next several years unless production was increased by at least 20% annually. (This was independently confirmed by the bank.)

4.   The present board and principal stockholders were strongly in favor of the project, and willing to invest additional equity.

5.   The company's projections indicated that once it was in full production, it would generate a substantial cash flow quickly (by mid-1983), and that cash flow would be very adequate to service its debt, assuming that the debt was structured properly.

6.   The business would create a minimum of 100 new jobs in the community, and make a significant contribution to the local economy.

7.   If successful, the business would become an excellent account customer of the bank.

Although lacking several necessary items of information, such as a detailed profit projection and pro forma balance sheet, Brown felt that there was sufficient potential in the proposal that it merited further consideration. He felt that with a larger injection of equity capital, an SBA 503 program loan to assist in financing the purchase of capital assets, and an SBA guaranteed working capital loan, the financing of the project might be feasible.

Several days later, Brown called Robins and his associates to the bank and explained his plan. He proposed that approximately 30%, or $675,000, of the company's needs be funded by equity. This would involve raising $475,000 more equity than company management had anticipated. Brown suggested that a venture capital company be contacted, and explained that venture capital companies are businesses that specialize in equity investments in small companies that have significant growth and profit potential. In return for its investment of risk capital, such a company usually demands options to purchase additional stock at a fixed price, a voice in management and an agreement giving the venture capital company a certain amount of control of the business. Robins agreed to contact several venture capital companies.

Brown also explained SBA's 503 program (see chapter 17). He suggested that an application be made to the local Certified Development Company which processes 503 program applications. Under that program, Hi-Tec Corporation could apply for long term, fixed rate debentures which SBA would guarantee and sell in the secondary market, for 40% of the cost of its land, buildings and equipment, up to a maximum of $500,000. The bank would be required to make a loan for 50% of the cost of the fixed assets, secured by a first mortgage and first security interest in those assets. The SBA debentures would be secured by a mortgage and security interest subordinate to the bank's. The remaining cost of the fixed assets would be funded by equity.

Brown also suggested that approximately half of the company's working capital needs be funded by equity, and the remaining half be funded by a seven-year loan to be guaranteed to the extent of 90% by SBA under its Section 7(a) program.[1] This loan would be collateralized by a first security interest in the company's inventory and receivables.

In summary, loan officer Brown's proposal for structuring the financing package was as follows:

Capital Loan

Commercial Bank term loan	$ 766,000.
SBA 503 program debentures	500,000.
From equity	265,600.
Total Required	$1,531,600.

Working Capital Loan

Commercial Bank loan with SBA Section 7(a) guaranty	$ 360,000.
From equity	344,000.
Total Required	$ 704,000.

With the financing package structured in this manner, Brown analyzed the bank's exposure as follows:

Amount of the term loan	$ 766,000.
Secured by:	
Real estate, at 80% of cost	$ 400,000.
Equipment and Vehicles presently owned, at 40% of value	58,280.
Equipment to be purchased, at 40% of cost (due to its specialized nature)	389,840.
Office furniture, at 50% of cost	8,500.
Vehicles, at 70% of cost	28,000.
Total net collateral value	$ 884,620.
Collateral coverage (percent)	115%
Amount of working capital loan	$ 360,000.

[1]   At that time it was permissable for a borrower to have a Section 7(a) guaranteed loan and Section 503 loan, each in a maximum amount of $500,000. In December, 1983, the U.S. Small Business Administration issued a ruling that the *total* of a borrower's loans uner Section 7(a) and Section 503 could not exceed $500,000.

Secured by:

Inventory (based on initial inventory) at 50% of cost	$	20,000.
Accounts Receivable (estimated to reach $200,000 by June 1983) at 75%		150,000.
Total net collateral value	$	170,000.
Lender's exposure	$	190,000.
Bank's share of exposure, based on 90% SBA guaranty	$	19,000.

Despite the fact that the bank's collateral coverage on the term loan was somewhat less adequate than the bank wished, and the bank had a potential exposure of approximately $19,000 on the working capital loan, Brown felt that the risk was within an acceptable range (in view of the potential benefits to the bank and the community), and that steps could be taken to further reduce the risk. Therefore, preparation of both a 503 program application and an SBA 7(a) working capital loan application was begun. Requirements for the 503 application are comprehensive, and include a history of the business, a statement detailing the exact uses of the loan proceeds, personal financial statements of proposed guarantors, personal history statements on all principals, balance sheet and income and expense information for the past three years (if the business has been in existence for that period of time), pro forma balance sheet, two-year income projection, and a monthly cash flow for at least the first year of operation. See figure 20-5, Hi-Tec Corporation's income projection for 1983 and 1984.

Bob Brown prepared a proposal for his bank loan committee requesting approval of a ten-year term loan in the amount of $766,000 and a seven-year working capital loan in the amount of $360,000. The rate on both loans was to be prime rate plus 2%. A loan service fee of 1.5% was to be paid on the term loan. Each loan would require an amortized monthly payment, except that in its first year monthly payments of interest only would be required on the term loan.

Brown's proposal included the following recommendations:

1. That the company be required to raise no less than $675,000 of new equity.
2. That both loans be personally guaranteed by Donald Robins and Fred Hutchins. (Personal statements received from Robins and Hutchins indicated that they had net worths of $368,000 and $112,000, respectively.)

FIGURE 20-5   Hi-Tech Corporation, Projection of Two-Years' Earnings

	First Yr.	% of Sales	Second Yr.	% of Sales
Gross Sales	$3,218,228	100.0	$9,136,162	100.0
Cost of Goods Sold	1,532,545	47.6	4,016,337	44.0
Gross Profit	$1,685,683	52.4	5,119,825	56.0
Officers Salaries	100,000	3.1	160,000	1.7
Employee Salaries	100,000	3.1	140,000	1.5
Accounting and Legal	45,000	1.4	45,000	.5
Advertising	60,000	1.9	90,000	1.0
Depreciation	137,189	4.3	162,300	1.8
Supplies	45,000	1.4	70,000	.8
Electrical Power	108,000	3.4	210,000	2.3
Telephone	12,000	.4	18,000	.2
Interest	156,000	4.8	180,000	2.0
Maintenance and Repair	14,000	.4	28,000	.3
Taxes	0	—	12,000	.1
Insurance	40,000	1.2	45,000	.5
Miscellaneous	0	—	8,000	.1
Total Expenses	$ 817,189	25.4	$1,168,300	12.8
Net Profit Before Taxes	$ 868,494	27.0	$3,951,525	43.2
Taxes	0		1,663,216	18.2
Net Profit After Taxes	$ 868,494	27.0	$2,288,309	25.0

3. That the term loan be secured by a first mortgage on the real estate to be purchased, and a security interest in all equipment, vehicles, fixtures and furnishings, including both those currently owned by the company and those to be purchased with the loan proceeds.
4. That the working capital loan be secured by a security interest in all receivables and inventory.
5. That SBA approve the issuance of $500,000 of debentures under its 503 program.
6. That SBA guarantee 90% of the working capital loan.

7. That the bank's existing $65,000 loan be paid off with funds provided by the new equity injection.

8. That the company purchase and assign to the bank at least $750,000 of life insurance on both Donald Robins and Fred Hutchins.

9. That prior to disbursement of the loan proceeds the company present evidence that it had at least $1,000,000 in orders forthcoming.

10. That the company be required to sign a comprehensive loan agreement (see Exhibit S, chapter 9) agreeing to all the bank's terms and requirements, and containing certain restrictive covenants which would give the bank a degree of control over company management.

The bank's loan committee approved the application as presented, and a 503 program application was immediately submitted to the local Certified Development Company (CDC), which processed the application and submitted it to its loan committee. CDC's loan committee requested that Robins, Hutchins, and Brown present the company's request, and after a two-hour in-depth presentation that stressed the potentially strong repayment capacity of the company and the contribution the company would make to the local economy, the application was approved by CDC's loan committee. The next step was the submission of the application to SBA for final approval. Within 20 days approval was received from SBA in the form of an Authorization and Debenture Guaranty. The bank had submitted the application for the SBA Section 7(a) guaranty of the working capital loan directly to SBA, and this was also approved. Both SBA approvals included the following additional stipulations:

1. That the company sign an agreement that it would fund any cost overruns of its building and equipment with additional equity.

2. That the shareholder holding the $8818 note from the company be required to sign SBA Form 155, a Standby Agreement (usually referred to as a subordination agreement).

3. That the working capital loan be additionally secured by a third security interest in all equipment, and a third mortgage on the real estate, subordinate to those securing the bank's term loan and the SBA 503 program debentures.

All requirements set by both the bank and SBA were agreed to by the management of Hi-Tec Corporation, and a concerted effort was begun to raise the necessary equity capital.

At this point both the bank and Hi-Tec Corporation realized that one aspect of the financing package had been overlooked. The $500,000 of Section

503 debentures would not be issued until the project, including construction of the building and placement of the equipment, was completed in April 1983. The bank would therefore be required to make an interim construction loan to fund construction costs, with this loan to be paid off with the net proceeds of the debenture issue. Since the net proceeds of the debenture issue, after deductions of a 3% reserve fund, the fiscal agent's fee of 1.5%, and the CDC's processing fee of .25%, would be $476,250, the bank's interim loan commitment was for $475,000. The interim loan was to be secured by a second security interest in the equipment and a second mortgage on the real estate, subordinate to those the bank held to secure its term loan. At the closing of the denture issue in April, the bank would than either release this mortgage and security interest or assign them to SBA.

Negotiations with ABC Venture Capital Company resulted in a commitment for a $375,000 injection of equity. Hi-Tec and ABC entered into an agreement giving ABC purchase options for additional stock, the right to seat its representative on Hi-Tec's board, and entitled ABC to a certain amount of management control of the company. The present stockholders of the company and four new investors pledged to invest the remaining $300,000 of equity. A stock escrow account was set up at the bank and the funds from the sale of stock were placed in this account pending closing of the various loans.

Bids from contractors and suppliers were received for the erection of the building and for the purchase of the major components of the production machines, which would be custom built by Hi-Tec personnel. Although supplier bids for the equipment were in line with Hi-Tec's projections, the lowest bid for the building was $128,000 higher than anticipated, resulting from Hi-Tec underestimating the cost of a sizeable "clean room" required for one step of the manufacturing process. It therefore appeared that it would be necessary for the company to raise an additional $128,000 in equity. As an alternative, company management proposed that job training grants from CETA (Comprehensive Education Training Act) and from a state job training program totaling $141,000 which had not been shown in their pro forma cash flow statement (at that time approval was in doubt) be considered a set-off to the cost overrun, since these funds would provide $141,000 of working capital funds not previously anticipated. Both the bank and SBA agreed to this arrangement. The necessary purchase orders for $1,000,000 of product were also procured, although there was considerable hesitancy on the part of prospective purchasers in dealing with a company that had not yet erected a production facility. As a result, a number of these orders had escape clauses which made their enforceability questionable.

The bank's term loan and interim loan were closed in October 1982. The SBA guaranteed working capital loan was closed in early November. A contract for construction of the building was awarded in early October and orders were placed for the necessary equipment. The $265,600 of equity funds allocated for capital purposes were used first to make progress payments on the building construction and to purchase equipment, and thereafter, funds from the term and interim loans were used. The remaining equity funds were used for payroll and other operating expenses. With the assistance of CETA, the hiring and training of production line workers was begun.

In early January the building was complete and construction of the equipment was progressing well. By February 1, the first machine was in production. Problems of lack of consistency in quality caused a four-week delay in getting the machine into full production, but once these were solved, it performed as anticipated. Two weeks thereafter the second machine was brought into full production. The third machine presented serious problems which only the eventual dismantling and rebuilding of the machine resolved. The five other machines were brought into production with only minor problems, but the problems with the first and third machines had created a two-month delay that resulted in the company reaching full production in mid-June instead of early April as projected.

Hi-Tec Corporation's product has been well accepted in the market-place and it has been readily able to sell all disks produced. As a result of quality control problems and the delay in achieving full production, its first year's sales were $2,200,000 instead of the $3,218,000 originally projected. The company's projections of its costs also proved to be low, and its profits for its first year of operation were $172,000 (projected first year's profit were $868,494). It is improving its operating efficiency and its second year's performance should be a significant improvement over its first year. It has been able to make all its loan payments on time.

Although the company has fallen short of its projections, it appears everyone involved has benefited. The community gained a desirable new business which has created 112 new jobs to date. The bank has gained a good new commercial customer, as well as the accounts of approximately 35 of the business' employees. The company's officers, employees, and stockholders can look forward to a bright future.

1984 Bankruptcy Amendments

On July 11, 1984, President Reagan signed "The Bankruptcy Amendments and Federal Judgeship Act of 1984." This law establishes a new bankruptcy court system and significantly modifies "The Bankruptcy Reform Act of 1978."

Although several of the changes took effect immediately, the amendments of the greatest concern to lenders will only affect bankruptcies filed after October 8, 1984. The most important changes are:

Substantial Abuse—The new law permits a bankruptcy judge to decide whether a Chapter 7 filing represents a "substantial abuse" of the system and should be dismissed for that reason. Although creditors are not allowed to initiate this proceeding, it is anticipated that judges will deny discharges to debtors who could have easily repaid their debts under a Chapter 13 Plan.

Bankruptcy Alternatives—In an effort to encourage Chapter 13 Plans instead of Chapter 7 filings, bankruptcy clerks will be required to give debtors a written notice explaining the differences between Chapters 7 and 13 prior to filing. Also, the debtor will be required to file a sworn statement that he or she understands the alternatives provided by both Chapter 7 and 13, and where the debtor has legal counsel the attorney will be required to file an affidavit stating that the differences between Chapter 7 and 13 have been explained to the debtor. Finally, in a Chapter 7 filing, the debtor will be required to submit a schedule of his or her *current* income and expenses, thereby providing fiscal data that should assist the judge in ruling upon the issue of "substantial abuse."

Chapter 13 Plan and Payments—The new law will require that all of the debtor's "disposable income" be devoted to the repayment plan which seems to be a departure from the "good faith" standard of the 1978 law. This change may tend to eliminate many of the nominal payment plans which have been approved in recent years, although there will obviously be disagreements over the definition of "disposable income." Also, the debtor will now be required to commence payments under a Chapter 13 Plan within 30 days after the filing, regardless of when the plan is approved. The trustee is required to insure compliance by the debtor with this provision and a creditor can use the lack of timely payments as grounds for obtaining a dismissal.

Collateral—Within 30 days after a Chapter 7 filing, but no later than the first meeting of creditors, the debtor must file a statement of his or her intention to retain or surrender collateral. The debtor must also specify whether such property is claimed as exempt or whether a redemption or reaffirmation is intended. The debtor is required to perform accordingly within 45 days following the creditor's meeting and the trustee is authorized to enforce compliance, as the creditor will remain under the automatic stay during this period of time.

Exemptions—Joint debtors in states that have not preempted the federal exemptions will be required to make a joint election of either the state or the federal exemptions. In addition, the federal exemption will now limit household goods to $4,000.00 and the "wild card exemption" for any unused homestead exemption to $3,750.00.

Reaffirmation—Under the new law, court approval of reaffirmation agreements will not be required in every case. In order to bypass court approval, the debtor must have an attorney and the agreement must be filed with the court, with the debtor's attorney filing an affidavit indicating that the debtor was fully informed and voluntarily entered into the agreement and that the reaffirmation does not impose an "undue hardship" on the debtor or a dependent. If the debtor is unrepresented by counsel, court approval will be required. In any event, the debtor can rescind the agreement by so notifying the creditor within 60 days after the agreement is filed with the court or at any time prior to discharge, whichever occurs later.

Since the new law, in most cases, seems to have eliminated the need for a judicial finding that a reaffirmation agreement is in the "best interest" of the debtor and does not impose an "undue hardship," more debtors should be in a position to reaffirm unsecured debts, particularly where co-makers or guarantors are involved.

Automatic Stay—Chapter 13 Co-debtor—Since the 1978 Code became effective, a cosignor to a Chapter 13 Plan was protected under the automatic stay until a creditor obtained a court order lifting the stay. Under the new amendments, the stay for Chapter 13 co-makers will automatically expire 20 days after the creditor requests relief from the stay, unless the debtor files a timely objection with the court. Of course, the creditor can still only recover from the cosignor the difference between the amount of the debt and what the Chapter 13 Plan proposes to pay. Another change provides that a Chapter 13 Plan may now categorize cosigned consumer debts differently than other unsecured debts for repayment purposes and this may result in limiting the need for legal action against co-makers.

Automatic Stay-Violation—A significant change affecting creditors allows debtors to recover punitive damages from anyone who "willfully" violates the automatic stay. Interestingly, a creditor who continues to receive payment by way of payroll deduction or direct deposit following an automatic stay is probably not willfully violating the new provision.

Voidable Preferences—A transfer by a debtor of amounts less than $600.00 within 90 days of bankruptcy filing will not be considered a preference.

Non-Dischargeable Debts—The new law establishes a presumption that debts of more than $500.00 for "luxury goods or services incurred within 40 days prior to filing cannot be discharged. Also, cash advances of more than $1,000.00 under an open-end consumer credit plan that are obtained within 20 days before filing are presumed to be non-dischargeable. Finally, debts incurred as a result of an accident caused by drunk driving are now deemed to be non-dischargeable in bankruptcy.

There are many other significant amendments to the bankruptcy laws which affect lenders and their procedures, in addition to those set forth above. Again, the lender is admonished to consult with his or her attorney concerning any of these recent amendments.

This Addendum written by Jim Evans.

Bibliography

American Bankers Association. *Bankruptcy Manual—Banker's Guide to the Bankruptcy Reform Act of 1978*. Washington, D.C., 1980.

American Bankers Association. *Bankers School Directory 1983-1984*. Washington D.C., 1982.

Behrens, Robert H. *Commercial Problem Loans*. Boston: Bankers Publishing Company, 1983.

Clark, Barkley. *The Law of Secured Transactions Under the Uniform Commercial Code*. Boston: Warren, Gorham and Lamont, Inc., 1980.

Cowans, Daniel R. *Cowans Bankruptcy Law and Practice, Practice and Procedure Under the New Bankruptcy Code*. Interim edition, St. Paul, Minnesota: West Publishing Company, 1980.

Hamilton, Dee. *Successful Business Development For the Community Bank*. Washington, D.C.: American Bankers Association, 1978.

Herzog, Asa S., and Lawrence P. King, Co-editors-in-chief. *Colliers Bankruptcy Practice Guide*. New York: Matthew Bender and Company, 1981.

Hillman, William C. *Commercial Loan Documentation*. New York: Practicing Law Institute, 1982.

O'Malia, Thomas J. *Banker's Guide to Financial Statments*. Boston: Bankers Publishing Company, 1982.

Quinn, Thomas M. *Uniform Commercial Code Commentary and Law Digest*. Boston: Warren, Gorham and Lamont, Inc., 1978.

Reiley, Eldon H. *Guidebook to Security Interests in Personal Property*. New York: Clark Boardman Company, Ltd., 1981.

Robert Morris Associates. *Classics in Commercial Lending*. Philadelphia, 1981.

Robert Morris Associates. *Report on Domestic and International Loan Charge-offs*. Philadelphia, 1983.

United States Council of the International Chamber of Commerce. "Uniform Customs and Practice for Documentary Credits." I.C.C. Publication No. 290, New York, 1975.

Periodicals:

Bel Air, Roger. "Business Development and the Loan Officer." *The Journal of Comercial Bank Lending*, Robert Morris Associates, Philadelphia, June 1982.

Brenner, Ronald D. "Lending to the Small High Technology Firm." *Journal of Commercial Bank Lending*, Robert Morris Associates, Philadelphia, October 1982.

Edmonds, Thomas P. "Judgment and the Lending Decision." *The Bankers Magazine*, Warren, Gorham and Lamont, Inc., Boston, November-December 1981.

Harl, Neil E. "New Subchapter S Rules." *Agri Finance*, Century Communications, Inc., Skokie, Illinois, Vol. 24, No. 10, December 1982.

Harl, Neil E. "Bankruptcy: Chapters 11 and 13 Reorganizations." *Agri Finance*, Century Communications, Inc., Skokie, Illinois, Vol. 25, No. 7, September 1983.

Harper, Courtland B. "Taking the Chill out of Cold Calling." *The Journal of Commercial Bank Lending*, Robert Morris Associates, Philadelphia, March 1983.

The Bankers Letter of the Law. "More Trouble on the Repo." Management Reports, Inc., Boston, Vol. 11, No. 1, January 1977.

The Uniform Commerical Code Law Letter. "Arm Twisting on the Repo." Management Reports, Inc., Boston, Vol. 9, No. 9, November 1975.

The Uniform Commercial Code Law Letter. "Guarantors: Handle With Care." Management Reports, Inc., Boston, Vol. 14, No. 8, October 1980.

The Uniform Commercial Code Law Letter. "Coping With Migratory Collateral." Management Reports, Inc., Boston, Vol. 16, No. 10, December 1982.

Weissman, Michael L. "A Banker's Guide to Business Workouts and Bankruptcy." *Commercial Lending Report*. Friedman, Eisenstein, Raemer and Schwartz, Certified Public Accountants, Chicago, Vol. 4, No. 3, May 1983.

Index